In the name of Allah,
The Compassionate, The Merciful

FAITH FIRST
A Guide to Awakening Iman

FAITH FIRST

A GUIDE TO AWAKENING IMAN

Adapted and translated from
the book *Al-Imān Awwalan*

Dr. Magdy Al-Hilali

MAS PUBLISHING

MASPUBLISHING.ORG

Published by MAS Publishing
712 H Street NE, Suite 1258
Washington, DC 20002
www.muslimamericansociety.org

ISBN 978-0-9792113-3-1

Printed in the U.S.A

TABLE OF CONTENTS

⊰(TRANSLATOR'S NOTE)⊱

Faith First was translated and adapted from the Arabic *Al-Iman Awwalan* by Dr. Magdy Al-Hilali, originally published in 2000 by *Dar An-Nashr wa at-Tawzee'*. The Muslim American Society (MAS) presents this translation of Dr. Al-Hilaly's book to the English-speaking Muslim audience.

The translators combined several prefaces into a single introduction and condensed and adapted the translation to allow for easier reading. Abdelminem Mustafa was the lead writer and translator, with Maha Ezzeddine translating and adapting portions of the book and editing the final work. Rayhan El-Alami translated the chapter on Prayer. A team of volunteers from Project 100 contributed to the final editing process.

Translation decisions were the product of consideration of meaning, priorities, and target audience. God and Allah are used interchangeably throughout the text. When a term could not be translated without compromising its meaning (*iman, khushoo'*, etc.), the Arabic word is used along with the closest English equivalent in parentheses. Definitions can be found in margins upon first mention of many Arabic words, and a glossary is included in the opening pages for the reader's convenience. Translation of Quran verses were taken primarily from The Clear Quran by Mustafa Khattab, and from M.A.S. Abdelhaleem's translation.

An upcoming second edition of this book will include an appendix of the Arabic Hadith texts as well as improvements to the current text. As this book is a work in progress and we value our readers' feedback, please send any textual recommendations and corrections to publishing@muslimamericansociety.org.

May Allah bless and reward Dr. Magdy Al-Hilali for authoring this inspiring and thorough text and granting MAS Youth permission many years ago to translate his writings. May Allah reward those who translated, edited, and contributed financially to this English version, and forgive the mistakes made in the process.

GLOSSARY

Allah: the Arabic name for God

Ansar: the native inhabitants of Medina who believed in and supported the Prophet and the migrants from Mecca (Muhajirun)

Athan: the call to prayer

Ayah: a verse of the Quran

Companions: Those who converted to Islam and lived alongside Prophet Muhammad ﷺ

Dawah: an invitation; the mission of calling others to worship God and follow the religion of Islam

Dua: supplication or prayer; the act of calling upon God

Fitrah: the initial state of creation of a person; the collection of attributes and tendencies the human was initially given

Hadith: a saying of Prophet Muhammad ﷺ transmitted through a chain of narrators. The sayings and traditions of the Prophet were meticulously recorded and verified after his death.

Hadith qudsi: a saying of the Prophet Muhammad ﷺ in which he conveys a statement of God

Hajj: pilgrimage to Mecca once in a lifetime, if physically and financially able to do so

Iman: translated as faith, belief. Derived from *'amn* (safety), *iman* linguistically means taking something as true, accepting it, and believing in it. In Islam, *iman* is belief, action, and intention stemming from certainty and complete acceptance of the existence of God and His attributes, and the Prophet and revelation. Iman is not only expressed in the heart, but also through worship, good deeds, and intentions. It can increase and decrease, and its strength or weakness reaches the depths of the self and affects all its aspects.

Insha'Allah: God willing

Israa' and Miraj: The Night Journey and Ascension; the Prophet's journey in a single night from Mecca to Jerusalem, and from there he ascended to the Heavens.

Jihad: striving in God's cause. It includes striving for self-improvement, striving for knowledge, striving against temptation, vices, and evil, and striving on the battlefield.

Jinn: a creation similar to human beings, but created of fire; also given free choice and commanded to worship God alone

Jum'a: Friday, the day of congregation in which Muslims gather mid-day to hear a sermon (khutba) in the mosque and perform the noon prayer.

Ka'bah: the house of worship built by Abraham and Ismael in the desert of Mecca. Muslims face the Ka'bah in their daily prayers as a symbol of their global unity.

Khushu': reverence, concentration, humility, a presence of heart and mind; often in the context of worship, especially prayer

Muhajirun: emigrants; Muslims from Mecca who migrated to Medina

Nafs: the self, ego; may be inspired with good or evil tendencies

Qiyam: the night prayer

Quran: the final revelation from God to all of mankind, sent through Prophet Muhammad

Quraysh: the dominant tribe controlling Mecca and the Ka'bah, and the tribe in which Prophet Muhammad ﷺ was born

Rabbaniyah: derived from *rabb* (Lord); dedicated to and for God in every way; Someone is "rabbani" when they have a strong connection with God, know His religion and His book, and convey it to others

Ramadan: the month of fasting for Muslims in which they abstain from food, drink, intimacy, and all indecency from dawn to sunset; the fourth pillar of Islam

Riya': showing off, seeking admiration of people

Salah: prayer; derived from *silah*, meaning connection; the fifth pillar of Islam

Salla Allahu alaihi wa sallam (ﷺ): This is a prayer that means, "May God's peace and blessings be upon him," which Muslims say whenever Muhammad's name is mentioned or written.

Seerah: the biography of Prophet Muhammad

Shirk: associating partners with God; worshipping anyone or anything alongside God.

Sunnah: the way, course, or conduct of life; the example set by Prophet Muhammad which all Muslims should strive to follow as best as they can. It can also refer to extra acts of worship that one can perform in order to gain favor with God.

Surah: a chapter of the Quran

Tabi'een: the second generation of Muslims: those who met the Companions but did not meet the Prophet ﷺ

Tafseer: the science of explaining the Quran and deriving its rulings

Tarbiyah: the holistic development and nurturing of Islamic spirituality and character

Taqwa: piety, mindfulness of God; being cautious in order to avoid God's displeasure

Tazkiyah: self-purification

Thikr: remembrance of God

'Ubudiyah: derived from the word *'abd* (servant); the state of submission, servitude, and worship of God

Ummah: the collective body of Muslims

Wudu: a ritual washing before prayer

Zakah: a prescribed percentage of a Muslim's wealth that must be given in charity; one of the pillars of Islam

Introduction

We are on a journey to grow closer to God, but at times the road seems blocked. *What is holding me back in my faith? Why don't I feel connected to God?* Those who seek God have asked the same questions over centuries:

وَإِذَا سَأَلَكَ عِبَادِى عَنِّى فَإِنِّى قَرِيبٌ

If My servants ask you about Me, I am near. [2:186]

Muslims understand that God is near, but still suffer a lack of spiritual connection. On the outside, we appear to be doing fine, busy with things to do and places to go, brandishing the latest gadget in our pockets and accessing information with the click of a finger. Entertainment and consumption are distractions from an empty feeling in our hearts. Although are couched in luxury, our collective human spirit is anxious, lonely, and spiritually starved.

وَمَنْ أَعْرَضَ عَن ذِكْرِى فَإِنَّ لَهُ مَعِيشَةً ضَنكًا

But whoever turns away from My remembrance will certainly
have a miserable life... [20:124]

Our Lord, the Creator of our souls, revealed that there is only one way for us to feel whole, and only one formula for a good life:

مَنْ عَمِلَ صَلِحًا مِّن ذَكَرٍ أَوْ أُنثَىٰ وَهُوَ مُؤْمِنٌ فَلَنُحْيِيَنَّهُ حَيَوٰةً طَيِّبَةً
وَلَنَجْزِيَنَّهُمْ أَجْرَهُم بِأَحْسَنِ مَا كَانُواْ يَعْمَلُونَ ۝

Whoever does good, whether male or female, and is a believer,
We will surely bless them with a good life. [19:97]

The need to be God-centered is etched in our DNA. We are beings created for worship. We knew God in another dimension, before our existence on this earth, and so we yearn for Him from deep within our soul. Just like the one who is dehydrated may crave unhealthy food, we feed on distractions in order to forget the thirst of being disconnected from Him.

There is one road out of our spiritual desert, and it is to awaken *iman* (faith). **Faith comes first.** It is our most precious resource and the starting point for everything truly good. As we awaken our faith, we become conscious of our surroundings, as though waking from a long sleep. Faith motivates us to pursue a closeness to God, and in that closeness we find safety and peace.

ٱلَّذِينَ ءَامَنُواْ وَلَمْ يَلْبِسُوٓاْ إِيمَٰنَهُم بِظُلْمٍ أُوْلَٰٓئِكَ لَهُمُ ٱلْأَمْنُ وَهُم مُّهْتَدُونَ ۝

Those who are faithful and do not tarnish their faith with falsehood will be secure, and it is they who are rightly guided. [6:82]

Every Muslim on earth has some trace of faith in their heart; we have all experienced its highs and lows. We have felt remorse when we remember our shortcomings in fulfilling what He asked of us on earth. No matter how hard our hearts have become, we understand that we belong to Him. Every now and then, we make bold resolutions to become more God-centered. But while the journey to God is truly sweet, this enthusiasm is usually a temporary phase. We grow distracted from our worship by family, work, school, and other pursuits. Our relationship with God is continually sidelined; it is easy to be frustrated by this cycle. Is it possible to maintain a high level of *iman* while living in such a demanding and materialistic society?

Scholars and philosophers have asked this question many times over the centuries. As Muslims, we are in possession of a practical methodology for living a faith-centered life in a material world. The legacy of the Prophet's Companions is timeless proof of the power, adaptability, and possibility of strong faith.

The Companions were not superhuman—in fact, the more we learn about them, the more we appreciate how they wrestled with the same challenges that we do. As narrations indicate, it was not the quantity of their deeds that surpassed every other generation, but something powerful that rested within their hearts. The Prophet ﷺ taught them to engage fully with their livelihood, families, and communities while also pursuing closeness to God. Throughout the book, we will take a closer look at examples of the Companions who sought the highest levels of faith while maintaining balance in every aspect of their lives.

The methodology used in nurturing the character of the Companions emphasized *iman* as a prerequisite to the rest of religion. It wasn't until the Medina period, more than 13 years after the first revelation, that fasting was mandated, intoxicants were prohibited, and other rulings regarding dress, financial dealings and social conduct were revealed. Even the five daily prayers were not prescribed until the *Isra' and Mi'raj*, roughly ten years after the beginning of Prophethood. But consider this: *qiyam* (night prayer) was prescribed at the very beginning for the early Muslims!

◆◆◆

S a'd ibn Hisham asked Aishah, the Prophet's wife and Mother of the Believers, "Tell me about the night prayers of the Prophet." She said, "Haven't you read Surah Al-Muzzammil? Allah Exalted prescribed night prayers at the beginning of the chapter. So Allah's Prophet and his Companions prayed that way for a year. Allah held back the revelation of the end of the surah for twelve months. Then Allah revealed the last verses, which lightened the burden, and night prayer became voluntary after it had been obligatory."[1]

This is a revealing point about how to awaken and rekindle faith. Standing for prayer in the middle of the night is quite difficult even once or twice a week. Nevertheless, the early Muslims spent the greater part of every night in prayer.

$$\text{يَـٰٓأَيُّهَا ٱلۡمُزَّمِّلُ ۝ قُمِ ٱلَّيۡلَ إِلَّا قَلِيلًا ۝ نِّصۡفَهُۥٓ أَوِ ٱنقُصۡ مِنۡهُ قَلِيلًا ۝ أَوۡ زِدۡ عَلَيۡهِ وَرَتِّلِ ٱلۡقُرۡءَانَ تَرۡتِيلًا ۝}$$

You, enfolded in your cloak! Stand all night (in prayer) except a little–half, or a little less, or a little more; recite the Quran slowly and distinctly [73:1-4]

In that first year, they prayed every night with the diligence later observed during the nights of Ramadan, according to Ibn Abbas.[2] But why was night prayer the first religious prescription for early Muslims? The Quran points to the reason:

$$\text{إِنَّ نَاشِئَةَ ٱلَّيۡلِ هِيَ أَشَدُّ وَطۡـًٔا وَأَقۡوَمُ قِيلًا ۝}$$

Indeed, the hours of the night are more impactful and suitable for recitation. [73:6]

Praying, reciting the Quran and calling upon God in the dark and stillness of the night was a stark departure from the typical rhythm of human life. Worshipping at night sharpens the words of the Quran, and forgoing sleep is a sacrifice worthy of a momentous message.

These pioneers among the Companions were being prepared for a difficult mission, and their hearts had to be primed to receive guidance. They would require rich reservoirs of faith to survive the long and hard road ahead.

Because the hearts of the Companions had been nurtured with faith over the years, it was easier for them to implement religious prescriptions later on. The verse to give up alcohol and gambling concluded with the question,

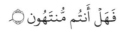

Will you not give them up? [5:91]

The Companions reaction was immediate. Streams of wine flowed in the streets of Medina as the vessels of alcohol were overturned. "We have given it up, our Lord!" they cried. It was an easy choice for hearts that had been nurtured in faith from the very beginning.

The first step in reforming ourselves and our community is to awaken faith and strengthen the connection with God. This rekindled faith is the fuel behind all good actions. Iman is not something that is inspired once; rather it must be rejuvenated continously. As the heart beats with a strong pulse of faith, the actions of the limbs follow. Developing faith is the most important form of *tarbiyah* (holistic training and development of the individual), and takes precedence over other forms of development.

Faith First was originally published as *Al-Iman Awwalan* by Magdy Al-Hilali. Adapted and translated by the Muslim American Society (MAS), this book is a much-needed resource for Muslims struggling with the practical steps of increasing faith. Some adaptations have been made to the original text to make the English version more readable. MAS' team of translators and editors strived to make this work relatable to contemporary readers, young and old.

As we prepare for the journey of faith and awaken our hearts, what is the best way to start? We understand the importance of faith but cannot always envision the best strategies for strengthening it, nor do we understand why our efforts in building faith may not always succeed. In order to grow our faith and connect our hearts to Allah, who is already nearer to us than we can imagine, we need to address what is blocking our hearts. We must revive and prime the heart first before we can expect it to work correctly.

This book is a how-to guide that focuses on the first steps of awakening the heart and awakening faith. *Faith First* helps readers to understand how faith works and then presents practical methods to root faith more deeply in the heart. The methods laid out in these pages are grounded in the Quran and the teachings of the Prophet ﷺ. With a multitude of verses, hadiths, and examples illustrating each method, readers will better understand the process of awakening faith in themselves and others. This book is unique in its emphasis on using the Quran to inspire and extract wisdoms in dealing with the heart, and readers may find themselves reflecting on familiar verses in a new light. Most importantly, we hope readers put into practice the methods presented here, using them to renovate their hearts, awaken their *iman*, and guide others in their journey to God.

A Heart Assessment

If God is close, as the verse in the beginning of this chapter indicated, then why do we feel disconnected? Why do we experience a perceived distance from God? The Quran has a straightforward answer to this:

كَلَّا بَلْ رَانَ عَلَىٰ قُلُوبِهِم مَّا كَانُوا يَكْسِبُونَ ۞

*No, verily their hearts are encrusted
with what they have done.* [43:14]

Sins and ambivalence create a physical crust on our heart, and this is why we feel detached. The encased heart becomes hard and numb, and does not easily respond to reminders and invitations to do good. The effort it takes to break through the crust and revive the heart is different for every person.

For some, there is a living, beating heart just under a thin layer of crust. Others will find their true, living heart through some effort, chipping away at the accumulated layers of neglect. It is not always a matter of time — if God wills, His guidance can free a trapped heart in an instant. No one can tell you exactly where your living, spiritual heart is hidden or how much excavation is needed to awaken it. One thing is certain: a vibrant faith-centered heart is within reach of anyone who is sincerely searching and willing to do some effort.

How will you know when you are on track, and your heart is working properly? You can assess the state of your heart by looking for these signs. They are described in the Quran as symptoms of a living heart, one that is free of distortion and tuned to guidance.

«(Is My Heart Awake?)»

- *Does my heart feel open and bright?*
- *Do I feel a sense of awe when God is mentioned?*
- *How sensitive am I to spiritual reminders?*
- *Do I taste enjoyment during worship?*
- *Is it easy for me to obey God's commands?*

◃ EXPANSIVENESS AND LIGHT ◃

أَوَمَن كَانَ مَيْتًا فَأَحْيَيْنَـٰهُ وَجَعَلْنَا لَهُۥ نُورًا يَمْشِى بِهِۦ فِى ٱلنَّاسِ كَمَن مَّثَلُهُۥ فِى ٱلظُّلُمَـٰتِ لَيْسَ بِخَارِجٍ مِّنْهَا ۚ كَذَٰلِكَ زُيِّنَ لِلْكَـٰفِرِينَ مَا كَانُواْ يَعْمَلُونَ ۝

Is a dead person brought back to life by Us, and given light with which to walk among people, comparable to someone trapped in deep darkness who cannot escape? [6:122]

A healthy heart is light and expansive. It feels alive when it is doing good deeds. Ibn Mas'ood and some others of Companions asked the Prophet ﷺ about this verse:

أَفَمَن شَرَحَ ٱللَّهُ صَدْرَهُۥ لِلْإِسْلَـٰمِ فَهُوَ عَلَىٰ نُورٍ مِّن رَّبِّهِۦ

What about the one whose chest God has opened in devotion to Him, so that he walks in light from his Lord? [39:22]

'What is this opening, Messenger of Allah?" The Prophet ﷺ answered, 'It is a light that is cast into the heart, and so it expands." The Companions asked, "Messenger of Allah, are there signs of that happening?" He ﷺ replied, "Yes...a yearning for the space of eternal life, shunning the world of desires, and preparation for death before it is met."[3]

◃ SHIVERING ◃

إِنَّمَا ٱلْمُؤْمِنُونَ ٱلَّذِينَ إِذَا ذُكِرَ ٱللَّهُ وَجِلَتْ قُلُوبُهُمْ وَإِذَا تُلِيَتْ عَلَيْهِمْ ءَايَـٰتُهُۥ زَادَتْهُمْ إِيمَـٰنًا وَعَلَىٰ رَبِّهِمْ يَتَوَكَّلُونَ ۝

True believers are those whose hearts tremble with awe when God is mentioned [8:2]

The shivering or trembling when you think of Allah is a sign that life is returning to your heart. Shivers run down your spine when you reflect upon God and His words. Um ad-Darda' said, "The shivering of the heart is like the burning of a palm leaf."[4] One can imagine the image she was evoking, similar to a piece of paper quivering, trembling and twisting in a flame.

◃(REVERENCE)▹

أَلَمْ يَأْنِ لِلَّذِينَ ءَامَنُوٓاْ أَن تَخْشَعَ قُلُوبُهُمْ لِذِكْرِ ٱللَّهِ وَمَا نَزَلَ مِنَ ٱلْحَقِّ وَلَا يَكُونُواْ كَٱلَّذِينَ أُوتُواْ ٱلْكِتَٰبَ مِن قَبْلُ فَطَالَ عَلَيْهِمُ ٱلْأَمَدُ فَقَسَتْ قُلُوبُهُمْ ۖ وَكَثِيرٌ مِّنْهُمْ فَٰسِقُونَ ۝

Is it not time for believers to humble (takhsha') their hearts to the remembrance of God and the Truth that has been revealed, and not to be like those who received the Scripture before them, whose time was extended but whose hearts hardened and many of whom were law-breakers? [57:16]

Khushoo' is usually translated as humility, but the meaning is actually a blend of emotions and physical sensations. *Khushoo'* encompasses meanings of awe, fear, reverence, and humility. It is a humble awe; the surrendering and deference of the heart as it acknowledges power-lessness and need for God. Ibn Al-Qayyim explains that the linguistic roots of *khushoo'* communicate a physical softening and stillness.[5]

On the Day of Judgment, voices will be hushed in awe and surrender:

وَخَشَعَتِ ٱلْأَصْوَاتُ لِلرَّحْمَٰنِ فَلَا تَسْمَعُ إِلَّا هَمْسًا ۝

Every voice will be hushed [khasha'at] for the Lord of Mercy; only whispers will be heard. [20:108]

The word *khushoo'* is used in the Quran to describe the earth: sub-missive, flattened, and still.

وَمِنْ ءَايَٰتِهِۦٓ أَنَّكَ تَرَى ٱلْأَرْضَ خَٰشِعَةً فَإِذَآ أَنزَلْنَا عَلَيْهَا ٱلْمَآءَ ٱهْتَزَّتْ وَرَبَتْ

Another of His signs is this: you see the earth lying desolate [khaashi'ah], but when We send water down on to it, it stirs and grows. [41:39]

---

khushoo':

reverence, awe, humility; often in the context of worship

خشوع

⊰ SENSITIVITY ⊱

The heart should not be a bystander in worship; it should be sensitive and alert. A healthy heart engages fully with worship, and there is a harmony of heart, tongue and limbs, each interacting with the other in the remembrance of God. Such a sensitive heart is response-ready, summoning tears and emotion during prayer, recitation of Quran, remembrance *(thikr)*, and supplication *(dua)*. The heart is present not only at those times, but also in daily situations that call for a compassionate response.

Another manifestation of a healthy heart is an increase in reverence and humility (*khushu'*), not just during, but *after* worship. Following acts of worship, we should check our heart for increased humility and sensitivity. This is a sign that our heart is responding to the worship and remembrance of Allah.

وَيَخِرُّونَ لِلْأَذْقَانِ يَبْكُونَ وَيَزِيدُهُمْ خُشُوعًا ۩

They fall down on their faces, weeping, and it increases their humility. [17:109]

⊰ TASTING THE SWEETNESS OF FAITH ⊱

The sweetness of faith is a delight like no other. The Prophet ﷺ said, **"There are three states in which the sweetness of faith can be found: when Allah and His messenger are more beloved than anything else, to love someone only for the sake of Allah, and to hate to return to disbelief just as one would hate to be thrown into the fire."**[6]

Al-Hasan Al-Basri said, "Look for the sweetness of faith amidst three things: during prayer, in the remembrance of God, and during the recitation of Quran. If you cannot find it there, you should know that your door is blocked."[7]

⊰ LOVING TO STRIVE FOR THE SAKE OF GOD ⊱

Some people mistakenly understand working and striving for the sake of Allah as a volunteer opportunity or extra credit, something to do when all of our other life responsibilities are taken care of. This verse indicates that it should be our highest priority, a sign of our faith:

قُلْ إِن كَانَ ءَابَآؤُكُمْ وَأَبْنَآؤُكُمْ وَإِخْوَٰنُكُمْ وَأَزْوَٰجُكُمْ وَعَشِيرَتُكُمْ
وَأَمْوَٰلٌ ٱقْتَرَفْتُمُوهَا وَتِجَٰرَةٌ تَخْشَوْنَ كَسَادَهَا وَمَسَٰكِنُ تَرْضَوْنَهَآ أَحَبَّ

إِلَيْكُم مِّنَ ٱللَّهِ وَرَسُولِهِۦ وَجِهَادٍ فِى سَبِيلِهِۦ فَتَرَبَّصُواْ حَتَّىٰ يَأْتِىَ ٱللَّهُ بِأَمْرِهِۦ وَٱللَّهُ لَا يَهْدِى ٱلْقَوْمَ ٱلْفَٰسِقِينَ ۝

Say (Prophet), 'If your fathers, sons, brothers, wives, tribes,
decline, and the dwellings you love are dearer to you than
Allah and His Messenger and the struggle in His cause, then
wait until God brings about His punishment.' Allah does
not guide those who break away. [9:24]

◄ SUBMISSION TO GOD'S RULINGS ►

A living heart finds it easier to obey God's rules:

فَإِن تَنَٰزَعْتُمْ فِى شَىْءٍ فَرُدُّوهُ إِلَى ٱللَّهِ وَٱلرَّسُولِ إِن كُنتُمْ تُؤْمِنُونَ بِٱللَّهِ وَٱلْيَوْمِ ٱلْءَاخِرِ

If you are in dispute over any matter, refer it to God and
the Messenger, if you truly believe in God and the Last
Day. [4:59]

Faith serves as a fortification against disobedience to God. It makes it easier to fulfill God's commands and stay away from what displeases Him:

يَٰٓأَيُّهَا ٱلَّذِينَ ءَامَنُواْ ٱتَّقُواْ ٱللَّهَ وَذَرُواْ مَا بَقِىَ مِنَ ٱلرِّبَوٰٓاْ إِن كُنتُم مُّؤْمِنِينَ ۝

You who believe, beware of God: give up any
outstanding dues from usury, if you are true believers.
[2:278]

This doesn't mean that the believer never makes mistakes or commits sins. Believers are as fallible and human as anyone else. But due to their faith and resilient hearts, believers rise up quickly after mistakes and return to God. They don't spiral out of control, prolonging their sinful state, and they avoid repeating the same sins:

يَعِظُكُمُ ٱللَّهُ أَن تَعُودُواْ لِمِثْلِهِۦٓ أَبَدًا إِن كُنتُم مُّؤْمِنِينَ ۝

God warns you never to do anything like this again, if
you are true believers. [24:17]

إِنَّ ٱلَّذِينَ ٱتَّقَوۡاْ إِذَا مَسَّهُمۡ طَٰٓئِفٌ مِّنَ ٱلشَّيۡطَٰنِ تَذَكَّرُواْ فَإِذَا هُم مُّبۡصِرُونَ ۝

*Those who are aware of God think of Him when Satan
prompts them to do something and immediately they can
see clearly.* [7:201]

◁{ FEELING CLOSE TO GOD }▷

When your heart is free of distortion, you feel close to Allah. You sense His presence when you pray and supplicate. You know that He is listening when you call upon Him, so you call upon Him even more. Day by day you grow closer until you reach a level of intimate nearness, delighting in worship and being alone with Him. Ibn Al-Qayyim says,

> When the heart lets go of fretting over this life with its money, status and image, and instead clings to the hereafter, bracing itself to stand before Allah, this is the first of its triumphs. It is the beginning of an inner sunrise, in which the heart tries to discover what will please Allah in order to do more and increase in closeness to Him. Whatever displeases Him is avoided. This is the sign of a true desire for God.

> When the heart is awakened and begins to move freely in this way, it learns to relish moments of solitude and privacy with God. Never noticing those empty pauses before, the heart now seeks out spaces where voices and sounds are hushed. The heart feels alienated by the constant chatter of life. In the silence, it finds the necessary space to rejuvenate while recovering from the distractions and low morale.

> As you continue on this road, you'll find a door open for your heart, and you'll feel yourself well up with love and sweetness. You'll feel that you can never get your fill of worship—you'll find comfort and joy beyond any mundane happiness. You might find yourself wishing prayer will never end, and you will long to hear more of the speech of Allah because your heart is put at ease—just as the heart of a child is at ease when it is surrounded by love.[8]

❧❧❧

These are some of the signs mentioned by the Quran and Prophet Muhammad ﷺ that we can use as benchmarks to measure how healthy our heart is. Don't be discouraged if you do not recognize any of these signs in yourself! It does not mean that you aren't a believer, nor does it mean your heart is permanently sealed. It certainly does not mean there is no hope — only that there is work to do.

If you are like many, you occasionally experience a closeness with Allah, but those moments fade quickly and do not last. Faith still resides in your heart, by the grace of Allah, but you should take this weakening pulse as a warning. It is urgent that you nurture yourself on a program of awakening and developing faith. As you work through this regimen, you just may find along the way that your heart achieves a sublime consciousness of God and tastes the joy described earlier. Allah says in the Quran:

يَـٰٓأَيُّهَا ٱلَّذِينَ ءَامَنُوا۟ ٱسْتَجِيبُوا۟ لِلَّهِ وَلِلرَّسُولِ إِذَا دَعَاكُمْ لِمَا يُحْيِيكُمْ
وَٱعْلَمُوٓا۟ أَنَّ ٱللَّهَ يَحُولُ بَيْنَ ٱلْمَرْءِ وَقَلْبِهِۦ وَأَنَّهُۥٓ إِلَيْهِ تُحْشَرُونَ ۝

Believers, respond to God and His Messenger when he calls
you to that which gives you life. Know that God comes
between a man and his heart, and that you will be gathered to
Him. [8:24]

The call of God and His Messenger is truly life-giving; we must respond to it with our hearts. minds, tongues, and limbs. The task of awakening our own faith and the faith of others is an urgent matter—beware of the temptation to brush it aside. Do not be content with a shallow spirituality; even a sick heart may still taste the sweetness of worship and public reminders on collective occasions such as Ramadan, Hajj, conventions, and organized activities. For a short time, this disadvantaged heart may enjoy these pious gatherings, but such staged moments of spirituality are inadequate and short-lasting.

Once this heart is submerged in the sludge of its day-to-day, the experience of God-mindfulness disappears; just as someone asleep is startled into consciousness, looks around for a few seconds, then drifts off to sleep again. The one who possesses a pure, living heart is continuously alert and works hard to maintain this state amidst the competing priorities of life. This is the goal we will try to reach together in this book, *insha'Allah.*

....

ENDNOTES

1. Muslim (1/512-513 #746)
2. Ibn Abi Shaibah (7/266 #35942) Abu Dawud (2/475 #1305) and Al-Hakim (2/548 #3864)
3. Al-Hakim, Al-Bayhaqi in *Az-Zuhd*
4. *Al-Jami' li Ahkam al-Quran* by al-Qurtubi (15/163)
5. *Tahtheeb Madarij As-Salikeen* by Ibn Al-Qayyim, 275
6. *Sahih*: Bukhari, Muslim; *Sahih al-Jami' as-Sagheer,* 1044
7. *Tahtheeb Madarij as-Salikeen,* p. 463
8. *Tahtheeb Madarij As-Salikeen* by Ibn Al-Qayyim, p. 631-632

MOTIVATION

HOW FAITH WORKS

FAITH AND THE ANSAR

WHEN FAITH IS WEAK

FAITH AND CHANGE

BEGIN WITH FAITH

PART I

why faith first?

Motivation

There is a motive behind every deed, decision and act of worship; our motives are the engines driving our actions. Motives stem from our most fundamental feelings of love, dislike, fear and desire. In order to awaken our faith, we must develop a strong source of motivation for it.

It is expected that we will do anything to please our beloved ones and guard them from harm, even at great inconvenience to ourselves. Every day, we do things that are difficult or outwardly inefficient because we are motivated by something larger than the action itself. Our actions as worshippers of God can be viewed in the same way.

When our worship arises from feelings of love and need, it takes on an entirely new spirit. Practicing our religion is easier when our actions are motivated by the fundamental emotions of love, fear, hope, and so on. Allah says in the Quran:

وَلَٰكِنَّ ٱللَّهَ حَبَّبَ إِلَيْكُمُ ٱلْإِيمَٰنَ وَزَيَّنَهُۥ فِى قُلُوبِكُمْ وَكَرَّهَ
إِلَيْكُمُ ٱلْكُفْرَ وَٱلْفُسُوقَ وَٱلْعِصْيَانَ أُوْلَٰٓئِكَ هُمُ ٱلرَّٰشِدُونَ فَضْلًا
مِّنَ ٱللَّهِ وَنِعْمَةً وَٱللَّهُ عَلِيمٌ حَكِيمٌ ۝

God has endeared faith to you and made it beautiful
to your hearts; He has made disbelief, mischief, and
disobedience hateful to you. It is people like this who are
rightly guided through God's favor and blessing: God is
all knowing and all wise. [49:7-8]

When our feelings of love and fear of God are undeveloped, worshipping and obeying Him feels difficult. Faced with two conflicting choices, we will choose the option backed by a stronger motive.

Our love for God becomes more powerful when connected to our sense of need for Him. To understand the relationship between faith, love, and need, take the example of a student who thrives on competition and recognition. The satisfaction of coming out on top keeps her motivated. She is willing to sacrifice sleep because her love for achievement outweighs life's pleasures. She is motivated to succeed, but is it because she loves success or because she needs it? The line between need and love is blurred; we love what we need, and often convince ourselves that we need what we love.

When we are motivated by love of God and our hatred of angering Him, then our faith is complete. Our life becomes a living expression of what is pleasing to God, and the self-serving ego is suppressed. Abu Umamah related that the Prophet ﷺ said, **"Whoever loves for God's sake, hates for God's sake, gives for God's sake and withholds for God's sake, has completed faith."**[1]

$$\text{وَٱلَّذِينَ ءَامَنُوٓاْ أَشَدُّ حُبًّا لِّلَّهِ}$$

Believers have greater love for God. [2:165]

Deep need and love ignite determination. The teasings of desire fade away in light of our greatest loves and deepest needs, whatever they may be. The more convinced we are that we need something, the more determined we are in its pursuit.

Our Need for God

Let's return now to the questions we asked earlier. Why do so many people fall short in fulfilling the duties of worship to God? Why do I feel distant from God? Why can good deeds be so burdensome, while sin seems effortless? We now have the beginnings of an answer. It is because people do not feel a deep need for Allah:

$$\text{كَلَّآ إِنَّ ٱلْإِنسَٰنَ لَيَطْغَىٰٓ ۝ أَن رَّءَاهُ ٱسْتَغْنَىٰٓ ۝}$$

But man exceeds all bounds, when he thinks he is self-sufficient. [96: 6-7]

Unless we are mindful, we slip into an illusion of self-sufficiency. We assume we are independent and have control over our lives. But when life constricts with hardship, our perspective changes dramatically. Humanity's deep need for God is realized in those moments of distress. Raising our hands and tilting our faces to the sky, we turn toward God as we should have all along. We call upon God eagerly in moments of dire need, humbled and broken.

$$\text{هُوَ ٱلَّذِى يُسَيِّرُكُمْ فِى ٱلْبَرِّ وَٱلْبَحْرِ حَتَّىٰٓ إِذَا كُنتُمْ فِى ٱلْفُلْكِ}$$
$$\text{وَجَرَيْنَ بِهِم بِرِيحٍ طَيِّبَةٍ وَفَرِحُواْ بِهَا جَآءَتْهَا رِيحٌ عَاصِفٌ وَجَآءَهُمُ}$$

ٱلْمَوْجُ مِن كُلِّ مَكَانٍ وَظَنُّواْ أَنَّهُمْ أُحِيطَ بِهِمْ دَعَوُاْ ٱللَّهَ مُخْلِصِينَ
لَهُ ٱلدِّينَ لَئِنْ أَنجَيْتَنَا مِنْ هَذِهِ لَنَكُونَنَّ مِنَ ٱلشَّاكِرِينَ ۝

It is He who enables you to travel on land and sea
until, when you are sailing on ships and rejoicing in the
favouring wind, a storm arrives: waves come at those
on board from all sides and they feel there is no escape.
Then they pray to God, professing sincere devotion
to Him, 'If You save us from this we shall be truly
thankful.' [10:22]

All Prophets, in their practice of calling people to God, emphasized humanity's profound need for God. The prophetic message reminded people of their dependence on God's blessings, and their miserable condition when they deny His presence. Prophet Hud said to his people,

وَٱتَّقُواْ ٱلَّذِى أَمَدَّكُم بِمَا تَعْلَمُونَ ۝ أَمَدَّكُم بِأَنْعَامٍ
وَبَنِينَ ۝ وَجَنَّاتٍ وَعُيُونٍ ۝ إِنِّى أَخَافُ عَلَيْكُمْ عَذَابَ يَوْمٍ
عَظِيمٍ ۝

Be mindful of Him who has provided you with everything
you know — He has given you livestock, sons, gardens,
springs — for I truly fear that the torment of a grievous
day will overtake you. [26:132-13]

How to Generate Motivation

Good, sincere deeds are motivated by love and a sense of need for Allah's forgiveness and reward. Learning the value of a specific deed motivates us to carry it out to seek its reward. For example, we are motivated to increase our donation when reminded about the status of charity and when we can visualize the need and impact it can have.

This process of enabling people to realize their need is a powerful method of *tarbiyah* (the holistic development of Islamic character and spirituality). Think about the sheer number of *hadiths* spelling out the merits and incentives of different actions. The Prophet ﷺ associated concrete rewards with good deeds in order to evoke our need for those deeds. Similarly, he associated bad deeds with dreaded consequences to motivate our flight from what displeases our Lord.

But forgetfulness is our second nature. God says,

وَلَقَدْ عَهِدْنَآ إِلَىٰٓ ءَادَمَ مِن قَبْلُ فَنَسِىَ وَلَمْ نَجِدْ لَهُۥ عَزْمًا ۝

We also commanded Adam before you, but he forgot and We
found him lacking in constancy. [20:115]

It is a mistake to think that when we hear or learn something once, we have no need of it
again. W might be inspired and convinced today, but that enthusiasm fades over time. This is
why the practice of reminding and remembering is so central to our faith; we should perpetually remind ourselves and one another of the significance behind our actions, motivations,
and commitments. Remembrance and renewal is the constant rhythm of the believer's life:

وَذَكِّرْ فَإِنَّ ٱلذِّكْرَىٰ تَنفَعُ ٱلْمُؤْمِنِينَ ۝

And go on reminding people, it is good for those
who believe to be reminded. [51:55]

Along with remembrance and mutual reminding, we must develop a clear vision of our
highest desire. Our greatest, encompassing goal should be winning God's pleasure and
avoiding His anger, admission to Paradise and evading Hell. We should organize our entire
life around this purpose, pursuing every action that is a means to reach this lofty aim. When
you are motivated by faith-based goals, your lifestyle will look very different from those who
lack such motivation. When your sense of need is centered on God, everything that crosses
your path in life must pass a litmus test: does this align with my goal of attaining God's
pleasure? Embrace it if it does, and discard if it doesn't.

The Quran repeatedly encourages us to develop our love and longing for Paradise to
motivate us to work hard and invite others to aspire to the hereafter:

وَسَارِعُوٓاْ إِلَىٰ مَغْفِرَةٍ مِّن رَّبِّكُمْ وَجَنَّةٍ عَرْضُهَا ٱلسَّمَٰوَٰتُ وَٱلْأَرْضُ
أُعِدَّتْ لِلْمُتَّقِينَ ۝

Hurry towards your Lord's forgiveness and a Garden as wide
as the heavens and earth prepared for the righteous. [3:133]

فَمَن زُحْزِحَ عَنِ ٱلنَّارِ وَأُدْخِلَ ٱلْجَنَّةَ فَقَدْ فَازَّ ۝

Whoever is drawn away from the Fire and admitted to the
Garden will have triumphed. [3:185]

Contrasting with the pursuit of forgiveness and Paradise, we find stern warnings of the horrors of hell that motivate our flight from sin:

إِنَّ جَهَنَّمَ كَانَتْ مِرْصَادًا ۝ لِّلطَّٰغِينَ مَـَٔابًا ۝ لَّٰبِثِينَ فِيهَآ
أَحْقَابًا ۝ لَّا يَذُوقُونَ فِيهَا بَرْدًا وَلَا شَرَابًا ۝ إِلَّا حَمِيمًا وَغَسَّاقًا ۝

Hell lies in ambush, a home for oppressors to stay in for a long, long time, where they will taste no coolness nor drink, except one that is scalding and dark — a fitting requital. [78:21-26]

إِنَّ لَدَيْنَآ أَنكَالًا وَجَحِيمًا ۝ وَطَعَامًا ذَا غُصَّةٍ وَعَذَابًا أَلِيمًا ۝

We have fetters, a blazing fire, food that chokes and an agonizing torment in store for them. [73:12-13]

Maintaining a regular connection with the Quran by reading and reflecting upon it ensures that we receive continual reminders that renew our motivation. The Quran sets alight our love for pleasing God and our dread of displeasing Him. It brings heaven and hell to life before our eyes so that we are deeply motivated in our pursuit of one and flight from the other.

....

ENDNOTES

1. Abu Dawud 8/69 # 4681; Al-Albani in *Saheeh Al-Jami'* #5965

How Faith Works

Among the meanings of faith (*iman*) is belief and certainty in Allah's names, attributes, promises and warnings. Faith is understanding that God did not create us to wander through life, but for a great purpose:

أَفَحَسِبْتُمْ أَنَّمَا خَلَقْنَـٰكُمْ عَبَثًا وَأَنَّكُمْ إِلَيْنَا لَا
تُرْجَعُونَ ۞ فَتَعَـٰلَى ٱللَّهُ ٱلْمَلِكُ ٱلْحَقُّ ۖ لَّا إِلَـٰهَ إِلَّا هُوَ رَبُّ ٱلْعَرْشِ
ٱلْكَرِيمِ ۞

*Did you think We had created you in vain, and that
you would not be brought back to Us? Exalted be
Allah, the true King, there is no god but Him, the Lord
of the Glorious Throne!* [23:115-116]

وَمَا خَلَقْتُ ٱلْجِنَّ وَٱلْإِنسَ إِلَّا لِيَعْبُدُونِ ۞

I created Jinn and Mankind only to worship Me. [51:56]

We are beings created for worship and servitude, similar to the rest of creation. To believe is to join the congregation of creatures and creation, the vast ensemble of worshippers in the universe expressing surrender, reverence, and humility before God. This magnificent scale of worship is encompassed in the faith of a Muslim.

تُسَبِّحُ لَهُ ٱلسَّمَـٰوَٰتُ ٱلسَّبْعُ وَٱلْأَرْضُ وَمَن فِيهِنَّ ۚ وَإِن مِّن شَىْءٍ إِلَّا يُسَبِّحُ
بِحَمْدِهِ وَلَـٰكِن لَّا تَفْقَهُونَ تَسْبِيحَهُمْ ۗ إِنَّهُۥ كَانَ حَلِيمًا غَفُورًا ۞

---

iman:

faith, belief;
*Derived from the word 'amn (safety),
iman linguistically means taking
something as true, accepting it, and
believing in it. In Islam, it is certainty
and complete acceptance of the existence of God and His attributes, and
belief in the Prophet and revelation.
Iman is speech, action, and intention,
not merely conviction. It can increase
and decrease, and its strength or
weakness reaches the depths of the
self and affects all its aspects.*

إيمان

The seven heavens and the earth and everyone in them glorify Him. There is not a single thing that does not celebrate His praise, though you do not understand their praise: He is most forbearing, most forgiving. [17:44]

From crickets to comets, single-celled organisms to gravitational fields, mountains and rivers, volcanoes and the shifting continents: every phenomenon and creature is conscious of God and has its own form of worship. Only the human being turns away from this overwhelming reality. This perspective changes the Muslim's mindset from being an anomaly to being among the vast majority of creation; disbelief and ignorance of God are deviations from the norms of the universe.

There is one aspect in which the worship of the human being is unique: free will. We choose to worship or not—and bear the consequences of that decision. In this way, we are distinct from the rest of creation. We are called upon to worship God despite competing forces drawing us away. These forces include a selfish ego and a devil sworn to mislead us:

قَالَ فَبِعِزَّتِكَ لَأُغْوِيَنَّهُمْ أَجْمَعِينَ ۝ إِلَّا عِبَادَكَ مِنْهُمُ ٱلْمُخْلَصِينَ ۝

Iblis said, 'I swear by Your might! I will tempt all but Your true servants.' [38:82-83]

Our worth before God is measured by our worship of Him. Allah says in His book,

قُلْ مَا يَعْبَؤُاْ بِكُمْ رَبِّي لَوْلَا دُعَآؤُكُمْ فَقَدْ كَذَّبْتُمْ فَسَوْفَ يَكُونُ لِزَامًا ۝

Say, 'What are you to my Lord if not for your supplication? But since you have written off the truth as lies, the inevitable will happen.' [25:77]

According to Ibn Abbas, *'your supplication'* in this verse represents our faith in God.[1] But faith can only be measured by Him. It is beyond the authority of any human to rule on whether or not faith exists within a heart, or whether it may exist someday in the future.

Forces of Earth And Sky

The human being was created from both spirit and clay. The origin of the soul is a divine spirit, one of God's secrets which no mind can comprehend, while the body is formed from the clay of the earth.

إِذْ قَالَ رَبُّكَ لِلْمَلَـٰئِكَةِ إِنِّي خَـٰلِقٌ بَشَرًا مِّن طِينٍ ۝ فَإِذَا سَوَّيْتُهُۥ
وَنَفَخْتُ فِيهِ مِن رُّوحِى فَقَعُواْ لَهُۥ سَـٰجِدِينَ ۝

Your Lord said to the angels, 'I will create a human being
from clay. When I have shaped him and breathed from My
Spirit into him, bow down before him.' [38:71-72]

The human being was created to be connected to God, holding to a rope that connects him to the sky and the origins of his soul. When a servant is connected in this way, he or she becomes God-centered (*rabbani*) — of God and for God in every aspect.

وَمَن يُسْلِمْ وَجْهَهُۥٓ إِلَى ٱللَّهِ وَهُوَ مُحْسِنٌ فَقَدِ ٱسْتَمْسَكَ بِٱلْعُرْوَةِ ٱلْوُثْقَىٰ
وَإِلَى ٱللَّهِ عَـٰقِبَةُ ٱلْأُمُورِ ۝

Whoever directs himself wholly to God and does good
work has grasped the surest handhold, for the outcome of
everything is with God. [31:22]

On the other hand, if we reduce ourselves to our worldly desires alone, our heavenly essence diminishes. We become earthbound, wrapped in its illusions and glamour. The Quran describes the different manifestations of these earthly forces:

زُيِّنَ لِلنَّاسِ حُبُّ ٱلشَّهَوَٰتِ مِنَ ٱلنِّسَآءِ وَٱلْبَنِينَ وَٱلْقَنَـٰطِيرِ ٱلْمُقَنطَرَةِ
مِنَ ٱلذَّهَبِ وَٱلْفِضَّةِ وَٱلْخَيْلِ ٱلْمُسَوَّمَةِ وَٱلْأَنْعَـٰمِ وَٱلْحَرْثِ ذَٰلِكَ مَتَـٰعُ ٱلْحَيَوٰةِ
ٱلدُّنْيَا وَٱللَّهُ عِندَهُۥ حُسْنُ ٱلْمَـَٔابِ ۝

The love of desirable things is made alluring for people —
women, children, gold and silver treasures piled up high, horses
with fine markings, livestock, and farmland- these may be the
joys of this life, but God has the best place to return to. [3:14]

Wealth, beauty, status, sleek transportation, and luxurious dwellings are all forms of earthly forces that tie us down to the mud. Our hearts covet such possessions, regardless of whether we own them or not. When we are too preoccupied by these worldly attractions, our love for the afterlife shrinks.

· ◆◆◆ ·

"Whoever loves this earthly life will hurt his afterlife, and whoever loves his afterlife will hurt his earthly life. So favor what is permanent over what is temporary."[2] -Prophet Muhammad

· ·

fitrah:

*the original state of
creation; the innate
spiritual sense; the
collection of attri-
butes and tenden-
cies the human was
initially given*

فطرة

The Great Witnessing

God took an oath from all human beings, in another existence where we were called as witnesses upon ourselves:

وَإِذْ أَخَذَ رَبُّكَ مِنْ بَنِى ءَادَمَ مِنْ ظُهُورِهِمْ ذُرِّيَّتَهُمْ وَأَشْهَدَهُمْ عَلَىٰ أَنفُسِهِمْ أَلَسْتُ بِرَبِّكُمْ قَالُوا۟ بَلَىٰ شَهِدْنَا۟ أَن تَقُولُوا۟ يَوْمَ ٱلْقِيَـٰمَةِ إِنَّا كُنَّا عَنْ هَـٰذَا غَـٰفِلِينَ ۝

*When your Lord took out the offspring from the loins
of the Children of Adam and made them bear witness
about themselves, He said, 'Am I not your Lord?'
and they replied, 'Yes, we bear witness.' So you
cannot say on the Day of Resurrection, 'We were not
aware of this.'* [7:172]

The memory of this oath and testimony is etched onto our innate spiritual sense (*fitrah*).

فَأَقِمْ وَجْهَكَ لِلدِّينِ حَنِيفًا فِطْرَتَ ٱللَّهِ ٱلَّتِى فَطَرَ ٱلنَّاسَ عَلَيْهَا لَا تَبْدِيلَ لِخَلْقِ ٱللَّهِ ذَٰلِكَ ٱلدِّينُ ٱلْقَيِّمُ وَلَـٰكِنَّ أَكْثَرَ ٱلنَّاسِ لَا يَعْلَمُونَ ۝

*So as one of pure faith, stand firm and true in
your devotion to the religion. This is the natural
disposition (fitrah) God instilled in mankind –
there is no altering God's creation – and this is
the right religion, though most people do not
realize it.* [30:30]

The Prophet ﷺ said, "Every child is born on the fitrah, then it is his parents who make him a Jew, Christian or Zoroastrian."[3] God made it clear to us from the beginning of time that human beings are held accountable for how well they fulfill the purpose of their creation:

أَيَحْسَبُ ٱلْإِنسَـٰنُ أَن يُتْرَكَ سُدًى ۝

*Does man think he will be left
without purpose?* [75:36]

وَعُرِضُوا۟ عَلَىٰ رَبِّكَ صَفًّا لَّقَدْ جِئْتُمُونَا كَمَا خَلَقْنَـٰكُمْ أَوَّلَ مَرَّةٍۭ بَلْ زَعَمْتُمْ أَلَّن نَّجْعَلَ لَكُم مَّوْعِدًا ۝

They will be lined up before your Lord: 'Now you have come to Us as We first created you, although you claimed We had not made any such appointment for you.' [18:48]

At the center of our worship-based identity lies our heart, wherein resides our most essential emotions and motives: love, dislike, fear, hope, joy, and sorrow. God created the heart to be a dwelling place for servitude to Him, and as we travel towards God to awaken our faith, our heart is our primary instrument.

Heart, Mind and Ego

nafs:

the self, ego; may be inspired with good or evil tendencies

نفس

God created the heart's miraculous apparatus within every human being, making it the central motivator in our lives. Every limb of the body is at the heart's command. The heart has the final word in decision-making, while all other motions of the body follow along. The Prophet ﷺ said, **"In the body there is a muscle. If it is good, the whole body is good. If it is spoiled, the whole body is spoiled — truly, it is the heart."**[4] From this great *hadith*, we understand the link between the state of our heart and our outward behavior. A good heart will translate into righteous actions, while a diseased heart will not.

If the heart is the center of our being, what about the mind? The heart has deputies, among them the mind and the self. The mind, or the intellect, directs our knowledge and thought processes. Because the mind has the power to recognize consequences and regulate emotions, it is the heart's chief advisor. The ego or self (*nafs*) is also a deputy of the heart, but it can be an undermining force. It is the nucleus of instinct and desire. It seeks to dominate the heart and control decision-making.

The mind and self are not the only elements competing for influence over the heart. Allah created two Companions for every one of us: one angel and one devil. These personal advisors attempt to sway our motivations and judgment. The angel encourages good and warns us to stay away from evil. The devil whispers false promises in our ear and lures us into danger, leveraging the self's love for instant gratification.

Ibn Masud related that the Prophet ﷺ said, **"Among human beings** there is a company of devils and a company of angels. As for the devils, they promise evil consequences and deny the truth. The angels promise goodness and confirm the truth. Whoever finds the angels' presence in his life should know that it is from Allah, thanking and praising Him. Whoever finds himself with the other presence, should seek refuge in Allah from the cursed devil."[5] Then the Prophet ﷺ recited Allah's words,

$$ ٱلشَّيْطَٰنُ يَعِدُكُمُ ٱلْفَقْرَ وَيَأْمُرُكُم بِٱلْفَحْشَآءِ $$

Satan threatens you with the prospect of poverty and commands you to do foul deeds... [2:268]

Faith Versus Desire

We've identified the heart as the nucleus of innermost feelings: love, hate, joy, sorrow, and so on. *Iman* (faith) and desire both speak to the heart, extending their respective invitations. *Iman* invites the heart to contentment: to internalize the truths recognized by the mind and to act accordingly. When people respond to faith wholeheartedly, their feelings become aligned with what the mind has accepted.

Iman cannot flourish while the heart is full of desires. If we do whatever we want, whenever we want, obeying the whims of our *nafs* (ego) at any given moment, *iman* will not have room to take root. We must learn to control the pull of our *nafs*—this self-control is a requirement in order to progress in our journey of faith.

Every decision made by the heart and put into action by the limbs translates into a victory of faith over desire, or the opposite. If faith is the victor, the limbs execute acts of obedience and worship. If desires prevail, they domineer the rest of the body and drive the limbs to satisfy its bidding. Abu Hurayrah related that the Prophet ﷺ said, **"The adulterer is not a believer while he commits adultery, the drunkard is not a believer while he drinks alcohol, and the thief is not a believer while he steals."**[6] In the moment of adultery, stealing, or committing a crime, desire has won over faith and assumed control of the heart.

While we accept that none can see into the heart of another, Islam does affirm that inward conditions are reflected in outward behavior, one way or another. We must use our own actions as indicators to guage the state of our heart. Self-evaluation is unsettling and uncomfortable, but it is a necessary practice. We should be diligent in evaluating our actions and use our behavioral patterns to measure the strength of our iman.

You can assess the degree of faith and desire within you by looking at your actions. The actions of the body and limbs are often a reflection of the strength and weakness of faith. Allah says in the Quran,

$$ ذَٰلِكَ ۖ وَمَن يُعَظِّمْ شَعَـٰٓئِرَ ٱللَّهِ فَإِنَّهَا مِن تَقْوَى ٱلْقُلُوبِ ۝ $$

All this (is ordained by God): those who honour God's rites
show the piety of their hearts. [22:32]

We can also see the connection between faith and action in a supplication (*duaa*), taught to us by the Prophet ﷺ: **"Allah, allocate for us enough fearful awe of You, so that it comes between us and disobeying You."**[7]

Faith and Servitude

The Arabic word for servitude, *'ubudiyyah*, comes from the word *'abd*, often translated as servant, worshipper or slave. *'Ubudiyyah* means the state of complete submission and worship. When faith is alive and well, the heart submits to Allah — it loves for His sake and hates for His sake, follows His commands, rejoices in His blessings and hates to fall short in His service. When the Muslim embraces this spirit of servitude, he or she submits totally to Allah in every aspect of life, an implementation of the verse:

$$ قُلْ إِنَّ صَلَاتِي وَنُسُكِي وَمَحْيَايَ وَمَمَاتِي لِلَّهِ رَبِّ ٱلْعَـٰلَمِينَ لَا شَرِيكَ لَهُۥ ۖ $$
$$ وَبِذَٰلِكَ أُمِرْتُ وَأَنَا۠ أَوَّلُ ٱلْمُسْلِمِينَ ۝ $$

Say, 'My prayers and sacrifice, my life and death, are all
for God, Lord of all the Worlds; He has no partner. This
is what I am commanded, and I am the first to devote
myself to Him.' [6: 162-163]

Our servitude to God is proportional to the amount of faith in the heart at a given time. We've already understood that the motivation behind any action is love and hate. We could be motivated by the love of Allah and pleasing Him, or we could be motivated by self-gratification and desire. When our faith is weak, we relinquish this spirit of servitude to God, no longer loving for His sake. In order to restore *'ubudiyyah*, we must allow our love for Him to triumph over our desires and prioritize what pleases Him over anything else.

'ubudiyyah · 'abd:

the state of complete submission, servitude and worship. The word is derived from 'abd (servant, worshipper, slave)

عبودية · عبد

يَـٰٓأَيُّهَا ٱلَّذِينَ ءَامَنُوٓا۟ إِن تَنصُرُوا۟ ٱللَّهَ يَنصُرْكُمْ وَيُثَبِّتْ أَقْدَامَكُمْ ۞

O believers! If you stand up for Allah, He will help you
and make your steps firm. [47:7]

Whatever decision the heart makes in terms of priorities in love, the limbs obey and translate into action — preferring either the love of Allah over the love of the self or the opposite.
Every decision is a duel between faith and desire, and only one of them can have the upper
hand. If faith is given preference, the limbs will follow, seeking obedience and nearness to
Allah. If the self is preferred, it drives the limbs to execute what pleases it. In this way, our
actions are an expression of the amount of faith present in our heart.

إِنَّ ٱلَّذِينَ هُم مِّنْ خَشْيَةِ رَبِّهِم مُّشْفِقُونَ ۞ وَٱلَّذِينَ هُم بِـَٔايَـٰتِ رَبِّهِمْ يُؤْمِنُونَ ۞
وَٱلَّذِينَ هُم بِرَبِّهِمْ لَا يُشْرِكُونَ ۞ وَٱلَّذِينَ يُؤْتُونَ مَآ ءَاتَوا۟ وَّقُلُوبُهُمْ وَجِلَةٌ أَنَّهُمْ إِلَىٰ
رَبِّهِمْ رَٰجِعُونَ ۞ أُو۟لَـٰٓئِكَ يُسَـٰرِعُونَ فِى ٱلْخَيْرَٰتِ وَهُمْ لَهَا سَـٰبِقُونَ ۞

Those who stand in awe of their Lord, who believe in His
messages, who do not ascribe partners to Him, who always
give with hearts that tremble at the thought that they must
return to Him – it is they who race toward good things, and
they will be the first to get them." [23:57-61]

In these verses, we see that those whose hearts are mindful of God will be the ones in the
forefront of doing good deeds; the spiritual state of their heart translates into actions of the
body and limbs. Once a man was playing with his beard in prayer and it was commented,
"If the heart of this person was in awe, his limbs would reflect that."[7] Faith is the force that
pushes us to do what is right, and good deeds are its reflections upon the limbs, the harvest
of a strong faith.

....

ENDNOTES

1. As-Suyooti in *ad-Durr al-Manthur* (6/286)
2. Ahmad in Musnad vol. 32 p.470 #19697 and Ibn Hibban vol. 2 p. 486 #709
3. *Sahih*: Bukhari, Muslim; al-Albani in *Sahih al-Jami'* (5784)
4. Bukhari (1/20 #52), Muslim (3/1219 #1599)
5. Tirmithi (5/219 #2988) and Ibn Hibban (3/278 #997)
6. Bukhari (7/104: 5578) Muslim (1/76: 57)
7. Tirmithi 5/528:3502: Hasan Gharib; Al-Hakim (1/709:1934): authenticated by Al-Albani in Sahih Al-Jami
8. Ibn Abi Shaibah, saying by Sai'd ibn al-Musayyib (2/86 #6787)

Faith and the Ansar

The Companions of the Prophet ﷺ were motivated by the powerful force of faith and accomplished the incredible. We learn from their stories and examples the transformative power of faith, both on the individual and communal level.

The *Muhajirun* (Companions who migrated from Mecca to Medina) endured vicious persecution in Mecca. They migrated to a new land out of love for Allah, seeking His reward and leaving behind wealth, family connections, and homes. One can imagine what a sacrifice this was in a desert society where the tribe was the source of security for the individual.

$$وَمِنَ ٱلنَّاسِ مَن يَشْرِي نَفْسَهُ ٱبْتِغَآءَ مَرْضَاتِ ٱللَّهِ ۗ وَٱللَّهُ رَءُوفٌ بِٱلْعِبَادِ ۞$$

And there are those who would give their life to please
God, and God is most compassionate to His servants.
[2:207]

Faith was deeply established in another group as well: the *Ansar* (the Companions in Medina who sheltered and supported the Prophet and the Muhajirun). God describes them as follows:

$$وَٱلَّذِينَ تَبَوَّءُو ٱلدَّارَ وَٱلْإِيمَٰنَ$$

Those who were already settled in the city and
settled in faith... [59:9]

Instead of describing faith as having entered their hearts, God described the Ansar themselves as having themselves settled wholly and entirely into faith. It is a surprising turn of phrase; let's explore this notable wording further.

The Ansar settled deeply into faith to the point that it encompassed their heart, flesh and blood. Their behavior was so imbued with faith that it stood out among others, for they are the only people described as "settled in faith" in the Quran. They competed with each other in hospitality and brotherhood, each trying to outdo the other in generosity toward the Muslim refugees in their city. It was said that the competition was so fierce that the Ansar drew straws to decide whose homes the emigrant guests were to be hosted in.[1]

وَٱلَّذِينَ تَبَوَّءُو ٱلدَّارَ وَٱلْإِيمَٰنَ مِن قَبْلِهِمْ يُحِبُّونَ مَنْ هَاجَرَ إِلَيْهِمْ وَلَا يَجِدُونَ فِي صُدُورِهِمْ حَاجَةً مِّمَّآ أُوتُواْ وَيُؤْثِرُونَ عَلَىٰٓ أَنفُسِهِمْ وَلَوْ كَانَ بِهِمْ خَصَاصَةٌ وَمَن يُوقَ شُحَّ نَفْسِهِۦ فَأُوْلَٰٓئِكَ هُمُ ٱلْمُفْلِحُونَ ۝

Those who were already settled in the city and settled in their faith show love for those who migrated to them and harbour no desire in their hearts for what has been given to the emigrants. They give them preference over themselves, even if they too are poor: those who are saved from their own souls' greed are truly successful. [59:9]

The verse describes the Ansar as feeling no need in their hearts for what they gave to the *Muhajirun*. They had so much love for God that no sacrifice felt like it was too much. The Ansar preferred their brothers over themselves, not because they were wealthy — in fact, they were quite poor themselves — but because of how rooted they were in their faith.

◆◆◆

In a touching story about a family of the Ansar, Abu Hurayrah said that a man came to the Prophet ﷺ and said, "I am in need." The Prophet himself sent word to his wives who replied, "By the One who sent you with truth, we have nothing but water." Prophet Muhammad ﷺ then asked his Companions, "Who can host him for one night? Allah have mercy on you."
One of the Ansar volunteered, "I can, Messenger of Allah."
The Ansari man brought the guest home and took his wife aside, "Do you have anything we can serve him?" She said, "No, only enough to feed my children." The man said, "Then distract them with something small. When our guest comes in to eat, turn down the lamp and pretend that we are eating with him." So they sat while their guest ate, and they spent the night hungry. The next morning, the Prophet ﷺ said, "Allah is amazed at what you did for your guest last night."[2]

The *Muhajirun* emigrants remained under the care of the Ansar up until the expulsion of the tribe of Banu Nadir from Medina, when the Muslim army claimed the property and wealth left behind by the Jewish tribe. At that time, the Prophet ﷺ summoned all of the Ansar, making supplication *(dua)* for them and thanking them for their selfless support of the emigrants. Then he ﷺ said, "If you choose, I can distribute what God has turned over to me from the wealth of Banu Nadir among both you and the Muhajirun, in which case the Muhajirun shall remain under your care and hospitality. Or if you like, I can give all of this wealth to the Muhajirun only, and they will no longer be your responsibility."

Sa'd ibn Ubadah and Sa'd ibn Mu'ath, two leaders of the Ansar, spoke up on behalf of the group, "Rather, we choose to give all of this to the Muhajirun, while they will still remain under our care." The crowd of Ansar agreed in unison, "We are pleased and surrender our right, Messenger of Allah!" The Prophet then prayed for them, "Allah, have mercy on the Ansar and the children of the Ansar."[3]

In order to appreciate the deep change that faith created in the lives of the Ansar, we should take a look at what their habits were like before faith settled in their hearts. Before Islam, the Ansar were divided into two rival, belligerent tribes, manipulated by their enemies and unable to unify their city.

وَٱعْتَصِمُوا۟ بِحَبْلِ ٱللَّهِ جَمِيعًا وَلَا تَفَرَّقُوا۟ وَٱذْكُرُوا۟ نِعْمَتَ ٱللَّهِ عَلَيْكُمْ
إِذْ كُنتُمْ أَعْدَآءً فَأَلَّفَ بَيْنَ قُلُوبِكُمْ فَأَصْبَحْتُم بِنِعْمَتِهِۦٓ إِخْوَٰنًا
وَكُنتُمْ عَلَىٰ شَفَا حُفْرَةٍ مِّنَ ٱلنَّارِ فَأَنقَذَكُم مِّنْهَا كَذَٰلِكَ يُبَيِّنُ ٱللَّهُ
لَكُمْ ءَايَٰتِهِۦ لَعَلَّكُمْ تَهْتَدُونَ ۝

Hold fast to God's rope all together; do not split into
factions. Remember God's favour to you: you were
enemies and then He brought your hearts together and
you became brothers by His grace. [3:103]

Anyone who hopes to achieve the Ansar's spirit of generosity must look to the incredible roots of faith that drove their actions. The tree of faith extends its branches in every direction and yields a steady harvest of exceptional fruit.

أَلَمْ تَرَ كَيْفَ ضَرَبَ ٱللَّهُ مَثَلًا كَلِمَةً طَيِّبَةً كَشَجَرَةٍ طَيِّبَةٍ أَصْلُهَا
ثَابِتٌ وَفَرْعُهَا فِى ٱلسَّمَآءِ ۝ تُؤْتِىٓ أُكُلَهَا كُلَّ حِينٍ بِإِذْنِ رَبِّهَا وَيَضْرِبُ
ٱللَّهُ ٱلْأَمْثَالَ لِلنَّاسِ لَعَلَّهُمْ يَتَذَكَّرُونَ ۝

Do you not see how God makes comparisons? A good
word is like a good tree whose root is firm and whose
branches are high in the sky, yielding constant fruit
by its Lord's leave—God makes such comparisons for
people so that they may reflect. [14:24-25]

....

ENDNOTES

1. Sahih Bukhari (2/72)
2. Muslim (3/1624 #2053)
2. Al-Qurtubi in *al-Jami' li Ahkam al-Quran* (18/17)

When Faith is Weak

Faith has a profound effect on our character and manners. When faith weakens, our ego and desire take the helm of our character instead. In order to measure the extent of our faith's weakness, we must do more than reflect inwardly. We should also observe our outward behavior, because it is a clear indicator of the strength or weakness of faith.

Signs of Weak Faith

These outward signs differ from person to person and depend on the degree of weakness of iman. Some of these indicators of weak faith are:

Laziness and distraction in worship

Skipping prayers

Not attending Friday Jumu'ah prayers or arriving late.

Ignoring recommended, sunnah acts of worship, thinking no harm is done

Neglecting the Quran: tongue is present, but heart is disengaged.

Tiring quickly of remembrance, supplication and seeking forgiveness.

Weighing deeds strictly by whether they are prohibited or not

Lack of diligence in fulfilling our promises and appointments.

Decreased reverence for religion.

No sense of responsibility to Islam and failing to call others to it.

Over indulgence, excessiveness, and wasting time

Failing to avert the eyes from sinful images

Enjoying poor company and negative conversation, either in person or on social media

Addiction to worldly concerns and consumption

Impact of Weak Faith on Community

If we recognize any of the previous symptoms, chances are that our faith is in a weak state, and our heart is attached to something that it was not created to love. This worldly life is a grand competition in accumulation of wealth, influence, beauty, and luxuries, but the nature of the heart is that nothing in this life can satisfy it. The poor man dreams of wealth, while the rich man envies the opulent.

On the parental level, even our duties towards our children could be compromised by weak faith. Instead of worrying about the resilience of their faith, we worry about their status, even when the environments in which they excel are hurtful to their religion and *iman*. When our faith is weak, our respect for the sacred aspects of Islam declines. We may excuse behaviors that contradict Allah's commandments and brush aside the responsibilities of our faith.

On the community level, our tolerance and patience with our community decreases. Relationships are tinged with suspicion as every person magnifies the flaws in the other. Everyone is a skeptic and assumes his or her viewpoint deserves to be broadcasted. When faith is weak, a person may become deluded about who he or she really is, convinced they are entitled to admiration, leadership and an audience.

In the same thread, an inflated ego leads to a decrease in sacrifice, generosity and spending for the sake of Allah. We perceive scarcity in every direction and hold tight to what we think belongs to us. We cannot muster the optimism to strive for the sake of God — to put our lives and possessions on the line for a just and noble cause. Instead, we fear drawing attention to ourselves and being persecuted like so many Muslims around the world. We fear making mistakes and being criticized. We fear losing what we hold in our hands today and fear the trials that might befall those who devote their lives to Islam.

Think about how much potential good is lost when faith is neglected. Good manners deteriorate rapidly when faith is weak. People become out of touch with their own hearts and character, indignant at other people's faults while overlooking their own. Everyone falls short in their responsibilities and, as a result, everyone feels deprived of their rights: parents, children, spouses, relatives, and co-workers. Brotherhood and sisterhood between Muslims becomes weak, vulnerable people are not cared for, and neighbors do not know each other.

One of the gravest consequences of weak faith is that we lose our hope in Allah's promises, as individuals and as communities. Although our religion instructs us to do otherwise, we pursue a material happiness, displeased with the mission Allah charted for us on earth. Pessimism dominates, and community volunteers are too easily frustrated by obstacles. We care little for the worries of other people and cannot be troubled by serving the distressed and vulnerable.

People are reluctant to join the ranks of those who are striving for the sake of Islam's message and call. Most of us are well-versed in the long list of excuses and justifications for why we cannot fulfill the responsibilities that Islam asks of us. Everyone is too busy, desensitized or disillusioned to do the work that must be done on this earth, the work for which we were created. This bleak state of the heart feeds into a dangerous listlessness that has repercussions on the individual, communal, and global level.

Faith and Change

Weak faith cannot be fixed simply by changing a single behavior, nor does awareness alone solve the problem. Weak faith is the result of an accumulation of choices which have created habits and behaviors. Attempting to fix a specific behavior alone, without addressing the root cause, is a superficial approach; the problem will only resurface in another form. Instead, we must dig deeper, focusing on creating motivation through awakening, or reviving, faith.

When someone is approaching faith for the first time, they should not be burdened with tasks and technical rituals. The first task at hand is not adjusting clothing, learning fiqh, or attending a lecture, at least not in most cases. A person with weak faith will find this tedious and ineffective in bringing life to their heart. ***The solution is to begin with faith, growing it in the heart. Awakening iman comes before religious assignments.***

◆◆◆

" While we were spirited and energetic youth with the Prophet, we learned iman before the Quran. Then we would memorize the Quran, and our iman would increase." Jundub ibn Abdullah[1]

Awakening faith should be a primary goal of learning the Quran and take priority over the quantity of verses memorized. This method of learning and growing faith before anything else was highlighted by the Companion Abdullah ibn Umar, who said,

> We lived for a short time when one would be given iman before the Quran. Then a surah would be revealed to Muhammad ﷺ, and we would learn its halal and haram, its commandments and warnings, and what our stance should be. Later, a man would be given the Quran before *iman*. He would read from *Al-Fatiha* to the end without understanding its commandments and prohibitions, or what his stance should be, strewing it around like scattering dates.[2]

Aisha, may Allah be pleased with her, said, "The first passages revealed from the Quran were the shorter surahs containing descriptions of Paradise and Hell. When people were established in their Islam, the halal and haram (permissible and prohibited) were revealed. If the first thing revealed had been, 'Do not commit adultery,' people would have said, 'We will never leave adultery,' and if the first thing revealed had been, 'Do not drink alcohol,' people would have said, 'We will never abandon alcohol.' When I was a young girl, still at a playful age, this verse from Surah Al-Qamar was revealed to the Prophet ﷺ, "But the Hour is their appointed time, the Hour is more severe and bitter." Surah Al-Baqarah and An-Nisa' were not revealed until I was living with him in Medina."[3]

The Quran describes the condition of one who has knowledge of revelation without an accompanying presence of *iman*:

فَخَلَفَ مِنْ بَعْدِهِمْ خَلْفٌ وَرِثُوا۟ ٱلْكِتَٰبَ يَأْخُذُونَ عَرَضَ هَٰذَا ٱلْأَدْنَىٰ وَيَقُولُونَ سَيُغْفَرُ لَنَا وَإِن يَأْتِهِمْ عَرَضٌ مِّثْلُهُۥ يَأْخُذُوهُ

And they were succeeded by generations who, although they inherited the Scripture, took the fleeting gains of this lower world, saying, 'We shall be forgiven,' and indeed taking them again if other such gains came their way. [7:169]

These people described in the verse learned the technicalities of their religion without a corresponding activation of faith. The teachings of the revealed books are supposed to be springs of guidance, but for these people, their knowledge of technicalities gave them a false sense of immunity from God's punishment.

Resetting Priorities

By now, we should be convinced that we have to rearrange our priorities so that *iman* is our primary source of motivation. This does not imply neglecting every other inclination of the heart, rather that *iman* should be the dominant force and influencer within the heart.

Iman imparts synergy and blessing to all good pursuits, aligning them together and making them mutually inclusive. It makes doing good deeds easier, while naturally reordering our priorities according to what Allah loves. The Quran demonstrates that the relationship between iman and good deeds is an explicit one:

ذَٰلِكَ وَمَن يُعَظِّمْ شَعَٰٓئِرَ ٱللَّهِ فَإِنَّهَا مِن تَقْوَى ٱلْقُلُوبِ ۝

All this (is ordained by Allah): those who honour Allah's rites show the piety of their hearts. [22:9]

The extent to which we honor God's commandments is proof of how much faith and piety we have attained. The greater our faith, the greater our esteem for the sacred. Reflect on how you respond to the call to prayer (*athan*); does it inspire reverence and urgency for the impending worship or is it just background noise to your ears?

The forthcoming verse describes the believers as having sufficient motivation in their hearts to struggle in the way of God, without requiring special permission or someone to justify why their participation is required. Their faith is deep enough to be motivation in itself — no extra incentives needed.

$$لَا يَسْتَـْٔذِنُكَ ٱلَّذِينَ يُؤْمِنُونَ بِٱللَّهِ وَٱلْيَوْمِ ٱلْءَاخِرِ أَن يُجَٰهِدُواْ بِأَمْوَٰلِهِمْ وَأَنفُسِهِمْ ۗ وَٱللَّهُ عَلِيمٌ بِٱلْمُتَّقِينَ ۝$$

Those who have faith in God and the Last Day do not ask you for exemption from struggle with their possessions and their persons — God knows exactly who is mindful of Him. [9:44]

Focus on the Heart

For those who are in the practice of mentorship and encouraging the good and forbidding evil, it's important to take the right approach in awakening faith in others. It can be easy to take the shorcut of fixating on outward negative behavior, an approach that causes the heart to suffer.

Guiding, correcting, and advising must be done with the end goal in mind: to grow faith and love for Allah. This approach of awakening *iman* first yields better results in the long run. It teaches a person to self-correct as they learn to love what Allah loves and hate what Allah hates.

If we want to motivate people to improve themselves, we cannot focus only on the evil of their actions and the corresponding punishment. Such negativity can backfire and lead to an aversion towards religion in general. We should instead use a positive approach of awakening faith in the heart so that the individual is motivated to change. This doesn't mean we should never correct bad behaviors or warn people against them — rather, we should do so with sensitivity and an understanding of priorities. Activating faith is the first step in changing behavior. The rest will follow with God's help and guidance.

Faith Covers Shame

Do not let your frustration with bad habits deter your faith journey. By its nature, *iman* will better equip you to tackle those issues. Faith and mindfulness of God clothe the self, covering its vulnerability and shame. Faith can also be compared to a stream that flows naturally through us — when faith is weak, the self is unnaturally exposed like a dry riverbed.

$$
\text{يَـٰبَنِىٓ ءَادَمَ قَدْ أَنزَلْنَا عَلَيْكُمْ لِبَاسًا يُوَٰرِى سَوْءَٰتِكُمْ وَرِيشًا ۖ وَلِبَاسُ ٱلتَّقْوَىٰ ذَٰلِكَ خَيْرٌ ۚ ذَٰلِكَ مِنْ ءَايَٰتِ ٱللَّهِ لَعَلَّهُمْ يَذَّكَّرُونَ ۝}
$$

Children of Adam, We have given you garments to cover your nakedness and as adornment for you; the garment of God-mindfulness is the best of all garments. [7:26]

Bad habits naturally recede as faith and God-mindfulness are nurtured. The Quran points to the example of prayer as a method of reducing shameful behaviors:

$$
\text{وَأَقِمِ ٱلصَّلَوٰةَ ۖ إِنَّ ٱلصَّلَوٰةَ تَنْهَىٰ عَنِ ٱلْفَحْشَآءِ وَٱلْمُنكَرِ ۗ وَلَذِكْرُ ٱللَّهِ أَكْبَرُ ۗ وَٱللَّهُ يَعْلَمُ مَا تَصْنَعُونَ ۝}
$$

Keep up the prayer: prayer restrains outrageous and unacceptable behaviour. Remembering God is greater: God knows everything you are doing. [29:45]

Once the Prophet ﷺ was told that there was a man who prayed the night prayer but engaged in theft during the day. The Prophet ﷺ said, **"His prayer will stop him (from stealing)."**[4] Abu Bakr ibn Ayyash said, "Whoever observes the night prayers will not behave immorally. Have you not heard the verse, 'Prayer restrains outrageous and unacceptable behavior.'"[5]

<table>
<tr><td>

....
《 3 Seerah Examples 》

*Surah al-Anfal &
spoils at Badr*

Battle of Hunayn

*Going Home with
the Prophet*
....

</td><td>

Examples from the Prophet's Life

No society is exempt from challenges and problems, but people differ in how they tackle them. The *seerah*, the life of the Prophet ﷺ, is replete with examples of faith's transforming power and its tangible impact. When the early Muslim community faced daunting obstacles, the Prophetic approach was to strengthen faith before, during, and after the experience. Here are more examples of how faith was prioritized in the development of the Companions, may God be pleased with them.

</td></tr>
</table>

《 SURAH AL-ANFAL AND SPOILS OF BADR 》

After the first Muslim victory at the Battle of Badr, problems arose. For the first time, the spoils of battle fell into the hands of the fledgling

Muslim community. Most of the Muslims were poor and in great need of this wealth, and so some began to argue over how the spoils should be distributed. Young warriors argued that they deserved a larger share than those who were less skilled or older in age. Those on the front line surely deserved more than those who had barely fought. Voices were raised, and tempers escalated.

Then Surah Al-Anfal came down. It began with:

$$\text{يَسْـَٔلُونَكَ عَنِ ٱلْأَنفَالِ قُلِ ٱلْأَنفَالُ لِلَّهِ وَٱلرَّسُولِ فَٱتَّقُوا۟ ٱللَّهَ وَأَصْلِحُوا۟ ذَاتَ بَيْنِكُمْ وَأَطِيعُوا۟ ٱللَّهَ وَرَسُولَهُۥ إِن كُنتُم مُّؤْمِنِينَ ۝}$$

They ask you (Prophet) about the spoils of war. Say, 'that is a matter for God and His Messenger, so be mindful of God and make things right between you. Obey God and His Messenger if you are true believers. [8:1]

With this opening verse, the spoils of war were taken out of the Muslim army's hands completely; they had no claim to it. Decision-making regarding the spoils belonged exclusively to Allah and His Messenger ﷺ.

The next forty verses of Surah Al-Anfal flow through a series of reminders designed to increase faith. Tangible descriptions offered a yardstick of *iman* by which Muslims could measure themselves:

$$\text{إِنَّمَا ٱلْمُؤْمِنُونَ ٱلَّذِينَ إِذَا ذُكِرَ ٱللَّهُ وَجِلَتْ قُلُوبُهُمْ}$$

True believers are those whose hearts tremble with awe when God is mentioned)...[8:2]

The hearts of true believers shiver and tremble, sensitive to the remembrance of Allah. This is a tangible expression of faith that is easy to detect in our own hearts. Have *you* ever felt this trembling before? The verses continues describing the believers:

$$\text{وَإِذَا تُلِيَتْ عَلَيْهِمْ ءَايَٰتُهُۥ زَادَتْهُمْ إِيمَٰنًا وَعَلَىٰ رَبِّهِمْ يَتَوَكَّلُونَ ۝ ٱلَّذِينَ يُقِيمُونَ ٱلصَّلَوٰةَ وَمِمَّا رَزَقْنَٰهُمْ يُنفِقُونَ ۝ أُو۟لَٰٓئِكَ هُمُ ٱلْمُؤْمِنُونَ حَقًّا لَّهُمْ دَرَجَٰتٌ عِندَ رَبِّهِمْ وَمَغْفِرَةٌ وَرِزْقٌ كَرِيمٌ ۝}$$

...whose faith increases when His revelations are recited to them, who put their trust in their Lord, who keep up the prayer and give to others out of what We provide for them. Those are the ones who truly believe. They have high standing with their Lord, forgiveness, and generous provision.' [8:2-4]

Could anyone still be thinking about the spoils of war after hearing these verses? Faced with vivid descriptions of belief, it would be hard to think of anything other than where you stand in your faith and how you measure up.

The most incredible experience in human history was to experience the transmission of revelation from the sky to earth. Divine solutions came down in real-time to guide the early Muslim community. While we will never experience firsthand the live unfolding of revelation, we have the entirety of the Quran in our hands, which documents solutions to the challenges faced by individuals, communities, and nations.

The surah continues, reminding the Muslims how Allah blessed them with a tremendous victory at Badr. They were reminded that victory came directly from Allah, not from their own efforts. It was He who enveloped them with sleep when they most needed it, sent down gentle rain and reinforcements from among the angels, sharpened their aim, made them stand firmly, and caused the disbelievers to lose their morale.

Then the surah calls the believers to respond to Allah and the Messenger ﷺ and frightens them with a warning that Allah stands between a person and their own heart. The verses take them back to the days of Mecca, when they were weak and oppressed.

وَٱذْكُرُوٓاْ إِذْ أَنتُمْ قَلِيلٌ مُّسْتَضْعَفُونَ فِى ٱلْأَرْضِ تَخَافُونَ أَن يَتَخَطَّفَكُمُ ٱلنَّاسُ فَـَٔاوَىٰكُمْ وَأَيَّدَكُم بِنَصْرِهِۦ وَرَزَقَكُم مِّنَ ٱلطَّيِّبَٰتِ لَعَلَّكُمْ تَشْكُرُونَ ۝

Remember when you were few, victimized in the land, afraid
that people might catch you, but God sheltered you and
strengthened you with His help, and provided you with good
things so that you might be grateful. [8:26]

This stirring journey of faith awakening spreads across many verses. Finally, several pages later in the forty-first verse of the surah, the answer to the problem comes. This is after the listener desires only Allah and has disconnected from everything else; after every soul has searched and examined the condition of its faith. Only then does the surah address practically how to distribute the spoils of war:

وَٱعْلَمُوٓاْ أَنَّمَا غَنِمْتُم مِّن شَىْءٍ فَأَنَّ لِلَّهِ خُمُسَهُۥ وَلِلرَّسُولِ وَلِذِى ٱلْقُرْبَىٰ وَٱلْيَتَٰمَىٰ وَٱلْمَسَٰكِينِ وَٱبْنِ ٱلسَّبِيلِ إِن كُنتُمْ ءَامَنتُم بِٱللَّهِ وَمَآ أَنزَلْنَا عَلَىٰ عَبْدِنَا يَوْمَ ٱلْفُرْقَانِ يَوْمَ ٱلْتَقَى ٱلْجَمْعَانِ وَٱللَّهُ عَلَىٰ كُلِّ شَىْءٍ قَدِيرٌ ۝

Know that one-fifth of your battle gains belongs to God and
the Messenger, to close relatives and orphans, to the needy and
travelers, if you believe in God and the revelation We sent down
to Our servant on the day of the decision, the day when the two
forces met in battle. God has power over all things. [8:41]

⟪ RALLYING AT THE BATTLE OF HUNAYN ⟫

Let's fast forward six years later to the Battle of Hunayn, shortly after the great conquest
of Mecca. People had just entered Islam in droves, and the Muslim forces were so numerous
that many among the Muslims imagined they were undefeatable:

وَيَوْمَ حُنَيْنٍ إِذْ أَعْجَبَتْكُمْ كَثْرَتُكُمْ فَلَمْ تُغْنِ عَنكُمْ شَيْئًا وَضَاقَتْ
عَلَيْكُمُ ٱلْأَرْضُ بِمَا رَحُبَتْ ثُمَّ وَلَّيْتُم مُّدْبِرِينَ ۝

Even on the day of the Battle of Hunayn. You were well
pleased with your large numbers, but they were of no use
to you: the earth seemed to close in on you despite its
spaciousness, and you turned tail and fled. [9:25]

As the Muslim forces descended into the Hunayn Valley, the enemy launched a surprise
attack on the steep hillside, striking with shocking ferocity and coordination. Despite num-
bering more than 12,000, the Muslim army scattered in every direction, and was on the verge
of a terrible defeat. Blinded and confused, the Muslim soldiers were intent only on escaping
the deadly ambush. Abu Sufyan ibn Harb, a new Muslim at the time, said of the retreating
army, "They will flee in defeat until they reach the Red Sea!"

The Prophet ﷺ attempted to rally the right side of the army by calling out, "To me,
people! I am the Messenger of Allah! I am Muhammad son of Abdallah!" Only a few of the
Muhajirun and a few members of the Prophet's household remained by his side in this dire
moment.[6] So what did the Prophet ﷺ do next? The story is narrated in Sahih Muslim: the
Prophet ﷺ instructed his uncle Al-Abbas: "Call out: O people of the Ansar! People of the
Tree! People of Surah Al-Baqarah!" Through these words, the Prophet ﷺ was reminding the
Companions of their commitment and appealing to the *iman* in their hearts.

Al-Abbas, may Allah be pleased with him, had a booming voice, and so the words of
the Prophet reached everyone on the battlefield. The fleeing Muslims, those whose faith
was awakened by the call of the Prophet ﷺ, stopped in their tracks at the sound of the call.
Hearts now awakened, they turned around, hurrying back to the scene of the fight franti-
cally like a mother camel afraid for her calf, crying, "*Ya labbayk ya labbayk!* We're coming!
We're coming!" Some of them had been riding horses and camels that were fleeing too fast to

control, and so they slid off the backs of their frantic animals. They threw their armor around their necks, grabbed their swords and shields, and flocked to the Prophet's side in crowds.

.... ✦✦✦ ....

O nlookers described the scene as a forest of men that suddenly grew around the Prophet ﷺ. So fervently did the Ansar cluster around the Messenger, protecting him and making amends for their mistake, that Al-Abbas recounted, "I was more afraid that the arrows of the Ansar would strike the Prophet than the arrows of the enemy."

....

The Prophet ﷺ ordered the rallied army to relaunch their attack. "Now the battle is truly underway!" he ﷺ said. Gathering a handful of dirt from the ground in his noble hand, the Prophet ﷺ threw it at the faces of the enemies, saying, "The faces are blackened!" It is said that every enemy soldier felt the dust in his eyes. Allah turned the tide, dividing the ranks of the enemy and forcing them to retreat.[7]

⊰ GOING HOME WITH THE PROPHET ⊱

In the Battle of Hunayn and Ta'if, the Muslims gained tremendous spoils and wealth unlike any they had encountered before. A few days after the battle, the Prophet ﷺ distributed the majority of the spoils among the leaders of the tribes that had just accepted Islam, giving nothing to the Ansar. Many of these leaders were the very same ones who had fled the battlefield and failed to regroup at the Prophet's side a few days earlier.

The Ansar struggled to make sense of this, and began to whisper among themselves. They were to receive nothing of the spoils, although they had rallied to the Prophet's ﷺ side and fought fiercely with him, reversing the course of the battle. Now, they watched great wealth piling into the hands of those who had retreated,while the hands of the Ansar were left empty.

Let us see what happens next. Abu Said Al-Khudri narrates the story: "When the Messenger of Allah ﷺ gave those generous gifts to Quraysh and the Arab tribes, the Ansar did not get anything. Some of the Ansar felt resentment, and they began to talk amongst themselves. One of them said, "By Allah, the Prophet ﷺ finally found his real people!"

Sa'd ibn Ubadah, one of the leaders of the Ansar, went to the Prophet ﷺ and said, "Messenger of Allah, some of the Ansar are bothered by what you have done with the spoils you received. You gave huge shares to your people, and to the Arab tribes, but gave nothing to the Ansar." The Prophet asked, "And what do you think of this, Sa'd?" Sa'd said, "Messenger of Allah, I am just a man from my people."

The Prophet 🕊 told Sa'd to gather his people in a certain place. He allowed some men from the Muhajirun to enter, while others he turned away. When they had all gathered, Sa'd came to the Prophet and said, "The Ansar have assembled for you."

The Messenger of Allah 🕊 then came to where they were gathered and began to speak. He glorified Allah and praised Him in a way that is worthy of Him. "People of the Ansar," the Prophet 🕊 said, "What have you been saying? Have you taken offense? Did I not come to you while you were lost, and then Allah guided you? Were you not in need, and then Allah enriched you? Were you not enemies of one another, and then Allah bound your hearts together?"

"Allah and His Messenger are generous and bountiful!" they replied.

The Prophet 🕊 insisted, "*Why don't you answer me,* people of the Ansar?"

"How shall we answer you, Messenger of God? We are indebted to God and His Messenger!" The Prophet 🕊 responded with a most beautiful response:

> By Allah, you could, if you wish, say what is true and what people would confirm. You could say, 'You (Prophet) came to us when people denied your message, and we believed you. You were abandoned, and we backed you. You were driven out, and we sheltered you. You were in need, and we supported you.'

> People of the Ansar, are you upset at losing a trifle of this world, that I gave people to win their hearts over to Islam, while I entrusted you to your Islam? Are you not satisfied, people of the Ansar, that other people will return home with sheep and camels while you go home with God's Messenger? I swear by the One in whose hand is Muhammad's soul, if it were not for the emigration, I would wish to be one of the Ansar. If all people were to take one road, while the Ansar took another, I would take the road of the Ansar. My Lord, shower your mercy on the Ansar, the children of the Ansar, and the grandchildren of the Ansar!

As they listened to the Prophet's words, the men wept until their beards were soaked. "We are pleased with the Messenger of Allah 🕊 as our share and portion!" they cried.[8]

Dealing with Lapses

See how the discontent of the Ansar transformed when their faith was strengthened. They embraced the richness of their own faith, content with the companionship of the Prophet 🕊 as their only share of the spoils. Do you see how the Messenger of Allah 🕊 appealed to their faith and hearts instead of focusing on their mistake? Many problems in our lives can be lightened by the increase of iman in our hearts.

But it is human nature to stumble and forget, so most people experience phases when their iman is weak. In those moments, a person's behavior may be misaligned with what he or she believes. As friends and mentors, we shouldn't rush to condemn someone because of a slip-up resulting from a temporary lapse. Rather, in these situations, we should be gentle, give excuses, and turn a blind eye to mistakes. We can help people rekindle faith in their hearts, surrounding them with a nurturing environment, reminders, and good companionship. When we find ourselves in this faith-centered atmosphere, the *nafs* (the ego or self) and its desires recede, and many lapses in character and spirituality are resolved without direct confrontation. With a faith-centered mindset, it is easier to forgive the shortcomings of others and overlook their trespasses. Problems seem less significant in our eyes, for faith reforms the heart and calms the most restless souls.

Consider the state of the Companions before Islam and after. People used to say about Umar ibn Al-Khattab before he accepted Islam, "Umar won't believe until his donkey believes." On what basis was this statement made? Umar was notoriously stubborn and aggressive, but when faith entered his heart, it transformed his stubbornness into a force for good, and he became a great advocate of Islam.

The Nafs

The *nafs* (the self or the ego) is a creation unlike anything else in the universe. God granted it the capacity for piety and transgression:

$$وَنَفْسٍ وَمَا سَوَّىٰهَا ۝ فَأَلْهَمَهَا فُجُورَهَا وَتَقْوَىٰهَا ۝$$

*By the nafs and how He formed it, and inspired it to
know its own rebellion and piety!* [91:7-8]

When the *nafs* is left to its own devices, without the tempering influence of mindfulness and faith, it is reckless and destructive. This is the same *nafs* that led Prophet Salih's people, the Tribe of Thamud, to deny his prophethood and reject belief. They demanded that Salih bring forth a sign proving his truthfulness. So God caused a camel to come forth from stone, proving without a doubt that their Prophet was truthful. God tells us the words of Prophet Salih, peace be upon him:

$$وَيَـٰقَوْمِ هَـٰذِهِۦ نَاقَةُ ٱللَّهِ لَكُمْ ءَايَةً فَذَرُوهَا تَأْكُلْ فِىٓ أَرْضِ ٱللَّهِ
وَلَا تَمَسُّوهَا بِسُوٓءٍ فَيَأْخُذَكُمْ عَذَابٌ قَرِيبٌ ۝$$

My people, this camel belongs to God, a sign for you, so

leave it to pasture on God's earth and do not harm it, or
you will soon be punished.' [11:64]

Instead of submitting to God and believing in their prophet's message, they committed the unspeakable:

$$فَعَقَرُواْ ٱلنَّاقَةَ وَعَتَوْاْ عَنْ أَمْرِ رَبِّهِمْ وَقَالُواْ يَٰصَٰلِحُ ٱئْتِنَا بِمَا تَعِدُنَآ$$
$$إِن كُنتَ مِنَ ٱلْمُرْسَلِينَ ۝ فَأَخَذَتْهُمُ ٱلرَّجْفَةُ فَأَصْبَحُواْ فِي دَارِهِمْ$$
$$جَٰثِمِينَ ۝ فَتَوَلَّىٰ عَنْهُمْ وَقَالَ يَٰقَوْمِ لَقَدْ أَبْلَغْتُكُمْ رِسَالَةَ رَبِّي$$
$$وَنَصَحْتُ لَكُمْ وَلَٰكِن لَّا تُحِبُّونَ ٱلنَّٰصِحِينَ ۝$$

And then they hamstrung the camel. They defied their Lord's
commandment and said, 'Salih, bring down the punishment you
threaten, if you really are a messenger!' An earthquake seized them:
by the next morning they were lying dead in their homes. So he
turned away from them, saying, 'My people, I delivered my Lord's
messages to you and gave you sincere advice, but you did not like
those who gave sincere advice.' [7:77-79]

How could a people's shamelessness reach that extent, when clear signs were laid before them? The Quran responds to this question. When the self is left without tempering and purification, it becomes self-destructive. God says,

$$وَنَفْسٍ وَمَا سَوَّىٰهَا ۝ فَأَلْهَمَهَا فُجُورَهَا وَتَقْوَىٰهَا ۝ قَدْ أَفْلَحَ مَن$$
$$زَكَّىٰهَا ۝ وَقَدْ خَابَ مَن دَسَّىٰهَا ۝ كَذَّبَتْ ثَمُودُ بِطَغْوَىٰهَآ ۝$$

By the nafs and how He formed it, and inspired it to know
its own rebellion and piety! The one who purifies his
soul succeeds and the one who corrupts it fails. Thamud
rejected the truth out of ignorance. [91:7-11]

This is the same *nafs* that led the brothers of Yusuf to betray their father and sibling:

$$وَجَآءُو عَلَىٰ قَمِيصِهِ بِدَمٍ كَذِبٍ قَالَ بَلْ سَوَّلَتْ لَكُمْ أَنفُسُكُمْ$$
$$أَمْرًا فَصَبْرٌ جَمِيلٌ وَٱللَّهُ ٱلْمُسْتَعَانُ عَلَىٰ مَا تَصِفُونَ ۝$$

And they showed him his shirt, deceptively stained with blood.
He cried, 'No! Your selves (nafs) have prompted you to do
wrong! But it is best to be patient: from God alone I seek help
to bear what you are saying.' [12:18]

The *nafs* led As-Samiri to deceive this people, a story told in the Quran:

$$\text{قَالَ فَمَا خَطْبُكَ يَسَمِرِيُّ ۝ قَالَ بَصُرْتُ بِمَا لَمْ يَبْصُرُواْ بِهِ فَقَبَضْتُ}$$
$$\text{قَبْضَةً مِّنْ أَثَرِ الرَّسُولِ فَنَبَذْتُهَا وَكَذَلِكَ سَوَّلَتْ لِى نَفْسِى ۝}$$

Moses said, 'And what was the matter with you, Samiri?'
He replied, 'I saw something they did not; I took in some
of the teachings of the Messenger but tossed them aside:
my nafs prompted me to do what I did.' [20:95-96]

Perhaps no story sheds more light on how the *nafs* can mislead us than the story of the sons of Adam. Two brothers grew up in the same home; one of them restrained his *nafs* with mindfulness of God, while the other brother left his *nafs* unchecked. This unrestrained, destructive self is what drove the latter to kill his brother, as God says in the Quran:

$$\text{فَطَوَّعَتْ لَهُ نَفْسُهُ قَتْلَ أَخِيهِ فَقَتَلَهُ فَأَصْبَحَ مِنَ الْخَاسِرِينَ ۝ فَبَعَثَ اللَّهُ}$$
$$\text{غُرَابًا يَبْحَثُ فِى الْأَرْضِ لِيُرِيَهُ كَيْفَ يُوَارِى سَوْءَةَ أَخِيهِ قَالَ يَوَيْلَتَىٰ أَعَجَزْتُ أَنْ}$$
$$\text{أَكُونَ مِثْلَ هَذَا الْغُرَابِ فَأُوَارِىَ سَوْءَةَ أَخِى فَأَصْبَحَ مِنَ النَّادِمِينَ ۝}$$

But his nafs prompted him to kill his brother: he killed him and
became one of the losers. God sent a raven to scratch up the
ground and show him how to cover his brother's corpse and
he said, 'Woe is me! Could I not have been like this raven and
covered up my brother's body?' He became remorseful." [5:30-31]

As we see throughout our history, the *nafs* has the capacity to be guided or self-sabotaging. Everyone on earth has these two potential forces within. The inclination towards guidance tends to weaken as the heart hardens and delves into sin. However, that does not mean recovery is impossible. Just as God, glory to Him, revives the dead earth with life, so does He revive dead hearts with renewed faith:

$$\text{اعْلَمُوٓاْ أَنَّ اللَّهَ يُحْىِ الْأَرْضَ بَعْدَ مَوْتِهَا قَدْ بَيَّنَّا لَكُمُ الْآيَتِ}$$
$$\text{لَعَلَّكُمْ تَعْقِلُونَ ۝}$$

Remember that God revives the earth after it dies; We have
made Our revelation clear to you so that you may use your
reason. [57:17]

Don't be like a Candle

A trap awaits those who are active in Islamic work. Sometimes we become so busy serving the needs of people and solving their problems that we ignore our spiritual needs. Serving people is a noble and worthy calling that everyone should pursue. But losing sight of the end goal is easy when we are busy, even if our intentions are good. When this busyness has no spirituality behind it, fueled instead by habit or some other motive, then there will be an inevitable negative effect on the soul.

The Prophet ﷺ warned us about this problem, saying, **"The learned one who teaches people good while forgetting his own self is like the candle. It gives light to people while it burns itself up."**[9] Imam Ar-Rafi'i, a 12th century Shafi' scholar, said: "It is a big mistake to organize the lives of people around you, while leaving your heart in disarray."[10]

Faith is the Answer

When we say that iman is the starting point and solution to every problem, this is not a new-fangled idea. The Quran is full of verses that spur us to faith and God-mindfulness, promising brilliant incentives for those who believe:

يَـٰٓأَيُّهَا ٱلَّذِينَ ءَامَنُوا۟ ٱتَّقُوا۟ ٱللَّهَ وَقُولُوا۟ قَوْلًا سَدِيدًا ۝ يُصْلِحْ لَكُمْ أَعْمَـٰلَكُمْ وَيَغْفِرْ لَكُمْ ذُنُوبَكُمْ ۗ وَمَن يُطِعِ ٱللَّهَ وَرَسُولَهُۥ فَقَدْ فَازَ فَوْزًا عَظِيمًا ۝

Believers, be mindful of God, speak in a direct fashion and to good purpose, and He will put your deeds right for you and forgive you your sins. Whoever obeys God and His Messenger will truly achieve a great triumph. [33:70-71]

وَمَن يَتَّقِ ٱللَّهَ يَجْعَل لَّهُۥ مَخْرَجًا ۝ وَيَرْزُقْهُ مِنْ حَيْثُ لَا يَحْتَسِبُ ۚ وَمَن يَتَوَكَّلْ عَلَى ٱللَّهِ فَهُوَ حَسْبُهُۥٓ ۚ إِنَّ ٱللَّهَ بَـٰلِغُ أَمْرِهِۦ ۚ قَدْ جَعَلَ ٱللَّهُ لِكُلِّ شَىْءٍ قَدْرًا ۝

And whoever is mindful of God, He will make a way out for them, and will provide for them from an unexpected source; God will be enough for those who put their trust in Him. God achieves His purpose; God has set a due measure for everything. [65:2-3]

Whoever wants to develop good character must begin with faith. The Prophet ﷺ said, **"The believer with the most complete *iman* is the one with the best character."**[11] Whoever aspires to abandon sin must join the night school of *iman*, as the Prophet ﷺ said, **"Observe the night prayer, for it was the diligent habit of the righteous before you, a drawing closer to Allah the Almighty, eraser of past evils, and a blocker of sin."**[12] *Iman* is also a gateway to greater consistency; the Prophet ﷺ said, **"If you see a man who frequents the masjid, bear witness to his *iman*."**[13]

Stories of Transformation

When the light of iman enters the heart, darkness dissipates and desires are extinguished. Consider the story of the people of the trench in Surah Al-Buruj. What made a group of newly converted believers so ready to face death by fire? Consider the Companions of the Prophet ﷺ, may God be pleased with them. What led them to abandon their hometowns, their wealth and connections, in order to migrate to a strange new place where they had no connections or property? Perhaps we should reword the question, for given what we have seen of the powerful effects of faith on the heart, how could it be otherwise? Allah the Exalted says,

بَلۡ نَقۡذِفُ بِٱلۡحَقِّ عَلَى ٱلۡبَٰطِلِ فَيَدۡمَغُهُۥ فَإِذَا هُوَ زَاهِقٌ وَلَكُمُ ٱلۡوَيۡلُ مِمَّا تَصِفُونَ ۝

No! We hurl the truth against falsehood, and truth obliterates it — see how falsehood vanishes away! Woe to you (people) for the way you describe God! [21:18]

⟪ THE PHAROAH'S SORCERERS ⟫

The sorcerers were hired by the Pharoah, in order to create an illusion of power and invincibility. Before their encounter with Prophet Musa, the sorcerers aspired to monetary reward and status:

فَلَمَّا جَآءَ ٱلسَّحَرَةُ قَالُوا۟ لِفِرۡعَوۡنَ أَئِنَّ لَنَا لَأَجۡرًا إِن كُنَّا نَحۡنُ ٱلۡغَٰلِبِينَ ۝

When the sorcerers came, they said to Pharaoh, 'shall we be rewarded if we win?' [26:41]

But when faith entered their hearts, the sorcerers transformed into God-centered beings, their souls reaching for the heavens. They saw this world for what it was and regretted opposing the cause of Allah. Now, only one thing matter:

إِنَّآ ءَامَنَّا بِرَبِّنَا لِيَغۡفِرَ لَنَا خَطَٰيَٰنَا وَمَآ أَكۡرَهۡتَنَا عَلَيۡهِ مِنَ ٱلسِّحۡرِۗ وَٱللَّهُ خَيۡرٌ وَأَبۡقَىٰٓ ۝

'We believe in our Lord, (hoping) He may forgive us our sins and the sorcery that you forced us to practise –God is better and more lasting.' [20:73]

◅{ SUHAIB AR-RUMI }►

Suhaib ar-Rumi was one of the early Companions, and when he tried to make the *hijrah* (migration), the people of Mecca blocked him. They said to him, "Suhaib, remember when you came to us with nothing to your name, and now you wish to leave us and take your money with you. By God, we won't let you go!" Suhaib answered the people, "What if I gave you all my wealth, would you let me go?" The leaders of Quraysh responded that they would. And so Suhaib narrates, "I gave them everything I owned, and they let me go. I traveled until I reached Medina, where the Prophet ﷺ heard my story and said, "Suhaib has won the profit! Suhaib has won the profit!"[14] Referring to Suhaib and other Companions like him, the verse was revealed,

$$وَمِنَ ٱلنَّاسِ مَن يَشْرِى نَفْسَهُ ٱبْتِغَآءَ مَرْضَاتِ ٱللَّهِ ۗ وَٱللَّهُ رَءُوفٌ بِٱلْعِبَادِ ۞$$

*But there is also a kind of man who gives his life away to please
God, and God is most compassionate to His servants.* [2:207]

◅{ AL-KHANSAA', MOTHER OF MARTYRS }►

Faith transformed al-Khansaa into a superstar of Islam. Before she accepted Islam, her beloved brother Sakhr died. She spent her days wailing and eulogizing her brother with famous lines of poetry:

> *I am reminded of Sakhr by the sunrise
> And remember him with every sunset.
> If there were not around me so many cries,
> For other lost brothers, I would kill myself.*

After she accepted Islam, al-Khansaa transformed entirely: we find a woman urging her sons to strive in the way of Allah. Historians relate that al-Khansaa' witnessed the Battle of Al-Qadisiyyah between the Persian empire and the Muslim armies, under the leadership of Sa'd ibn Abi Waqqas. Her four sons were with her.

During one of the fiercest nights of combat, al-Khansaa' gathered her sons and encouraged them to remain steadfast. She said,

> My sons, you accepted Islam out of submission to Allah, and you migrated willingly. By the One whom there is no god but Him, you are all of the same father, as you are all from the same mother. I never betrayed your father, nor did I change

your lineage. You know what abundant reward Allah has prepared for the Muslims who face the oppressive enemy in battle. Know that the lasting home is better than the temporary home, and Allah the most High says, "You who believe, be steadfast, more steadfast than others; be ready; always be mindful of God, so that you may prosper." [3:200] If you wake up, by the will of God, safe and sound in the morning, then go forth to fight for the sake of God, with your eyes wide open, triumphing over your enemy. If you find that war has overtaken you, then cleanse yourself in its heat, strike it with your sword, and win your reward in the next life.

The next morning, the sons of al-Khansaa' fought with brave hearts until they fell in battle, one after the other. Al-Khansaa' received news of the death of her four sons all in one day. She did not wail and tear her clothes, as she once did for her brother. Rather, her reaction was a reflection of her strong faith and how it alleviated her sorrow. Her response to the news was, "Praise be to Allah who honored me with their deaths. I hope my Lord reunites me with them under His mercy."[15]

⊰ THE HUNGRY BEDOUIN ⊱

There is another short story that illustrates the tangible, transformative effects of iman. A man was once a guest in the Prophet's home, and the Prophet ﷺ requested that a sheep be milked for him.[16] The man drank all of the milk, so the Prophet ﷺ asked that another sheep be milked, and another, and another, until the guest drank the milk of seven sheep.

Over the course of the night, this man's heart opened to Islam. He became Muslim at the hands of the Prophet ﷺ, bearing witness to his faith in Allah and His messenger. The next morning, the Prophet ordered that a sheep be milked for the guest. The man drank the milk, but when a second sheep was milked, he could not finish it. Upon this the Prophet ﷺ said, "The believer drinks with one stomach, while the disbeliever drinks with seven stomachs."[17] In just one night, a man who insisted on overindulging evolved into a man who was easily satisfied. Iman has the ability to transform innumerable aspects of character, personality, and habit.

Changing Behaviors

The first step in solving any problematic behavior is building up faith, whether the individual is young or old, and whether the behavior is isolated or recurring. In this section, we will explore three types of wrong behaviors and how to address them with faith.

1 INCIDENTAL BEHAVIORS, or one-time actions that are uncharacteristic of the person's character. These behaviors may, or may not, mark the start of a bad pattern.

2 EMBEDDED BEHAVIORS are those that have become habit, either because they were inherited through genetics or upbringing, or because they were repeated so often over time that they became part of one's character and personality. A person engages in these behaviors and patterns automatically without thinking.

3 BEHAVIORS RESULTING FROM A DISEASE OF THE HEART. These diseases are not only weaknesses in character, but signify a major flaw in our relationship with God. Examples of these diseases of the heart are arrogance, self-admiration, disdain, showing off, hypocrisy, and worshipping desires.

Let's look at the role iman can play in amending each of these problematic behaviors. In the case of **incidental behaviors,** they are usually the result of weakness and inattention in restraining the *nafs* (self). When faith is awakened, many of these negligent behaviors will disappear as a matter of course, without requiring a treatment plan. In fact, when sharp criticism comes on the heels of a one-time lapse, it may create the opposite of the desired effect, causing the individual to resent the advice and feel misunderstood.

We can think of these momentary weaknesses as similar to catching a bad cold. Someone could be in general good health, but this sickness knocked them off their feet, spoiled their mood and behavior, and led them to behave in an uncharacteristic manner. What he or she requires most are elements to strengthen the body so the immune system can fight off the virus. Once the virus is eliminated, the negative symptoms will disappear.

Embedded Behaviors

Embedded behaviors are traits and attitudes that have taken root as a result of lack of development and attention. These errant habits, which may start out as occasional mistakes, eventually take hold of the heart and become second-nature. Someone who struggles with these habits may even acknowledge their laziness, quick temper, lack of organization, or sensitivity to criticism, and may have a plan to address those habits.

If we go long enough without self-accountability, or find ourselves in a toxic environment, we may pick up negative traits and mannerisms that become new bad habits. Our behaviors and habits are not static; they are constantly evolving and responding to the environments and company we associate with. A passive attitude and lack of vigilance in self-development can lead to new negative habits taking root in our personality.

Planning is one thing, and creating change is another. You will develop new positive qualities only through intentional practice over time. Similar to learning to ride a bike, every movement is calculated in the beginning. Control of the handlebars is precarious, and there are inevitable scrapes and falls. Once a child finds her center of balance, and the pedaling motions become automatic, she can ride confidently with much less attention. There is a period when a desired habit requires utmost focus and intentionality. Over time, the movements become easier and more natural.

This approach is reflected in the rhythms of the Quran itself. Repetitiveness in meanings and principles, conveyed through multiple methods within the flow of Quranic verses, establishes grounding beliefs and principles in the heart. Throughout the Quran, similar ideas are expressed from different angles and through various examples, until the concepts become part of our mental framework and our soul's fabric.

A character trait, attitude, or behavior, must be rehearsed for a time before it becomes an intrinsic quality. No matter how much you wish to be organized or disciplined, it will never become a habit unless you strive to build it with small conscious steps over time. Prophet Muhammad ﷺ said, "**Knowledge comes only through trying to learn, and forbearance comes only through trying to be forbearing. Whoever pursues goodness will be given it, and whoever avoids evil will be spared from it.**"[18] He ﷺ also said, "**Whoever strives to be chaste, Allah will make him chaste; whoever strives to gain lawfully, Allah will enrich him; and whoever strives to be patient, Allah will make him patient.**"[19]

Ideas and convictions alone are not enough for change. Most people are convinced that justice and equality are noble causes and think of themselves as advocates. However, when it comes to implementation and sacrifice, many of us fall short. Without commitment and the hard labor of practice, most people will default to the less principled habits and behaviors they are accustomed to, even if those habits contradict their proclaimed convictions.

The Importance of Practice

To address negative behaviors embedded in our character, we must practice and work hard. Our community faces a serious problem in how we isolate knowledge from actionable steps. It is not uncommon for someone to be knowledgeable in all of the religious commandments: what is allowed and prohibited, rights and obligations, opinions of different scholars and schools of thoughts, and all the recommended acts of worship. He or she may even memorize extensive passages of the Quran and *hadith* texts. Yet if we look at this person's reality, we find a dissonance between what he is calling for and what he is practicing. This is because he failed to train himself in the practical dimension. *Tarbiya*, the gradual nurturing and shaping of the individual, is different from learning. A person improves not through knowledge in itself, but through its application. Noble character qualities can be attained through training and practice until they become part of our nature.

Abu Hamid Al-Ghazali, the great 11th century Islamic theologian and scholar, wrote in his magnificent volume *Ihya' 'uloom ad-Din* (Revival of the Islamic Sciences):

> Beautiful character qualities can be attained through practice. In the beginning, the behaviors associated with that character quality require effort, but in the end they become part of one's nature. Such is the strange relationship between the heart and the limbs.

> This can be illustrated by the example of a person who wishes to become an expert in handwriting. There is no way to become a truly skilled handwriter without immersing oneself in practice, taking on the habits of the skilled writer and imitating their motions. After much painstaking practice and time, the amateur writer begins to see signs of skill in their work, although only with effort and sustained attention to every motion. He continues to work on his form until he is able to produce beautiful handwriting almost effortlessly. What once was only achievable through great effort and attention becomes elementary to him.

> And so it is with whoever wishes to change himself to be more generous, modest or easygoing. One must consciously take on the associated actions until it becomes part of his nature. There is no cure for behavior flaws other than this.[20]

Faith Motivates Behavior Change

The process of training yourself to change habitual negative behavior is not easy. Your *nafs* will evade any attempt at restraint. Here again, we see the importance of strong motivation. Notice how the Messenger ﷺ began many of his directives with, "Whoever believes in Allah and the Last Day…" He ﷺ reminds us that doing good and avoiding bad deeds requires an internal motivation springing from faith and mindfulness of God. In one of these specially worded directives, the Prophet ﷺ said, "**Whoever believes in Allah and the Last Day should treat his neighbor most finely. Whoever believes in Allah and the Last Day should be generous to his guest. Whoever believes in Allah and the Last Day should say something good or keep quiet.**"[21]

In fact, *iman* is what compels us to heed the Quran's reminders. Allah says,

ذَٰلِكَ يُوعَظُ بِهِۦ مَن كَانَ مِنكُمْ يُؤْمِنُ بِٱللَّهِ وَٱلْيَوْمِ ٱلْآخِرِ

Let those of you who believe in God and the Last Day take this to heart… [2:232]

لَّا تَجِدُ قَوْمًا يُؤْمِنُونَ بِٱللَّهِ وَٱلْيَوْمِ ٱلْآخِرِ يُوَآدُّونَ مَنْ حَآدَّ ٱللَّهَ وَرَسُولَهُۥ
وَلَوْ كَانُوٓا۟ ءَابَآءَهُمْ أَوْ أَبْنَآءَهُمْ أَوْ إِخْوَٰنَهُمْ أَوْ عَشِيرَتَهُمْ ۚ أُو۟لَٰٓئِكَ كَتَبَ
فِى قُلُوبِهِمُ ٱلْإِيمَٰنَ وَأَيَّدَهُم بِرُوحٍ مِّنْهُ ۖ

You will not find people who truly believe in God and the Last Day giving their loyalty to those who oppose God and His Messenger, even though they may be their fathers, sons, brothers, or other relations: these are the people in whose hearts God has inscribed faith, and whom He has strengthened with His spirit. [58:22]

Diseases of the Heart

We spoke about how to address two common patterns of wrong behaviors through gentle reminders, practice, and *tarbiyah*. The third category of wrong behaviors are those resulting from a disease infecting the heart. Curing the problem of a diseased heart is challenging, because the disease has embedded itself in more than just our habits, but also our heart, mind, and worldview. Knowledge of the diseases of the heart is important to our discussion because *iman* cannot take root properly in a diseased heart.

ONE OF THE GRAVEST forms of spiritual disease is arrogance or feeling superior to others. This terrible sickness can be due to several causes, such as growing up in a home that takes excessive pride in lineage and status or a series of academic and career achievements

taken out of perspective. Depending on how we interpret these life events and how our character receives social distinctions, the disease of arrogance may take root.

Arrogance is a great obstacle to entering Paradise. Prophet Muhammad ﷺ said, **"Whoever has a mustard seed's weight of arrogance in his heart shall not enter the Garden."**[22] Its most dangerous manifestation is rejecting any truth that does not originate within oneself. The Prophet ﷺ said, **"Arrogance is to reject the truth and to look down on people."**[23]

Abu Hamid Al-Ghazali writes:

> Arrogance is a barrier to Paradise, for it comes between a servant and the best character qualities of believers. These character qualities are embodied by the doors of Paradise, and arrogance and self-importance close each of these doors. When a person believes he is superior to others, he cannot love for the believers what he loves for himself nor can he be humble, the crowning characteristic of the pious.
>
> Such a person cannot stop himself from envy, cannot advise others tactfully, nor can he accept advice while this arrogance is in him. He cannot resist belittling others and backbiting about their faults. In fact, there is no nasty, mean characteristic except that the arrogant person is compelled toward it in order to maintain his self-importance. And there is no praiseworthy character quality except that he finds himself incapable of practicing it in order to preserve his superior position.[24]

Arrogance blocks every window of insight and understanding. It causes one to think of himself or herself as more exceptional than others, maybe even a creation apart—quite in line with Satan's school of thought. Arrogance is to belittle other people while reserving exceptionality for yourself or an elite group. You refuse to apply to yourself the same standards that you apply to others.[25]

The Quran demonstrates the effects of arrogance through the story of pharaoh and his entourage. Allah's signs came to them clearly, with no room for doubt, and still they refused Prophet Musa's warning and fought the Messenger of God:

$$\text{فَلَمَّا جَآءَتْهُمْ ءَايَٰتُنَا مُبْصِرَةً قَالُواْ هَٰذَا سِحْرٌ مُّبِينٌ ۝ وَجَحَدُواْ بِهَا وَٱسْتَيْقَنَتْهَآ أَنفُسُهُمْ ظُلْمًا وَعُلُوًّا فَٱنظُرْ كَيْفَ كَانَ عَٰقِبَةُ ٱلْمُفْسِدِينَ ۝}$$

But when Our enlightening signs came to them, they said, 'this is clearly (just) sorcery!' They denied them, in their wickedness and their pride, even though their souls acknowledged them as true. See how those who spread corruption met their end! [27:13-14]

It was arrogance and a craving for supremacy that made them turn away from faith. This is the case with those who deny the truth, much like the Tribe of Aad, Prophet Hud's people:

$$فَأَمَّا عَادٌ فَٱسْتَكْبَرُوا۟ فِى ٱلْأَرْضِ بِغَيْرِ ٱلْحَقِّ وَقَالُوا۟ مَنْ أَشَدُّ مِنَّا قُوَّةً$$
$$أَوَلَمْ يَرَوْا۟ أَنَّ ٱللَّهَ ٱلَّذِى خَلَقَهُمْ هُوَ أَشَدُّ مِنْهُمْ قُوَّةً وَكَانُوا۟ بِـَٔايَـٰتِنَا$$
$$يَجْحَدُونَ ۞$$

The people of 'Ad behaved arrogantly throughout the land without any right, saying, "Who could be stronger than us?" Did they not realize that God, who created them, was stronger than them?' They continued to reject Our message.
[41:15]

It is extremely difficult to cure the disease of arrogance. Preserving one's self-superiority is the highest priority for the arrogant soul, making it impossible to accept advice or warning. To admit to a mistake would tarnish the sacred image of the self. It is much easier to dismiss the warnings in a way that preserves the inflated image of self: *"No one understands me; they are just jealous; I know the right way to do things,"* and so on.

. . . .   ◆◆◆   . . . .

A man at the time of the Prophet ﷺ was eating with his left hand. The Messenger ﷺ instructed him to eat with his right hand, knowing the man was capable of changing the habit. The man refused to comply with the Prophet's advice, claiming that he couldn't eat with his other hand. The Prophet ﷺ said, "Then may you not be able." Only pride stopped him from following the Prophet's instructions.[26]

. . . .

In order to overcome the disease of arrogance, in most cases, the individual must experience a severe shock that shatters their false perceptions. He or she must go through a spiritual earthquake that shakes their identity and brings them to their knees. It is the only way to expose the flaws in this creed of self-importance. Ibn Al-Qayyim wrote:

> If Allah wants good for this servant, He will cast him into a sin that will break him and force him to acknowledge his weakness, overwhelming him with guilt and regret, turning him upside down, drawing out the disease of arrogance and false superiority over His other servants. In this case, the sin is more beneficial to this servant than many acts of obedience, for it is the medicine that cured a fatal illness.[27]

If one thinks they are afflicted with this disease, they should immerse themselves in an environment of faith, seeking to lessen the effects of the disease. They should humble themselves and pray to God to cure them, while preparing mentally for the possibility of a harsh wake-up call in the future.

RIYA' (SHOWING OFF) is another form of disease that also impairs the influence of *iman* on the heart. *Riya'* is love of attention, prestige and recognition. Developing strong iman and deep mindfulness of God is crucial to the process of curing *riya'*.

يَـٰٓأَيُّهَا ٱلَّذِينَ ءَامَنُوا۟ لَا تُبْطِلُوا۟ صَدَقَـٰتِكُم بِٱلْمَنِّ وَٱلْأَذَىٰ كَٱلَّذِى
يُنفِقُ مَالَهُۥ رِئَآءَ ٱلنَّاسِ وَلَا يُؤْمِنُ بِٱللَّهِ وَٱلْيَوْمِ ٱلْءَاخِرِ فَمَثَلُهُۥ كَمَثَلِ
صَفْوَانٍ عَلَيْهِ تُرَابٌ فَأَصَابَهُۥ وَابِلٌ فَتَرَكَهُۥ صَلْدًا لَّا يَقْدِرُونَ عَلَىٰ شَىْءٍ
مِّمَّا كَسَبُوا۟ وَٱللَّهُ لَا يَهْدِى ٱلْقَوْمَ ٱلْكَـٰفِرِينَ ۝

You who believe, do not cancel out your charitable deeds with
reminders and hurtful words, like someone who spends his
wealth only to be seen by people, not believing in God and the
Last Day. Such a person is like a rock with earth on it: heavy
rain falls and leaves it completely bare. Such people get no
rewards for their works: God does not guide the disbelievers.
[2:264]

The people described in the previous verse gave charity only to be seen, seeking to enhance their social status. They failed in their intentions because of a lack of true faith and a fear of God.

وَٱلَّذِينَ يُنفِقُونَ أَمْوَٰلَهُمْ رِئَآءَ ٱلنَّاسِ وَلَا يُؤْمِنُونَ بِٱللَّهِ وَلَا بِٱلْيَوْمِ ٱلْءَاخِرِ
وَمَن يَكُنِ ٱلشَّيْطَـٰنُ لَهُۥ قَرِينًا فَسَآءَ قَرِينًا ۝

(Nor does He like those) who spend their wealth to show off,
who do not believe in Him or the Last Day. [4:38]

The cure for *riya'* is to develop a fear of Allah, for it is fear of God that pushes us to be deeply sincere in our actions, not desiring any other exchange for our deeds. God Exalted says:

وَيُطْعِمُونَ ٱلطَّعَامَ عَلَىٰ حُبِّهِۦ مِسْكِينًا وَيَتِيمًا وَأَسِيرًا ۝ إِنَّمَا
نُطْعِمُكُمْ لِوَجْهِ ٱللَّهِ لَا نُرِيدُ مِنكُمْ جَزَآءً وَلَا شُكُورًا ۝ إِنَّا نَخَافُ
مِن رَّبِّنَا يَوْمًا عَبُوسًا قَمْطَرِيرًا ۝

And they give food—despite their love for it—to the poor, the

> *orphan, and the captive, (saying to themselves,) "We feed you only for the sake of Allah, seeking neither reward nor thanks from you. We fear from our Lord a horribly distressful Day."* [76:8-10]

These righteous people possess a fear of their Lord that motivates their choices. This fear, along with their love for God, drives them to serve others while expecting no return, not even a word of thanks or praise.

....

ENDNOTES

1. Ibn Majah (1/42 #61), al-Albani (Sahih ibn Majah) and al-Busiri (1/12)
2. al-Maruzi in *Mukhtasar Qiyam al-Lail* (1/179), at-Tahawi in *Mushakal al-Athar* (4/154 #1453) and al-Hakim in *al-Mustadrak* (1/91 #101)
3. al-Bukhari (6/185 #4993)
4. Ahmad (15/483 #9776); al-Bazzar (16/130); ibn Hibban (6/300 #2560); authenticated by al-Arna'ut
5. *Book of Tahajud and Qiyam Al-Layl* by Ibn Abi Ad-Dunia, p. 419
6. *al-Raheeq al-Makhtum*, p. 467-468
7. Muslim (3/1398 #1775) and Muhammad Rasul Allah by Muhammad as-Sadiq Arjun, 4/374.
8. *Seerah ibn Hisham* (2/499-500) and *ar-Raheeq al-Makhtum* (473-474)
9. Al-Khatib in *Iqtida' al-'Ilm al-'Amal*, no. 71, and Al-Albani in *Sahih Al-Jami*, #5837
10. Ar-Rafi'i in *Wahy al-Qalam*, 2/42
11. Hasan Sahih, Ahmad (12/364 #7402); Tirmithi; Abu Dawud; Al-Albani in as-Silsilah as-Sahihah (284)
12. Tirmithi (5/552 #3549) and others;, authenticated by Al-Albani in Takhreej Mishkat al-Masabih (1227)
13. Ahmad (18/194 #11651) Tirmithi (5/12 #2617), Ibn Majah, Ibn Hibban in his Sahih
14. *Seerah ibn Hisham* (1/477); reason for verse revelation from as-Suyooti in *ad-Durr al-Manthur* (1/575)
15. *Al-Iman wa Al-Hayah* by Dr. Yusuf Al-Qaradawi, 267-269; al-Kila'i (2/475)
16. This story is included in Imam Muslim's Sahih, Burhan Mubeen ala Mablagh Athar Al-Iman; al-Iman wa al-Hayah by al-Qaradawi, 268.
17. Muslim (3/1632 #2063)
18. Ibn Abi Dunya in al-Hulm #4; al-Albani in as-Silsilah as-Sahihah #342
19. Part of a *hadith* that is agreed upon: Bukhari (6470) and Muslim (1053)
20. *Ihya' Uloom Ad-Din* vol. 3: p. 96-97
21. al-Bukhari (8/11 #6019); Muslim (1/69 #48)
22. Muslim (1/93 #91)
23. Part of a *hadith* in Sahih Muslim (1/93 #91)
24. *Ihya' Uloom ad-Din*, 3/344-345.
25. *Kun ka Ibn Adam*, p. 25
26. Sahih Muslim (3/1599 #2021)
27. *Tahtheeb Madarij As-Salikeen*, p. 170

Begin with Faith

A skilled physician knows not to treat every symptom individually, but tries to diagnose the underlying condition. Painkillers relieve symptoms, but the underlying condition will resurface eventually. The spiritual heart is much the same. When the heart is infected with desire, the limbs pursue the various sources of pleasure and stimulation. It is not enough to instruct people to stop certain actions; we must address the heart's underlying attachments.

In our haste to correct the outer appearance, we neglect the inner aspects: the heart, the mind, and the *nafs*. We focus on the limbs instead of addressing a heart that is unmotivated to restrain the *nafs* and fight against evil whispers.

Some people may object to this shift in approach, saying that we must speak out against evil whenever we see it. This is true conceptually, since prohibiting evil is a religious obligation. However, there are many degrees and methods of prohibiting evil. Among the many methods of prohibiting evil is addressing the root causes and nurturing the good that will eventually replace it. This understanding and gentle approach is the best way to inspire human beings to change themselves. So let us start with what is good. Let us begin with faith. As we work to mend our hearts and the hearts of others, our actions will follow.

The Awakening

In order to begin the process of journeying to Allah, the first step is to awaken the heart so that it becomes aware of its need for God. This is a necessary step that startles the sleepers and snaps the daydreamers to attention. Ibn al-Qayyim wrote,

> The first step of servitude to God is awakening. It is when the heart is startled, coming to a realization after a period of oblivious ignorance. By God, what a valuable realization this is! And how meaningful and crucial—a great help to

changing behavior. Whoever experiences this realization has tasted success, by God! If not, then he still lies in the drunken stupor of ignorance. When a person becomes aware, he rolls up his sleeves and gets to work, advancing along the journey to God.[1]

This seems to be what is described as the standing up in the Quran: to wake up from a drowsy state of ignorance and stagnancy.

$$أَن تَقُومُواْ لِلَّهِ مَثْنَىٰ وَفُرَٰدَىٰ ثُمَّ تَتَفَكَّرُواْ$$

Say (Prophet), 'I advise you to do one thing only: stand before
God, in pairs or singly, and think...' [34:46]

Without this awakening, life will be aimless. Good deeds will be performed mechanically with little spirit or motivation behind them. Any positive effect is fleeting, lasting only for a few moments before a relapse into ambivalence.

Acts of worship, when performed with life and spirit, are supposed to increase the *iman* in our heart. Allah The Exalted describes this increase of faith:

$$إِنَّمَا ٱلْمُؤْمِنُونَ ٱلَّذِينَ إِذَا ذُكِرَ ٱللَّهُ وَجِلَتْ قُلُوبُهُمْ وَإِذَا تُلِيَتْ
عَلَيْهِمْ ءَايَٰتُهُۥ زَادَتْهُمْ إِيمَٰنًا وَعَلَىٰ رَبِّهِمْ يَتَوَكَّلُونَ ۝$$

True believers are those whose hearts tremble with awe when
God is mentioned, whose faith increases when His revelations
are recited to them, who put their trust in their Lord. [8:2]

Worship that is dull and lifeless may be a problem of heart, not necessarily of execution. The solution then, is not the introduction of more rituals to be performed by the limbs, but restoration of life to the heart.

Are You Motivated?

Whether you are the seeker or the mentor, the preliminary motivation is essential. This motivation comes from the initial awakening: realizing that our heart is devoid of real life, that external good deeds are inadequate, and fearing the consequences of weak faith. Ibn al-Qayyim said,

> There is little doubt that performing external actions without mindfulness or turning toward Allah is of little benefit and low yield in this life and the afterlife... Even if the actions are many, they are burdensome and without benefit. They are like wheat bran, appearing substantial but of little nutritional value. Allah only

records the parts of a servant's prayer that he is mentally present for, and it is similar for the rest of actions that we are supposed to perform consciously, such as the rituals of Hajj and so on.[2]

The prospect of our deeds amounting to little should frighten us and spur us to take steps to improve our internal state.

The Quran shows us that although the world is full of signs pointing to God, these will only impact people who want guidance for themselves. As for the self-sufficient one who feels no need for guidance, then the world with all its signs and proofs makes no difference.

$$قُلِ ٱنظُرُواْ مَاذَا فِى ٱلسَّمَـٰوَٰتِ وَٱلْأَرْضِ ۚ وَمَا تُغْنِى ٱلْـَٔايَـٰتُ وَٱلنُّذُرُ عَن قَوْمٍ لَّا يُؤْمِنُونَ ۝$$

Say, 'Look at what is in the heavens and on the earth.'
But what use are signs and warnings to people who
will not believe? [10:101]

Abu Raqid al-Laythi narrated that the Prophet ﷺ was sitting with the people in the mosque, when three people approached. Two of them walked toward Allah's Messenger ﷺ while the third was distant. One of the men found an opening in the circle of people and sat there. The second man sat behind the circle. The third turned away and left. When the Messenger of Allah ﷺ was finished with his task, he said, **"Shall I tell you about three individuals? One of them sought shelter with Allah and so Allah sheltered him. The other was shy, so Allah was shy from him. And the last turned away, so Allah turned away from him."**

When someone is motivated in seeking guidance, it shows. Their behavior testifies to the eagerness within. The Quran paints a picture of what this motivation looks like in its human form:

$$وَأَمَّا مَن جَآءَكَ يَسْعَىٰ ۝ وَهُوَ يَخْشَىٰ ۝$$

But the one who has hurried to you, full of
eagerness and awe [80:8-9]

As we graduate to exploring the methods of awakening iman, make sure you keep this motivation alive in yourself and others. Kindle your sense of urgency, make haste, plead with Allah, and remind yourself of your need for His help and guidance. As fellow travelers, we should remind each other often of the meanings of God-centeredness:

⟨ True Motivation ⟩

The verse to the right describes the blind man who came to the Prophet asking for guidance. It outlines qualities of the seekers of guidance:

» Taking initiative
» Seeking out benefit
» Haste
» *Khushoo' (reverence)*

how much we are in need of a revival of our hearts and how much we require help from God on our journeys.

A Note on Chapter Order

The remainder of this book explores methods of bringing the heart to life. These are not new techniques, rather, they are well-established in the Quran and Sunnah. This book lays them before the reader in an organized fashion, suggesting practical tips and exploring each one at length. You can read them in any sequence and skip ahead to chapters of interest. However, the first chapter *Fear* and the second chapter *Quran* have a special significance to their ordering.

All of the strategies for bringing the heart to life and strengthening iman are important, but keep this in mind: the Quran is the key! It should be the beginning, middle, and end of our spiritual journey in life. It is the miraculous blessing that God gave to us all, and it is the most direct method to heal the hearts and restore iman.

However, hearts do not always respond to the Quran immediately. They must first be sensitive and awake. Hence, the next section begins with a chapter on fear of Allah, despite the superiority of the Quran. As you can see in the verses cited to the right, the heart requires an element of fear and awe of God in order to interact most effectively with the Quran.

So we begin our journey of awakening faith at the station of fear, which will pave the way to benefitting more fully from the words of God in the Quran.

يَـٰٓأَيُّهَا ٱلنَّاسُ قَدْ جَآءَتْكُم مَّوْعِظَةٌ مِّن رَّبِّكُمْ وَشِفَآءٌ لِّمَا فِى ٱلصُّدُورِ وَهُدًى وَرَحْمَةٌ لِّلْمُؤْمِنِينَ ۝

People, a teaching from your Lord has come to you, a healing for what is in (your) hearts, and guidance and mercy for the believers. [10:57]

سَيَذَّكَّرُ مَن يَخْشَىٰ ۝

Those who stand in awe of God will heed the reminder. [87:10]

فَذَكِّرْ بِٱلْقُرْءَانِ مَن يَخَافُ وَعِيدِ ۝

So remind, with this Quran, those who fear My warning. [50:45]

....

ENDNOTES

1. *Tahtheeb Madarij as-Salikeen*, p. 101
2. *Tahtheeb Madarij as-Salikeen*, p. 153

PART II

the methods

Fear

◄(the jumpstart)►

Often, the heart requires a wake-up call. It is not easy to abandon temptation; we need compelling motivations to jolt us into action and shift our course. Fear is one of the most powerful forces driving change within the heart.

Whenever we hear a reminder, attend a funeral prayer, or witness a close call, we recognize our precarious reality. We shed a few tears and pronounce somber insights, but quickly move on from the discomfort. Fear should be more than a fleeting emotion, however. In order for the heart to be awakened, our fear of God must reach a befitting level. Fear jumpstarts the engine of our heart and propels us in God's direction, for there is nowhere to flee but towards Him.

◆◆◆

One of the great twentieth-century callers to Allah, Hasan al-Banna, observed that youth paid little attention to the imams of the mosque and flocked instead to cafes.

One evening, Al-Banna walked into a coffee house, took some burning charcoal and flung it onto one of the tables. People scrambled to avoid the burning embers. In the midst of this commotion, Al-Banna stood on a chair and called out,

"If this piece of ember can cause so much panic, what will you do when you are surrounded by fire on all sides, above and below, with no way to turn it back? Today you escaped being burned, but what will you do in Hell, where there is no escape?"

The hearts and minds of the young audience were shocked into attention, and they listened to his reminders as they never had before. Some of these young people approached al-Banna after his talk and became part of a movement that would have worldwide impact.

Prophet Noah's address to his people:

إِنَّآ أَرْسَلْنَا نُوحًا إِلَىٰ قَوْمِهِۦٓ أَنْ أَنذِرْ قَوْمَكَ مِن قَبْلِ أَن يَأْتِيَهُمْ عَذَابٌ أَلِيمٌ ۝ قَالَ يَٰقَوْمِ إِنِّى لَكُمْ نَذِيرٌ مُّبِينٌ ۝

We sent Noah to his people: 'Warn your people, before a painful punishment comes to them.' And so he said, 'My people, I am here to warn you plainly.' [71:1-2]

...and the words of Prophet Abraham:

وَإِنَّ مِن شِيعَتِهِۦ لَإِبْرَٰهِيمَ ۝ إِذْ جَآءَ رَبَّهُۥ بِقَلْبٍ سَلِيمٍ ۝ إِذْ قَالَ لِأَبِيهِ وَقَوْمِهِۦ مَاذَا تَعْبُدُونَ ۝ أَئِفْكًا ءَالِهَةً دُونَ ٱللَّهِ تُرِيدُونَ ۝ فَمَا ظَنُّكُم بِرَبِّ ٱلْعَٰلَمِينَ ۝

Abraham was of the same faith: he came to his Lord with a devoted heart. He said to his father and his people, 'What are you worship-ping? How can you desire false gods instead of the true God? What then do you expect from the Lord of all worlds?' [37:83-87]

Prophet Hud warned his people:

وَٱذْكُرْ أَخَا عَادٍ إِذْ أَنذَرَ قَوْمَهُۥ بِٱلْأَحْقَافِ وَقَدْ خَلَتِ ٱلنُّذُرُ مِنۢ بَيْنِ يَدَيْهِ وَمِنْ خَلْفِهِۦٓ أَلَّا تَعْبُدُوٓاْ إِلَّا ٱللَّهَ إِنِّىٓ أَخَافُ عَلَيْكُمْ عَذَابَ يَوْمٍ عَظِيمٍ ۝

And remember the brother of 'Ad, when he warned his people, who inhabited the sand-hills—there were certainly warners before and after him—saying, "Worship none but Allah. I truly fear for you the torment of a tremendous day." [46:21]

...and Prophet Moses with Pharoah:

وَلَقَدْ جَآءَ ءَالَ فِرْعَوْنَ ٱلنُّذُرُ ۝

The people of Pharaoh also received warnings. [54:41]

Opening Address of Prophets

When we read the stories in the Quran of the Prophets and those who called to God, we observe that their opening addresses convey a sense of alarm. Their words warn their people of the dire consequences of continuing down the current path. The dual role of the Messengers has always been to warn and to give glad tidings to the believers; to invoke both fear and hope.

Prophet Muhammad ﷺ is our best example. When this verse was revealed:

وَأَنذِرْ عَشِيرَتَكَ ٱلْأَقْرَبِينَ ۝

Warn your nearest kinsfolk.
[26:214]

He ﷺ climbed Mount Safa and sounded the call of alarm that was used to summon the different tribes of Quraysh in case of emergency. When they had all gathered, the Messenger of Allah ﷺ said, "If I were to tell you that armed horsemen are behind this mountain waiting to attack Mecca, would you believe me?" They answered, "Yes, of course! We have only known you to tell the truth." The Prophet ﷺ said, "Then, I am sent to warn you against grievous suffering!"[1]

In another narration, the Prophet ﷺ called out individually to every tribe, "Tribe of Ka'b ibn Lu'ay, save yourselves from the fire! Tribe of Murrah ibn Ka'b, save yourselves from the fire!" and so on, until he ﷺ mentioned his own family members: "Tribe of Abdulmutalib, save yourselves from the fire! Fatima (the Prophet's own daughter) save yourself from the fire, for I cannot save you from Allah in the least. I am only related to you, and will fulfill my obligations toward you (in this life)."[2]

Take Precautions

All of the Prophets and callers to God utilized this method of kindling a sense of fear in their people. Through their efforts, Allah opened up hearts that were crusted over, eyes that were blind, and ears that were deaf. Fear is the surest way to awaken a heart intoxicated by desire.

Fear is the setting out on a journey to God, while taking the necessary precautions for the journey. In this hadith, setting out in the early night is a metaphor for the sense of urgency and precautionary measures one might take if there is peril on the journey:

◆◆◆

> "Whoever fears attack sets out in the early part of the night. And the one who sets out in the early part of the night reaches home. Truly, God's merchandise is precious. Truly, God's merchandise is Paradise." -Prophet Muhammad[3]

Many scholars have described this sense of urgency and fear in the heart of the believer. Ibrahim ibn Shaiban said, "When fear inhabits the heart it burns away desire and expels love for this life. It hushes the tongue from speaking too much about this world."[4] Fear keeps the individual on the right track, while losing fear can cause us to go astray as another scholar explained, "People are on the right path so long as they have fear. When they lose their sense of fear, they lose their way."[5] Abdullah ibn Mas'ood considered fear to be the precursor to wisdom, saying, "The best provision is *taqwa* (mindfulness of God), and the crux of wisdom is fear of Allah Almighty."[6]

Abu al-Darda', a famous Companion, described fear most vividly:

> If you all realized what awaited you after death, you would not be able to enjoy food or drink nor would you enjoy the shelter of your homes. You would flee to the hills, striking your chests, crying for your souls. People would wish their existence was reduced to some shrubbery that grew each year and was eaten.[7]

Fear in the Quran

The Quran brims with descriptions of Prophets and righteous people who had strong, abiding fear of God and His judgment. Even the best of creation, the Messengers of God, imbued their worship of God with a sense of fear.

Prophet Yahya and his wife called upon Allah together in hope and fear:

فَٱسْتَجَبْنَا لَهُ وَوَهَبْنَا لَهُ يَحْيَىٰ وَأَصْلَحْنَا لَهُ زَوْجَهُ إِنَّهُمْ كَانُوا۟ يُسَٰرِعُونَ فِى ٱلْخَيْرَٰتِ وَيَدْعُونَنَا رَغَبًا وَرَهَبًا وَكَانُوا۟ لَنَا خَٰشِعِينَ ۝

We answered him—We gave him John (Yahya), and cured his wife of barrenness- they were always keen to do good deeds. They called upon Us out of longing and fear, and humbled themselves before Us. [21:90]

Even those who do good deeds and live a righteous life-style should be acquainted with an element of fear:

وَٱلَّذِينَ يَصِلُونَ مَآ أَمَرَ ٱللَّهُ بِهِۦ أَن يُوصَلَ وَيَخْشَوْنَ رَبَّهُمْ وَيَخَافُونَ سُوٓءَ ٱلْحِسَابِ ۝

Those who join together what God commands to be joined; who are in awe of their Lord and fear the harshness of the Reckoning. [13:21]

The angels are praised in the Quran for their fear:

يَعْلَمُ مَا بَيْنَ أَيْدِيهِمْ وَمَا خَلْفَهُمْ وَلَا يَشْفَعُونَ إِلَّا لِمَنِ ٱرْتَضَىٰ وَهُم مِّنْ خَشْيَتِهِۦ مُشْفِقُونَ ۝

He knows what is ahead of them and what is behind them. They do not intercede except for whom He approves, and they tremble in awe of Him. [21:28]

It was fear that stopped one of the sons of Adam from striking the other:

لَئِنۢ بَسَطتَ إِلَىَّ يَدَكَ لِتَقْتُلَنِى مَآ أَنَا۠ بِبَاسِطٍ يَدِىَ إِلَيْكَ لِأَقْتُلَكَ إِنِّىٓ أَخَافُ ٱللَّهَ رَبَّ ٱلْعَٰلَمِينَ ۝

If you raise your hand to kill me, I will not raise mine to kill you. I fear God, the Lord of all worlds. [5:28]

When God commanded the Children of Israel to enter the sacred city, they refused, fearing the enemies within. Two men came forward to encourage their people to obey God's command to enter the sacred city. The Quran describes those two heroes as men who feared God:

قَالَ رَجُلَانِ مِنَ ٱلَّذِينَ يَخَافُونَ أَنْعَمَ ٱللَّهُ عَلَيْهِمَا ٱدْخُلُوا۟ عَلَيْهِمُ ٱلْبَابَ فَإِذَا دَخَلْتُمُوهُ فَإِنَّكُمْ غَٰلِبُونَ وَعَلَى ٱللَّهِ فَتَوَكَّلُوٓا۟ إِن كُنتُم مُّؤْمِنِينَ ۝

Yet two men whom God had blessed among those who were afraid said, 'Go in to them through the gate and when you go in you will overcome them. If you are true believers, put your trust in God.' [5:23]

فَأَوْحَىٰ إِلَيْهِمْ رَبُّهُمْ لَنُهْلِكَنَّ ٱلظَّٰلِمِينَ ۝ وَلَنُسْكِنَنَّكُمُ ٱلْأَرْضَ مِنۢ بَعْدِهِمْ ذَٰلِكَ لِمَنْ خَافَ مَقَامِى وَخَافَ وَعِيدِ ۝

But their Lord inspired the messengers: 'We shall destroy the evildoers, and leave you to dwell in the land after them. This reward is for those who are in fear of meeting Me, and of My warnings.' [14:13-14]

إِنَّمَا نُطْعِمُكُمْ لِوَجْهِ ٱللَّهِ لَا نُرِيدُ مِنكُمْ جَزَآءً وَلَا شُكُورًا ۝ إِنَّا نَخَافُ مِن رَّبِّنَا يَوْمًا عَبُوسًا قَمْطَرِيرًا ۝

We feed you for the sake of God alone: We seek neither recompense nor thanks from you. We fear the Day of our Lord—a woefully grim Day.' [76:9-10]

وَمَن يُطِعِ ٱللَّهَ وَرَسُولَهُۥ وَيَخْشَ ٱللَّهَ وَيَتَّقْهِ فَأُولَٰٓئِكَ هُمُ ٱلْفَآئِزُونَ ۝

Whoever obeys God and His Messenger, stands in awe of God, and keeps his duty to Him will be triumphant. [24:52]

فَمَا لَهُمْ عَنِ ٱلتَّذْكِرَةِ مُعْرِضِينَ ۝ كَأَنَّهُمْ حُمُرٌ مُّسْتَنفِرَةٌ ۝ فَرَّتْ مِن قَسْوَرَةٍ ۝ بَلْ يُرِيدُ كُلُّ ٱمْرِئٍ مِّنْهُمْ أَن يُؤْتَىٰ صُحُفًا مُّنَشَّرَةً ۝ كَلَّا بَل لَّا يَخَافُونَ ٱلْآخِرَةَ ۝

What is the matter with them? Why do they turn away from the warning, as if they were spooked zebras, fleeing from a lion? Each one of them demands that a scripture be sent down to him and unrolled before his very eyes—but no! Truly they have no fear of the life to come. [74:49-53]

۞ ۞ ۞

Fear will also be a signature characteristic of those whom Allah will cause to prevail over oppressors on earth.

The Quran gives the example of people who give, sacrifice, and work for the sake of God while expecting no recognition or thanks from anyone. Note their reference to fear.

Fear is one of the pathways to salvation and success on the Day of Judgment.

We might think that the reason people turn away from religion is that they are not convinced of the arguments, which is sometimes the case, but often it is inadequate fear of consequences.

The Stigma of Fear

In modern culture, fear and sorrow are seen as negative emotions to be avoided at all costs. Such a superficial approach ignores the complexity of the heart and its multifaceted needs. Fear of God, sorrow, and mindfulness are very much at home in the heart. They heighten our sensitivity and reap much benefit in this life and the next.

Scholars have spoken about the desirable streak of sorrow and fear in the hearts of believers: "Lack of fear results from a lack of sorrow in the heart. When the heart feels no sorrow, it becomes empty like an abandoned house," and "Sorrow pollinates good actions."[8]

◆◆◆

" I see what you do not see and hear what you do not hear. The skies are groaning, and they have every right to groan, for there is no space of four fingers except that it is occupied by an angel in prostration. If you knew what I knew, you would laugh less and weep often. You wouldn't be able to enjoy your spouses, and you would flee to the hills crying to Allah for help."
Prophet Muhammad ﷺ[9]

The Quran tells us how the people of Paradise will remember the sorrow and fear of their former lives:

وَقَالُوا۟ ٱلْحَمْدُ لِلَّهِ ٱلَّذِى أَذْهَبَ عَنَّا ٱلْحَزَنَ إِنَّ رَبَّنَا لَغَفُورٌ شَكُورٌ ۝

They will say, 'Praise be to God, who has separated us from all sorrow! Our Lord is truly most forgiving, most appreciative. [35:34]

قَالُوٓا۟ إِنَّا كُنَّا قَبْلُ فِىٓ أَهْلِنَا مُشْفِقِينَ ۝

'When we were still with our families (on earth) we used to live in fear. [52:26]

taqwa:

piety, mindfulness of God; being cautious and fearful in order to avoid God's displeasure

تقوى

Taqwa is a Goal of Worship

Worship, when performed correctly, nurtures *taqwa* (God-mindfulness), fear, *khashyah* (reverence and humility) in our hearts. The Quran spells out the relationship between the believer and worship in many verses:

إِنَّ أَكْرَمَكُمْ عِندَ اللَّهِ أَتْقَىٰكُمْ

*In God's eyes, the most honoured of you are the
ones most mindful of Him.* [49:13]

Our rank before God goes
up and down depending
on the amount of *taqwa*
(God-mindfulness) in
our heart.

يَـٰٓأَيُّهَا ٱلنَّاسُ ٱعْبُدُوا۟ رَبَّكُمُ ٱلَّذِى خَلَقَكُمْ وَٱلَّذِينَ مِن
قَبْلِكُمْ لَعَلَّكُمْ تَتَّقُونَ ۝

*People, worship your Lord, who created you and
those before you, so that you may be mindful.* [2:21]

Worship and good deeds
are meant to tune us into a
higher level of *taqwa* and
fear of God.

لَن يَنَالَ ٱللَّهَ لُحُومُهَا وَلَا دِمَآؤُهَا وَلَـٰكِن يَنَالُهُ ٱلتَّقْوَىٰ مِنكُمْ

*It is neither their meat nor their blood that reaches
God but your piety.* [22:37]

Acts of worship are not
technical items on a check-
list. Rather, the heart is the
goal, as the Quran empha-
sizes using the example of
the sacrifice at Hajj.

يَا أَيُّهَا ٱلَّذِينَ آمَنُوا كُتِبَ عَلَيْكُمُ ٱلصِّيَامُ كَمَا كُتِبَ عَلَى
ٱلَّذِينَ مِن قَبْلِكُمْ لَعَلَّكُمْ تَتَّقُونَ ۝

*You who believe, fasting is prescribed
for you, as it was prescribed for those
before you, so that you may be mindful
of God.* [2:183]

So it is with all forms of
worship. The connection
between fasting and *taqwa*
is often cited.

وَيَخِرُّونَ لِلْأَذْقَانِ يَبْكُونَ وَيَزِيدُهُمْ خُشُوعًا ۝

*And they fall down upon their faces weeping, and
it increases them in humble awe.* [17:109]

Prostration (*sujood*) is
meant to increase our fear.

وَأَنذِرْ بِهِ ٱلَّذِينَ يَخَافُونَ أَن يُحْشَرُوا إِلَىٰ رَبِّهِمْ لَيْسَ لَهُم مِّن
دُونِهِ وَلِيٌّ وَلَا شَفِيعٌ لَّعَلَّهُمْ يَتَّقُونَ ۝

*Use the Quran to warn those who fear being
gathered before their Lord- they will have no one
but Him to protect them and no one to intercede—
so that they may beware.* [6:51]

And the Quran's warnings
are most readily received by
those who fear their Lord.

⫸ ⫸ ⫸

Stories of the God-fearing

You cannot miss this signature quality of all Prophets and righteous people: they all feared God. Abraham, the father of all Prophets, is described in the Quran:

$$\text{إِنَّ إِبْرَهِيمَ لَحَلِيمٌ أَوَّهٌ مُّنِيبٌ ۝}$$

Truly, Abraham was forbearing, grieving, and ever turning to His Lord. [11:75]

Abu Bakr once exclaimed to the Prophet ﷺ, "Messenger of Allah, your hair is turning gray!" He ﷺ responded, **"Surah Hud has grayed my hair, along with al-Waqiah, al-Mursalat, *'Amma yatasa'alun*, and *Itha ash-shamsu kuwwirat*** [two other surahs]."[10] The Companions said that when the Prophet ﷺ prayed, he weeped so much that a wheezing sound like the boiling of a pot would escape his chest.[11]

Once the Prophet ﷺ came upon a group of people and asked, "Why have they gathered?" The Prophet ﷺ was told that the people had gathered to dig a grave. His face became alarmed, and he hastened forward until he reached the location of the grave. There, he sank to his knees and wept until the ground became wet. Then, he turned to his Companions and said, **"My brothers, you must prepare for a day like this!"**[12]

How do we reconcile these descriptions with what we know about the Prophet's ﷺ manners: that he smiled widely, cheered those around him, and made things easy for people? The appropriate fear of God is one that motivates one to call upon God, to rush to please Him, to be merciful toward the needy, and to emulate the restorative teachings of Prophet Muhammad ﷺ. Far from paralyzing, fear of God should be a great motivator when properly balanced.

Ibn al-Qayyim wrote, "Whoever reflects on the Companions will find that they were in a state of perpetual proactivity while also being in a state of fear. Today we are in a state of inactivity, truly falling short, while enjoying a false sense of security."[13]

Abu Bakr, the most excellent of the Companions, whose faith is equal to the faith of all other Muslims put together, used to say, "Cry! And if you cannot cry, then force yourself to cry."[14] Umar once came upon Abu Bakr and found him pulling at his tongue. Umar exclaimed in surprise, "Stop that, Allah forgive you!" Abu Bakr responded, "This (tongue) has brought me to the brink of disaster!"[15] Abu Bakr often expressed his wish that he was something insignificant so he could escape being called to account: "I wish that I were just a piece of greenery that the wild animals eat!"[16]

Take the example of Umar ibn al-Khattab, who had two dark marks on his face, rivulets left by tears. When he read the verse,

$$\text{إِنَّ عَذَابَ رَبِّكَ لَوَاقِعٌ}$$

Indeed, the punishment of your Lord will come to pass. [52:7]

He recited it over and over again, weeping so hard that he was incapacitated, and people visited him thinking he was ill.[17] On his deathbed, Umar ordered his son, "Put my cheek on the floor." His son was reluctant to do so, and Umar insisted. Umar was heard saying over and over again until he fell unconscious, "Woe to me, and woe to my mother, if God does not forgive me."[18] Ibn Abbas once tried to console Umar, "Allah used you decisively in many situations and victories, you have lived through so many great events!" Umar responded, "I can only hope that I am saved, gaining neither reward nor sin."[19]

We cannot help but feel humbled by the examples of the Companions and their robust sense of fear. Uthman ibn Affan stood at a grave, weeping until his beard was soaked, saying, "If I found myself somewhere between heaven and hell, not knowing which one I would be sent to, I would prefer to be turned into sand before finding out my destination."[20] And Abu al-Darda' used to say, "What I fear most about standing to account is that I will be asked, "You knew! So why did you not act upon what you knew?"[21]

There are many examples of Companions who were overwhelmed by a single verse. Tameem ad-Dari once read Surah al-Jathiyah in his night prayer, and came across this verse,

$$\text{أَمْ حَسِبَ ٱلَّذِينَ ٱجْتَرَحُوا ٱلسَّيِّئَاتِ أَن نَّجْعَلَهُمْ كَٱلَّذِينَ}$$
$$\text{ءَامَنُوا وَعَمِلُوا ٱلصَّٰلِحَٰتِ سَوَآءً مَّحْيَاهُمْ وَمَمَاتُهُمْ سَآءَ مَا}$$
$$\text{يَحْكُمُونَ}$$

Do those who commit evil deeds really think that We will deal with them in the same way as those who believe and do righteous deeds, that they will be alike in their living and their dying? How badly they judge! [45:21]

He cried and repeated this one verse until the morning.[22]

Once a man declared that he didn't just want to be among the people of Paradise, but hoped to be among those who are closest to Allah (*muqarraboon*). Abdullah ibn Mas'ood heard him and responded, "But here you have a man who wishes only that when he dies, he will not be resurrected!"[23] Abdullah ibn Mas'ood here was referring to himself; although his deeds and knowledge were of the highest level, he did not see himself that way.

Abu Hurayrah was the great Companion who spent every moment he could at the Prophet's side and narrated thousands of hadith. Despite his rank, he greatly feared facing His Lord. When he fell sick, he cried bitterly and was asked the reason for that. He said, "I am crying over how long my journey is and how little my provision. I am on a hill between heaven and hell, and I have no idea which one I will be taken to."[24]

Fatima bint Abdulmalik described the habits of her husband, Umar ibn Abdul Azeez, considered the fifth of the righteous Caliphs. She said, "There may be men who pray and fast more than Umar ibn Abdul Azeez, but I never saw a man who was more fearful of his Lord than him. He would come home and retreat to his prayer space, where he would continue to cry and supplicate until he fell asleep. When he would wake up, he would continue doing the same all night long."[25] She continued, "Sometimes he would cry, so I would cry, and the entire household would cry, with no one knowing why they were crying." Fatima asked him on one of these occasions, "My father be sacrificed for you, Leader of the Believers, why were you crying?" He replied, "Fatima, I remembered how people will be before God, a group to Paradise and a group to Hell." He then cried out and fell unconscious.[26]

Ahmad ibn Hanbal used to think about death and be overcome with emotion. He said,

> Fear makes me lose my appetite. When I think of death, the affairs of this life seem simple: food for one day at a time and clothing for one day at a time. Life is but a few days. If there was a way, I would prefer that no one knew or remembered me.[27]

Reasons for Fear

Why were these people so fearful of God while they were so pious? Surely they were destined for Paradise! If they worried so, then what hope is there for people like us? The truth is that there are many reasons for fear, not all which depend upon our level of faith and piety. Some of these reasons for fear are listed in the following pages; familiarize yourself with them and use them to nurture the softness of your heart and motivate your flight towards God.

⟨15 Reasons for Fear⟩

We should fear...

God's power
Falling short in worship
Consequences of sin
God's anger
Gradual decline into sin
Canceled good deeds
Unaccepted good works
Fear of being forsaken
Fear of losing faith
Fear of a bad ending
Sudden death
Agonies of death
Narrowness of the grave
Day of Judgment
Being Trapped in Hell

1. FEAR OF ALLAH'S OVERWHELMING POWER

The Quran recounts the words of Prophet Nuh when he asked his people:

$$مَّا لَكُمْ لَا تَرْجُونَ لِلَّهِ وَقَارًا ۝$$

What is the matter with you that you are not in awe of the
Majesty of Allah. [71:13]

The more we grow closer to Allah, we come to know better His names and attributes. We reflect in awe on His perfection and recognize His overwhelming power in the universe. He is the One who directs the course of history, alternating power and strength among peoples and civilizations:

$$قُلِ ٱللَّهُمَّ مَٰلِكَ ٱلْمُلْكِ تُؤْتِى ٱلْمُلْكَ مَن تَشَآءُ وَتَنزِعُ ٱلْمُلْكَ مِمَّن تَشَآءُ وَتُعِزُّ مَن تَشَآءُ وَتُذِلُّ مَن تَشَآءُ ۖ بِيَدِكَ ٱلْخَيْرُ ۖ إِنَّكَ عَلَىٰ كُلِّ شَىْءٍ قَدِيرٌ ۝$$

Say, 'God, holder of all control, You give control to whoever
You will and remove it from whoever You will; You elevate
whoever You will and humble whoever You will. All that is
good lies in Your hand: You have power over everything. [3:26]

Nations are overturned—one falls while the other rises. The angels are perpetually descending with divine commands. What He wills will come to pass at the time that He wants, in the way He wants, without any deviation, advance, or delay. His will and power is enforced in the limitless expanse of the heavens and in the smallest details of the earth, from the atomic scale to the intergalactic. He changes and creates therein what He wills.

$$يُدَبِّرُ ٱلْأَمْرَ مِنَ ٱلسَّمَآءِ إِلَى ٱلْأَرْضِ ثُمَّ يَعْرُجُ إِلَيْهِ فِى يَوْمٍ كَانَ مِقْدَارُهُۥٓ أَلْفَ سَنَةٍ مِّمَّا تَعُدُّونَ ۝$$

He runs everything, from the heavens to the earth, and
everything will ascend to Him in the end, on a Day that will
measure a thousand years in your reckoning. [32:5]

There is no particle in the heavens or earth except that He knows it and has counted it, nor is there a living cell swimming in the depth of the oceans or subsisting in the layers of the earth except that He knows it and has control of it.

$$وَعِندَهُۥ مَفَاتِحُ ٱلْغَيْبِ لَا يَعْلَمُهَآ إِلَّا هُوَ ۚ وَيَعْلَمُ مَا فِى ٱلْبَرِّ وَٱلْبَحْرِ ۚ وَمَا تَسْقُطُ مِن وَرَقَةٍ إِلَّا يَعْلَمُهَا وَلَا حَبَّةٍ فِى ظُلُمَٰتِ ٱلْأَرْضِ وَلَا$$

$$\text{رَطْبٍ وَلَا يَابِسٍ إِلَّا فِي كِتَٰبٍ مُّبِينٍ} ۝$$

He has the keys to the unseen: no one knows them but Him.
He knows all that is in the land and sea. No leaf falls without
His knowledge, nor is there a single grain in the darkness of
the earth, or anything, fresh or withered, that is not written in
a clear Record. [6:59]

How can we not tremble at what we can glimpse of Allah's overwhelming power?[29] Ibn al-Qayyim quoted these lines of poetry:

He is the All-Knowing
whose knowledge includes
Everything in the universe,
secret and obvious.
He knows what will come tomorrow
what is now becoming, and what has been.
He knows what did not happen,
And He knows, had it happened,
How it would have been.

Allow your mind to revel in the variety and scope of God's creation. The more you learn about the inner workings of science, the human body and the natural world, the more you will be in awe of God's power of creation. Your mind will go back and forth between the minutiae of the smallest particles and organisms and the vast systems of time and space, making connections and increasing in reverence.

Reflect on how His mercy and wisdom touches everything in the most creative of ways. He hears and understands the languages of every human, animal, and inanimate structure. To God, the unseen is witnessed reality, and secrets are in plain sight. He sees every angle and dimension, even the scurrying of a black ant and the wing of a gnat in the darkness of the night. He sees their flimsy forms, their inner workings, and trembling joints.

He hears every single supplication of his creation and knows their exact conditions, needs, and state of mind. Multiple supplications do not confuse Him, nor does He become tired of those who are persistent in their calling upon Him. The one who calls out loud does not drown out the voice of the whisperer.[23]

$$\text{وَأَسِرُّواْ قَوْلَكُمْ أَوِ ٱجْهَرُواْ بِهِۦٓ إِنَّهُۥ عَلِيمٌۢ بِذَاتِ ٱلصُّدُورِ} ۝$$

Whether you keep your words secret or state them openly, He
knows the contents of every heart. [67:13]

$$\text{يَعْلَمُ خَآئِنَةَ ٱلْأَعْيُنِ وَمَا تُخْفِى ٱلصُّدُورُ}$$

*God is aware of the most furtive of glances, and of all that
hearts conceal.* [40:19]

Aishah, the mother of the believers, said, "Praise be to God whose hearing encompasses every sound. When the woman came to the Prophet to complain about her husband, I was in the house but could not hear what she said." Yet Allah heard her complaint and revealed[30]:

$$\text{قَدْ سَمِعَ ٱللَّهُ قَوْلَ ٱلَّتِي تُجَادِلُكَ فِي زَوْجِهَا}$$

*Allah has heard the words of the woman who disputed with
you (Prophet) about her husband...* [58:1]

There is no one dominant except that He is higher; no one intimate except that He is Closer. There is no first except that Allah is before, no final except that He is after. There is no piece of sky or earth that is hidden, and no outer layer that can conceal the inner from Him.

$$\text{هُوَ ٱلْأَوَّلُ وَٱلْآخِرُ وَٱلظَّاهِرُ وَٱلْبَاطِنُ وَهُوَ بِكُلِّ شَيْءٍ عَلِيمٌ ۞ هُوَ ٱلَّذِي}$$
$$\text{خَلَقَ ٱلسَّمَوَاتِ وَٱلْأَرْضَ فِي سِتَّةِ أَيَّامٍ ثُمَّ ٱسْتَوَى عَلَى ٱلْعَرْشِ يَعْلَمُ مَا}$$
$$\text{يَلِجُ فِي ٱلْأَرْضِ وَمَا يَخْرُجُ مِنْهَا وَمَا يَنزِلُ مِنَ ٱلسَّمَاءِ وَمَا يَعْرُجُ فِيهَا وَهُوَ}$$
$$\text{مَعَكُمْ أَيْنَ مَا كُنتُمْ وَٱللَّهُ بِمَا تَعْمَلُونَ بَصِيرٌ}$$

*He is the First and the Last; the Outer and the Inner; He has
knowledge of all things. It was He who created the heavens and
earth in six Days and then established Himself on the throne. He
knows what enters the earth and what comes out of it; what
descends from the sky and what ascends to it. He is with you
wherever you are; He sees all that you do.* [57:3-4]

Everything shall perish except for His face, and every kingship will fall except for His. Every favor will be cut off except for His favor. He cannot be obeyed except by His permission and mercy, and cannot be disobeyed except with His knowledge and wisdom. When He is obeyed, He is the Most Appreciative, and when He is disobeyed, He overlooks and forgives. Every chastisement from Him is just, and every blessing from Him is a favor. He is the closest observer and protector. He comes between us and our own hearts, holds our foreheads in His hand, records every footstep and the exact second of our death:

$$\text{إِنَّمَآ أَمْرُهُ إِذَآ أَرَادَ شَيْئًا أَن يَقُولَ لَهُ كُن فَيَكُونُ ۞ فَسُبْحَانَ ٱلَّذِي}$$
$$\text{بِيَدِهِ مَلَكُوتُ كُلِّ شَيْءٍ وَإِلَيْهِ تُرْجَعُونَ}$$

When He wills something to be, His way is to say, "Be"—and
it is! So glory be to Him in whose Hand lies control over all
things. It is to Him that you will all be brought back.' [82:83]

Allah is most deserving of remembrance, worship, praise and thanks. Whoever invokes Him will receive the greatest help, for Allah is the gentlest King and the most Generous provider. He is both Mighty and Forgiving, pardoning us while He is All-Powerful.

Allah, The Glorified and Absolute, is greater than anything, and nothing lies beyond the grip of His power. To comprehend the scale of these words we must let them unfold in our hearts. He is wise beyond wisdom and has knowledge beyond comprehension. Nothing is beyond His reach or slips His notice. Contemplate this *hadith* qudsi, in which Allah's words are retold by the Prophet ﷺ:

···   ✦✦✦   ···

"O my servants! I have forbidden injustice for Myself, and I have made it forbidden amongst you, so do not oppress one another. My servants, all of you are lost except those whom I have guided, so seek guidance from Me—I will guide you. My servants, all of you are hungry except those whom I have fed, so seek food from Me—I will feed you. My servants, all of you are naked except those whom I have clothed, so seek clothing from Me—I will clothe you. My servants, you commit sins by night and day, and I forgive all sins, so seek forgiveness from Me—I will forgive you. My servants, you are incapable of harming Me, and you are incapable of benefitting Me. My servants, if the first of you and the last of you, the humans and the jinn, were all as pious as the most pious heart amongst you, then this would not add anything to My Kingdom. My servants, if the first of you and the last of you, the humans and the jinn, were all as wicked as the most wicked heart amongst you, then this would not decrease anything from My Kingdom. My servants, if the first of you and the last of you, the humans and the jinn, were all to stand together in one place and ask of Me, and I were to give everyone what they requested, that would not decrease what I have any more than a needle can decrease from the ocean. My servants, it is your deeds that I account for you, then I recompense you for them. So he who finds good, let him praise Allah, and he who finds other than that, let him blame no one but himself."[31]

···

His words are perfect in truth, justice, and every noble sense. His attributes cannot be measured by our standards, and His being does not resemble our concept of being. His doings are just, wise, merciful, perfect, and kind. He teaches His servants about Himself in many ways and provides them with a variety of signs, verses, and proofs pointing to His presence.

قُل لِّمَنِ ٱلْأَرْضُ وَمَن فِيهَآ إِن كُنتُمْ تَعْلَمُونَ ۞ سَيَقُولُونَ لِلَّهِ قُلْ أَفَلَا
تَذَكَّرُونَ ۞ قُلْ مَن رَّبُّ ٱلسَّمَٰوَٰتِ ٱلسَّبْعِ وَرَبُّ ٱلْعَرْشِ ٱلْعَظِيمِ ۞ سَيَقُولُونَ
لِلَّهِ قُلْ أَفَلَا تَتَّقُونَ ۞ قُلْ مَنۢ بِيَدِهِ مَلَكُوتُ كُلِّ شَىْءٍ وَهُوَ يُجِيرُ وَلَا يُجَارُ
عَلَيْهِ إِن كُنتُمْ تَعْلَمُونَ ۞ سَيَقُولُونَ لِلَّهِ قُلْ فَأَنَّىٰ تُسْحَرُونَ ۞

Say (Prophet), 'Who owns the earth and all who live in it, if
you know (so much)?' And they will reply, 'God.' Say, 'Will
you not take heed?' Say, 'Who is the Lord of the seven
heavens? Who is the Lord of the Mighty Throne?' and they
will reply, 'God.' Say, 'Will you not be mindful?' Say, 'Who
holds control of everything in His hand? Who protects, while
there is no protection against Him, if you know (so much)?'
and they will reply, 'God.' Say, 'then how can you be so
deluded?' [23:84-89]

Contemplating the greatness of Allah and understanding His Names and Attributes should elicit a powerful sense of fear and reverence before our great Lord, to whom all is surrendered:

وَلِلَّهِ يَسْجُدُ مَن فِى ٱلسَّمَٰوَٰتِ وَٱلْأَرْضِ طَوْعًا وَكَرْهًا وَظِلَٰلُهُم بِٱلْغُدُوِّ
وَٱلْءَاصَالِ ۞

All that are in heaven and earth submit to God alone, willingly
or unwillingly, as do their shadows in the mornings and in the
evenings. [13:15]

2. FEAR OF FALLING SHORT IN WORSHIP

God created human beings and preferred us over all of His creation. The angels were commanded to prostrate before our father Adam, and Satan was expelled from the heavens because of his refusal to do so. We were created in the best form and given the means to live comfortably on earth.

وَلَقَدْ كَرَّمْنَا بَنِىٓ ءَادَمَ وَحَمَلْنَٰهُمْ فِى ٱلْبَرِّ وَٱلْبَحْرِ وَرَزَقْنَٰهُم مِّنَ ٱلطَّيِّبَٰتِ
وَفَضَّلْنَٰهُمْ عَلَىٰ كَثِيرٍ مِّمَّنْ خَلَقْنَا تَفْضِيلًا ۞

We have honoured the children of Adam and carried them by
land and sea; We have provided good sustenance for them
and favoured them specially above many of those We have
created. [17:70]

God appoints angels to protect and watch over us as we walk the earth:

وَإِنَّ عَلَيْكُمْ لَحَافِظِينَ ۝

Appointed over you are Keepers. [82:10]

And He promises to provide for us:

وَفِى ٱلسَّمَآءِ رِزْقُكُمْ وَمَا تُوعَدُونَ ۝

In the sky is your sustenance and all that you are promised. [51:22]

He created the earth to accommodate human life; the skies, the soil, the phases of the moon, the mountains' equilibrium, rivers, oceans, forests, livestock, and raw materials of the earth.

وَسَخَّرَ لَكُم مَّا فِى ٱلسَّمَٰوَٰتِ وَمَا فِى ٱلْأَرْضِ جَمِيعًا مِّنْهُ إِنَّ فِى ذَٰلِكَ لَءَايَٰتٍ لِّقَوْمٍ يَتَفَكَّرُونَ ۝

He has subjected all that is in the heavens and the earth for your benefit, as a gift from Him. There truly are signs in this for those who reflect. [45:13]

We are blessed with millions of facilitations and gifts that cannot be counted.

وَإِن تَعُدُّواْ نِعْمَةَ ٱللَّهِ لَا تُحْصُوهَآ إِنَّ ٱللَّهَ لَغَفُورٌ رَّحِيمٌ ۝

If you tried to count Allah's blessings, you could never take them all in: He is truly most forgiving and most merciful. [16:18]

In light of this facilitation and design, is it reasonable to think that we were created for no purpose? Are we meant to drift aimlessly through our living existence—our joy and suffering meaning nothing? Could it be that the great expanse of the universe with its wondrous precision and scale, the earth teeming with life and beauty, exists for no particular reason? Surely not:

وَمَا خَلَقْنَا ٱلسَّمَٰوَٰتِ وَٱلْأَرْضَ وَمَا بَيْنَهُمَا لَٰعِبِينَ ۝ مَا خَلَقْنَٰهُمَآ إِلَّا بِٱلْحَقِّ وَلَٰكِنَّ أَكْثَرَهُمْ لَا يَعْلَمُونَ ۝

We were not playing a pointless game when We created the heavens and earth and everything in between; We created them for a true purpose, but most people do not comprehend. [44:38-39]

Contemplation should deepen the realization of our purpose. Look at something as straightforward as our daily meal, as we are invited to in the Quran:

$$\text{فَلْيَنظُرِ ٱلْإِنسَٰنُ إِلَىٰ طَعَامِهِۦٓ ۞}$$

Let people then consider their food. [80:24]

There are intricate natural systems and balances in the atmosphere, the soil, at the molecular level, and even within the casing of a seed, that are involved in the production of our food. The fact that God created the food supply to be scalable through farming and man-made processes is a sign for us to reflect upon.

The human body is another landscape for endless reflection. Heart and lungs work together in perfect, congruent timing, replenishing the blood with oxygen and distributing it to billions of individual cells in the body. When we read with our eyes, taste food with our tongue, relive a memory, or cry tears of sorrow, each cell joins together with millions of others to perform its specific job in an incredible symphony of biological systems. How often do we pause to contemplate such things?

$$\text{وَفِى ٱلْأَرْضِ ءَايَٰتٌ لِّلْمُوقِنِينَ ۞ وَفِىٓ أَنفُسِكُمْ ۚ أَفَلَا تُبْصِرُونَ ۞}$$

*On earth there are signs for those with sure faith–and within
yourselves too, do you not see?* [51:20-21]

The Quran points us to ponder the miracle of water, how it pours from the skies as an elixir of life. The precise orbits of the sun and moon set the rhythm of our life and worship routines. Since the beginning of history, there has been no delay of the sun's rising nor a single night that came earlier than scheduled. There is not an iota of randomness in creation: everything is counted, measured, and balanced. As we consider this brilliant vista of creation, we ask ourselves if it is possible that it is all for no reason:

$$\text{يَٰٓأَيُّهَا ٱلنَّاسُ ٱذْكُرُوا۟ نِعْمَتَ ٱللَّهِ عَلَيْكُمْ ۚ هَلْ مِنْ خَٰلِقٍ غَيْرُ ٱللَّهِ}$$
$$\text{يَرْزُقُكُم مِّنَ ٱلسَّمَآءِ وَٱلْأَرْضِ ۚ لَآ إِلَٰهَ إِلَّا هُوَ ۖ فَأَنَّىٰ تُؤْفَكُونَ ۞}$$

*People, remember God's grace towards you. Is there any
creator other than God to give you sustenance from the
heavens and earth? There is no god but Him. How can you be
so deluded?* [35:3]

$$\text{هَٰذَا خَلْقُ ٱللَّهِ فَأَرُونِى مَاذَا خَلَقَ ٱلَّذِينَ مِن دُونِهِۦ ۚ بَلِ ٱلظَّٰلِمُونَ}$$
$$\text{فِى ضَلَٰلٍ مُّبِينٍ ۞}$$

*All this is God's creation. Now, show Me what your other
gods have created. No, the disbelievers are clearly astray.*
[31:11]

Once we have accepted that such a magnificent universe cannot be pointless, the next question is what is our place? We were provided with every means of development and upliftment, but for what purpose? Allah says:

وَمَا خَلَقْتُ ٱلْجِنَّ وَٱلْإِنسَ إِلَّا لِيَعْبُدُونِ ۝

I did not create jinn and humans except to worship Me. [51:56]

The goal of our existence is to worship God through our own free will. It is the great purpose and weighty trust from which the sky, the earth, and the mountains shied away. We committed to this promise to worship God and serve as the earth's stewards:

رَبُّكَ مِنۢ بَنِىٓ ءَادَمَ مِن ظُهُورِهِمْ ذُرِّيَّتَهُمْ وَأَشْهَدَهُمْ عَلَىٰٓ أَنفُسِهِمْ أَلَسْتُ بِرَبِّكُمْ قَالُوا۟ بَلَىٰ شَهِدْنَآ أَن تَقُولُوا۟ يَوْمَ ٱلْقِيَـٰمَةِ إِنَّا كُنَّا عَنْ هَـٰذَا غَـٰفِلِينَ ۝

And when your Lord took out the offspring from the loins of the Children of Adam and made them bear witness about themselves, He said, 'Am I not your Lord?' and they replied, 'Yes, we bear witness.' So you cannot say on the Day of Resurrection, 'We were not aware of this.' [7:172]

Every human being is born with a longing to worship God alone:

فَأَقِمْ وَجْهَكَ لِلدِّينِ حَنِيفًا فِطْرَتَ ٱللَّهِ ٱلَّتِى فَطَرَ ٱلنَّاسَ عَلَيْهَا لَا تَبْدِيلَ لِخَلْقِ ٱللَّهِ

So (Prophet) as a man of pure faith, stand firm and true in your devotion to the religion. This is the natural disposition God instilled in mankind- there is no altering God's creation... [30:30]

Allah created the universe around us in such a way that it would point to His existence, speaking to our innate nature:

سَنُرِيهِمْ ءَايَـٰتِنَا فِى ٱلْآفَاقِ وَفِىٓ أَنفُسِهِمْ حَتَّىٰ يَتَبَيَّنَ لَهُمْ أَنَّهُ ٱلْحَقُّ أَوَلَمْ يَكْفِ بِرَبِّكَ أَنَّهُۥ عَلَىٰ كُلِّ شَىْءٍ شَهِيدٌ ۝

We shall show them Our signs in the horizons and in themselves, until it becomes clear to them that this is the Truth. Is it not enough that your Lord witnesses everything? [41:53]

Prophets and revelations were sent to remind us of a purpose we already sense deep within ourselves. And so Allah asks in the Quran,

فَمَا ظَنُّكُم بِرَبِّ ٱلْعَـٰلَمِينَ ۝

What then do you expect from the Lord of all worlds?" [37:87]

What do people expect from their Lord when they have become distant from Him, abandoned His worship, and busied themselves with other than what they were created for? What do you expect when He has given us every blessing and facilitation to fulfill our purpose? The Prophet ﷺ said in a *hadith* narrated by Abu Hurayrah: "**The first blessing that you will be asked about on the Day of Judgment is, 'Did we not give you a healthy body? Did we not provide you with cool water?'**"[32] It is the most serious matter; nothing is more grave and consequential in our lives than this purpose.

$$قُلْ هُوَ نَبَؤٌاْ عَظِيمٌ ۝ أَنتُمْ عَنْهُ مُعْرِضُونَ ۝$$

*Say, 'this message is a mighty one, yet you
ignore it.* [36:67-68]

This message is one that should summon tears and urgency:

$$أَفَمِنْ هَٰذَا ٱلْحَدِيثِ تَعْجَبُونَ ۝ وَتَضْحَكُونَ وَلَا
تَبْكُونَ ۝ وَأَنتُمْ سَٰمِدُونَ ۝$$

*Do you find this revelation astonishing, Laughing and not
weeping, while persisting in heedlessness?* [53:59-61]

◆◆◆

The Messenger ﷺ said, "If someone were to be dragged on his face from the day he was born to the day he died as an old man, all for the sake of Allah, he would still deem it too little on the Day of Judgment."[33] In another *hadith*, the Prophet ﷺ said, "If God were to punish the inhabitants of His skies and the inhabitants of His earth, His punishing of them would not be unjust. And if He were to show them mercy, His mercy would be greater than the amounting of their own deeds..."[34]

All of the Prophets affirmed this purpose of our existence and called their people to worship God and uphold His religion, as told in the Quran,

$$شَرَعَ لَكُم مِّنَ ٱلدِّينِ مَا وَصَّىٰ بِهِۦ نُوحًا وَٱلَّذِىٓ أَوْحَيْنَآ إِلَيْكَ وَمَا وَصَّيْنَا بِهِۦٓ
إِبْرَٰهِيمَ وَمُوسَىٰ وَعِيسَىٰٓ أَنْ أَقِيمُواْ ٱلدِّينَ وَلَا تَتَفَرَّقُواْ فِيهِ كَبُرَ عَلَى ٱلْمُشْرِكِينَ مَا
تَدْعُوهُمْ إِلَيْهِ ٱللَّهُ يَجْتَبِىٓ إِلَيْهِ مَن يَشَآءُ وَيَهْدِىٓ إِلَيْهِ مَن يُنِيبُ ۝$$

*In matters of faith, He has laid down for you (people) the
same commandment that He gave Noah, which We have
revealed to you (Muhammad) and which We enjoined on*

*Abraham and Moses and Jesus: 'Uphold the faith and do not
divide into factions within it'- what you (Prophet) call upon
the idolaters to do is hard for them; God chooses whoever He
pleases for Himself and guides towards Himself those who
turn to Him.* [42:13]

If we turn away from His worship, the punishment will surely come. How can we not fear that?

قُلْ مَا يَعْبَؤُاْ بِكُمْ رَبِّي لَوْلَا دُعَآؤُكُمْ فَقَدْ كَذَّبْتُمْ فَسَوْفَ يَكُونُ لِزَامًا ۝

*(Prophet, tell the disbelievers), 'What are you to my Lord
without your supplication? But since you have written off the
truth as lies, the inevitable will happen.'* [25:77]

3. FEAR OF THE CONSEQUENCES OF SIN

We have so much to fear in this aspect, for every one of us carries the dark weight of sin. Whose glance hasn't fallen upon on what God forbade, and whose tongue hasn't strayed into gossip and ridicule? Who has never thought ill of another Muslim? Have we never wasted away the hours of the night in useless talk or entertainment? Have we never told a lie, felt superior or belittled someone else?

Everyone passes through times when they fall short in their worship and remembrance. Our character may falter in our kindness towards our parents and relatives and giving our spouses and children their due rights. We forget to inspect our food and make sure it is pure and halal. We fail to encourage the good, forbid the evil and give good advice to people, deciding it is too awkward. We neglect to appreciate our blessings and engage in wastefulness and excessive consumerism.

Who among us has not wronged another? Have we never preferred our desires to the Allah's command? As we learn about the terrible conditions facing Muslims around the world, who among us has done their duty in supporting them? Are we doing all that we can to alleviate the suffering of our communities? Are we speaking out against injustice, sharing our wealth, and feeding the hungry as we should?

In truth, we fall short of our responsibilities and are guilty of many trespasses. But it is our nature to gloss over our past sins. That is why we often think we are better off than we actually are. Our Lord, however, does not forget.

أَحْصَىٰهُ ٱللَّهُ وَنَسُوهُ

*Allah has kept account of it all, while they have
forgotten it.* [58:6]

$$\text{هَٰذَا كِتَٰبُنَا يَنطِقُ عَلَيۡكُم بِٱلۡحَقِّ ۚ إِنَّا كُنَّا نَسۡتَنسِخُ مَا كُنتُمۡ تَعۡمَلُونَ ○}$$

*Here is Our record that tells the truth about you: We have
been recording everything you do.' [45:29]*

We should have no illusions about our righteousness. We should be humbled by our doubt
of the validity of our good deeds, unsure whether they are worthy or clouded by mixed intentions. As for our sins and shortcomings, those are a certainty.

.... ❖❖❖ ....

Abdullah ibn Mas'ood narrated that the Prophet ﷺ said, "Do not underestimate
the small sins, for they pile upon a person until they ruin him." The Prophet
continued to put forth an analogy of a people camped out in a valley who are
preparing their food. One man goes out and retrieves a stick, and another brings a
stick, and so on until they build a pile and are able to cook their food.[35]

....

The Prophet ﷺ himself used to make these supplications: **"I seek refuge from any evil I have
done,"**[36] and **"We seek refuge in Allah from the evil of ourselves and our wrong deeds."**[37]
How can we not fear our sins when Allah, Exalted, says,

$$\text{فَلۡيَحۡذَرِ ٱلَّذِينَ يُخَالِفُونَ عَنۡ أَمۡرِهِۦٓ أَن تُصِيبَهُمۡ فِتۡنَةٌ أَوۡ يُصِيبَهُمۡ عَذَابٌ أَلِيمٌ ○}$$

*Do not treat the Messenger's summons to you [as lightly] as
your summons to one another. Allah certainly knows those
of you who slip away, hiding behind others. So let those who
disobey his orders beware, for an affliction may befall them,
or a painful torment may overtake them. [24:63]*

One statement, even one word, can land a person in Hell for seventy years. The Prophet
ﷺ said, **"A servant might say something thoughtlessly, but in fact the words plummet him
into Hell further than the distance between the east and west."**[38] This habit of belittling our
sins is dangerous. Even if we brush off our sins and forget about them, there remains the
possibility that they are brazen stains on our record of deeds:

$$\text{إِذۡ تَلَقَّوۡنَهُۥ بِأَلۡسِنَتِكُمۡ وَتَقُولُونَ بِأَفۡوَاهِكُم مَّا لَيۡسَ لَكُم بِهِۦ عِلۡمٌ وَتَحۡسَبُونَهُۥ هَيِّنٗا وَهُوَ عِندَ ٱللَّهِ عَظِيمٌ ○}$$

When you took it up with your tongues, and spoke with your

mouths things you did not know, you thought it was trivial
but to God it was very serious. [24:15]

Anas ibn Malik, may Allah be pleased with him, lived for many decades after the Prophet ﷺ, and once warned the people around him, "You commit deeds that in your eyes are finer than the thickness of a hair, but we used to view them at the time of the Prophet ﷺ as major sins."[39] Bilal ibn Sa'd, among the *tabi'een*, the generation that followed the Companions, used to say, "Don't look at the smallness of your mistake, but look at the Greatness of Whom you disobeyed."[40]

Ibn al-Qayyim advises,

> This is a crucial point that people get wrong in regard to sins. They do not see the immediate consequence of sin, and because its effects are delayed, the sin is forgotten. *SubhanAllah*! How many people have been ruined because of this! How many blessings have been forfeited and how much suffering has this caused? Even the scholars and pious have fallen for this, not to mention the naive majority! If only the people would realize that a sin will always strike back, even if after a time, just as poison strikes or a previous wound becomes infected.[41]

Even though the consequences of sin are often delayed, there is still a subtle but immediate effect: a black dot on the heart and a dull countenance. Sulaiman at-Taimi said, "Someone may commit a sin secretly, but comes out with a shamefulness hanging over him."[42]

The Quran is replete with warnings about the consequences of sin.

لَّيْسَ بِأَمَانِيِّكُمْ وَلَآ أَمَانِيِّ أَهْلِ ٱلْكِتَـٰبِ مَن يَعْمَلْ سُوٓءًا يُجْزَ
بِهِۦ وَلَا يَجِدْ لَهُۥ مِن دُونِ ٱللَّهِ وَلِيًّا وَلَا نَصِيرًا ۝

It will not be according to your hopes or those of the People of
the Book: anyone who does wrong will be requitted for it and
will find no one to protect or help him against God. [4:123]

وَمَا ظَلَمَهُمُ ٱللَّهُ وَلَـٰكِن كَانُوٓا۟ أَنفُسَهُمْ يَظْلِمُونَ ۝ فَأَصَابَهُمْ
سَيِّـَٔاتُ مَا عَمِلُوا۟ وَحَاقَ بِهِم مَّا كَانُوا۟ بِهِۦ يَسْتَهْزِءُونَ ۝

God did not wrong them; they wronged themselves. So the
evil they had done hit them and they were surrounded by the
very thing they had mocked. [16:33-34]

When we do commit a sin, our greatest priority should be erasing that sin and gaining Allah's forgiveness as soon as possible. Many people have been ruined before for their sins, and many people will be ruined after us. We should not think that we are an exception.

The devil was cast down from his lofty position and turned into the most despicable of beings. The people of Nuh were drowned because of what they used to do, and the tribe of 'Aad were destroyed by pulverizing winds that left them like the dead stalks of uprooted trees. The rolling dark clouds that brought the people of Shu'ayb their doom and the sudden sinkhole that swallowed up Qarun's property were due to a trail of unremorseful sins that brought ruin upon their souls.

$$فَكُلًّا أَخَذْنَا بِذَنۢبِهِۦ فَمِنْهُم مَّنْ أَرْسَلْنَا عَلَيْهِ حَاصِبًا وَمِنْهُم مَّنْ أَخَذَتْهُ ٱلصَّيْحَةُ وَمِنْهُم مَّنْ خَسَفْنَا بِهِ ٱلْأَرْضَ وَمِنْهُم مَّنْ أَغْرَقْنَا وَمَا كَانَ ٱللَّهُ لِيَظْلِمَهُمْ وَلَٰكِن كَانُوٓا۟ أَنفُسَهُمْ يَظْلِمُونَ ۝$$

And We seized each one of them for their sins: some We struck with a violent storm; some were overcome by a sudden blast; some We made the earth swallow; and some We drowned. It was not God who wronged them; they wronged themselves.
[29:40]

Some of the obstructions we face currently in our lives may be due to a sin we committed in the past and forgot about. The Prophet ﷺ said, **"A man could be denied *rizq* (sustenance) due to a sin he committed."**[43] Righteous people have observed that they can see the negative consequences of sins in daily life situations, such as the reliability of their transport and interactions with their spouse.[44] We should fear the fallout of our sins—they will creep back and catch up with us if we are not constantly fleeing back to God. Aishah related that she once awoke at night to find the Prophet ﷺ absent from his bed. As she felt for him in the dark, her hands touched his standing feet as he prayed, reciting, **"Allah, I seek refuge in Your pleasure from Your anger, and in Your forgiveness from Your punishment. I seek refuge in You, from You. I cannot count Your praises enough. You are as You have praised Yourself."**[45]

We cannot know for sure whether our past sins have been resolved. Has Allah forgiven them or are they lying in wait for us? Do we have any proof of forgiveness, a signed paper that attests to our absolved sins? Such a guarantee does not exist in this life; this is why we must fear our sins and repent often.

$$أَمْ لَكُمْ أَيْمَٰنٌ عَلَيْنَا بَٰلِغَةٌ إِلَىٰ يَوْمِ ٱلْقِيَٰمَةِ إِنَّ لَكُمْ لَمَا تَحْكُمُونَ ۝ سَلْهُمْ أَيُّهُم بِذَٰلِكَ زَعِيمٌ ۝$$

Have you received from Us solemn oaths, binding to the Day of Resurrection, that you will get whatever you yourselves decide? Ask them (Prophet) which of them will guarantee this. [68:39-40]

4. FEAR OF GOD'S ANGER

God says in His Quran,

أَفَأَمِنَ أَهْلُ ٱلْقُرَىٰٓ أَن يَأْتِيَهُم بَأْسُنَا بَيَٰتًا وَهُمْ نَآئِمُونَ ۝ أَوَأَمِنَ أَهْلُ ٱلْقُرَىٰٓ أَن يَأْتِيَهُم بَأْسُنَا ضُحًى وَهُمْ يَلْعَبُونَ ۝ أَفَأَمِنُوا۟ مَكْرَ ٱللَّهِ فَلَا يَأْمَنُ مَكْرَ ٱللَّهِ إِلَّا ٱلْقَوْمُ ٱلْخَٰسِرُونَ ۝

Did the people of those societies feel secure that Our punishment would not come upon them by night while they were asleep? Or did they feel secure that Our punishment would not come upon them by day while they were at play? Do they feel secure against God's plan? Only the losers feel secure against God's plan. [7:97-99]

God's forgiveness precedes His punishment, but there are actions that can bring about the anger of The Almighty. Many people before us reached such an extent of heedlessness and audacity that God's punishment finally stopped them in their tracks.

وَكَذَٰلِكَ أَخْذُ رَبِّكَ إِذَآ أَخَذَ ٱلْقُرَىٰ وَهِىَ ظَٰلِمَةٌ إِنَّ أَخْذَهُۥ أَلِيمٌ شَدِيدٌ ۝

Such is the [crushing] grip of your Lord when He seizes the societies entrenched in wrongdoing. Indeed, His grip is [terribly] painful and severe. [11:102]

The Messenger ﷺ used to make this *dua'* (supplication): **"O Allah! I seek refuge in You from the confiscation of Your blessings, the withdrawal of Your protection, the suddenness of Your wrath, and anything that could displease You."**[46]

Just because we are not committing blatant sins does not mean we are safe from God's anger. Even people who spend their lives worshipping God privately, isolating themselves from the corruption surrounding them, may be struck by God's anger if they do not try to change the society around them. Allah warns us in His book,

وَٱتَّقُوا۟ فِتْنَةً لَّا تُصِيبَنَّ ٱلَّذِينَ ظَلَمُوا۟ مِنكُمْ خَآصَّةً وَٱعْلَمُوٓا۟ أَنَّ ٱللَّهَ شَدِيدُ ٱلْعِقَابِ ۝

Beware of a trial that will not only affect the wrongdoers among you. And know that Allah is severe in punishment. [8:25]

Ibn Abi ad-Dunya narrated that, "Allah revealed to Yusha' ibn Nun (a successor of Prophet

Musa) that He would punish 40,000 good people and 70,000 evil people among his tribe. Yusha' asked, 'My Lord, the evil ones, I understand, but the good ones too?' God answered, 'they were not angry for My Sake, and they would share food and drink with the evil ones.'"[47]

◆◆◆

Zainab bint Jahsh narrates that the Prophet ﷺ entered her home in a state of alarm, saying, "La ilaha illah Allah! Woe to the Arabs from an approaching evil. Today, a hole of this size has opened in the barrier holding back Gog and Magog." He made a circle with his thumb and index finger. Zainab, his wife, asked, "Messenger of Allah, will we be destroyed even when there are righteous people amongst us?" He answered, "Yes, if evil becomes widespread enough."[48]

When we give up on calling to good and speaking out against evil, resigned to the corruption around us, this will incur God's anger and punishment. In a *hadith* narrated by Huthayfah, the Prophet ﷺ said, "**By Him in whose hands is my soul, you must encourage the good and forbid the evil, or else Allah will send his punishment upon you. You will call upon Him, and you will not be answered.**"[49]

In another chilling *hadith*, the Prophet ﷺ warns, "**When people hoard dinars and dirhams, engage in 'eenah, pursue the tails of cows, and give up striving for the sake of Allah, Allah will send upon them an affliction that will not be lifted until they return to their religion.**"[50] ('*Eenah* is a type of interest-based financial transaction and pursuing the tails of cows is a metaphor for being consumed with growing wealth and property). Al-'Umri az-Zahid, one of the early pious of Medina, said, "It is a form of ignorance of the self and a turning away from Allah when you see something that angers Allah but you overlook it, neither advising nor attempting to change it, fearing people who cannot bring about harm or benefit."[51]

Whenever there would be a strong wind or dark clouds on the horizon, the Prophet ﷺ would appear worried, and he would walk to and fro in agitation. Then, when it rained he would finally relax. Aishah asked him about this, and he ﷺ said, "**I fear it may be a punishment descending on my people.**"[52] One of the *tabi'een* relates that once the sky darkened so much that the day became like night. They asked the Companion Anas ibn Malik if that had ever happened during the life of the Prophet, and Anas responded, "I seek refuge in Allah! When the wind grew strong, we would race to the mosque fearing the Day of Resurrection."[53]

5. FEAR OF GRADUAL DECLINE INTO SIN

The Quran speaks about this danger; there are people who will be showered with outward blessings so that they may gradually sink into sinfulness. It is a slow erosion of morals that people may not detect. Just because one lives in material ease does not mean he is safe from God's anger. On the contrary, freedom and amenities can lead us astray if we are not mindful.

$$أَيَحْسَبُونَ أَنَّمَا نُمِدُّهُم بِهِۦ مِن مَّالٍ وَبَنِينَ ۞ نُسَارِعُ لَهُمْ فِى ٱلْخَيْرَٰتِ بَل لَّا يَشْعُرُونَ ۞$$

Do they think, since We provide them with wealth and children, that We race to honor them with good things? They really have no idea! [23:55-56]

Good things in life, as well as afflictions, are a reminder to turn back to Allah:

$$وَبَلَوْنَٰهُم بِٱلْحَسَنَٰتِ وَٱلسَّيِّئَاتِ لَعَلَّهُمْ يَرْجِعُونَ ۞$$

We tested them with blessings and misfortunes, so that they might all return (to righteousness). [7:168]

When people are tested and do not turn back to God, the next stage is sometimes one of excessive bounties. These misguided people become deluded by their comfortable circumstances, thinking that all is right between them and God. Lower and lower they sink into evil until they meet their end:

$$وَلَقَدْ أَرْسَلْنَآ إِلَىٰٓ أُمَمٍ مِّن قَبْلِكَ فَأَخَذْنَٰهُم بِٱلْبَأْسَآءِ وَٱلضَّرَّآءِ لَعَلَّهُمْ يَتَضَرَّعُونَ ۞ فَلَوْلَآ إِذْ جَآءَهُم بَأْسُنَا تَضَرَّعُوا۟ وَلَٰكِن قَسَتْ قُلُوبُهُمْ وَزَيَّنَ لَهُمُ ٱلشَّيْطَٰنُ مَا كَانُوا۟ يَعْمَلُونَ ۞ فَلَمَّا نَسُوا۟ مَا ذُكِّرُوا۟ بِهِۦ فَتَحْنَا عَلَيْهِمْ أَبْوَٰبَ كُلِّ شَىْءٍ حَتَّىٰٓ إِذَا فَرِحُوا۟ بِمَآ أُوتُوٓا۟ أَخَذْنَٰهُم بَغْتَةً فَإِذَا هُم مُّبْلِسُونَ ۞ فَقُطِعَ دَابِرُ ٱلْقَوْمِ ٱلَّذِينَ ظَلَمُوا۟ وَٱلْحَمْدُ لِلَّهِ رَبِّ ٱلْعَٰلَمِينَ ۞$$

We sent messengers before you (Prophet) to many communities and afflicted their people with suffering and hardships, so that they could learn humility. If only they had learned humility when suffering came from Us! But no, their hearts became hard and Satan made their foul deeds alluring to them. So, when they had forgotten the warning they had received, We opened the gates to everything for them. Then, as they revelled in what they had been given, We struck them suddenly and they were dumbfounded. [6:42-45]

There are many ways to be drawn into sin; no one should feel immune. The Quran says in the words of the Prophet ﷺ:

وَإِنْ أَدْرِى لَعَلَّهُ فِتْنَةٌ لَّكُمْ وَمَتَـٰعٌ إِلَىٰ حِينٍ ۞

I do not know: this (time) may well be a test for you, and
enjoyment for a while.' [21:111]

Ibn al-Qayyim wrote,

> It is up to the individual to differentiate between the blessings that facilitate good
> deeds, leading to eternal happiness, and the bounties that might lead to distraction,
> heedlessness, and sin. So many people are deceived by their apparent blessings,
> enchanted by people's admiration, and proud that God is meeting their needs and
> concealing their sins. For most people, these are the only indicators they use for
> success, and that is the unfortunate extent of their knowledge.[54]

Ibn al-Qayyim continues to explain that the blessings that bring us closer to Allah are true
blessings, and whatever distracts us from Him is really a test disguised as a blessing. It can be
hard to differentiate between the two. Good things that give us the strength and motivation
to obey Allah and pursue His pleasure are true gifts and blessings. Everything else is a test
and can potentially count against us. We should look at every element, bounty, and situation
in our life, and question whether they are gifts or tests.

6. FEAR OF GOOD DEEDS BEING CANCELED

It is frightening that many of our good deeds may end up nullified without our knowledge.
There are several things we may do, intentionally or not, that can spoil our good deeds; we
should learn about these causes of deed cancellations and avoid them at all costs.

Shirk (worshipping anything alongside God) can cancel out good deeds. There are many
forms of *shirk*, some of which we may commit unaware. It is truly terrifying that we might
strive and sacrifice and do many good deeds, but because we are subconsciously worshipping
or seeking approval of someone else, our efforts will be erased.

وَلَقَدْ أُوحِىَ إِلَيْكَ وَإِلَى ٱلَّذِينَ مِن قَبْلِكَ لَئِنْ أَشْرَكْتَ لَيَحْبَطَنَّ عَمَلُكَ
وَلَتَكُونَنَّ مِنَ ٱلْخَـٰسِرِينَ ۞

It has already been revealed to you (Prophet) and to those
before you: 'If you ascribe any partner to God, all your work
will come to nothing: you will be one of the losers. [39:65]

Riya' (showing off and craving admiration) will turn our actions to dust, even if we toiled
for those actions. The disease of *riya'* was discussed in more detail in Part I.

$$\text{يَـٰٓأَيُّهَا ٱلَّذِينَ ءَامَنُواْ لَا تُبْطِلُواْ صَدَقَـٰتِكُم بِٱلْمَنِّ وَٱلْأَذَىٰ كَٱلَّذِى يُنفِقُ}$$
$$\text{مَالَهُۥ رِئَآءَ ٱلنَّاسِ وَلَا يُؤْمِنُ بِٱللَّهِ وَٱلْيَوْمِ ٱلْـَٔاخِرِ فَمَثَلُهُۥ كَمَثَلِ صَفْوَانٍ}$$
$$\text{عَلَيْهِ تُرَابٌ فَأَصَابَهُۥ وَابِلٌ فَتَرَكَهُۥ صَلْدًا لَّا يَقْدِرُونَ عَلَىٰ شَىْءٍ مِّمَّا كَسَبُواْ}$$
$$\text{وَٱللَّهُ لَا يَهْدِى ٱلْقَوْمَ ٱلْكَـٰفِرِينَ ۝}$$

You who believe, do not cancel out your charitable deeds with
reminders and hurtful words, like someone who spends his wealth
only to be seen by people, not believing in God and the Last Day.
Such a person is like a rock with earth on it: heavy rain falls and
leaves it completely bare. Such people get no rewards for their
works: God does not guide the disbelievers. [2:264]

••••

Umar once found Mu'ath ibn Jabal crying near the grave of the Prophet ﷺ.
Umar asked why he was crying, so Mu'ath explained that he once heard the
Prophet ﷺ say, "Even the slightest of *riya'* is *shirk*. Allah loves the hidden God-con-
scious people, those who are not missed when they are absent, and who are not
noticed when they are present. Their hearts are lamps of guidance, shining from
every dark, dusty corner."[55]

The Quran likens *riya'* to a man who tends very carefully to a lush orchard, flourishing
with beautiful trees, ripe fruit, and flowing streams. When its fruit is at last ready for har-
vesting, the orchard catches on fire and burns to ashes, while the owner still has a family
and young children to support. Imagine the loss and bitter taste of regret this man would
feel—this is exactly the metaphor put forth in the Quran:

$$\text{أَيَوَدُّ أَحَدُكُمْ أَن تَكُونَ لَهُۥ جَنَّةٌ مِّن نَّخِيلٍ وَأَعْنَابٍ تَجْرِى مِن تَحْتِهَا}$$
$$\text{ٱلْأَنْهَارُ لَهُۥ فِيهَا مِن كُلِّ ٱلثَّمَرَٰتِ وَأَصَابَهُ ٱلْكِبَرُ وَلَهُۥ ذُرِّيَّةٌ ضُعَفَآءُ فَأَصَابَهَآ}$$
$$\text{إِعْصَارٌ فِيهِ نَارٌ فَٱحْتَرَقَتْ كَذَٰلِكَ يُبَيِّنُ ٱللَّهُ لَكُمُ ٱلْـَٔايَـٰتِ لَعَلَّكُمْ}$$
$$\text{تَتَفَكَّرُونَ ۝}$$

Would any of you like to have a garden of palm trees and
vines, graced with flowing streams and all kinds of produce,
which, when you are afflicted with old age and dependent
offspring, is struck by a fiery whirlwind and burnt down? In
this way God makes His messages clear to you, so that you
may reflect on them. [2:266]

Another attitude that can cancel our good deeds is being impressed by our good works. This self-enamor was counted by the Prophet ﷺ as one of three spiritual destroyers, which also include greed and desires. He ﷺ said, "**There are three salvations and three destroyers. The salvations are *taqwa* (God-mindfulness) in secret and in public, speaking truth when pleased and when angered, and moderation in affluence and in poverty. As for the destroyers, they are greed that is obeyed, desire that is followed, and being impressed by oneself.**"[56] Aishah, may God be pleased with her, was once asked how to tell if you are on the wrong track. She responded simply, "When you are convinced that you are doing remarkably well."[57]

A sin that humiliates you sometimes may be better than a good deed that causes you to feel superior to others. When we are self-enamored, our good deeds become as insubstantial as dust. The woeful, regretful tears of the sinners are more beloved to God than the humming of worshippers who crave admiration and praise.[58]

Giving charity with a patronizing and condescending attitude is another cause for the cancellation of good works. When we expect something subtle in return for our charity or service, perhaps a seat at the table, influence, appreciation, or some form of recognition, we are destroying our own deeds.

$$يَـٰٓأَيُّهَا ٱلَّذِينَ ءَامَنُوا۟ لَا تُبْطِلُوا۟ صَدَقَـٰتِكُم بِٱلْمَنِّ وَٱلْأَذَىٰ$$

You who believe, do not cancel out your charitable deeds
with reminders and hurtful words...[2:264]

Just as good deeds can wipe out bad deeds, so can an entitled attitude wipe out good deeds. The Quran warns,

$$يَـٰٓأَيُّهَا ٱلَّذِينَ ءَامَنُوٓا۟ أَطِيعُوا۟ ٱللَّهَ وَأَطِيعُوا۟ ٱلرَّسُولَ وَلَا تُبْطِلُوٓا۟ أَعْمَـٰلَكُمْ ۝$$

Believers, obey God and the Messenger and do not let
your deeds go to waste. [47:33]

We have to tend our good deeds carefully and monitor our intentions, before, during and after, in order to preserve them on our record. The thought that many of our good deeds that we worked hard for might have been canceled out should inspire fear in our hearts. Ibn Sireen once heard a man chastising another, "I did this and that for you!" Ibn Sireen told the man, "Be quiet! There is no good in a service that is recounted."[59]

7. FEAR OF UNACCEPTED GOOD DEEDS

This should be a constant fear in the heart of a believer. Allah says,

$$وَٱلَّذِينَ يُؤۡتُونَ مَآ ءَاتَواْ وَّقُلُوبُهُمۡ وَجِلَةٌ أَنَّهُمۡ إِلَىٰ رَبِّهِمۡ رَٰجِعُونَ ۝$$

Those who always give with hearts that tremble at the thought
that they must return to Him. [23:60]

They offer their good deeds with a lingering fear that they will not be accepted. They are conscious of all the ways they may have fallen short and do not take for granted that their actions are accepted. Aishah asked the Prophet ﷺ specifically about the previous verse—whether they trembled because of their bad deeds. He ﷺ responded, "No, daughter of Abu Bakr, daughter of as-Siddeeq, they pray and fast and give charity while they are fearful of Allah, the Exalted and Glorious."[60]

> If the Companions, who excelled in every aspect, were worried over whether their actions would be accepted, then surely we have cause to worry as well. Abu al-Darda', may God be pleased with him, said, "If I could be sure that Allah accepted one single prayer, that would be more beloved to me than anything in the world. Allah says, 'God only accepts from those who are mindful of Him." [5:27]

The Companions, as devoted as they were to Allah and His messenger, did not consider themselves beyond hypocrisy. Ibn Abi Mulaykah said, "I met thirty of the Prophet's ﷺ Companions; each one was worried about being a hypocrite."[61]

Huthayfah ibn al-Yaman, the secret-keeper of the Prophet ﷺ, was the only individual who was told the names of the hypocrites of Medina. Umar ibn al-Khattab would go to Huthayfah and beg him, "I beg you, by Allah, did the Prophet ﷺ mentioned my name (on the list of hypocrites)?" After much pressure from Umar, Huthayfah finally said, "No, but I will not say this to anyone after you."[62] Imagine Umar worrying about whether he was counted among the hypocrites!

Yahya ibn Mu'ath, a great scholar in the generation after the Companions, said, "How can the believer be truly happy in this life? If he commits a sin, he is afraid that his soul will be taken with that sin. If he does a good deed, he fears that it won't be accepted."[63] Another scholar said, "Do not feel confident in your good deeds, for you cannot be sure they were accepted or not. Do not feel safe from your sins, for you cannot be sure they were forgiven or not. Your past actions are unseen, removed, and you cannot know what Allah did with them."[64]

8. FEAR OF BEING FORSAKEN

In the expedition of Tabuk, the Muslims were given adequate time to prepare and mobilize their resources for the long journey. Because the expedition was to take place at the hottest time of year and during the harvest season, some people were reluctant. They delayed their preparations for the journey and came up with last-minute excuses. The Quran describes this,

وَلَوْ أَرَادُواْ ٱلْخُرُوجَ لَأَعَدُّواْ لَهُۥ عُدَّةً وَلَـٰكِن كَرِهَ ٱللَّهُ ٱنبِعَاثَهُمْ فَثَبَّطَهُمْ وَقِيلَ ٱقْعُدُواْ مَعَ ٱلْقَـٰعِدِينَ ۝

If they had really wanted to go out (to battle) with you, they would have made preparations, but God was loath to let them rise up and made them hold back. It was said, 'stay with those who stay behind.'
[9:46]

We need Allah's support and help in every aspect of our life. Even our successes in performing good deeds require His guidance and support. The alternative is being abandoned and left to our own devices. In this case we would receive no help in our pursuits; everything becomes cloaked in failure and sin. We would be left to our own selfishness, desires, laziness, and delusions.

The Prophet ﷺ used to make this supplication, **"If You entrust me to myself, you have entrusted me to weakness, exposure, sin, and mistakes. I only have confidence in Your mercy."**[65] He ﷺ once instructed his daughter Fatima, **"Won't you listen to my advice, when I tell you to say every morning and evening: "O Ever-Living, Sustainer, I beg Your mercy! Set right all of my problems, and do not leave me alone for the blink of an eye."**[66] On the night before the Battle of Badr, he ﷺ made the dua, **"O Allah, do not abandon me."**[67]

Ibn al-Qayyim wrote that whoever reflects on the true meanings of success and failure will find they are in constant need of their Lord's help in everything, with every breath and blink of the eye. Our faith and belief lies in His Hand, and if He were to let our hearts go for just a moment, our conviction would crumble and the sky of our faith would come crashing to the ground. We should be begging God for His Help at all times and seek His protection from abandonment. We should throw ourselves at His door, surrendering entirely to Him, lowering our heads to the ground in helplessness. We cannot control any harm or benefit to our own selves, nor do we have any power in the face of death, life, or resurrection.[68]

It was the habit of guided and righteous leaders to discourage any praise for their good works. They would redirect all praise to God, for He alone provides blessings, foresight, and opportunities for good. The Caliph Umar ibn Abd al-Azeez was particularly keen on this point. Once he wrote a letter to the people at Hajj, reminding their leaders to treat them well and relieve any difficulties or corruption they had to face. In the letter he mentioned, "Do not praise anyone for these measures except for Allah, for if He were to entrust me to myself I would be like anyone else."[69]

9. FEAR OF LOSING FAITH

No one is considered safe from God's plan. No one can guarantee they will possess iman until the end of their life.

$$ أَفَأَمِنُوا مَكْرَ اللَّهِ ۚ فَلَا يَأْمَنُ مَكْرَ اللَّهِ إِلَّا الْقَوْمُ الْخَاسِرُونَ ۝ $$

Do they feel secure against God's plan? Only the losers feel secure against God's plan. [7:99]

If any one was safe from Allah's plan, it would have been the Prophets. But they also feared turning to disbelief, and prayed that their hearts would remain firm. Consider the plea of Prophet Ibrahim:

$$ وَاجْنُبْنِي وَبَنِيَّ أَن نَّعْبُدَ الْأَصْنَامَ ۝ $$

Keep me and my children away from the worship of idols. [14:35]

And the supplication of Prophet Yusuf:

$$ تَوَفَّنِي مُسْلِمًا وَأَلْحِقْنِي بِالصَّالِحِينَ ۝ $$

Allow me to die as one who submits and join me with the righteous. [12:101]

Our beloved Messenger Muhammad ﷺ would often supplicate, "O Turner of Hearts, make my heart firm on Your religion."[70] He ﷺ would also say, "O Protector of Islam and its people, help me hold to Islam until I meet You upon it."[71] Another one of the Prophet's supplications is, "O Allah, I submit to You. I believe in You, I rely on You. I turn to You. I oppose and resist for Your sake. Allah, I seek refuge in Your Power—there is no God but You—from going astray. You are The Living who does not die, while the jinn and humans die."[72]

The Companion Abu Hurayrah used to say toward the end of his life, "Allah, I seek refuge in You from committing adultery or from committing a major sin of Islam." The other Companions exclaimed, "Abu Hurayrah, how can someone like you fear such a thing, when you have reached old age and your desire is decreased, when you have witnessed the Prophet ﷺ, learned from him and given your oath to him?" Abu Hurayrah responded, "Be careful!

There is no guarantee of safety so long as Satan lives."[73]

.... ♦♦♦ ....

Jubayr ibn Nafeer once entered upon the home of the Companion Abu al-Darda' and found him praying. When Abu al-Darda' sat for the tashahhud, he sought refuge in God from hypocrisy. Jubayr asked him afterwards, "May Allah forgive you Abu al-Darda'! What have you to do with hypocrisy?" Abu al-Darda' said three times, "Your forgiveness, Allah!" Then he remarked, "Who is safe from being tested? Who is safe from being tested? By Allah, a man can be tested and turn away from his religion in an hour."[74] Abu al-Darda' also used to say, "Why don't I see the signs of faith's sweetness in all of you? By the One in whose Hand is my soul, if wild animals were able to taste faith you would see even them enjoying its sweetness. Any servant who worries about his faith will be bestowed with it, while any servant who feels secure in his faith will have it stolen from him."[75]

....

Al-Hasan, may Allah be pleased with him, used to say, "By Allah, there has never been on the face of the earth a believer who did not fear hypocrisy within himself. The only one who feels safe from hypocrisy is, in fact, the hypocrite."[76] The sage Ibn Al-Mubarak said,

> Those with insight will never feel safe from four things: a past sin which they don't know how the Lord has dealt with, a future containing unknown tribulations, a favor that could be a test or a means of slipping into sin, and misguidance that was made appealing and so could have been mistaken for guidance. This is how the hearts deviate time after time, until, suddenly in the blink of an eye, religion is snatched away without a person realizing.[77]

10. FEAR OF A BAD ENDING

Our life will be judged by the actions and deeds of our final days. Since no one knows how or when their final days will be, it is appropriate to fear a bad ending, even if one lived an outwardly righteous life. Listen to what the Messenger of Allah ﷺ said about life's end,

> By the One and Only God, someone may perform the actions of the people of Paradise until he is so close that there is only an arm's length between him and Paradise, but then what is written overtakes him, so he commits the actions of the people of Hell and enters it. And someone may perform the actions of the people of Hell until there is only an arm's length between him and Hell, but what is written overtakes him, so he performs the actions of the people of Paradise and enters it.[78]

Is this not a terrifying prospect? It brings both hope and fear to the heart—hope that it is never too late, and fear of never being safe from Hell in this life. The believer is always cautious and aware of the possibility of being overtaken by hypocrisy in the final moments of life; even the great Companions and scholars feared for their own hearts. Ibn Rajab elaborates on this, "This is why the early Muslims greatly feared a bad ending to their lives... Many of the Companions would cry on their deathbeds, and when they were asked about this, they would say, "I heard the Messenger of Allah ﷺ say, 'Verily Allah Exalted gripped His creation in two groups, and said, "These are in Paradise, and these are in Hell,' and I do not know in which group I am."[79]

Those who are truthful with themselves will be wary of putting too much faith in their own devices, instead calling out to Allah in fear and hope that they may live their final hours upon His religion. These are the people described in the Quran who do good deeds while their hearts are hesitant, unsure of whether their initiatives are acceptable to their Lord,

وَالَّذِينَ يُؤْتُونَ مَا آتَوا وَّقُلُوبُهُمْ وَجِلَةٌ أَنَّهُمْ إِلَى رَبِّهِمْ رَاجِعُونَ ۝

[Those] who always give with hearts that tremble at the
thought that they must return to Him. [23:60]

11. FEAR OF SUDDEN DEATH

The Quran describes death as a calamity awaiting each one of us:

فَأَصَابَتْكُم مُّصِيبَةُ الْمَوْتِ

And the disaster of death should strike you... [5:106]

There is no escaping or putting off death—when its time has come, it is ruthless and unyielding. A thinking person should anticipate death at any moment in order to not be surprised by its sudden appearance.

قُلْ إِنَّ الْمَوْتَ الَّذِى تَفِرُّونَ مِنْهُ فَإِنَّهُ مُلَاقِيكُمْ

Say, "The death you are running away from will
inevitably come to you." [62:8]

Living with an anticipation of death certainly generates a sense of fear, as the individual is prepared to meet his or her Lord at any moment, and we are not always in a state of obedience. We should not entertain any assumptions about how long we will live nor when, where, or in what state we might die.

$$وَمَا تَدْرِى نَفْسٌ مَّاذَا تَكْسِبُ غَدًا ۖ وَمَا تَدْرِى نَفْسٌ بِأَيِّ أَرْضٍ تَمُوتُ ۚ$$
$$إِنَّ اللَّهَ عَلِيمٌ خَبِيرٌ ۝$$

No soul knows what it will reap tomorrow, and no soul
knows in what land it will die; it is God who is all knowing
and all aware. [31:34]

12. FEAR OF THE AGONIES OF DEATH AND THE SOUL'S EXTRACTION

Imam Abu Hamid Al-Ghazali writes,

> Realize that if there were no other anguish or terror awaiting a person other than the throes of death, it would be enough to trouble him deeply, cloud his happiness, and snap him out of heedlessness. The approach of the agonies of death merits attention and great preparation, especially since every breath draws us closer to its onset...

> If one were to find himself in the midst of a most delightful and entertaining gathering, but knew there was a guard ready to barge in at any moment and strike him five sharp blows with a wooden stick, his enjoyment would be utterly spoiled. It is surprising then that the same person enjoys life heedlessly while drawing closer with every breath to the Angel of Death, who waits to strike with the agonies of death and the soul's extraction.

> The extraction of the soul from the body is a visceral pain, extending to each fragment of the soul. Every wisp of the soul dispersed in the body will be engulfed in this pain. Imagine each vein and artery being stripped from the limbs - even the pain of tugging out a single vein from the flesh is something unimaginable. What then is felt by the extraction of the soul that perceives pain? The soul is stripped from every vein and limb, gradually with the feet growing cold, then the legs, then every organ and faculty, spasm upon spasm, agony upon agony, until the soul reaches the throat, where it loses sight of this world and its people, where the doors of repentance close, and it is overwhelmed by regret and sorrow.[80]

The Prophet ﷺ would seek refuge from the agonies and throes of death, supplicating, **"Allah, help me with the agonies of death."**[81] Righteous people would sometimes ask questions of the dying in order to catch a glimpse of the experience of death. When Amr ibn al-Aas was upon his deathbed, he described the sensation, "It feels as though the sky has collapsed upon the earth, and my soul is passing through the eye of a needle."[82] Umar, may Allah be pleased with him, once asked Ka'b al-Ahbar, a wise Jewish scholar who converted to Islam, about what it felt like to die. Ka'b answered, "Death feels like a stick covered in thorns that is placed in the body, every thorn catching and ensnaring a vein. Then someone violently rips the stick out of the body, extracting what comes out, and leaving behind the remains."[83]

Mixed in with the fear of the pains of death is the terror of seeing the Angel of Death for the first time, and the panic that will surge forth when the heart realizes its moment has come. Imam al-Qurtubi describes the situation, "The alarm and panic that will enter the heart in this moment is something that cannot be described, so terrifying is the sight of the Angel of Death. It is such that only those who have seen him can fathom."[84]

If these experiences are not enough to reflect upon, an even more frightening trial is receiving the results of our life's test and realizing our eventual destination. Will we be among those to whom the angels will say, "Do not fear, nor grieve. Rather, rejoice in the good news of Paradise, which you have been promised," or will we be in an entirely different situation?

$$ وَلَوْ تَرَىٰ إِذْ يَتَوَفَّى الَّذِينَ كَفَرُواْ الْمَلَائِكَةُ يَضْرِبُونَ وُجُوهَهُمْ وَأَدْبَارَهُمْ وَذُوقُوا عَذَابَ الْحَرِيقِ ۝ $$

If only you (Prophet) could see, when the angels take the souls
of the disbelievers, how they strike their faces and backs: it
will be said, 'taste the punishment of the Fire. [8:50]

The Prophet ﷺ said, **"Whoever loves to meet Allah, Allah loves to meet him, and whoever hates to meet Allah, Allah hates to meet him."** Aishah, may Allah be pleased with her, said, "But we all hate to die!" So he ﷺ responded,

> It is not that. Rather, when the believer is dying, he is given the good tidings of Allah's pleasure and generosity, and so there is nothing more beloved to him than what lies before him. He loves to meet Allah, and Allah loves to meet him. When the disbeliever dies, he will be given the tidings of Allah's punishment, and there is nothing more dreaded than what lies before him. So he hates to meet Allah, and Allah hates to meet him.[85]

One can imagine the sheer terror of the wretched soul when it comprehends its eventual outcome. Contrast this with the unparalleled joy felt by the righteous. In another *hadith*, Prophet Muhammad ﷺ described the sweet-scented soul of the believer that will be clasped by two angels who will take it up to the skies. The inhabitants of heaven will notice, saying, "A good soul that has just come from the earth! Allah's blessings upon you and the body you used to occupy." The soul will be taken to its Lord, Exalted and Glorious, who will say, "Take the soul until the end of time." As for the disbeliever, when his soul comes, it is cursed and smelly. The inhabitants of Heaven will say, "A bad soul that has just come from the earth!" And it will be said, "Take it back until the end of time."[86]

13. FEAR OF THE GRAVE'S NARROWNESS AND THE QUESTIONING

No one will escape the claustrophobic pressure and narrowness of the grave. The Prophet ﷺ said, "**There is constriction in the grave—if any one were to have been spared, it would have been Sa'd ibn Mu'ath.**"[87]

Every soul must also pass through the questioning of the angels. The Messenger of Allah said to Umar ibn Al-Khattab, "**Umar, how will you fare when you die, and your family will go to measure out [a shroud] three cubits by one and a span, then return to wash you, shroud and perfume you, then carry you, set you in [your grave], pour the earth over you and bury you? When they leave you, the two tormentors of the grave, Munkar and Nakir, shall come, whose voices are like rolling thunder, whose eyes are like dazzling lightning, who trail their hair and scour the grave with their fangs, grabbing hold of you and terrifying you? How will you fare then, Umar? ...**"[88]

Your grave can be, as the Messenger of Allah ﷺ said, "**...A pit from the pit-holes of Hell or a garden from the gardens of Paradise.**"[89] Every morning and evening, each servant in the grave will be shown his or her place in Paradise or Hell: "**When one of you dies, he will be shown his place in the morning and evening. If he is from the people of Paradise, his place will be among the people of Paradise. And if he is from the people of Hell, then his place will be among the people of Hell. It will be said, "This is your place until Allah resurrects you on the Day of Judgment."**"[90]

14. FEAR OF THE TERRORS OF THE DAY OF JUDGMENT

What can describe for us the magnitude and momentousness of the Day of Judgment? All will rise up from the dead, beginning from the first of humanity to the last living person on earth. Revelation gives us a glimpse into that tremendous event:

$$ يَا أَيُّهَا النَّاسُ اتَّقُوا رَبَّكُمْ إِنَّ زَلْزَلَةَ السَّاعَةِ شَيْءٌ عَظِيمٌ ۝ $$

*People, be mindful of your Lord, for the earthquake of the
Last Hour will be a mighty thing.* [22:1]

$$\text{يَوْمَ يَقُومُ النَّاسُ لِرَبِّ الْعَالَمِينَ} \, ﴿٦﴾$$

A Day when everyone will stand before the Lord of the
Worlds [83:6]

$$\text{إِنَّ فِي ذَلِكَ لَآيَةً لِّمَنْ خَافَ عَذَابَ الْآخِرَةِ ۚ ذَلِكَ يَوْمٌ مَّجْمُوعٌ لَّهُ النَّاسُ وَذَلِكَ}$$
$$\text{يَوْمٌ مَّشْهُودٌ} \, ﴿﴾$$

That is a Day in which all people will be gathered together, a
Day for all to see. [11:103]

Harith al-Muhāsibī, an eighth century scholar of Islamic philosophy from Baghdad, visualizes the scene of the Last Day:

> When death overtakes the last soul, the earth and sky will finally be devoid of their inhabitants, stillness after life. No being will exist to hear or see, except for God, The Compeller, The Most High (*Al-Jabbar Al-A'laa*), Eternal as He was and always will be, Singular in Greatness and Glory.
>
> Suddenly a call will startle your soul and that of all creation. Imagine the sound penetrating your consciousness for the first time after oblivion, your mind comprehending that you are being called to stand before The Highest King. Your heart will flutter and your hair will turn white at this call. No sooner will this call reach you than the earth will shiver and crumble away from your head and you will find yourself standing upright, covered from head to toe in the dirt of your grave. Your eyes will widen in terror, all of creation having risen covered with the earth's dust, staring in the direction of the Call.
>
> Imagine the collective terror and anticipation; imagine your nakedness, humility and worry amidst this crowd. Everyone will be exposed, barefoot, and silent, humbled by their fear and awe. There will be no sound except for shuffling feet on the earth. The rulers of the earth will be small and miserable, their power stripped away. Even their stature will appear smaller and weaker than the rest of the people, due to their oppression and transgression against God's servants on earth.
>
> When every being, human, jinn, devil, creature, animal, and insect, has assembled, the stars above their heads will scatter, the sun and moon will extinguish, and the earth will grow dark.
>
> As you and the rest of creation stand in the blackness, the sky will loom above. You will watch with your own eyes as a crack in the universe's sky will extend

500 years. How terrifying the splitting of the enduring sky be to our human sight!
How deafening the sound of its cracking dimensions to our ears! Then, the sky
will tear apart, the angels standing at its edges, and the Creator of the sky will
cause it to melt like molten copper:

$$\text{فَإِذَا انشَقَّتِ السَّمَاءُ فَكَانَتْ وَرْدَةً كَالدِّهَانِ ۝}$$

*When the heavens will split apart, becoming rose-red like
(burnt) oil!* [55:37]

Al-Muhāsibī continues with his breathtaking visualization of the Day of Judgment,

> The books will fly into right hands and left hands, and the scales will be laid out.
> Can you imagine eyeing the great scale, while you wait for your book to make its
> way to your right or left hand? Then, the wardens of Hell will be called to come
> forth carrying maces of iron, and again your chest will tighten with fear. In the
> midst of this terrible scene, a voice will call your name in front of all creation,
> "Where is so and so, son of so and so?" You hesitate and your body limpens,
> but giant angels grab you—imagine the feel of their hands and the tightness of
> their grip—and rush you forth toward the Throne of The Merciful where you
> will be cast forward to stand alone.
>
> Allah, Glorified, will address you, "Come closer to me, son of Adam." You will
> be engulfed in His light, standing before the Great Lord, Exalted, Generous.
> You will be humbled, terrified, and trembling like a newborn lamb. Will you
> feel embarrassed and ashamed before Your Lord who, even in that moment, is
> most kind and covers your sins? How can your tongue possibly answer Him
> when He asks you about your ugly deeds and crimes?[91]

15. FEAR OF BEING TRAPPED IN HELL

Every human being must cross the *sirat*, a razor-thin passageway over Hell, and will either
reach safety or fall into the abyss. Hell's heat is unbearable and its depth unfathomable; a
rock can fall for 70 years without reaching its bottom. Its passageways are constricted, the
raging fires groan and hiss, and there are no resources to avail. In the dungeons of Hell,
people finally meet with the anger of *Al-Jabbar*, The Mighty.

$$\text{يَا أَيُّهَا الَّذِينَ آمَنُوا قُوا أَنفُسَكُمْ وَأَهْلِيكُمْ نَارًا وَقُودُهَا النَّاسُ وَالْحِجَارَةُ عَلَيْهَا}$$
$$\text{مَلَائِكَةٌ غِلَاظٌ شِدَادٌ لَّا يَعْصُونَ اللَّهَ مَا أَمَرَهُمْ وَيَفْعَلُونَ مَا يُؤْمَرُونَ ۝}$$

Believers, guard yourselves and your families against a Fire fuelled by people and stones, over which stand angels, stern and strong; angels who never disobey God's commands to them, but do as they are ordered. [66:6]

وَذَرِ الَّذِينَ اتَّخَذُوا دِينَهُمْ لَعِبًا وَلَهْوًا وَغَرَّتْهُمُ الْحَيَاةُ الدُّنْيَا ۚ وَذَكِّرْ بِهِ أَن تُبْسَلَ نَفْسٌ بِمَا كَسَبَتْ لَيْسَ لَهَا مِن دُونِ اللَّهِ وَلِيٌّ وَلَا شَفِيعٌ وَإِن تَعْدِلْ كُلَّ عَدْلٍ لَّا يُؤْخَذْ مِنْهَا ۗ أُولَٰئِكَ الَّذِينَ أُبْسِلُوا بِمَا كَسَبُوا ۖ لَهُمْ شَرَابٌ مِّنْ حَمِيمٍ وَعَذَابٌ أَلِيمٌ بِمَا كَانُوا يَكْفُرُونَ ۝

Leave to themselves those who take their religion for a mere game and distraction and are deceived by the life of this world, but continue to remind them with the (Quran), lest any soul be damned by what it has done- it will have no one to protect it from God and no one to intercede; whatever ransom it may offer will not be accepted. Such are those who are damned by their own actions: they will have boiling water to drink and a painful punishment, because they used to defy (God). [6:70]

The descriptions of Hell-fire in the Quran are vivid and meant to strike fear and revulsion in our hearts, so that we flee to God and hold tight to His guidance.

وَتَرَى الْمُجْرِمِينَ يَوْمَئِذٍ مُّقَرَّنِينَ فِي الْأَصْفَادِ ۝ سَرَابِيلُهُم مِّن قَطِرَانٍ وَتَغْشَىٰ وُجُوهَهُمُ النَّارُ ۝

On that Day you will see the wicked bound together in chains, with garments of tar, and their faces covered with flames.
[14:49-50]

Hell is a dwelling-place of regret, despair, and endless burning. Bodies are doused in boiling water and flames, stomachs are filled with molten metal, and necks are weighed down with scalding chains. Foreheads will be branded with irons—feel the touch of Hell! Its inhabitants will raise their voices in a common plea:

وَهُمْ يَصْطَرِخُونَ فِيهَا رَبَّنَا أَخْرِجْنَا نَعْمَلْ صَالِحًا غَيْرَ الَّذِي كُنَّا نَعْمَلُ ۚ أَوَلَمْ نُعَمِّرْكُم مَّا يَتَذَكَّرُ فِيهِ مَن تَذَكَّرَ وَجَاءَكُمُ النَّذِيرُ ۖ فَذُوقُوا فَمَا لِلظَّالِمِينَ مِن نَّصِيرٍ ۝

They will cry out loud in Hell, 'Lord, let us out, and we will do righteous deeds, not what we did before!'—'Did We not give you a life long enough to take warning if you were going

to? The warner came to you, now taste the punishment.' The
evildoers will have nobody to help them. [35:37]

They will call out to the angel of death, invoking death over the endless punishment:

وَنَادَوْا يَا مَالِكُ لِيَقْضِ عَلَيْنَا رَبُّكَ ۖ قَالَ إِنَّكُم مَّاكِثُونَ ۝

They will cry, 'Malik, if only your Lord would finish us off,'
but he will answer, 'No! You are here to stay.' [43:77]

Their appeals will be of no avail, and no one will advocate for them. They will be unable to taste the comfort of sleep and will say to themselves,

سَوَاءٌ عَلَيْنَا أَجَزِعْنَا أَمْ صَبَرْنَا مَا لَنَا مِن مَّحِيصٍ ۝

It makes no difference now whether we rage or endure with
patience: there is no escape.' [14:21]

Al-Hasan Al-Basri used to speak as though he was seeing the Hereafter with his very eyes, and he used to weep as though Hell was created exclusively for him. He would approach people as though he was coming to bury a close friend, and he would sit down as though he were a prisoner shying away from a beating.[92] The fear of Hell is a lifeline for people who seek righteousness and truth:

إِنَّهَا لَإِحْدَى الْكُبَرِ ۝ نَذِيرًا لِّلْبَشَرِ ۝ لِمَن شَاءَ مِنكُمْ أَن
يَتَقَدَّمَ أَوْ يَتَأَخَّرَ ۝

Surely Hell is one of the mightiest catastrophes—a warning to
all mortals, to those of you who choose to go ahead and those
who lag behind. [74:35-37]

....

ENDNOTES

1. Bukhari (6/111 #4770) and Muslim (1/193 #207)
2. Muslim (1/192 #204)
3. al-Tirmidhi, #2450, al-Albani in *as-Silsilah as-Saheehah* #954
4. *Shu'ab Al-Iman* (2/268 #860)
5. *Tahtheeb Madarij as-Salikeen*, p. 27
6. *Shu'ab al-Iman* (2/201 #728)
7. Ibn Asakir in *Tareekh Dimashq* (56/268 #7111)
8. Sayings by Malik ibn Dinar and Ibrahim al-Taimi
9. Ahmed (35/405 #21516) and Ibn Majah (5/283 #4190) and at-Tirmithi (4/556 #2312)
10. Ibn Abi Shaibah in *al-Musannaf*, Tirmithi (5/402 #3297); al-Thahabi and al-Albani
11. Ahmad (26/238 #16312), Abu Dawud (2/173 #904) and others.

12. This incident is narrated by Ahmed (30/563 #18601) Ibn Majah (5/286 #4195) and declared Hasan by an-Nawawi and al-Albani.

13. Az-Zuhd by Ahmed ibn Hanbal #560

14. Az-Zuhd, narrated by Wakee' #29

15. Imam Malik in al-Muwatta' (5/1438 #3621)

16. Ad-Da' wa al-Dawa' by Ibn al-Qayyim p. 80

17. Ibn Kathir in Musnad al-Faruq (2/607)

18. At-Tabaqat by Ibn Sa'd (3/360)

19. Az-Zuhd by Ibn Hanbal #659

20. Hilyat al-Awliya (1/60) and az-Zuhd by Ibn Mubarak #1005

21. Az-Zuhd by Ibn Mubarak #39

22. az-Zuhd by Ahmad Ibn Hanbal #1015

23. az-Zuhd by Ahmad ibn Hanbal #869

24. Shu'b al-Iman by al-Bayhaqi (13/208 #10202)

25. az-Zuhd by Ibn al-Mubarak #884

26. ar-Riqah wa al-Buka' by Ibn Abu ad-Dunya #55

27. Siyar 'Alam an-Nubala' (11/215, 216)

28. These descriptions of God's power are summarized from al-Wabil as-Sayyib by Ibn al-Qayyim p. 62, 126.

29. Ibid

30. Ahmad (40/228 #24195)

31. Muslim; 40 Hadith Nawawi (hadith #24)

32. At-Tirmithi (5/448 #3358); Ibn Hibban (16/365 #7364); Al-Hakim (4/153 #7203) Authenticated by ath-Thahabi, Ibn al-Arabi and al-Albani in as-Saheehah #539

33. Ahmad (29/197 #17650); at-Tabarani in al-Kabeer (17/122 #303) authenticated by Al-Arna'ut.

34. Ahmad in al-Musnad (35/486 #21611), Ibn Majah (1/55 #77) Abu Dawud (7/84 #4699) authenticated by Al-Albani

35. Ahmad (6/376 #3817) and at-Tabarani (10/212), and several other similar narrations by Sahl ibn Sa'd, Aishah; authenticated by al-Albani

36. al-Bukhari (8/67 #6306)

37. Ahmad in al-Musnad (6/262 #3720) and Ibn Majah (3/88 #1892) and others.

38. Al-Bukhari (8/100 #6477) and Muslim (4/2290 #2988)

39. al-Bukhari (8/103 #6492)

40. az-Zuhd by Ibn Al-Mubarak #71

41. az-Zuhd by al-Wakee' #13

42. at-Tawbah by ibn Abi ad-Dunya #195

43. Ahmed (37/68 #22386), Ibn Majah (1/67 #90) and others

44. ad-Da' wa ad-Dawa' by Ibn al-Qayyim p. 54

45. Muslim (1/352 #486)

46. Muslim (4/2097 #2739)

47. al-Amr bil Ma'ruf wa an-Nahi an al-Munkar by Ibn Abi ad-Dunya #75

48. al-Bukhari (4/138 #3346) and Muslim (4/2207 #2770)

49. at-Tirmithi (4/468 #2169) Hasan; Ahmad (38/339 #23312)

50. Ahmed in al-Musnad (8/440 #4825) and Muslim (5/332 #3472); authenticated by al-Albani.

51. Ibn Abi Dunya in Al-Amr bil Ma'ruf wa an-Nahy an al-Munkar #14

52. al-Bukhari (4/109 #3206) and Muslim (2/616 #899)

53. al-Hakim (1/483 #1241) saheeh; al-Bayhaqi in Shu'b al-Iman (2/312 #965)

54. Tahtheeb Madarij as-Salikeen (116-117)

55. Ibn Abi ad-Dunya in Al-Awliya' (6) Al-Hakim (1/44 #4), graded sahih.

56. At-Tabarani in al-Awsat (5754) and others; al-Albani in as-Silsilah as-Saheehah #1802

57. Paraphrased from Wafiyyat al-Amal by Ibn Khalkan (3/17)

58. Tahtheeb Madarij as-Salikeen p. 116-117

59. Al-Jami' li Ahkam Al-Quran (3/202)

60. Ahmed (42/156 #25263) at-Tirmithi (5/327 #3175) Ibn Majah (5/288 #4199) authenticated by al-Albani #162.

61. al-Bukhari (1/18 Kitab al-Iman Chapter on A Believer's Fear of Actions being wasted)

62. Ibn Abi Shaibah in al-Musannaf (7/481 #3739)

63. *Shu'ab al-Iman* (1/504)

64. Ibn Rajab. al-Mahajjah fe Siyar al-Duljah p. 98

65. Ahmad (35/520 #21666) and at-Tabarani (5/119, 157)

66. al-Bazar (13/49 #6368) and an-Nasa'i in *as-Sunan al-Kubra* (6/212 #10330) al-Hakim (1/730 #2000) authenticated by al-Albani (#227)

67. Sa'id ibn Mansur in *Sunan* (2/362)

68. Summarized from Ibn al-Qayyim's *Tahtheeb Madarij as-Salikeen* (p. 218)

69. Ibn Rajab p. 42 and al-Asfahani in *Hilyat al-Awliya'* (5/292)

70. Ahmad (44/138 #26519); at-Tirmidhi (5/423 #3522); Al-Albani in *As-Silsilah As-Sahihah* (#2091)

71. At-Tabarani in Al-Awsat (1/206 #661); al-Baihaqi in *Ad-Da'waat* (1/346 #254); Al-Haithami in *Majma' az-Zawa'id* (10/176) Al-Albani in *As-Silsilah As-Sahihah* (1476)

72. Muslim (4/2068 #2717)

73. *Shu'ab al-Iman* (2/258 #831)

74. *Shu'ab al-Iman* (2/258 #830)

75. *Shu'ab al-Iman* (2/259 #832)

76. *Shu'ab al-Iman* (2/259 #833)

77. *Shu'ab al-Iman* (1/506-507)

78. Bukhari (8/122 #6594) and Muslim (4/2036 #2643)

79. Imam Ahmed (29/134 #17593) with a slightly different wording; Ibn al-Qayyim in *Ahkam ath-Thimah* (2/1003); authenticated by Al-Albani in *As-Silsilah As-Sahihah* (#50)

80. *Ihya' Uloom ad-Din* (5/61-62)

81. Ahmad (40/415 #24356) Ibn Majah (2/546 #1623) at-Tirmithi (3/299 #978) and others

82. Ibn Sa'd in at-Tabaqat (4/260)

83. Ibn Abi Shaibah in al-Musannaf (7/236 #35643)

84. At-Tathkirah by al-Qurtubi (1/113)

85. Bukhari (8/106 #6507) Muslim (4/2065 #2684)

86. Muslim (4/2022 #2872)

87. Ahmed (40/327 #24283) Ibn Hibban (7/379 #3112) and others; Al-Albani in *as-Saheehah* (#1695)

88. Al-Haithami in *Baghyat al-Bahith* (1/379 #281) and Al-Baihaqi in *Ithbat 'Athab al-Qabr* (1/81)

89. at-Tirmithi (4/640)

90. Al-Bukhari (2/99 #1379) and Muslim (4/2199 #2866)

91. Al-Harith al-Muhasibi in *At-Tawahhum*, p. 80-82

92. *Qoot al-Qulub* by Abi Talib al-Makki (1/381)

Fear

◀ how to nurture it ▶

We cannot start our journey of faith without first rising from our slumber, and the best way to do that is to use the alarm of fearing God. Fear keeps us moving and makes us uncomfortable with our status quo. We can use it to increase our sensitivity, fuel our voyage, and set a steady pace towards our Lord. When you kindle a sense of fear in your heart, you will find the other methods of awakening faith to be more effective.

Benefitting from the Quran, for example, requires that our heart be fearful. Allah says,

فَذَكِّرْ بِالْقُرْءَانِ مَن يَخَافُ وَعِيدِ ۝

So remind with the Quran those who fear My warning. [50:45]

The same is stipulated for prayer:

وَٱسْتَعِينُوا بِٱلصَّبْرِ وَٱلصَّلَوٰةِ وَإِنَّهَا لَكَبِيرَةٌ إِلَّا عَلَى ٱلْخَٰشِعِينَ ۝

And seek help through patience and prayer. Indeed, it is a burden except for the humble [and fearful] [2:45]

Giving charity consistently is something that can be sustained only by a heart that is mindful of its ultimate meeting with its Lord:

وَمِنَ الْأَعْرَابِ مَن يُؤْمِنُ بِاللَّهِ وَالْيَوْمِ الْآخِرِ وَيَتَّخِذُ مَا يُنفِقُ قُرُبَاتٍ عِندَ اللَّهِ

However, among the nomadic Arabs are those who believe in Allah and the Last Day, and consider what they donate as a means of coming closer to Allah... [9:99]

The signs and reminders that God places throughout His creation resonate more with hearts that are fearful and aware:

$$ إِنَّ فِى ذَٰلِكَ لَآيَةً لِّمَنْ خَافَ عَذَابَ ٱلْآخِرَةِ $$

Surely in this is a sign for those who fear the torment of the
Hereafter. [11:103]

One who attempts to journey to God without the aid of a fearful heart will find the various methods of awakening faith to be of feeble and temporary avail. Without fear as their facilitator, these methods cannot reach the proper depths within our hearts. On the other hand, someone who is fearful will perk their ears at advice and rush to implement means of security and salvation.

God clarifies that despite the plethora of reminders placed in creation for His servants, only those who are alert and vigilant will grasp them:

$$ إِنَّا لَمَّا طَغَا ٱلْمَآءُ حَمَلْنَـٰكُمْ فِى ٱلْجَارِيَةِ ۝ لِنَجْعَلَهَا لَكُمْ تَذْكِرَةً $$
$$ وَتَعِيَهَآ أُذُنٌ وَٰعِيَةٌ ۝ $$

Indeed, when the floodwater had overflowed, We carried you
in the floating Ark, so that We may make it a reminder to you,
and that attentive ears may grasp it. [69:11-12]

Droves of people might pass by the same reminder, but its effect will differ according to their states. Notice in the following ayah the qualification for benefitting from God's guidance and teachings:

$$ هَـٰذَا بَيَانٌ لِّلنَّاسِ وَهُدًى وَمَوْعِظَةٌ لِّلْمُتَّقِينَ ۝ $$

This is an insight to humanity—a guide and a lesson to the
God-fearing. [3:138]

Ibn al-Qayyim clarifies that fear is essential for the beginner on his or her journey:

A servant is more in need of warnings and encouragement when he is distracted and forgetful. As his level of repentance and mindfulness increases, he is less in need of reminders in this respect, and in more need of a good knowledge of what is required and what is forbidden in religion. So someone who is oft-repenting and spiritually aware is in need of knowing God's commands and prohibitions, while one who is heedless is in dire need of reminders that create a sense of longing and a sense of fear.[1]

In this chapter we present several methods of increasing fear in the heart. It is crucial that these methods are accompanied by deep engagement with the Quran, which will be explored in depth in the next chapter.

Remember Death Often

We live under the false illusion that death is a distant prospect, confident that our lives will stretch long enough for us to improve our relationship with God. When we see those who are older than us, we imagine what we will be doing at their age and how we will build our future in this world. The Prophet ﷺ commented on this universal phenomenon when he said, **"The human being grows old, while two things stay young within him: the aspiration for wealth, and the aspiration for long life."**[2]

The antidote to this poisonous delusion is to remember death often. The Messenger of Allah ﷺ said, **"Remember the destroyer of delights often: death. It comforts anyone who remembers it at a time of tightness, and tightens the condition of anyone who remembers it at a time of comfort."**[3] Death surely destroys all delights. Imam al-Ghazāli commented on this figurative description of death: "it kills [delights] immediately upon its mention, and it ends our emotional dependence on them, redirecting us to God."[4]

Ibn Umar narrates: I was with the Messenger of Allah ﷺ when a man from the Ansar came to him and greeted the Prophet ﷺ. **Then he said, "Messenger of Allah, which of the believers is the most superior?" He replied: "The best of them in character." He said, "And which of them is most astute?" He said, "The one who remembers death the most, and the one who works best for what comes after it. Those are the astute."**[5]

Umar bin Abdul-Aziz used to gather the scholars around him every night to discuss death, the resurrection, and the afterlife. They would cry to the point that it seemed as if they were at an actual funeral. Safiyyah remembers that when a woman once complained to Aishah about her heart becoming hard, Aishah said, "Remember death more often, and your heart will soften." Similarly, it is narrated that a man once asked her, "What is the cure for a hard heart?" She instructed him to visit the ill, to attend funerals, and to always be alert to the reality of death.[6]

When we remember death often, it alters our character and nature. We grow more soft-hearted, fearful, and humble. Our looming death informs our every decision and drives our every action. Ibn Ḥibbān wrote about how the wise could never afford to forget something so impending as death:

> They would never forget about the only thing that they are sure to encounter, nor would they attempt to escape their inevitable fate. Death leaves no one behind, and

catches all who try to flee from it ... Think about how many people are honored
by their families, revered by their communities, and regarded so highly by those
around them. They have no fear that their wealth would ever decrease, and have
never experienced any tragedy that ever grieved them.

But then the phenomenon that ends the reign of every king, overpowers every
oppressor, and subdues every tyrant finally reaches them, laying them flat in front
of all those who love them. Think about how many nations death has brought
an end to and how many towns death has neutralized. Think about how many
women it has turned to widows, and how many children it has turned to orphans.

The poet al-Kurayzi writes,

> *The money we made is for our heirs to taste*
> *The house we built will someday wither and waste*
> *We busy ourselves here in toil and haste*
> *Though the only salvation is through restraint*
> *Stay still and hide; you will not miss your fate*
> *Run as fast as you can; you can never escape*
> *It may creep secretly at night, or strike bright in the day*
> *Death has no preference, and does not discriminate.*

It is a huge mistake to live life without the central theme of death in mind. Abu al-Darda'
said, "Whenever you remember the deceased, consider yourself one of them."[8] Similarly, Umar
said, "Every day we hear, 'this man has died!' and 'that man has died!' It's only a matter of
time before the name they call is mine."[9] Ali ibn Abi Talib used to say, "If you are leaving,
and death is coming, then how soon it is that you will meet!"[10]

In his grand spiritual guide to anyone intending to study the Islamic sciences, Iḥyā' 'Uloom
al-Deen, Imam al-Ghazali suggests that we constantly remind ourselves of thoughts like these,
in addition to visiting the graveyards and tending to the ill, to keep the remembrance of death
fresh in our hearts until it motivates us to divest from this world of desire and delusion. He
tells a short anecdote to drive this point home:

> Ibn Mutee' looked at his house one day and was delighted by how beautiful it
> looked. But then he began to cry. He said "By God, were it not for death, I would
> be content with you! Were it not for the tightness of the graves, we would find our
> comfort in this world." He continued to cry for longer, sobbing in a high voice.[11]

Thinking of Death Develops Character

Dr. Umar al-Ashqar points out the impactful effect of remembering death on one's self improvement and refinement. The souls covet this world and its pleasures, yearning to stay here forever. "They easily fall into sin and temptation, and are reluctant towards worship and obedience. If death were constantly on our minds, this world would seem insignificant in our eyes, and this would help us work towards improving ourselves and correcting our mistakes."[12] One scholar also said that whoever remembers death often is granted three unique things: urgency for repentance, contentment at heart, and energy for worship. Likewise, whoever is oblivious to death fails in three regards: procrastinating in their repentance, an insatiable desire for more, and a laziness in worship.[13]

Visiting Graveyards and Washing the Dead

The most effective way to bring death to the forefront of our minds is to visit an actual graveyard. Ibn Mas'ood narrates that the Messenger of Allah ﷺ said, **"I used to forbid you from visiting graves, but now visit them. They make one austere in this world and mindful of the next."**[14]

When we pass by graves, we should remember all of our friends and loved ones who have beaten us to the finish line. Imam al-Ghazāli describes some of the thoughts that might pass through our minds when we visit a graveyard in Iḥyā' 'Uloom al-Deen:[15]

> Upon seeing the grave of someone we know, we remember how he used to look, all of his virtues, and all of the feats that he had accomplished. But then we remember his death, how he is now lying helplessly under the soil. The maggots have eaten away at his face without any regard for his beauty, and his body lies in pieces wrapped together in a box. His wife grieves over him, now spending her nights alone, and his children are still trying to adjust to this new life without him. The wealth he acquired can do nothing for him. Someone new now fills his usual spot in the mosque, and his friends cannot seem to shake the feeling that there is something missing in their gatherings. The time and energy he invested in preparing for his worldly dreams and aspirations have gone to waste. The future he so intricately planned for vanished the moment he saw the Angel of Death and heard the striking call to his end—a call either to the bliss of Paradise or to the doom of the Hellfire.

Imam al-Ghazāli concludes: "When this comes to mind, remember that you are just like him. You are just as oblivious to your fate as he was, and your final destination is the same as his."

Ibn al-Jawzi also gives some powerful and moving advice on what to do at a grave when we visit. He suggests, "Picture your grave among the rest, and think about what you will need while you are in there. Make sure to take a lot of it, for you will be there for a while!" He then clarifies that what he is alluding to is the accrual of good deeds. "Anything else," he says, "will only be a source of pain and regret in your grave." He then instructs, "Consider your current state. If it is befitting for you to die upon, then continue on! But if not, then repent to God therefrom, and return to what will be of benefit."[16]

◆◆◆

Another practical suggestion for keeping the reality of death clear in our minds is to take part in the ritual washing of deceased people and attending their funerals. The Messenger of Allah ﷺ said, "Visit graves, and you will remember the afterlife through that. Wash the deceased, for tending to a lifeless body is an impactful reminder. Take part in the funeral prayers so that it might grieve you, for the grieved is in God's shade on the Day of Resurrection."[17] We should be waiting for the next opportunity to wash a deceased body, pray their funeral prayer, ride in the group to their burial, and then pour the soil over them. Doing this often will keep us constantly aware of death, and God ultimately knows best.

There is much benefit in reflecting upon our own impending death. Every so often, we should sit alone in a quiet place, away from all of the ruckus of the worldly life to imagine the moment when the Angel of Death comes to meet us. Predict the reaction of our spouses, children, family, and friends to the news of your passing. Picture the dimly lit room and cold steel table where your corpse will lie. Who will pour the water over your head and body? What will they use to mask the putrid smell of your rotting cadaver? Your family and friends will carry you to the mosque, and then to the ditch where your journey to the afterlife begins. Pebbles and clots of dirt will rain over you as they seal your new home, and the patter of their footsteps will be the last thing you hear before you meet the angels who will interrogate you and investigate your faith. How will you answer their questions?

Preparing for death through action is perhaps the most productive and transformative way to prevent ourselves from slipping into heedlessness. Death is, after all, a calamity:

$$\text{فَأَصَبَتْكُم مُّصِيبَةُ ٱلْمَوْتِ}$$

If you are afflicted by the calamity of death... [5:106]

Any intelligent person would never ignore this inevitable calamity, as the only way to survive any calamity is to prepare for it before it strikes. The deceased is just as affected by his own death as his loved ones are. They are afflicted with the pain of loss, but the tragedy of the deceased is that the chance to do more good deeds has ended.

If, however, we prepare for our deaths, then death will not be a calamity for us. One practical step we can take to prepare for our own death is to write our will and revisit it from time to time. Ibn Umar narrates that the Messenger of Allah ﷺ said, **"It is a duty for the Muslim person who has something that they wish to bequeath to not go two nights except that his will is written with him."**[18] Ibn Umar said, "Not a single night has passed since I heard the Messenger of Allah ﷺ say that except that I kept my will with me."[19] This will is meant to be our parting advice for our children and loved ones for how they should live the rest of their lives, not just a document dictating the distribution of our estate.

Another way to prepare for the day of our departure is to invest in charity that will have continuing effects long after our death. This can even be as simple as planting a tree! We can also take private steps to prepare such as buying our own cloth to be wrapped in, keeping it stowed away and looking at it from time to time to remind ourselves of our end. We should also have straightforward and empathetic conversations with our spouses about how to handle certain matters in our absence. It is also important to rush to pay off our debts as soon as we can.

The early Muslims spent a lot of time and energy preparing for their own deaths. They would be clear with their wives on how to conduct their funerals. Ḥabeeb bin Muhammad al-Fārisi even appointed a specific person to wash his corpse. When his wife was asked how she knew these specific stipulations, she said, "He would repeat it every day!"[20]

Visualize the Hour of Death

It also serves us well to imagine what our last moments on our deathbeds might be like. Ibn al-Jawzi describes some of the emotions that we might feel at that time in his master work on self-purification, Ṣayd al-Khātir. He writes that the concluding moments of life invoke a feeling of pressing urgency, and quake the heart with a fear incomparable to anything we might have felt before. Every single regret of our past has now amassed and conglomerated into a gut-wrenching grief, and all we will want is just one more chance to do it all right. Death's palpable proximity wrings every ounce of sincerity from our hearts into our repentance. Ibn Jawzi recommends that we try to evoke these feelings before they actually take place. "The wise is one who pictures himself in that scene and acts on its effects," allowing himself to benefit from those emotions before they actually take place.

Hasan al-Baṣri once visited an ill friend and found that he was in the final stages before death. He noticed his friend's agony, and returned to his family with a visible difference in his face. When they called him to come eat, he said, "My dear beloved, keep your food and drink. By God, I have seen a great tragedy that I will continue to prepare for until I encounter it myself."[21]

Visiting the sick helps us remember death and reset our priorities. Doing so is highly beneficial, from a religious, moral, and social perspective, and is easier today than ever before. The hospitals are filled with sick people, and we can take a transformative lesson from each of them with their unique circumstances, some of which will unsettle our stomachs and incite us towards rectifying our affairs. Remember that you will find yourself struggling for your last breaths sooner than you expect. It helps us to realize the true value of this world, and that nothing herein is meant to last forever.

Just think back to the last time you were ill, and consider how much it affected even the most trivial daily activities. Your enthusiasm diminished, your determination dwindled, and your normal routine became difficult. Now imagine how much this discomfort will be multiplied when we are lying there on our deathbeds. Just as that illness struck you without any warning, you will find yourself struggling for your last breaths sooner than you expect. And just as you used to yearn with every bone in your body for your health to return back to its normal state, you will find yourself ready to give up anything for another chance to do better and focus your efforts on the afterlife.

Record Your Deeds

An exercise that will help us remember death more often is actually to write down on paper our strengths and weaknesses with regards to our worship. Perhaps seeing our deeds on paper may alert us to how little our accumulation of good deeds, or how lengthy our list of bad deeds. We shudder at the thought of being caught by surprise, realizing only too late that the ultimate assets we can accrue were good deeds. God says,

وَمَنْ عَمِلَ صَلِحًا فَلِأَنْفُسِهِمْ يَمْهَدُونَ ۝

Those who did good will have prepared for themselves [30:44]

It is only through our deeds that the environments of our graves are prepared, either a garden of Paradise, or a ditch from the Hellfire. By the time we regret the lost opportunities to do good, it will already be too late.

حَتَّىٰ إِذَا جَاءَ أَحَدَهُمُ ٱلْمَوْتُ قَالَ رَبِّ ٱرْجِعُونِ ۝ لَعَلِّي أَعْمَلُ صَلِحًا فِيمَا تَرَكْتُ ۝

When death approaches any of them, they cry, "My Lord! Let

me go back, so I may do good in what I left behind." [23:99-100]

We can hope to avoid this by writing down our regularly practiced good deeds that we might wish to come back to do again, identifying all of the missed opportunities in our day. This can be as straightforward as our daily prayers, our fasting in Ramadan, and the opportunities that we have had to make Hajj or Umrah, or more complex like our relationships, acts of service and the efforts we have exerted to spread and teach this religion to others.

It is important for us to realize that as long as we are breathing, we have something that so many wish for: the chance to improve our standing with God. This commodity is invaluable, and taking the time to chart out a plan to make ourselves better for God will serve us well. We must then hold ourselves to it, prioritizing the biggest threats to our salvation and constantly updating it according to our progress.

.... ◆◆◆ ....

The Messenger of Allah said that Gabriel came to him and said, "Muhammad! Live as you wish, for you will someday die. Love whomever you wish, for you will someday depart them. Do what you wish, for you will someday be repaid for it. Know that the believer's honor is his prayer at night, and his dignity is in his lack of need for others."[22]

....

Realize that the last person whose funeral you attended had high hopes much like you, but death grounded their aspirations and woke them up from the hallucination of an endless life. No matter how rich, powerful, or noble you may be, you will be left to rot under a pile of dirt one day. Your to-do list and goals will be left rudely unfinished. Ibn Umar narrates that the Prophet ﷺ once grabbed his shoulder and said, **"Be in this world like a stranger, or a passing visitor."**[23] Ibn Umar used to say, "When you reach the evening, don't expect to reach the morning; and when you reach the morning, don't expect to reach the evening. Take advantage of your good health for when you fall ill, and take advantage of your time alive for when you die."[21]

Abdullah bin 'Amr narrates that the Messenger of Allah ﷺ once passed by him as he was repairing his straw house. When the Prophet ﷺ asked what he was doing, he explained that the house had worn out a bit, and so he was just fixing it up. The Prophet ﷺ told him, **"I only see that our circumstance is more urgent than this!"**[24] Abu al-Dardā' once called out to the public, "People of Damascus! Come listen to what your sincerely concerned brother has to say!" They gathered around him, and he said, "Why do you build houses in which you never live, buy food that you do not eat, and aspire towards what you will never attain? There were those before you who certainly built impressive structures, made grand plans, and accumulated much, but their plans deceived them, their heaps of wealth eroded, and their homes are now their graves."[25]

One scholar shared that his father said, "Don't be deceived by your good health! Haven't you ever seen someone die while healthy? The Angel of Death has no regard for your wealth, nor any care for your strength! The moment of death is full of agony and distress. You will regret every shortcoming you chose to neglect."

Soften your Heart

Listening to powerful reminders, lectures, and reading books that soften the heart and remind of the afterlife are a sure way to nurture fear and sensitivity. A Companion by the name of al-'Irbāḍ bin Sāriyah said, "The Messenger of Allah ﷺ once delivered a speech to us that filled our eyes with tears and filled out hearts with fear."[26]

Ibn Rajab points out that the spiritual state of the teacher can have a transformative effect on listeners and students. He describes Ḥasan al-Baṣri as a man who "seemed like he had seen the afterlife, and had come to describe it," whenever he taught. His students, likewise, "would leave his presence without a care for this world at all."[27] The ability to be affected by reminders differs from one person to another. Some listeners will only engage superficially with a reminder, returning quickly to their prior state of carelessness. Others will react heartily to the reminders, as though a whip struck their heart into wakefulness. With modern day conveniences such as recorded lectures, videos, and podcasts, there is no excuse not to expose the heart to a steady diet of religious reminders that develop an attuned sense of fear and awareness.

In addition to listening to speeches and taking classes that help us build a lasting fear of God within us, we must also keep in mind that our literary heritage is filled with books that are as insightful and relevant as any modern psychological study on the human mind. The scholars of our past have spent their entire lives contemplating the human soul, outlining its stages for growth and warning against its pitfalls and traps. We have much to benefit from their wisdom and experience, and we can ask the learned members of our communities for help in building a personalized reading list for a more intimate experience with this tradition.

Remember Your Sins

This should not be the first, or only, method we use to develop fear, but it is most helpful when used in tandem with other methods. This is because identifying our sins without a cognizance of the afterlife will have little to no effect. When we remember our sins, in parallel with an awareness of the afterlife, it should distress our hearts and translate into an impetus for change. It is important to write them down physically, for putting them on paper helps them materialize into concrete facts instead of abstract memories. As one scholar said, "Whenever you find yourself having strayed from the path, retrace your sins to find your way back."

Seeing your sins written out and recorded crushes your ego and refreshes your sense of fear in God. This humility and fear is necessary for a sincere repentance. When we exist in narcissistic delusion, oblivious to our own flaws, there will remain a barrier between us and our Lord. In the process of self-examination, we should learn to identify specific types of sins that may be lurking in the shadows. There are sins of the limbs. including those of the tongue such as backbiting, gossip, lying, and insulting and mocking others. The eye is also considered in this category, and we must be vigilant against mindless glances at that which Allah forbade us to look at. Other important limbs that require supervision are our ears, our hands, and our private parts. All of these have their fair share in committing the sins we engage in every day, and we must be attentive to each one and the role it plays in keeping us from advancing closer to God.

The heart is a more subtle sinner. We might wear the masks of humility while feeling arrogance and conceit. We might claim with our tongue to love our brothers and sisters, but feel envy towards their blessings and accomplishments deep within. Some work night and day, exhausting themselves in doing good deeds, but are only doing so to feed their own ego and self-righteousness. These silent slips can turn into a fatal fall into hypocrisy.

While some sins are active, others are passive in that they entail a failure to uphold a duty or responsibility. This is often due to a misalignment of priorities. A person might devote their time to their friends or their career, or even make a commitment to serving their community, while falling short in their duties to their parents, spouses, or children. Others might invest all of their time in securing their own comfort, or that of their immediate family, while neglecting to play a role in developing and benefitting their local and global community, which are more in need of collaborative and cooperative efforts than ever before.

We may also be sinful in falling short in our worship of God. This can be assessed quantitatively or qualitatively. We can look to see whether or not we pray every prayer on time and pay the right amount of Zakah, but we can also consider whether the acts of worship are perfected with the proper conditions. These conditions include the external, which are necessary for the validity of the act, and the internal, which are required in order for these rituals to impact our hearts as God intended. Just as we must check to ensure that our hands and feet are in their proper place during prayer, we must also be vigilantly alert to the state of our hearts.

When assessing our sinful souls from the angle of falling short with God, we must not only take our ritual worship into account, but also the general state of our hearts in engaging God throughout our day. As we utilize and interact with His endless blessings, a humbling question to ask ourselves is whether or not we are grateful enough to Him for them. In order for the requirements of this gratitude to be fulfilled properly, we have to consider God's numerous blessings and bounties in all of their forms and facets of our life. Just as we realized the powerful effect of writing down our sins in order to come to terms with their gravity, we can apply the same approach in attempting to internalize the unmatched value of God's gifts. It is a task that can never be completed, and realizing that first hand instills within our hearts a deep and organic sense of gratitude. It is the ultimate internalization of God's words,

$$وَإِن تَعُدُّوا نِعْمَةَ ٱللَّهِ لَا تُحْصُوهَآ$$

If you tried to count Allah's blessings, you would never be able to number them. [16:18]

So after writing down the blessings you can count, think then about all of the sins and crimes that would have disqualified you from those blessings were it not for God's mercy and love. This exercise sheds light on the true degree to which we fall short in regards to our duty to our Lord. The Prophet ﷺ taught us this reality through some daily words of prayer: **"I admit to you, God, your blessings upon me, and I admit to you my sins, so forgive me. There is surely no one who can forgive sins but you."**

Between Fear and Hope

Some might object to this approach of building a foundation of fear to our faith, claiming that though fear might cause some to focus on God, it can cause others to completely despair in God's mercy. Imam al-Ghazali responds to these objections in his famous Iḥyā' 'Uloom al-Deen, saying that questioning which of the two is better is just like asking whether bread is better than water: "Bread is better for the hungry, and water is better for the thirsty." If both are present, he says the priority is given to the one we are most in need of, and if they are equal, then neither is better than the other.

> Fear and hope are two medicines with which the hearts are cured. Preference is given according to the malady: if the heart is plagued by the delusion of security from God's punishment, then fear is better; and if it is plagued by despair from God's mercy, then hope is better.

He adds that hope is better for someone who is drowning and despairing in their sins. Imam al-Ghazāli then points out that when something is sought out as a means to an end, it is more accurate to say that it is "more pertinent" than its counterpart, rather than saying it is "better." "And thus, we say that for most people, fear is more pertinent than hope," he explains, "because of the overwhelming presence of sins."[28]

For the pious people who have successfully rid themselves of the majority of outer and inner sins, al-Ghazāli recommends that they keep fear and hope equal. Umar once said, "If it were announced that all people will enter the Hellfire except for one person, I would hope to be him. If it announced that all people will enter Paradise except for one person, I would fear that I was him." Al-Ghazāli says that "someone like Umar has a right to keep both emotions equal, but for a sinner to believe that he is the one person who is exempted from the Hellfire is evidence of his self-delusion."

◆◆◆

" Fear Allah to the degree that you worry that if you were to bring forth all of the good deeds of the people on earth, he would not accept it from you. And have hope in Allah to the degree that you expect that if you were to bring forth all of the sins of the people on earth, He would forgive you." -Ali ibn Abi Talib writing to his son

Ibn al-Qayyim presents a metaphor that so uniquely and vividly outlines our relationship with fear and hope. He compares the heart to a bird: its head is love, and its two wings are hope and fear. He says, "When the head and both wings are intact, the bird flies well. When the head is cut, the bird dies, and when the wings are lost, then it is easy prey for any predator." Ibn al-Qayyim points out that the early Muslims would focus more on their fear of God when in good health, and lean on the wings of hope when they sensed that death was near.[29]

Fear is a Means

Given that fear is a means to awakening our hearts, what then is our actual goal, and what are its limits? We cultivate the fear of God in our hearts in hopes of purging our attachment to this world and turning away from distractions. Fear is the burst of electric current that burns away our sinful desires and restores life to our souls.

Fear also primes the heart to accept the most powerful message and reminder of all: the Quran. God even tells us that fear is a prerequisite in order to benefit from the Quran:

فَذَكِّرْ بِالْقُرْآنِ مَن يَخَافُ وَعِيدِ ۝

So remind with the Quran those who fear My warning. [50:45]

Fear, then, is an early stimulus in reviving our faith, which must be balanced with the Quran and other methods outlined in the upcoming chapters.

Being that fear varies in its types and degrees, it is important to define exactly what the fear that we hope for is. Imam al-Ghazāli describes the praiseworthy type of fear as,

> ...One that encourages action, disrupts all of our worldly passions, irritates the heart so that it divests from this world, and teaches it to turn away from this domain of disappointment. [Good fear] is somewhere between the weak conscience that fails to hold one back from sin and a severe intimidation that causes one to despair.[30]

The Prophet's Fear

The best guidance is that of the true Prophet ﷺ. There is nothing that can bring us closer to God that he failed to direct us to. God says,

$$وَإِن تُطِيعُوهُ تَهْتَدُوا$$

And if you obey him, you will be rightly guided. [25:54]

He is the best of all creation. He is the most perfect and the most knowledgeable of God. His guidance is the best guidance, his character is the most beautiful, and his Companions were the finest generation of human beings to walk the earth. If we study his life and personality, we will find that he feared God more than any other human being. He once said, **"By God, I am the most fearful of God out of all of you, and the most cognizant of Him."**[31]

His wife Aishah said that whenever he saw signs of rain in the sky, he would pace back and forth, nervously coming in and out of the house with his face noticeably different. Then when it rained, he would be relieved. When Aishah asked him about this, the Prophet ﷺ said, "I do not know; it may be as God said[32],

$$فَلَمَّا رَأَوْهُ عَارِضًا مُّسْتَقْبِلَ أَوْدِيَتِهِمْ قَالُوا هَٰذَا عَارِضٌ مُّمْطِرُنَا$$

Then when they saw the torment as a cloud approaching their valleys, they said, "This is a cloud bringing us rain!" [46:24]

The Prophet ﷺ was teaching us—leading by example—to always be on alert, fearful of God's power and might.[31] He would get up after a third of the night had passed, saying, **"People! Remember God! People! Remember God! People! Remember God! The blast is near, and the next one will follow! Death will soon come with all that it brings! Death will come soon with all that it brings!"**[33]

This heightened sense of urgency and fear naturally penetrated the hearts of those who spent their days and nights devoted to learning from the Prophet ﷺ. Anas narrates, "The Messenger of Allah ﷺ once delivered a speech to us, the likes of which I have never heard. He said, 'If you knew what I knew, you would laugh little and cry much.' The Companions of the Messenger of Allah ﷺ then covered their faces, sobbing audibly through their noses."[33]

◆◆◆

Towards the end of his life, Ali bin Abu Talib reminisced about the Companions to those who were with him. He said, "By God, I have seen the Companions of the Muhammad ﷺ, and I see no one who resembles them today. They would show up in the morning disheveled and dusty, with spots like the knees of goats on their foreheads; they had spent the night prostrating and standing for God, reciting His book, and alternatingly shifting their weight between their foreheads and their feet. Then once the morning came, they would sit to make remembrance of God, swaying like trees on a windy day. Their eyes would pour forth with tears, drenching their clothing. By God, it seems the people are now spending their nights in ignorance ..."[35]

Along with an intense provision of fear that never left their hearts, the Companions also had an optimistic hope in their Lord. They lived by the verse,

نَبِّئْ عِبَادِى أَنِّى أَنَا ٱلْغَفُورُ ٱلرَّحِيمُ ۝ وَأَنَّ عَذَابِى هُوَ ٱلْعَذَابُ ٱلْأَلِيمُ ۝

Inform My servants that I am truly the All-Forgiving, Most Merciful, and that My torment is indeed the most painful. [15:49-50]

Their hearts were forever fluctuating between fear and hope, a trait inherited by those who learned from them for generations thereafter. Yaḥya bin Muʿādh said, addressing his Lord, "How can I fear you, when You are so generous? How can I not hope in you, when You are so grand. I am forever between a fear that holds me back, and a hope that keeps me going. My hope shall not let me die from fear, and my fear shall not let me live in ignorant glee."[36]

Despite their inhibiting sense of fear and their eager sense of hope, the Companions and those who followed in their footsteps managed to live their lives in a natural state. They didn't go into recluse out of fear for their own souls, nor did they renounce all worldly engagements. They got married, had children, and worked to make a living for themselves and their families. Some were more inclined towards business and trade, others were more focused on learning, and some were craftsmen and laborers. It was the greatest of all human beings himself, our Prophet Muhammad ﷺ—who was the most fearful of God—who taught us to keep a balance and give everything the attention it deserves: **"Your body has a right over you, your eyes have a right over you, your guests have a right over you, and your spouse has a right over you."**[37]

We never hear or read about the Companions isolating themselves for the purpose of worshipping God away from all of the mundane distractions of life. If anyone around them ever began to lean towards this mindset, the others would rush to advise him against it and remind him of Islam's balanced approach. Abdullah bin Mas'ood once heard that some men left Kufa for a nearby village in order to devote themselves to worship away from the city life. He visited them, and they rejoiced at his arrival, assuming it was out of approval for their actions. But when they told him that they wanted to avoid the adversities of dealing with other people and focus solely on their ritual worship of God, Abdullah said, "If everyone did as you are doing, then who would fight against the enemy? I will not leave until you return."[38]

When al-Ḥasan al-Baṣri once requested that one of his peers named Thābit al-Bunāni go out to help someone in need, Thābit declined. He was in a state of i'tikāf, wherein one devotes themselves to staying in the mosque for a certain period of time to solely engage in ritual worship. Al-Ḥasan responded to him, "Don't you know that walking to serve your Muslim brother's need is better for you than performing Hajj one year after the other?!"[39]

Abdullah bin 'Umar was once asked, "Did the Companions used to laugh?" He said, "Yes, while the faith in their hearts was greater than mountains."[40] They were able to hold the remembrance of God and His greatness, His reward, and His punishment in their hearts while engaging in worldly matters with their bodies. They made sure their income was from pure sources, they took care of their families' needs, and they interacted with people in ways that brought them closer to Allah, making all of those actions acts of worship in and of themselves. They would always make sure to teach those whom they met, they physically put their lives on the line for just causes, and they made sure to promote virtue and call out evil actions. These are the successors of God's messengers. Ali bin Abu Ṭalib once said about them that they "participated in this world with their bodies, while their souls clung to the highest of realms."

This is what it looks like to put into practice the teachings of the Master of Messengers, who himself struck the perfect balance between his spiritual and worldly commitments. Jābir narrates about the Prophet ﷺ that when he would mention the Final Hour in his speech, his anger would intensify and his voice would rise as if he were warning against an imminent attack.[41] When Aishah was asked about how the Messenger of Allah ﷺ was when he was alone with his wives, she said, "He was the most gentle of all people, and the most respectable of all people. He was a man just like any of you, but he would laugh and smile often."[42] He ﷺ taught us by example how to strike the balance the spiritual dimensions of hope and fear and the practical concerns of living on earth and fulfilling the needs of our families, livelihood, communities, and ummah.[43]

When Fear is Counter-Productive

Sometimes, fear can grow so intense that it becomes a hindrance to our spiritual advancement. Fear is the fuel of self-purification and can propel us fast and far in our journey to coming closer to our Lord, but when it overwhelms our hearts and assumes control, then it will not be long until we burn out and give up.

Being alert to this tendency in ourselves and in those around us is of vital importance to our individual and communal welfare. If we take a look at how the Quran cultivates fear, we would see that its approach is assertive and direct. Fear is an important element of our relationship with God. But at the same time, the verses of fear are always invoked alongside hope, displaying the importance of balancing both emotions. Consider the following verses:

ٱلْحَمْدُ لِلَّهِ ٱلَّذِىٓ أَنزَلَ عَلَىٰ عَبْدِهِ ٱلْكِتَٰبَ وَلَمْ يَجْعَل لَّهُۥ عِوَجَا ۜ

قَيِّمًا لِّيُنذِرَ بَأْسًا شَدِيدًا مِّن لَّدُنْهُ وَيُبَشِّرَ ٱلْمُؤْمِنِينَ ٱلَّذِينَ يَعْمَلُونَ

ٱلصَّٰلِحَٰتِ أَنَّ لَهُمْ أَجْرًا حَسَنًا ۜ مَّٰكِثِينَ فِيهِ أَبَدًا ۜ

All praise is for Allah Who has revealed the Book to His servant, allowing no crookedness in it, perfectly upright, to warn of a severe torment from Him; and to give good news to the believers—who do good—that they will have a fine reward, in which they will remain forever... [18:1-3]

بَل كَذَّبُوا بِٱلسَّاعَةِ ۖ وَأَعْتَدْنَا لِمَن كَذَّبَ بِٱلسَّاعَةِ سَعِيرًا ۜ إِذَا رَأَتْهُم

مِّن مَّكَانٍ بَعِيدٍ سَمِعُوا لَهَا تَغَيُّظًا وَزَفِيرًا ۜ وَإِذَآ أُلْقُوا مِنْهَا مَكَانًا

ضَيِّقًا مُّقَرَّنِينَ دَعَوْا هُنَالِكَ ثُبُورًا ۜ لَّا تَدْعُوا ٱلْيَوْمَ ثُبُورًا وَٰحِدًا وَٱدْعُوا

ثُبُورًا كَثِيرًا ۜ قُلْ أَذَٰلِكَ خَيْرٌ أَمْ جَنَّةُ ٱلْخُلْدِ ٱلَّتِى وُعِدَ ٱلْمُتَّقُونَ ۚ كَانَتْ

لَهُمْ جَزَآءً وَمَصِيرًا ۜ لَّهُمْ فِيهَا مَا يَشَآءُونَ خَٰلِدِينَ ۚ كَانَ عَلَىٰ رَبِّكَ وَعْدًا

مَّسْـُٔولًا ۜ

In fact, they deny the Hour. And for the deniers of the Hour, We have prepared a blazing Fire. Once it sees them from a distance, they will hear it fuming and growling. And when they are tossed into a narrow place inside, chained together, then and there they will cry out for destruction. "Do not cry only once for destruction, but cry many times over!" Say, "Is this better or the Garden of Eternity

which the righteous have been promised, as a reward and an ultimate
destination? There they will have whatever they wish for, forever.
That is a promise, binding on your Lord." [25:11-16]

فَإِنَّمَا يَسَّرْنَٰهُ بِلِسَانِكَ لِتُبَشِّرَ بِهِ ٱلْمُتَّقِينَ وَتُنذِرَ بِهِۦ قَوْمًا لُّدًّا ۝

Indeed, We have made it easy with your tongue so that with it
you may give good news to the righteous and warn those who
are contentious. [19:97]

The Quran raises the heart's sense of fear without letting it reach the level of despair and hopelessness - so long as there is life, there is bright hope. The verses of admonishment and encouragement are intricately interwoven to form a transformational compound that keeps the soul balanced.

Hope in the promises of redemption and reward in the Quran can lead the inattentive reader to an imbalance as well. Someone who focuses purely on the verses of hope and mercy might mislead themselves to think that hard work and humility is not required on their end, and that God is bound by His boundless mercy to accept their unsatisfactory worship. But these verses are always paired with the mention of torment and punishment in order to recalibrate our senses.

نَبِّئْ عِبَادِىٓ أَنِّىٓ أَنَا ٱلْغَفُورُ ٱلرَّحِيمُ ۝ وَأَنَّ عَذَابِى هُوَ ٱلْعَذَابُ ٱلْأَلِيمُ ۝

Inform My servants that I am truly the All-Forgiving, Most
Merciful, and that My torment is indeed the most painful.
[15:49-50]

Let us emulate the Quran's wise approach to engaging fear and hope so as to strike the right balance between the two emotions. When we feel that we are nearing the point of despair, it would do us great benefit to pay more attention to the verses of hope, using them to restore optimism and brighten the depression in our hearts. It is of vital importance for us to understand the endless nature of God's mercy to counterbalance any intense fear that might drive us to the extreme of giving up. Hope is among the methods of increasing faith enumerated in this book, and the reader would do well to read closely the relevant chapter if they find that fear has a paralyzing effect on him or her. Imam Ahmad warned, "The traveler to God must remain between fear and hope. If either of them exceeds the other, the traveler will perish."

....

ENDNOTES

1. Tahtheeb Madārij al-Sālikeen, pp. 239-240
2. Muslim, #1048

3. al-Bazzār, #6987

4. *Ihyā' 'Uloom al-Deen*, v. 5, p. 44

5. Ibn Mājah, #4259

6. Al-Ghazali in *Ihyā' 'Uloom al-Deen* (4/451) and al-Qurtubi in *at-Tathkirah* (1/132)

7. *Rawdah al-'Uqalā'* by Ibn Hibban, pp. 285-286

8. al-Zuhd, Abu Dāwud, #73

9. Risālah al-Mustarshideen, al-Ḥārith al-Muḥāsibi with commentary by Shaykh Abdul-Fattāḥ Abu Ghuddah

10. Ibid, p. 111

11. *Ihyā' 'Uloom al-Deen* v. 5, p. 48

12. *al-Qiyāah al-Ṣughra* by Umar al-Ashqar, p. 81

13. al-Tadhkirah, al-QurTubi, v. 1, p. 27

14. Muslim, #1977; Ibn Mājah, #1571

15. *Ihyā' 'Uloom al-Deen* v. 5, pp. 47-48

16. *Bustān al-Wā'iẓeen*, p. 268

17. Al-Ḥākim, #7941

18. al-Bukhari, #2738 (in this wording); Muslim, #1627

19. This addition is found in the narration by Muslim cited above.

20. *Sifat al-Safwah* by Ibn al-Jawzi (2/189)

21. al-Qurtubi in *al-Tadhkirah*, v. 1, p. 32

22. al-Ṭayālisi, #1862, al-Hakim (4/360 #7921); al-Albani in *as-Silsilah as-Sahihah* (831)

23. al-Bukhari, #6416 (both hadith and saying of Ibn Umar)

24. Ahmad, #6502

25. Ibn Abu Dunyā, *Qasr al-Amal*, p. 169-170

26. Ahmad, #17142, and others

27. *Lata'if al-Ma'arif* by Ibn Rajab, p. 19-20

28. *Ihyā' 'Uloom al-Deen*, v. 4 pp. 254-255

29. Tahtheeb Madārij al-Sālikeen, p. 272

30. Ihyā' 'Uloom al-Deen, v. 4, p. 257

31. al-Bukhari, #5063, and Muslim #1108

32. The *hadith* is reported by al-Bukhari, #3206; and Muslim, #899

33. Ahmad (21241); Tirmithi (2457) and others

34. al-Bukhari, #4261; and Muslim, #2359

35. Ibn Abu Dunya, *Maqtal 'Ali bin Abi Ṭālib*, #6

36. al-Bayhaqi, *Shu'ab al-Iman*, #1003

37. al-Bukhari, #6134; and Muslim, #1159

38. Ibn al-Mubārak, al-Zuhd, #1104

39. Ibn Abu Dunyā, IṢṬinā' al-Ma'roof, #163

40. *Jami' Ma'mar ibn Rashid* (11/451) #20976)

41. Muslim, #867

42. *Musnad Ishāq bin Rāhooyah* #1750 and *Makarim al-Akhlaq* by ibn Abi Dunya (397)

43. Ibn Rajab, *Latā'if al-Ma'ārif*, p. 18-19 [with adaptations]

Quran

There is no greater way to increase faith than through interacting with the Quran. Once the heart has been rendered sensitive through fear and God-mindfulness, it can fully engage with the words of God. He, Glorified, says,

وَإِذَا تُلِيَتْ عَلَيْهِمْ ءَايَـٰتُهُۥ زَادَتْهُمْ إِيمَـٰنًا

...and when His verses are recited to them, it increases them in faith [8:2]

The Quran is a potent antidote for the illness of the heart.

يَـٰٓأَيُّهَا ٱلنَّاسُ قَدْ جَآءَتْكُم مَّوْعِظَةٌ مِّن رَّبِّكُمْ وَشِفَآءٌ لِّمَا فِى ٱلصُّدُورِ
وَهُدًى وَرَحْمَةٌ لِّلْمُؤْمِنِينَ ۝

O mankind, there has to come to you instruction from your Lord and healing for what is in the breasts and guidance and mercy for the believers. [10:57]

The Quran gives life to the heart and prepares for its journey to God.

وَكَذَٰلِكَ أَوْحَيْنَآ إِلَيْكَ رُوحًا مِّنْ أَمْرِنَا مَا كُنتَ تَدْرِى مَا ٱلْكِتَـٰبُ وَلَا ٱلْإِيمَـٰنُ
وَلَـٰكِن جَعَلْنَـٰهُ نُورًا نَّهْدِى بِهِۦ مَن نَّشَآءُ مِنْ عِبَادِنَا وَإِنَّكَ لَتَهْدِىٓ إِلَىٰ
صِرَٰطٍ مُّسْتَقِيمٍ ۝

And so We have sent to you (O Prophet) a revelation by Our command. You did not know of (this) Book and faith (before). But We have made it a light, by which We guide whoever We will of Our servants. And you are truly leading (all) to the Straight Path [5:42]

The Quran is a light that illuminates the path of those traveling
amidst the darkness of doubts.
It shines a light on the truth and
makes it easier to follow:
With the Quran as our lens, we are
able to see our way to Allah clearly:

قَدْ جَآءَكُم مِّنَ ٱللَّهِ نُورٌ وَكِتَٰبٌ مُّبِينٌ ۝ يَهْدِى بِهِ ٱللَّهُ مَنِ
ٱتَّبَعَ رِضْوَٰنَهُۥ سُبُلَ ٱلسَّلَٰمِ وَيُخْرِجُهُم مِّنَ ٱلظُّلُمَٰتِ إِلَى ٱلنُّورِ
بِإِذْنِهِۦ وَيَهْدِيهِمْ إِلَىٰ صِرَٰطٍ مُّسْتَقِيمٍ ۝

*There has come to you from Allah a light and a clear
Book. Allah guides with it those who pursue His
pleasure to the ways of peace and brings them out
from darknesses into the light, by His permission, and
guides them to a straight path.* [5:15-16]

هَٰذَا بَصَآئِرُ مِن رَّبِّكُمْ وَهُدًى وَرَحْمَةٌ لِّقَوْمٍ
يُؤْمِنُونَ ۝

*This (Quran) is an insight from your
Lord—a guide and a mercy for those who
believe."* [7:203]

Whoever abides by the Quran
has committed to the straight path
of God:

إِنَّا سَمِعْنَا قُرْءَانًا عَجَبًا ۝ يَهْدِىٓ إِلَى ٱلرُّشْدِ

*"Indeed, we have heard a wondrous recitation. It
leads to Right Guidance…"* [72:1-2]

The path of the Quran is one of
devotion. It is the path to *ar-Rab-
baniyah*, a God-centeredness in
every aspect of life.

وَلَٰكِن كُونُوا۟ رَبَّٰنِيِّۦنَ بِمَا كُنتُمْ تُعَلِّمُونَ
ٱلْكِتَٰبَ وَبِمَا كُنتُمْ تَدْرُسُونَ ۝

*Rather, he would say, "Be [rabbaniyeen]
devoted to the worship of your Lord
(alone)"—in accordance with what these
prophets read in the Scripture and what
they taught.* [3:79]

Whoever wishes to tread the
straight way must seek out the
Quran and hold to it.

إِنْ هُوَ إِلَّا ذِكْرٌ لِّلْعَٰلَمِينَ ۝ لِمَن شَآءَ مِنكُمْ أَن
يَسْتَقِيمَ ۝

*Surely this (Quran) is only a reminder
to the whole world— to whoever of you
wills to take the Straight Way.* [81:27-28]

Your Trusty GPS

The Quran is God's rope that never rips. Those who hold onto it tightly and follows its guidance reach unprecedented heights, ascending towards their Lord. The Messenger of Allah ﷺ once said to the Companions, **"Rejoice! Rejoice! Do you not testify that there is nothing worth of worship but God, and that I am the Messenger of Allah?"** They said, **"Certainly!"** He said, **"This Quran is a rope. One of its ends in God's hand, and the other end is in your hands. Hold onto it tightly, and you will never be lost or in danger."**[1]

يَـٰٓأَيُّهَا ٱلنَّاسُ قَدْ جَآءَكُم بُرْهَـٰنٌ مِّن رَّبِّكُمْ وَأَنزَلْنَآ إِلَيْكُمْ نُورًا مُّبِينًا ۝
فَأَمَّا ٱلَّذِينَ ءَامَنُوا۟ بِٱللَّهِ وَٱعْتَصَمُوا۟ بِهِۦ فَسَيُدْخِلُهُمْ فِى رَحْمَةٍ مِّنْهُ وَفَضْلٍ
وَيَهْدِيهِمْ إِلَيْهِ صِرَٰطًا مُّسْتَقِيمًا ۝

O humanity! There has come to you conclusive evidence
from your Lord. And We have sent down to you a brilliant
light. As for those who believe in Allah and hold fast to Him,
He will admit them into His mercy and grace and guide
them to Himself through the Straight Path. [4:174-175]

The Quran is the guide that leads you to God via the quickest route. Ibn al-Qayyim wrote,

> The primary tool in your migration to God must be constant contemplation of God's verses, to the point where it consumes your mind and preoccupies your heart. When the Quran is the filter through which your thoughts are produced, it becomes the heart's captain. Your journey becomes clear. You will be firm like the mountains, but light like the winds: "Now you see the mountains, thinking they are firmly fixed, but they are travelling like clouds. (That is) the design of God, Who has perfected everything. Surely He is All-Aware of what you do." [27:88][2]

Set the Quran as your GPS. Trust it will take you where you need to go. Listen to its commands, allow its words to settle deeply, and follow its exact directions to reach the most transcendent destination.

Don't Marginalize the Quran

People who neglect the Quran are truly disadvantaged, wasting their efforts searching for some other way to reach God. Can you imagine the regret they will feel upon realizing what was in front of them the whole time! They spent so much time and energy looking for a path to God, coming up with all sorts of arbitrary routines and theories, but refusing to see how easy the Quran makes it.

Some of us are impressed by these alternate routes to God, out of a sincere hope to come closer to Him. We might follow their regimens, hoping to find a faster route to God, but after a while we look down and find that we have not moved an inch. Ibn al-Qayyim draws our attention to this when he says:

> You must first remove your heart from being settled in this world to living in the next. Then expose it to the meanings of the Quran, uncover its hidden gems and contemplate upon it. You must understand what its objectives are and study its context, taking the time to look carefully into every single ayah for a cure for your heart. This, in reality, is the most direct, easy and accessible approach to the Highest Company. It is a safe path, protecting those who tread it from fear of any danger, sparing them the risk of hunger, thirst, and diseases that lie waiting for those who choose other paths. Allah placed on this path a guardian to protect and defend its travelers. Those who have been around, treading other paths and surviving their dangers, know the true value of this path.[3]

As Khabbāb bin al-Arat once said, "Come near to Allah however you can, but you will never come closer to Him through anything more beloved to Him than His own words."[4]

Miracle on our Bookshelf

The Quran is the blessing and miracle that Allah chose for us. He says,

$$أَوَلَمْ يَكْفِهِمْ أَنَّا أَنزَلْنَا عَلَيْكَ ٱلْكِتَٰبَ يُتْلَىٰ عَلَيْهِمْ إِنَّ فِى ذَٰلِكَ لَرَحْمَةً وَذِكْرَىٰ لِقَوْمٍ يُؤْمِنُونَ ۝$$

Is it not enough for them that We have sent down to you the Book, (which is) recited to them. Surely in this (Quran) is a mercy and reminder for people who believe. [29:51]

The miracle of the Quran is the greatest one that God has ever sent to mankind. It is greater than when Jesus revived the dead and healed the sick, greater than when Moses split the sea, and greater than all of the wonderful miracles that God gave to all other prophets. But what is the secret behind this miracle that makes it superior to all others?

One might say that the Quran's miracle is in its language and linguistic style, so clear and precise. Or one might claim that it lies in the extensive knowledge within it, its unparalleled legal code, or its universal applicability for all times and places. To answer this question, some point out that its greatest miracle is the challenge in its verses to produce a similar Quran and humanity's failure to meet that challenge.

These arguments are all ways in which the Quran is miraculous, but they miss the greatest point of all. The Quran is more than a divine proof from God; more than a book of healing and miracles. It is the catalyst for human transformation. The true secret of the Quran's miracle is the remarkable impact it has on an individual, whatever his or her condition. It has the ability to transform someone's mind, heart, and soul, raising them up as an individual who declares with confidence:

قُلْ إِنَّ صَلَاتِي وَنُسُكِي وَمَحْيَايَ وَمَمَاتِي لِلَّهِ رَبِّ ٱلْعَٰلَمِينَ ۝

"Surely my prayer, my worship, my life, and my death are all
for Allah—Lord of all worlds." [6:162]

This Quranic declaration encompasses the dimensions of the heart, the mind, and the *nafs* (ego or self). Attention is given in the Quran to every aspect of human identity.

The Quran nurtures the intellect, giving it due attention and activating its latent potential. It gives the mind the proper lens through which to view the world, planting the seed for Islam to grow deep within. The result is a fact-based, balanced intellectual perspective that is able to give everything its due right.

The Quran's effect on the heart is also extraordinary, as we shall explore further in this chapter. It plays a vital role in increasing the faith in our hearts and dispelling doubts from it. It brings listless hearts back to life and prepares it for its journey to God. As for the nafs, the Quran appeals to that aspect of human beings as well. The Quran tames our irascible self, equips it for battle and helps it stay firm upon obedience to God with true sincerity.

The Humbled Mountain

The Quran will have profound effects on those who take the time to engage with it. God gives an example of the power of the Quran:

لَوْ أَنزَلْنَا هَٰذَا ٱلْقُرْءَانَ عَلَىٰ جَبَلٍ لَّرَأَيْتَهُۥ خَٰشِعًا مُّتَصَدِّعًا مِّنْ
خَشْيَةِ ٱللَّهِ وَتِلْكَ ٱلْأَمْثَٰلُ نَضْرِبُهَا لِلنَّاسِ لَعَلَّهُمْ يَتَفَكَّرُونَ ۝

Had We sent down this Quran upon a mountain, you
would have certainly seen it humbled and torn apart
in awe of Allah. We set forth such comparisons for
people, (so) perhaps they may reflect. [59:21]

Imam al-Qurtubi, the great scholar of Islamic law and interpreter of the Quran, points out that if the mountains had intellect and could understand this Quran, they would have followed its commands, and you would have seen them crumble in awe of Allah despite how firm and solid they are. How should this revelation, which can pulverize the mountains, affect our hearts then? God tells us,

$$اللَّهُ نَزَّلَ أَحْسَنَ الْحَدِيثِ كِتَابًا مُتَشَابِهًا مَثَانِيَ تَقْشَعِرُّ مِنْهُ جُلُودُ$$
$$الَّذِينَ يَخْشَوْنَ رَبَّهُمْ ثُمَّ تَلِينُ جُلُودُهُمْ وَقُلُوبُهُمْ إِلَى ذِكْرِ اللَّهِ$$

Allah sent down the best message—a Book of perfect consistency and repeated lessons—which causes the skin (and hearts) of those who fear their Lord to tremble, then their skin and hearts soften at the mention of Allah. [39:23]

The Quran Sparks Faith

Part of believing in Allah is for our minds to be convinced of the truths that He revealed through His book and the Messenger ﷺ, while accepting and affirming those truths in our heart. Faith, however, naturally goes up and down. It rises when we busy our hearts with anything that is for Allah, and it falls when we respond to our desires. This is where the Quran plays a critical role in increasing our faith. It has a power—by Allah's permission—to activate our emotional connection and redirect our focus. Its deeply influencing lessons and magnetic effect on the soul provide us with fuel, in order to keep rising towards Allah with actions that He loves.

This spark coming from the Quran ignites an energy within us. This energy causes our faith to manifest on our limbs, causing us to cry in our prayers, humble ourselves, and do good deeds. The awareness of our heart increases, and so does our faith. Allah describes those who interact with the Quran in this way:

$$قُلْ آمِنُوا بِهِ أَوْ لَا تُؤْمِنُوا إِنَّ الَّذِينَ أُوتُوا الْعِلْمَ مِن قَبْلِهِ إِذَا$$
$$يُتْلَى عَلَيْهِمْ يَخِرُّونَ لِلْأَذْقَانِ سُجَّدًا ۝ وَيَقُولُونَ سُبْحَانَ رَبِّنَا إِن$$
$$كَانَ وَعْدُ رَبِّنَا لَمَفْعُولًا ۝ وَيَخِرُّونَ لِلْأَذْقَانِ يَبْكُونَ وَيَزِيدُهُمْ$$
$$خُشُوعًا ۝$$

Say, (O Prophet,) "Believe in this (Quran), or do not. Indeed, when it is recited to those who were gifted with knowledge before it (was revealed), they fall upon their faces in prostration, and say, 'Glory be to our Lord! Surely the promise of our Lord has been fulfilled.' And they fall down upon their faces weeping, and it increases them in humility."
[17:107-109]

Life to the Heart

A constant engagement with the Quran brings our hearts in harmony with it, and therefore increases our faith. With every square inch that faith grows in the heart, the portion controlled by our desires diminishes. We continue to interact with the Quran until finally we reach the point where faith becomes fully settled in our hearts, at home and taking full control, freeing us from lowly desires. This is the moment when our hearts become truly alive and aware. Ibn al-Qayyim says,

> The soul is born twice in this world: once when the human is actually born, and once again as a rebirth of the heart and soul. The heart gives birth to the soul anew, causing it to separate from its natural state just as the fetus separated from the womb upon its birth. Imam Ahmad reports in *Kitab al-Zuhd* (The Book on Austerity) that Jesus said to his disciples, "You will never surpass the realm of the sky until you are born a second time."[5]

It is upon this rebirth that the heart is brought back to life and begins its journey to Allah by knowing Him in this world and earning nearness to Him in the next.

There is nothing, then, more beneficial for the heart than reciting the Quran with contemplation and reflection, as Ibn al-Qayyim points out.[6] Doing so takes us through all of the stages and stations of spiritual development, garnering in our hearts love and yearning, fear and hope, motivation and trust, and unsurpassed enjoyment. It builds our sense of gratitude, patience, and all of the other qualities that maintain life in our hearts, while simultaneously driving us away from any sinful quality or action that corrupts them. The Quran creates a heart that is alive, sensitive and conscious of its purpose.

Examples of the Quran's Impact

What better model is there for Quranic transformation than the generation of the Prophet's Companions? Before Islam, they were uncultivated and ignorant. They fought wars over trivial matters, and many buried their infant daughters alive. The gods they worshipped were sometimes idols that they would craft out of food items, and when they got hungry, they would eat them. But then these men and women experienced the Quran. They went through the training program of the Quran, transforming into completely different people, exemplary models for generations to come.

This generational transformation testifies to the power of this Quran to reform people at their very roots. Who would believe that a group of barefoot, impoverished herdsmen in the desert who had nothing to show for themselves in the shadows of mighty, neighboring civilizations would, just a few decades later, become the most economically, militarily, and academically advanced empire on earth? A people who spent their days tending to livestock and their nights in drunken stupors, unable to see past tribal lines and class labels, suddenly began to set the standards for studying science, literature, and philosophy; redefined and revived the traditions of spirituality and austerity; practiced concepts of equality and social justice; and united under one banner of Islam to bring the rest of the world out of darkness and into light. It was nothing other than the Quran that transformed them. It recalibrated their priorities, broke their egos and established in their hearts a connection to God.

Within the span of one single generation, Allah's promise to those who act upon His revelation proved true:

$$إِنَّ ٱللَّهَ لَا يُغَيِّرُ مَا بِقَوْمٍ حَتَّىٰ يُغَيِّرُوا مَا بِأَنفُسِهِمْ$$

Indeed, Allah would never change a people's state until they change their own state. [13:11]

For such a radical transformation to occur in a short amount of time is nothing short of a miracle. In just a few years, a new world power emerged from the desert, dismantling empires, resetting priorities and establishing the model for just leadership.

$$وَمَنْ أَوْفَىٰ بِعَهْدِهِۦ مِنَ ٱللَّهِ$$

Who could be more faithful to his promise than God? [9:111]

The Prophet ﷺ and the Quran

The Companions' diligent engagement with the Quran and their never-ending pursuit to extract all of its benefits is what ultimately led to their transformation. They valued it and understood its true objective. Their teacher, after all, was none other than the Messenger of Allah ﷺ himself, leading them through his actions and demonstrating for them what it means to live by the Quran and devote one's life to it.

It was as if the Prophet ﷺ was a living and breathing version of the Quran. The Prophet's wife Aisha was once asked about the Prophet's manners and behavior. She responded by asking the questioner, "Don't you read the Quran? His manners were the Quran. He would be pleased and angered only according to it."[7]

The Prophet ﷺ once spent his entire prayer through the night repeating one single ayah:

$$إِن تُعَذِّبْهُمْ فَإِنَّهُمْ عِبَادُكَ وَإِن تَغْفِرْ لَهُمْ فَإِنَّكَ أَنتَ ٱلْعَزِيزُ ٱلْحَكِيمُ ۝$$

If You punish them, they belong to You after all. But if You forgive them, You are surely the Almighty, All-Wise." [5:118]

· ◆◆◆ ·

❝I prayed with the Prophet one night, and when he began to recite Surah al-Baqarah, I said to myself, 'He will bow after one hundred verses.' But then he passed it, so I said, 'He will recite it all in the first half of the prayer." When he came to the end of it, I said, "Now he will bow," but he began reciting Surah al-Nisa. He recited it all, and then began Surah Āli 'Imrān until its end. He recited slowly and smoothly, glorifying Allah after verses of glorification, requesting at verses of requests, and seeking refuge after verses of refuge."

Huthayfah ibn al-Yaman[8]

· ·

We can also marvel at the effect that the Quran had on the Prophet ﷺ himself. He says, "Surah Hud and its peers gave me grey hairs."[9] The Prophet ﷺ once stepped out of his house and heard an elderly woman reciting Surah al-Ghāshiyah, repeating the verses over and crying. She recited,

Has the news of the Overwhelming Event reached you? [88:1]

He started to cry as well, saying, "Indeed, it has. Indeed, it has."[10]

Quranic Generation

The Quran did not just impact the Companions as individuals, but it transformed their contextual reality and reordered their priorities. The story of Abbad bin Bishr illustrates this. He took turns with Ammar bin Yasir in guarding the Muslims during the battle of *Dhat al-Riqa*. He asked Ammar's permission to be the first one to stand guard for the first half of the night while Ammar rested. When he saw that the area was safe, Abbad stood in prayer during his watch. But then an enemy soldier shot him with an arrow. He carefully took out the arrow and continued to pray. The man shot him again, and again he took out the arrow and continued to pray. When the man shot him a third time, he was bowing down in prostration, and so he raised his voice to wake up Ammar.

Ammar later asked Abbad why he didn't wake him up after he had been shot by the first arrow. Abbad explained, "I was in the middle of reciting a surah, and I did not want to interrupt it until I completed it. Then when he shot me again, I bowed and called you. I swear by

Allah, if it were not for the fact that the Prophet ﷺ assigned me to keep this road safe, he would have killed me before I finished."[11]

Although unlikely to happen today, this behavior of Abbad's was not considered strange or crazy in the context of a community that grasped the significance of the Quran. Because they understood its critical value, the Companions were ever keen to learn from the Quran, contemplate its messages, and act upon it. Abdullah bin Mas'ood said, "When someone among us learned ten verses, he would not go further until he knew their meanings and acted upon them."[12]

◆◆◆

66 **W**e learned the Quran from people who told us that they would learn ten verses and would not move onto the next ten until they knew the applications of those verses. So we learned knowledge and action together. They told us that people will receive the Quran after us, drinking it like they drink water, not surpassing this," and then he pointed to his throat."

Abdul-Rahman al-Sullami, one of the students of the Companions[13]

Act upon the Quran

The Companions interacted with the Quran as if its instructions were immediate and urgent commands. They would race one another to act on what they learned verse by verse, even if it would take much longer to memorize the whole surah. Umar bin al-Khattab spent twelve whole years learning and memorizing Surah al-Baqarah. When he completed it, he sacrificed a camel out of gratitude.[14] His son Abdallah memorized al-Baqarah over eight years.[15]

Abdullah bin Mas'ood said, "Memorizing the words of the Quran was difficult for us, but acting upon it was easy. For those after us, memorizing the Quran will be easy, but acting upon it will be difficult."[16] Ibn Umar, who spent eight years memorizing Surah al-Baqarah, said,

> Some of the greatest Companions from the start of this religion only memorized a surah or two, but were blessed with the ability to act upon the Quran. Towards the end of this religion, even the children and the blind will memorize the Quran, but they will not act upon it.[17]

To Carry the Quran

The phrase "to carry" the Quran meant something special to the Companions. Abdullah bin 'Amr bin al-'As said, "Whoever memorizes the Quran carries something immense. His heart is promoted to the level of prophethood, except for the fact that he does not receive revelation."[18]

At the start of the Battle of Yamama, the Muslims took a big hit from the enemy apostates. The Muhajiroon rushed to pass their flag to Salim, the freed servant of Abu Hudhayfah. He knew that the reason he was entrusted with the standard was his mastery of the Quran, and so he was determined to stand his ground. During the heat of the battle, his right arm was cut off. He clung to the flag with his left, but it was soon cut as well. Salim brought the flag close to his chest, hugging it with whatever he had left of his limbs, and began reciting the verse:[19]

وَمَا مُحَمَّدٌ إِلَّا رَسُولٌ قَدْ خَلَتْ مِن قَبْلِهِ ٱلرُّسُلُ أَفَإِين مَّاتَ أَوْ قُتِلَ ٱنقَلَبْتُمْ
عَلَىٰٓ أَعْقَـٰبِكُمْ وَمَن يَنقَلِبْ عَلَىٰ عَقِبَيْهِ فَلَن يَضُرَّ ٱللَّهَ شَيْئًا وَسَيَجْزِى
ٱللَّهُ ٱلشَّـٰكِرِينَ وَمَا كَانَ لِنَفْسٍ أَن تَمُوتَ إِلَّا بِإِذْنِ ٱللَّهِ كِتَـٰبًا مُّؤَجَّلًا وَمَن
يُرِدْ ثَوَابَ ٱلدُّنْيَا نُؤْتِهِۦ مِنْهَا وَمَن يُرِدْ ثَوَابَ ٱلْءَاخِرَةِ نُؤْتِهِۦ مِنْهَا وَسَنَجْزِى
ٱلشَّـٰكِرِينَ ۝ وَكَأَيِّن مِّن نَّبِيٍّ قَـٰتَلَ مَعَهُۥ رِبِّيُّونَ كَثِيرٌ فَمَا وَهَنُوا لِمَآ
أَصَابَهُمْ فِى سَبِيلِ ٱللَّهِ وَمَا ضَعُفُوا وَمَا ٱسْتَكَانُوا وَٱللَّهُ يُحِبُّ ٱلصَّـٰبِرِينَ ۝

Muhammad is no more than a messenger; other messengers
have gone before him. If he were to die or to be killed, would
you regress into disbelief? Those who do so will not harm Allah
whatsoever. And Allah will reward those who are grateful.
No soul can ever die without Allah's Will at the destined time.
Those who desire worldly gain, We will let them have it, and
those who desire heavenly reward, We will grant it to them.
And We will reward those who are grateful.
(Imagine) how many devotees fought along with their prophets
and never faltered despite whatever (losses) they suffered in the
cause of Allah, nor did they weaken or give in! Allah loves those
who persevere. [3:144-146]

Even in his dying moments, Salim was carrying the Quran and bringing his actions to life through its powerful verses.

The respect of the early generations for those who not only memorized, but carried the Quran—and as we are learning, those terms were synonymous to them—is a significant shift from our default interactions with the Quran today. Carrying the Quran, and memorizing it along with action, require tremendous effort. The material conveniences we enjoy today certainly make it easy for us to learn and access information, but blind us to the hard work and diligence that education demanded in the past. The Quran you hold in your hands today was digitally printed on machine-cut paper and delivered to your local mosque on an airplane—some of us even think a hard copy book is too cumbersome, and so we only ever read or listen to the Quran app on our phones! Compare this to the method employed by Quran students for centuries: either memorizing purely through live dictation, or etching the verses by hand on wooden tablets, and then rubbing them away when it was time to move on to the next set of verses (this latter method is still employed in many schools throughout the world). This toil, though spiritually and intellectually fruitful, took its physical toll. One of the students of the Companions recalls that, "We used to know the students of the Quran by their pale faces."[20]

To carry the Quran does not mean to commit its words to memory through rote repetition. To carry the Quran means to internalize its meanings and act upon it as much as you can. Even as early as one or two generations after the Companions, this understanding of carrying the Quran began to be reduced to mere memorization. In an attempt to ralign the understanding of the rapidly growing Muslim community, Abu al-Darda' said in response to a man who came to him with news that his son had recently memorized the whole Quran, "O Allah, forgive! Only those who hear and obey truly carry the Quran."[21] In another report, Abu Mas'ood also clearly defines for us what it means to "carry" the Quran:

> The student of the Quran must be distinguished by praying during the night while others are asleep; by fasting during the day while others are eating; by crying while others laugh; by staying careful while others are negligent; by staying silent while others speak idly; by staying humble while others become conceited; and by staying grounded while others are overcome with emotion.[22]

Ignoring our Greatest Resource

The Quran is our scripture. It is the miracle which God chose to give to our Prophet ﷺ. It is the source of our honor and strength. It has the power to transform the lives of those who dedicate themselves to it, refining them to be God-centered (*rabbaniyoon*) servants. God instructs us to contemplate over the Quran in order for its objectives to solidify in our minds, its effects to settle in our hearts, and its lessons to manifest on our limbs. Allah, Exalted, says,

$$\text{كِتَٰبٌ أَنزَلْنَٰهُ إِلَيْكَ مُبَٰرَكٌ لِّيَدَّبَّرُوٓا۟ ءَايَٰتِهِۦ وَلِيَتَذَكَّرَ أُو۟لُوا۟ ٱلْأَلْبَٰبِ ۝}$$

(This is) a blessed Book which We have revealed to you (O Prophet) so that they may contemplate its verses, and people of reason may be mindful. [38:29]

Failing to contemplate over the Quran also puts our spiritual state at a great risk. God says,

أَفَلَا يَتَدَبَّرُونَ ٱلْقُرْءَانَ أَمْ عَلَىٰ قُلُوبٍ أَقْفَالُهَآ ۝

Do they not then reflect on the Quran? Or are there locks
upon their hearts? [47:24]

If only that were it! Instead it gets worse: someone who recites the Quran while heedless of its wonders and meanings has set himself up for grave failure, for there are lessons to be learned and teachings to be followed in every single ayah. These letters and verses will testify against you if you fail to heed their messages. The Messenger of Allah ﷺ said, **"Prayer is a light, charity is a testament, and patience is illumination. The Quran is a proof, either for you or against you."**[23] To take it even further, Ibn Umar said, "Every single letter in the Quran calls out to its reader, 'I am a messenger from God to you, so act upon me and take heed of my warnings!'"[24] Every time you sit down to read the Quran, you rise from your seat having either profited or lost, as one scholar from the early generations warned. This is related to the ayah,

وَنُنَزِّلُ مِنَ ٱلْقُرْءَانِ مَا هُوَ شِفَآءٌ وَرَحْمَةٌ لِّلْمُؤْمِنِينَ وَلَا يَزِيدُ ٱلظَّٰلِمِينَ إِلَّا خَسَارًا ۝

We send down the Quran as a healing and mercy for the
believers, but it only increases the wrongdoers in loss. [17:82]

The Messenger of Allah ﷺ took great care to warn his Companions against the Kharijites, a group of violent extremists that he said would emerge after his passing. Almost every report about them highlights their hollow relationship with the Quran. The Prophet ﷺ said, for example, **"Some people will emerge from the east who will recite the Quran, but it will not pass their throats. They will pass through the religion like an arrow passes through its target"**[25] (meaning that they will enter Islam, but take nothing from it). If they only let the Quran settle into their minds and hearts, they would have benefitted and maintained balance in their religion. But because their relationship with the Quran was shallow, they disastrously veered off the path.

Proper Recitation

A proper recitation of the Quran is one wherein we understand its meanings and act upon its lessons. The word used to describe recitation in the Quran is *tilawah*, from the verb *tala*, meaning to follow. Ibn Abbas explained the following verse,

ٱلَّذِينَ ءَاتَيْنَٰهُمُ ٱلْكِتَٰبَ يَتْلُونَهُۥ حَقَّ تِلَاوَتِهِ

Those We have given the Book recite it as it should be recited. [2:121]

He said that to "recite it as it should be recited," means to "follow it as it should be followed." One of his students, 'Ikrimah, points out that the verb is also used in Surah al-Shams:

$$وَٱلشَّمْسِ وَضُحَىٰهَا ۝ وَٱلْقَمَرِ إِذَا تَلَىٰهَا ۝$$

By the sun and its brightness, and the moon as it follows it. [91:1-2]

The proper recitation of the Quran does not only involve reciting the letters and words. It is a spiritual and intellectual activity as well. Ibn al-Qayyim emphasized this when he said,

> To properly recite the Quran is to ponder over and act upon the meanings. It means to believe in its statements and abide by its commands and prohibitions. It requires us to take the Quran as our guide, following wherever it takes us. To recite it means both to read its words and engage with its meanings, and engaging with its meanings is better than just reciting its words. The People of the Quran hold high ranks both in this life and the next, and they are none other than those who recite it "properly," as thus.[27]

Similarly, Umar bin al-Khattab says, "Do not be deluded by those who those who simply recite the Quran, for it is just words they pronounce. Look, instead, to those who act upon it."[28]

Al-Hasan al-Basri said in explaining the verse,

$$كِتَٰبٌ أَنزَلْنَٰهُ إِلَيْكَ مُبَٰرَكٌ لِّيَدَّبَّرُوٓا۟ ءَايَٰتِهِۦ وَلِيَتَذَكَّرَ أُو۟لُوا۟ ٱلْأَلْبَٰبِ ۝$$

(This is) a blessed Book which We have revealed to you (O Prophet) so that they may contemplate its verses, and people of reason may be mindful. [38:29]

> Only those who follow its actions contemplate its meanings, not those who memorized its words. One might even say, 'I recited the whole Quran without even missing a single letter!' while in reality he missed all of it, for you do not see the Quran manifest in his character or his actions.[29]

No Substitute for Reflection

Abdullah bin 'Amr narrates that he said, "Messenger of Allah, how often should the Quran be completed?" He responded, **"Recite it every month."** He said, "But I can do more than that," so he said, **"Recite it in twenty five days."** He said again, "But I can do more than that." He said, **"Recite it in twenty."** He repeated, "But I can do more than that," and he responded, **"Recite it in fifteen."** Again Abdallah said, "I can do more than that," and the Prophet ﷺ

said, **"Recite it in ten."** He prompted him with the same: "I can do more than that," and he responded, **"Recite it in seven."** When he asked him a last time, "I can do more than that," the Prophet ﷺ said, **"Anyone who recites it in less than three days does not comprehend it."**[30] Notice the Prophet's final response. He forbade him from reciting the entire Quran in less than three days because he would not comprehend what he recited if he did so. This shows us that reciting the Quran must be accompanied by reflection and deep thought.

Ibn Mas'ood said, "Do not prattle the Quran off like poetry, and don't scatter it as rotten dates are scattered on the ground. Stop to marvel at its wonders, move the hearts with it, and don't make your objective the end of the surah." Abu Jamrah once said to Ibn 'Abbas, "I recite quickly and complete the Quran in three days."[31] Ibn 'Abbas said, "I would prefer to recite only Surah al-Baqarah in one night, contemplating over it and reciting it smoothly, than to recite as you say you do."[32] To make things clearer, Ali ibn Abi Talib even said, "There is no good in reciting the Quran without contemplation."[33]

When reciting Quran, we must give priority to quality over quantity. This is something that the early scholars of our religion understood from the Quran itself. The tenth-century scholar from Baghdad, Abu Bakr al-Ājurri, wrote in his book about how the students of the Quran should act and behave: "I prefer to study only a little bit of Quran, with deep thought and reflection, over reciting a lot of it without thinking or reflecting at all. Anyone who recites the Quran would understand this!"[34] Mujāhid, the famous interpreter of the Quran, was once asked about one man who recited Surahs al-Baqarah and Āli 'Imrān in the same length of time that another man recited just Surah al-Baqarah.[35] He said that the one who recited only Surah al-Baqarah was better, and then recited the following verse as proof:

$$\text{وَقُرْءَانًا فَرَقْنَٰهُ لِتَقْرَأَهُۥ عَلَى ٱلنَّاسِ عَلَىٰ مُكْثٍ وَنَزَّلْنَٰهُ تَنزِيلًا ۝}$$

(It is) a Quran We have revealed in stages so that you may
recite it to people at a deliberate pace. [17:106]

A Common Misconception

Someone might say that they recite quickly in order to "stock up" on the rewards that come with recitation. The Prophet ﷺ did inform us, after all, **"Whoever recites one letter from Allah's book receives one reward, and each reward is multiplied by ten. I do not mean that 'Alif Lām Meem,' is one letter, but rather that 'Alif' is one letter, 'Lām' is another,' and 'Meem' is another."**[36]

The response to this zealous approach is that the true value and blessing of the Quran is found in its meanings, and the letters are the medium through which those meanings enter our hearts. The Prophet's objective was for people to recite more, encouraging them to do so by mentioning the great reward that comes with it. It is just like when a mother promises a reward for her child if he spends a certain amount of time on homework. Her objective is certainly not for the child to simply sit for that time staring at the paper or scribbling without any understanding. Rather it is an attempt to encourage her child to apply his efforts in thinking about the material and ensure his passing grade.

Considering the higher objectives of the Quran and connecting those to the reward that Allah attached to its recitation, we can see that this reward is an incentive for the Muslim to constantly keep the Quran close—not to tire their tongues with its recitation, but to have their hearts cling to its guidance. To recite the words only for their reward would, without a doubt, leave us in great loss of the life-changing guidance that the Quran contains. It would be missing the forest for the trees, and not benefitting from the purpose for which the Quran was revealed.

The Quran's Blessing

The value and blessing of the Quran lies in its deep meanings and its potential to transform those who read it, clarifying our minds, awakening our hearts, and training our nafs. When we read the Quran we learn who Allah is and how to worship Him sincerely. We become deeply insightful. Such benefits do not come out of simply reciting the text with our tongues, no matter the frequency or quantity of our recitation.

Ibn Taymiyah says that the point of any speech is to convey meaning, not to simply make sounds. Shouldn't this apply even more so to the Quran? He continues his point:

> Anyone with intellect can see that the objective for the revelation is for it to be followed and acted upon. Those who act upon it earn the title of "the People of the Quran." The objective of reciting it is to reflect upon it and understand its meanings, which is why Allah commanded for it to be recited smoothly and slowly, to give time for its insight to dawn upon its reader. We must adorn ourselves with the effects of its reminders.[37]

Getting the blessings of the Quran is not about how much you recite or memorize. It's not about how much of the Quran people hear you recite. Instead, it's about how much of the Quran they see in your actions. Now the only step between recitation and action is reflection.

Our Ailing Relationship

There is no doubt, even among non-Muslim historians, that the Quran we have in our hands is the very same Quran that the Companions read—the very same Quran that turned them into the giants they became. We must ask, then, what has changed today? Why is there this disparity in results? It would be a mistake to point to the Quran as the issue, thinking that it has lost its efficacy, relevance, or ability to touch people. It would be a mistake to think that Western Muslims cannot connect as effectively to the Quran simply due to a language barrier. Its miraculous effects are indeed universal and never-ending, transcending language, culture, and context, and Allah is the One who preserves its power.

The only logical conclusion, then, is that the fault is ours. Despite the fact that there is a Quran on every bookshelf, an ayah hanging in each one of our homes, hundreds of thousands of memorizers of the Quran walking in our midst, and Quran apps that cater to our preferences, it is rare to find evidence of the Quran's effects on our lives. We wander lost while the compass is in our own pockets.

This shocking disconnect is due to our failure to fulfill the Quran's right. We shortchange our relationship with the Quran, focusing solely on the words, neglecting to internalize the meanings. We mistakes the means for the end by focusing on recitation only for the reward, not realizing that we are cheating ourselves of the greater change that comes with deep reflection. We are impressed with ourselves when we reach the end of a long surah or finish a full schedule of reciting the entire Quran. But prioritizing quantity over quality prevents us from the true blessing and goal of reciting God's Scripture.

Consequences of Ignoring the Quran

A superficial relationship with the Quran has barred many people from being able to benefit from it as they should. Now the hearts of many Muslims are unmoved by it and they are blind to its wonders, widening the gap between where we should be and where we are and causing dissonance between what we say and what we do. Our priorities are misaligned, and our love for this world and attachment to it has only grown stronger. We must be proactive in improving our conditions, for God says,

$$ ذَٰلِكَ بِأَنَّ ٱللَّهَ لَمْ يَكُ مُغَيِّرًا نِّعْمَةً أَنْعَمَهَا عَلَىٰ قَوْمٍ حَتَّىٰ يُغَيِّرُوا مَا بِأَنفُسِهِمْ وَأَنَّ ٱللَّهَ سَمِيعٌ عَلِيمٌ ۟ $$

This is because Allah would never discontinue His favour to a people until they discontinue their faith. Surely Allah is All-Hearing, All-Knowing. [8:53]

We are actually falling into the very trap that the Messenger of Allah ﷺ feared for us. He once said, **"Your enemies will soon invite one another to devour you like a host invites his guests to his meal."** Someone asked, "Will this be due to our small numbers at that time?"

He responded, **"Rather you will be many at that time, but you will be shallow like scum on a stream. Allah will remove the fear of you from the hearts of your enemies, and Allah will cast weakness into your hearts."** Someone then asked, "O Messenger of Allah, what will that weakness be?" He said, **"Love for this world and an aversion to death."**[38]

It is clear now that we must come back to a true devotion to the Quran by giving it its due share of attention and engaging with it intellectually and spiritually. It is time for us to begin our journey of self-transformation by submitting ourselves wholeheartedly to the Quran, working to improve ourselves so that Allah will improve our conditions:

$$\text{إِنَّ ٱللَّهَ لَا يُغَيِّرُ مَا بِقَوْمٍ حَتَّىٰ يُغَيِّرُوا مَا بِأَنفُسِهِمْ}$$

*Indeed, Allah would never change a people's state until they
change their own state.* [13:11]

Any self-improvement method that does not start with the Quran will not produce sound results. Why should we begin with anything else when the Quran is a divine remedy, sent down by God to cure us of our illnesses and return our hearts to clarity?

$$\text{يَـٰٓأَيُّهَا ٱلنَّاسُ قَدْ جَاءَتْكُم مَّوْعِظَةٌ مِّن رَّبِّكُمْ وَشِفَآءٌ لِّمَا فِي ٱلصُّدُورِ}$$
$$\text{وَهُدًى وَرَحْمَةٌ لِّلْمُؤْمِنِينَ ۝}$$

*O humanity! Indeed, there has come to you a warning from
your Lord, a cure for what is in the hearts, a guide, and a
mercy for the believers.* [10:57]

Satan's Tricks

Many make the mistake of thinking that they are not qualified to contemplate the Quran's meanings. They think that it is a task reserved for scholars and the intellectual elite. But if this is the case, then why does Allah repeatedly implore everyone to reflect over it?

Imam al-Qurṭubi makes this point in his explanation of the verse,

$$\text{أَفَلَا يَتَدَبَّرُونَ ٱلْقُرْءَانَ وَلَوْ كَانَ مِنْ عِندِ غَيْرِ ٱللَّهِ لَوَجَدُوا فِيهِ ٱخْتِلَـٰفًا كَثِيرًا ۝}$$

*Do they not then reflect on the Quran? Had it been from
anyone other than Allah, they would have certainly found in
it many inconsistencies.* [4:82]

He says, "This ayah proves that reflecting over the Quran is mandatory, so that its meanings can be internalized."[39] Ibn Hubayrah, a 12th century scholar who served as vizier to the Caliph in Baghdad also affirms this. He says, "One of Satan's strategies is to divert God's servants from reflecting over the Quran, because he indeed knows how much knowledge comes with it. He will convince us that our reflection is just a passing and unqualified thought, causing us to refrain from sharing it out of a false sense of piety."[40]

It is true that more doors of understanding open with the more knowledge you have, and that limited knowledge would prevent one from understanding on a deeper level. But in either case, the main objective remains: to stimulate the heart and mind with God's words. Some scholars with the highest pedigrees in Islamic knowledge can make the critical mistake of engaging with the Quran solely through their knowledge and not with their hearts, while a layman who has some basic level of understanding can be profoundly impacted by his simple understanding of an ayah, changing his course in life. We all know people whose lives were changed because of a single ayah from the Quran, despite having little to no background knowledge of its linguistic breakdown or theological implications. This is living proof of those whom Allah describes in the ayah,

اللَّهُ نَزَّلَ أَحْسَنَ ٱلْحَدِيثِ كِتَٰبًا مُّتَشَٰبِهًا مَّثَانِيَ تَقْشَعِرُّ مِنْهُ جُلُودُ ٱلَّذِينَ يَخْشَوْنَ رَبَّهُمْ ثُمَّ تَلِينُ جُلُودُهُمْ وَقُلُوبُهُمْ إِلَىٰ ذِكْرِ ٱللَّهِ

Allah sent down the best message—a Book of perfect consistency and repeated lessons—which causes the skin (and hearts) of those who fear their Lord to tremble, then their skin and hearts soften at the mention of Allah. [39:23]

God does not honor certain people over others because of the amount of information held in their brains. It is, in fact, by the state of their hearts. God says,

إِنَّ أَكْرَمَكُمْ عِندَ ٱللَّهِ أَتْقَىٰكُمْ

Surely the most noble of you in the sight of Allah is the most righteous among you. [49:13]

Consider what happened when a bedouin man was sitting with the Messenger of Allah ﷺ, and he heard him recite,

فَمَن يَعْمَلْ مِثْقَالَ ذَرَّةٍ خَيْرًا يَرَهُ ۝ وَمَن يَعْمَلْ مِثْقَالَ ذَرَّةٍ شَرًّا يَرَهُ ۝

So whoever does a speck's weight of good will see it. And whoever does a speck's weight of evil will see it. [99:7-8]

The bedouin asked, "O Messenger of Allah, even a speck's weight?" He replied, "Yes." The bedouin man stood up abruptly, shouting, "How terrifying!" The Messenger of Allah ﷺ said, **"Faith has entered this bedouin man's heart."**[41]

No Excuses

No one has any excuse in failing to reflect over the Quran and develop a beautiful relationship with it. For those who deprive themselves of this by complaining that they don't have enough knowledge, Imam al-Qurṭubi has a response in his explanation of the ayah,

لَوْ أَنزَلْنَا هَٰذَا ٱلْقُرْءَانَ عَلَىٰ جَبَلٍ لَّرَأَيْتَهُۥ خَٰشِعًا مُّتَصَدِّعًا مِّنْ خَشْيَةِ ٱللَّهِ ۚ
وَتِلْكَ ٱلْأَمْثَٰلُ نَضْرِبُهَا لِلنَّاسِ لَعَلَّهُمْ يَتَفَكَّرُونَ ۝

Had We sent down this Quran upon a mountain, you would
have certainly seen it humbled and torn apart in awe of Allah.
We set forth such comparisons for people, (so) perhaps they
may reflect. [59:21]

Al-Qurtubi says,

> Allah commands us all to pay close attention to the lessons in the Quran, leaving
> no valid excuse for anyone to abandon reflecting over it. Even if a mountain were
> given the capacity to think, it would comply with the Quran's commands. And
> despite how firm and solid it is, you would see it crumble out of humility and awe
> of Allah. The phrase, "We set forth such comparisons for people," is a point for
> us to compare our lack of motivation by its promises and alarm by its threats to
> the hypothetical humility and awe of the mountain, which would have become
> humble and crumbled.[42]

No matter what your condition or educational background is, you do not compare to the strength of a mountain. And while this mountain would collapse into pieces if God's words were revealed to it, we—the Quran's audience—stand unconcerned and unimpressed due to the poor quality of our hearts. Allah did not designate a specific group of people to contemplate over the Quran to the exclusion of others. Anyone with a sound intellect, who uses their mind to coordinate their own personal affairs and distinguish between good and bad is able to reflect on the meanings of the Quran. Abu Imraan al-Juni said, "By Allah, our Lord has explained and varied the Quran for us in such a way that would have crumbled and leveled the mountain."

Mālik bin Deenār would often recite that same verse,

لَوْ أَنزَلْنَا هَٰذَا ٱلْقُرْءَانَ عَلَىٰ جَبَلٍ لَّرَأَيْتَهُۥ خَٰشِعًا مُّتَصَدِّعًا مِّنْ خَشْيَةِ
ٱللَّهِ ۚ وَتِلْكَ ٱلْأَمْثَٰلُ نَضْرِبُهَا لِلنَّاسِ لَعَلَّهُمْ يَتَفَكَّرُونَ ۝

Had We sent down this Quran upon a mountain, you would
have certainly seen it humbled and torn apart in awe of Allah.

> *We set forth such comparisons for people, (so) perhaps they*
> *may reflect.* [59:21]

Then he would say, "I swear to you all, any heart that truly believes in this Quran will crumble."[43]

The Quran is a book of guidance and a way of life. Allah sent it down to direct us to what is good for us in both this world and the next. If we don't actualize this purpose, then what good is the movement of our tongues? To recite the Quran properly is not only to perfect the way it sounds when you recite it. To recite the Quran properly is to reflect upon it and follow it.

When Hearts are Sick

Some people think that we must first purify our diseased hearts before coming to the Quran, and that a sick heart cannot really benefit from the Quran. They even misappropriate a maxim of Islamic self-development literature, "clean out before you decorate," to support their view. But if this was true in our relationship the Quran, then really what good would the Quran be? Did God not describe it as a cure for the hearts? You cannot cure something that is not ill. God says,

$$
\text{يَـٰٓأَيُّهَا ٱلنَّاسُ قَدْ جَآءَتْكُم مَّوْعِظَةٌ مِّن رَّبِّكُمْ وَشِفَآءٌ لِّمَا فِى ٱلصُّدُورِ}
$$
$$
\text{وَهُدًى وَرَحْمَةٌ لِّلْمُؤْمِنِينَ ۞}
$$

> *O mankind, there has to come to you instruction from your*
> *Lord and healing for what is in the breasts and guidance and*
> *mercy for the believers.* [10:57]

The Quran is the most effective treatment for a sick heart. Its light sears through darkness, extinguishing it and removing the doubts and desires that come with it. God says,

$$
\text{بَلْ نَقْذِفُ بِٱلْحَقِّ عَلَى ٱلْبَـٰطِلِ فَيَدْمَغُهُۥ فَإِذَا هُوَ زَاهِقٌ}
$$

> *In fact, We hurl the truth against falsehood, leaving it crushed,*
> *and it quickly vanishes.* [21:18]

Yes, we may not feel it at first. Our hearts might still be polluted with sins and lowly habits. We also may struggle with a language barrier, perceived lack of time, and deficiencies in mental focus. But this veil cannot stand long in the face of mindful effort, consistent recitation, and genuine reflection on the Quran. With every divine word that enters our heart, some filth is removed, and the heart comes one step closer to returning to its clear state. If we are persistent and diligent with the Quran for long enough, we will find our hearts functioning at full capacity. God says,

أَنزَلَ مِنَ ٱلسَّمَآءِ مَآءً فَسَالَتْ أَوْدِيَةٌ بِقَدَرِهَا فَٱحْتَمَلَ ٱلسَّيْلُ زَبَدًا
رَّابِيًا وَمِمَّا يُوقِدُونَ عَلَيْهِ فِي ٱلنَّارِ ٱبْتِغَآءَ حِلْيَةٍ أَوْ مَتَـٰعٍ زَبَدٌ مِّثْلُهُۥ
كَذَٰلِكَ يَضْرِبُ ٱللَّهُ ٱلْحَقَّ وَٱلْبَـٰطِلَ فَأَمَّا ٱلزَّبَدُ فَيَذْهَبُ جُفَآءً وَأَمَّا مَا
يَنفَعُ ٱلنَّاسَ فَيَمْكُثُ فِي ٱلْأَرْضِ كَذَٰلِكَ يَضْرِبُ ٱللَّهُ ٱلْأَمْثَالَ ۝

He sends down rain from the sky, causing the valleys to flow,
each according to its capacity. The currents then carry along
rising foam, similar to the slag produced from metal that
people melt in the fire for ornaments or tools. This is how
Allah compares truth to falsehood. The (worthless) residue is
then cast away, but what benefits people remains on the earth.
This is how Allah sets forth parables. [13:17]

If we attempt to purify our hearts before coming to the Quran, we will stagnate in our spiritual journey. The problem will not be fixed, and new issues will keep cropping up. There will never come a day when we can truly claim to be completely purified, and so those who take this approach will prevent themselves from the light of the Quran, deprived of its healing cure.

Tools for Interacting with the Quran

The Quran is the Companion guide to our hearts. It has a miraculous power to awaken and develop our *iman* (faith). In our pursuit of a close relationship with God, the Quran lies at the center of our quest. So, the natural question for us now is how do we return to the Quran? What are the methods available to us, and how can we make its effects on our heart more pronounced? Is it easier said than done? Before we delve into these answers, we must emphasize two important conditions that are necessary to unleash the Quran's potential: Fear (an action of the heart) and improving recitation skills (an action of the limbs).

Why Fear is Relevant

God, Mighty and Majestic, tells us in His book that the ones who benefit most from the Quran are those who are fearful and mindful of God. He says,

فَذَكِّرْ بِٱلْقُرْءَانِ مَن يَخَافُ وَعِيدِ ۝

So remind with the Quran those who fear My warning. [50:45]

The Quran—how could we begin to describe it in human words! But only those hearts that contain an element of fear and awe within them will be able to interact and heeds its lessons:

وَأَنذِرْ بِهِ ٱلَّذِينَ يَخَافُونَ أَن يُحْشَرُوٓا۟ إِلَىٰ رَبِّهِمْ لَيْسَ لَهُم مِّن دُونِهِۦ وَلِىٌّ وَلَا شَفِيعٌ لَّعَلَّهُمْ يَتَّقُونَ ۝

Warn with this (Quran) those who are awed by the prospect
of being gathered before their Lord—when they will have no
protector or intercessor besides Him—so perhaps they will be
mindful (of Him). [6:51]

Those who fear God are the only ones who benefit from His message. His words only increase their level of mindfulness, fear, and humility.

طه ۝ مَآ أَنزَلْنَا عَلَيْكَ ٱلْقُرْءَانَ لِتَشْقَىٰٓ ۝ إِلَّا تَذْكِرَةً لِّمَن يَخْشَىٰ

Tā-Hā. We have not revealed the Quran to you (O Prophet)
to cause you distress, but as a reminder to those in awe (of
Allah). [20:1-3]

Trying to find ways to benefit from the Quran—as important as it surely is—cannot come before increasing the sense of fear of God in your heart. It's the first step of preparation, priming your heart to accept easily the words of the Lord of All Creation, ensuring that its meanings reverberate. Fear is a piercing awareness of your helplessness and need for God, and an essential prerequisite in your journey of self-transformation through the Quran.

A heart without *taqwa* (God-mindfulness) cannot take much away from the Quran. Notice how God says,

هَٰذَا بَيَانٌ لِّلنَّاسِ وَهُدًى وَمَوْعِظَةٌ لِّلْمُتَّقِينَ ۝

This is an insight to humanity—a guide and a lesson to the
God-fearing. [3:138]

The verses in the Quran play different roles for different kinds of people. They are insightful verses for anyone who reads them, as many non-Muslims have acknowledged the wonders and wisdom of the Quran. But those same verses serve as something greater—guidance and lessons for hearts full with fear of God. If we truly want to feel the effects of the Quran, we need to prepare ourselves by instilling the fear and mindfulness of God that is due to Him.

The Student and the Exam

When we are fearful, our mindset is notably different. We are sensitive and on guard, listening to any advice that might soothe our worries and calm us down. Someone who perceives himself secure does the exact opposite, feeling no need for extra precautions.

Compare a student's attitude toward the final exam at the beginning of the year to her feelings towards the end. She is fully aware of the final exam, but feels safe for the most part because of how far away it seems. You'll find her taking it easy in her studies, not as keen on sticking to a study schedule or asking for help. She doesn't feel urgency yet to make such preparations.

As the final exam draws closer, the fear of failure intensifies. You'll notice her studying for longer periods of time, sitting in the silent section of the library instead of the group study area where friends might distract her. She is now organizing her notes and clarifying questions that she didn't understand the first time, asking her classmates for help and looking up explanations for specific topics online. All of this stems from the increased fear of the final exam. She may have even heard the same answer to her question and read the same material in the beginning of the semester, but didn't pay as much attention to it because she felt there was so much time.

This example helps us understand the attitude we should bring to our interactions with the Quran. We must approach the Quran's guidance and commands with an urgency rooted in fear if we wish to truly benefit. Come to the Quran with your heart trembling out of caution and awe of Allah. We should be afraid of a heart that is too encrusted to receive guidance. We should be afraid of the consequences of not giving the revelation its due attention. Isn't it true that death might strike tomorrow? Do you not fear your stance with your Lord? Even the Prophet's Companions—the most righteous men and women to walk the earth—felt this fear:

إِنَّمَا تُنذِرُ مَنِ ٱتَّبَعَ ٱلذِّكْرَ وَخَشِيَ ٱلرَّحْمَٰنَ بِٱلْغَيْبِ فَبَشِّرْهُ بِمَغْفِرَةٍ وَأَجْرٍ كَرِيمٍ ۝

You can only warn those who follow the Reminder and are in awe of the Most Compassionate without seeing Him. So give them good news of forgiveness and an honourable reward.
[36:11]

This element of fear as a prerequisite to scripture was even established at the time of Moses. Allah says,

وَلَمَّا سَكَتَ عَن مُّوسَى ٱلْغَضَبُ أَخَذَ ٱلْأَلْوَاحَ وَفِي نُسْخَتِهَا هُدًى وَرَحْمَةٌ لِّلَّذِينَ هُمْ لِرَبِّهِمْ يَرْهَبُونَ ۝

When Moses' anger subsided, he took up the Tablets whose text contained guidance and mercy for those who stand in awe of their Lord. [7:154]

Ibn al-Qayyim similarly points out,[44]

> The crux of happiness is to internalize the reality of God's promises. A heart that lacks conviction in these promises is completely ruined and has absolutely no chance of success. God, Most High, even tells us that his signs and warnings will only benefit those who believe in his threat of punishment in the afterlife. These are the primary audience of the warnings, and they are those who will benefit from God's verses to the exclusion of all others, as God says:

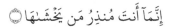

إِنَّمَآ أَنتَ مُنذِرُ مَن يَخْشَىٰهَا ۝

You are only sent to warn those who fear it. [79:45]

Improving Recitation skills

The other condition that we must seek out is to improve our pronunciation of the Quran and learn the rules of proper pronunciation and recitation. Reciting the Quran correctly is important in understanding its meanings. It makes the recitation more smooth and enjoyable, allowing it to have a greater effect on the heart and forcing the mind to pay attention to its words. You don't even have to memorize every technical term or know the points over which some scholars disagreed with others, as long as you can recite properly enough to achieve a smooth, rhythmic, meaningful recitation.

Some wonder why the rhythmic recitation is necessary. Shouldn't correct pronunciation be enough? What they fail to realize is that a smooth, rhythmic recitation helps us benefit from the Quran in many ways, such as extending the period of time that we recite any given ayah, giving meanings a chance to sink deeper into our hearts. Ibn Ḥajar, who wrote the most famous commentary on al-Bukhari's Sahih collection, pointed out that reciting slowly and steadily allows one to clearly pronounce each letter. "Giving more time to this process is more conducive to understanding its meanings," he wrote.[45]

Another benefit that comes from a rhythmic recitation is that it evokes emotion. Contemplation is not a strictly intellectual endeavor—you must engage the meanings with every facet of your existence in order for them to have a real effect on the heart and increase your faith. This is why we find the Prophet's instruction to beautify our voices with the Quran; it is meant to pull at your buried feelings within, and can do so more effectively when recited properly.

The Prophet ﷺ even gave instructions that seem off putting at first glance. He ﷺ said, **"This Quran came down with sorrow. When you read it, cry, and if you cannot cry, then make yourself cry. Recite it with melody, for whoever does not recite it with melody is not one of us."**[46] The command to "make yourself cry" must be understood to mean in private and for your own benefit—to break through the hardness of your own heart by force. It is obviously looked down upon to make yourself cry in front of others in order to impress them. This is similar to the idea of dressing for the job you want, not the job you have, and we should be aiming to be so soft at heart that God's words bring us to tears. Imam al-Ghazāli explains in his magnum opus Iḥyā' 'Uloom al-Deen:

> Reciting the Quran as it should be recited means for the tongue, the mind, and the heart to all take part in the act together. The tongue's duty is to pronounce the letters correctly and recite beautifully, the mind's duty is to explore the meanings, and the heart's duty is to take heed and be responsive to the words with alarm and eagerness to comply. So the tongue recites, the mind explains, and the heart internalizes.[47]

Daily Quran Prescription

In order to advance beyond just reciting the Quran with our tongue, you must be patient and persistent. Some hard work will be required - nothing ventured, nothing gained. As this chapter lays out the various recommendations that prepare you to be moved and shaken by the Quran, examine your motivations. Are you ready to stick to the plan and not give up at the first sign of resistance?

The most essential component of the plan is an uncompromising commitment to a daily Quran habit. This daily appointment is indispensable to having a meaningful relationship with God's revelation. In order for the Quran to have its effect, you must frequent your contact with it and increase the quality time you spend in its presence. Daily exposure to the Quran is essential for your soul as sunlight is to your body. Giving up even one day of recitation has detrimental effects.

The fact of the matter is that God knows how busy you are and how many items are left on your to-do list. He would never let a single second dedicated for His sake go unrewarded. The more time you dedicate to His revelation, the more of its treasures and secrets He will give to you.

This was experienced firsthand by Ibn Taymiyah when he was imprisoned and prevented from reading any books. He decided to dedicate his entire time in prison to reciting the Quran, and said about his experience, "In this fortress of solitude and seclusion, God has opened up to me many of the Quran's meanings. He has granted me a foundation in knowledge that so many other scholars wish they had. I regret wasting so much of my time with anything but the Quran!"[48]

We are constantly being bombarded by new ideas, products, and people, each coming with its own test and trial. In this state of flux, Muslims must be reminded of the constant principles of Islam. We live in an environment where our hearts require perpetual healing, and we thirst for doses of spirituality to counter the dominant materialistic culture. Here is where the Quran plays a great role in strengthening our immunity and reminding us of our goal.

Daily Quran Keeps the Heart Firm

God says in the Quran,

$$قُلْ نَزَّلَهُ رُوحُ ٱلْقُدُسِ مِن رَّبِّكَ بِٱلْحَقِّ لِيُثَبِّتَ ٱلَّذِينَ ءَامَنُوا وَهُدًى وَبُشْرَىٰ لِلْمُسْلِمِينَ ۝$$

Say that the Holy Spirit has brought the Revelation with the Truth step by step from your Lord, to strengthen the believers and as guidance and good news to those who submit. [16:102]

The Quran is one of the greatest ways to attain firmness, as God says to the Prophet ﷺ,

$$وَكُلًّا نَّقُصُّ عَلَيْكَ مِنْ أَنۢبَآءِ ٱلرُّسُلِ مَا نُثَبِّتُ بِهِۦ فُؤَادَكَ وَجَآءَكَ فِى هَٰذِهِ ٱلْحَقُّ وَمَوْعِظَةٌ وَذِكْرَىٰ لِلْمُؤْمِنِينَ ۝$$

So [Muhammad], We have told you the stories of the prophets to make your heart firm and in these accounts truth has come to you, as well as lessons and reminders for the believers.
[11:120]

The Quran relates for us in epic detail the struggles of Prophets in preaching God's message to their peoples. Reciting their stories so often makes us feel like we are there by their sides. Reflecting on how widespread injustice and evil was in their societies helps us put the struggles of modern-day scholars and teachers into perspective—they are, after all, the inheritors of the Prophets. It also makes very clear to us that although these modern struggles are difficult, they can be overcome, as Allah gave victory to those prophets who had fewer resources and more factors working against them than we do today. The tyrants among us today, who are undoubtedly deplorable, are still no match for the Pharaoh, and the arrogance and injustice today is still not at the level of Thamud and 'Ad.

Over and over, the Quran shows us how these prophets were rejected and fought against, and then tells us of their redemption and victory by God's help. It teaches us that history indeed repeats itself, and though we may currently be at a low point in the cycle of civilizations, the pious will ultimately emerge victorious. God says, addressing the Prophet ﷺ directly,

وَلَقَدْ كُذِّبَتْ رُسُلٌ مِّن قَبْلِكَ فَصَبَرُوا عَلَىٰ مَا كُذِّبُوا وَأُوذُوا حَتَّىٰ أَتَىٰهُمْ نَصْرُنَا
وَلَا مُبَدِّلَ لِكَلِمَٰتِ ٱللَّهِ وَلَقَدْ جَآءَكَ مِن نَّبَإِى ٱلْمُرْسَلِينَ ۝

Other messengers were disbelieved before you, and they
bore their rejection and persecution steadfastly until Our aid
arrived- no one can alter God's promises. You have already
received accounts of these messengers. [6:34]

He also says in Surah Hud, which is filled with mention of the struggles of the previous prophets,

تِلْكَ مِنْ أَنۢبَآءِ ٱلْغَيْبِ نُوحِيهَآ إِلَيْكَ مَا كُنتَ تَعْلَمُهَآ أَنتَ وَلَا قَوْمُكَ مِن
قَبْلِ هَٰذَا فَٱصْبِرْ إِنَّ ٱلْعَٰقِبَةَ لِلْمُتَّقِينَ ۝

This is one of the stories of the unseen, which we reveal to you
(O Prophet). Neither you nor your people knew it before this.
So be patient! Surely the ultimate outcome belongs (only) to
the pious. [11:49]

Anyone with a speck of doubt about this reality can travel all throughout the world and see what the tyrants of nations past have left to claim. God says,

أَفَلَمْ يَسِيرُوا۟ فِى ٱلْأَرْضِ فَيَنظُرُوا۟ كَيْفَ كَانَ عَٰقِبَةُ ٱلَّذِينَ مِن قَبْلِهِمْ كَانُوٓا۟ أَكْثَرَ
مِنْهُمْ وَأَشَدَّ قُوَّةً وَءَاثَارًا فِى ٱلْأَرْضِ فَمَآ أَغْنَىٰ عَنْهُم مَّا كَانُوا۟ يَكْسِبُونَ ۝

Have they not travelled throughout the land to see what was
the end of those who were (destroyed) before them? They were
far superior in might and (richer in) monuments throughout
the land, but their (worldly) gains were of no benefit to them.
[40:82]

And to the Meccans who lived in the same region of many of these ancient civilizations who were destroyed by their own wrongdoing, God says,

وَإِنَّكُمْ لَتَمُرُّونَ عَلَيْهِم مُّصْبِحِينَ ۝ وَبِٱلَّيْلِ أَفَلَا تَعْقِلُونَ ۝

You (Meccans) certainly pass by their ruins day and night.
Will you not then understand? [37:137-138]

Imagine living at the time of the Pharaoh. God tells us about his ruthless oppression and cruel tactics:

إِنَّ فِرْعَوْنَ عَلَا فِى ٱلْأَرْضِ وَجَعَلَ أَهْلَهَا شِيَعًا يَسْتَضْعِفُ طَآئِفَةً مِّنْهُمْ يُذَبِّحُ

أَبْنَآءَهُمْ وَيَسْتَحْىِ نِسَآءَهُمْ إِنَّهُۥ كَانَ مِنَ ٱلْمُفْسِدِينَ ۝

*Indeed, Pharaoh (arrogantly) elevated himself in the land and
divided its people into (subservient) groups, one of which he
persecuted, slaughtering their sons and keeping their women.
He was truly one of the corruptors.* [28:4]

Can you feel the terror that wrung the hearts of the Israelites? Can you see the tears falling from the eyes of the young mothers who lost their sons? How hopeless and miserable do you think they felt, seeing how much power and luxury the Pharaoh and his people had, compared to their own state of weakness and desperation?

But you'd be wrong to stop there, as that was not the end of the story. After many long and agonizing years following the birth of Moses, it was the Pharaoh who became humiliated. He and his army were crushed by the sea, left for dead as Moses and his followers marched on to safety. Now, bask in their redemption and victory. Picture the tears, now of relief, from seeing the Pharaoh's bitter end. Their certainty in God's promise now made them regret their despair, and all whispers of doubt faded to silence as the masses cheered in glee as God's victory and power was now clear.

Such stories are repeated all throughout the Quran. God is assuring us of His victory so that we don't fall into the trap of despair when we encounter injustice, pain, and rejection. God encourages us, instead, to see these oppressors and tyrants as insignificant. We must trust and have certainty that Allah's promise is indeed true.

فَٱصْبِرْ إِنَّ وَعْدَ ٱللَّهِ حَقٌّ وَلَا يَسْتَخِفَّنَّكَ ٱلَّذِينَ لَا يُوقِنُونَ ۝

*So be patient, for the promise of Allah certainly is true. And
do not be disturbed by those who have no sure faith.* [30:60]

When we engage on a daily basis with these heart-strengthening stories that pour from the pages of the Quran, we are less likely to despair when we encounter difficulty.

Daily Quran wards away doubts

On our long journey to God, we will certainly encounter some puzzling questions and obstacles to understanding (which are, in reality, due to our own biases and limitations). Our hearts may be confused by them, and we may consider compromising or even giving up on our goal reaching God. So part of the Quran's role in our journey is to prevent these doubts from blocking our path. The Quran reassures us, reminds us of our limits, and exposes the flaws of our baseless skepticism. A regular dosage of the Quran keeps our vision clear and our hearts firmly grounded, as Allah says,

وَلَا يَأْتُونَكَ بِمَثَلٍ إِلَّا جِئْنَـٰكَ بِٱلْحَقِّ وَأَحْسَنَ تَفْسِيرًا ۝

Whenever they bring you an argument, We come to you with
the right refutation and the best explanation. [25:33]

Daily Quran Reaffirms our Priorities

It can be easy to forget our foundational principles when we encounter adversity. How many times have we held assumptions about our own capabilities that proved wrong when put to the test? This is where a daily routine of reciting the Quran must come to play its role, for it reminds us to stay firm.

When was the last time you were put under pressure, whether from your family, coworkers, or just your personal desires, to go against what you knew to be right? How many people do you know who engage in business practices that are dubious—or even outright forbidden—but absolve themselves of guilt by claiming that otherwise, they and their family would be out on the streets? You may even know people who have built their careers in industries that are rooted in sin. Perhaps if they came across this ayah sooner, they would have chosen to dedicate their lives to a job that would benefit them both now and in the afterlife:

قُلْ إِن كَانَ ءَابَآؤُكُمْ وَأَبْنَآؤُكُمْ وَإِخْوَٰنُكُمْ وَأَزْوَٰجُكُمْ وَعَشِيرَتُكُمْ
وَأَمْوَٰلٌ ٱقْتَرَفْتُمُوهَا وَتِجَـٰرَةٌ تَخْشَوْنَ كَسَادَهَا وَمَسَـٰكِنُ تَرْضَوْنَهَآ أَحَبَّ
إِلَيْكُم مِّنَ ٱللَّهِ وَرَسُولِهِ وَجِهَادٍ فِى سَبِيلِهِ فَتَرَبَّصُوا حَتَّىٰ يَأْتِىَ ٱللَّهُ بِأَمْرِهِ ۗ
وَٱللَّهُ لَا يَهْدِى ٱلْقَوْمَ ٱلْفَـٰسِقِينَ ۝

Say, "If your parents and children and siblings and spouses
and extended family and the wealth you have acquired and
the trade you fear will decline and the homes you cherish—
(if all these) are more beloved to you than Allah and His
Messenger and struggling in His Way, then wait until Allah
brings about His Will. Allah does not guide the rebellious
people." [9:24]

We often believe that our efforts to benefit our local communities, or even to support our brothers and sisters who are suffering around the world, is our chance to help and give back. The idea that these needy people are in need of us is ironically what often leads to our stinginess. We drop a few quarters into the beggars cup and feel that we've done our duty to serve humanity. We attend fundraisers and feel irritated when, after we've already signed the check, the organization is still asking for more to meet their goal for the night. But instead of looking at the ones asking as needy, we should realize that we are in need of the opportunity to give more than they are in need of our money. This realization should come easily if we read this ayah often:

هَـٰٓأَنتُمْ هَـٰٓؤُلَآءِ تُدْعَوْنَ لِتُنفِقُوا۟ فِى سَبِيلِ ٱللَّهِ فَمِنكُم مَّن يَبْخَلُ وَمَن يَبْخَلْ فَإِنَّمَا يَبْخَلُ عَن نَّفْسِهِۦ وَٱللَّهُ ٱلْغَنِىُّ وَأَنتُمُ ٱلْفُقَرَآءُ وَإِن تَتَوَلَّوْا۟ يَسْتَبْدِلْ قَوْمًا غَيْرَكُمْ ثُمَّ لَا يَكُونُوٓا۟ أَمْثَـٰلَكُم ۝

Here you are, being invited to donate in the cause of Allah.
Still some of you withhold—and whoever withholds only
withholds from himself. For Allah is the Self-Sufficient,
whereas you are the ones who are in need. If you turn away,
He will replace you with another people, and they will not be
like you. [47:38]

The glamour of this worldly life constantly puts our sincerity to the test. Whether it be shiny cars, pretty faces, or validation from people who know nothing of our internal conditions, our hearts are subjected to many forms of temptation. With verses like the following, which are plentiful in God's book, the Quran is our daily reminder to divest from this world and shift our focus to that which is better and everlasting:

وَٱضْرِبْ لَهُم مَّثَلَ ٱلْحَيَوٰةِ ٱلدُّنْيَا كَمَآءٍ أَنزَلْنَـٰهُ مِنَ ٱلسَّمَآءِ فَٱخْتَلَطَ بِهِۦ نَبَاتُ ٱلْأَرْضِ فَأَصْبَحَ هَشِيمًا تَذْرُوهُ ٱلرِّيَـٰحُ وَكَانَ ٱللَّهُ عَلَىٰ كُلِّ شَىْءٍ مُّقْتَدِرًا ۝

And give them a parable of this worldly life: it is like the plants
of the earth, thriving when sustained by the rain We send
down from the sky. Then they turn into chaff scattered by the
wind. And Allah is fully capable of all things. [18:45]

The Quran also reminds us that results cannot be hastened. Things will come in their right time. It is love of this world that causes us to be impatient and feel like the road is too long:

أَلَمْ تَرَ إِلَى ٱلَّذِينَ قِيلَ لَهُمْ كُفُّوٓا۟ أَيْدِيَكُمْ وَأَقِيمُوا۟ ٱلصَّلَوٰةَ وَءَاتُوا۟ ٱلزَّكَوٰةَ فَلَمَّا كُتِبَ عَلَيْهِمُ ٱلْقِتَالُ إِذَا فَرِيقٌ مِّنْهُمْ يَخْشَوْنَ ٱلنَّاسَ كَخَشْيَةِ ٱللَّهِ أَوْ أَشَدَّ خَشْيَةً وَقَالُوا۟ رَبَّنَا لِمَ كَتَبْتَ عَلَيْنَا ٱلْقِتَالَ لَوْلَآ أَخَّرْتَنَآ إِلَىٰٓ أَجَلٍ قَرِيبٍ قُلْ مَتَـٰعُ ٱلدُّنْيَا قَلِيلٌ وَٱلْءَاخِرَةُ خَيْرٌ لِّمَنِ ٱتَّقَىٰ وَلَا تُظْلَمُونَ فَتِيلًا ۝

[Prophet], do you not see those who were told, 'Restrain yourselves
from fighting, perform the prayer, and pay the prescribed alms'?
When fighting was ordained for them, some of them feared men as

much as, or even more than, they feared God, saying, 'Lord, why
have You ordained fighting for us? If only You would give us just a
little more time.' Say to them, 'Little is the enjoyment in this world,
the Hereafter is far better for those who are mindful of God: you
will not be wronged by as much as the fibre in a date stone. [4:77]

But despite being surrounded by danger and difficulty, God has given us all the tools necessary to defend ourselves. When we feel like our grip is slipping and we are losing sight of our ultimate goal, it's likely due to the lack of both quantity and quality of time spent with the Quran. Reciting it every day and engaging with its powerful reminders will ensure that we are maintaining our principles and sticking to our priorities.

Daily Quran is Shelter from the Storm

As chaos and confusion intensifies and the truth of our world appears murky, the importance of the Quran as a means of protection conversely becomes more clear. The Messenger of Allah ﷺ once said to his Companions, **"Rejoice! Rejoice! Do you not testify that there is nothing worth of worship but God, and that I am the Messenger of Allah?"** They said, "Certainly!" He said, **"This Quran is a rope. One of its ends in God's hand, and the other end is in your hands. Hold onto it tightly, and then you will never be lost or in danger."**[49]

The Quran exposes Satan's tactics and addresses the different types of trials and tribulations in human life. The more we familiarize ourselves with its discourse, the more prepared we are for tests that will inevitably come our way. Allah tells us in His Quran about the heroic response of the believers when they were attacked by an army made up of all of their enemies in a single alliance.

وَلَمَّا رَءَا ٱلْمُؤْمِنُونَ ٱلْأَحْزَابَ قَالُوا هَٰذَا مَا وَعَدَنَا ٱللَّهُ وَرَسُولُهُۥ وَصَدَقَ
ٱللَّهُ وَرَسُولُهُۥ وَمَا زَادَهُمْ إِلَّآ إِيمَٰنًا وَتَسْلِيمًا ۝

When the believers saw the enemy alliance, they said,
"This is what Allah and His Messenger had promised
us. The promise of Allah and His Messenger has
come true." And this only increased them in faith and
submission. [33:22]

Because of their intimacy with the Quran, the Companions recognized God's promise, and that the Quran had prepared them for such a day.

A daily recitation of the Quran endows the heart with certainty in Allah and His attributes. It increases our conviction in the fundamentals of our faith. These matters are repeated throughout the Quran in different styles with different approaches, drilling the meaning into our minds in order to establish them firmly. Allah says in the magnificent verse which refers to, according to different scholars of tafseer, to the falling of the rain in different patterns over the earth or to the showering of the Quran on the hearts:

وَلَقَدْ صَرَّفْنَٰهُ بَيْنَهُمْ لِيَذَّكَّرُوا فَأَبَىٰ أَكْثَرُ ٱلنَّاسِ إِلَّا كُفُورًا ۝

We certainly disperse it among them so they may be mindful... [25:50]

To "disperse," here, means to repeat in different styles.

Designing your Daily Quran Session

The Glorious Quran revives, nourishes, and heals our hearts. It is a rope that secures those who hold onto it tightly, and leads whoever follows it to the straight path of God. It is our means of security, sustenance, and guidance. But in order for the Quran to play its proper role in our lives, we must commit to it and hold space for it in our lives. It requires a one-on-one appointment: a consistent daily recitation session with deep reflection on its meanings. Once we make this daily commitment to the Quran, there are a few elements we can incorporate before and during our recitation that will help us maximize the benefit of our daily session. These will set us up for success and facilitate a deeper connection with the Quran.

◖ Daily Quran Essentials ◗

Right Environment
Ask God for Help
Seek Protection
Take your Time
Maintain Mindfulness
Be Shy before God
Accept Limitations
Value of Tafseer
Talk to Allah
Lean into Verses

1. THE RIGHT ENVIRONMENT

For the Quran to actualize its potential of transformation, we have to prepare the right setting for our engagement with it. We should find a place of tranquility to be with the Quran, away from all of the clamor and commotion of our everyday nonsense. A serene setting will help us focus and perfect our understandings. While there is benefit in reciting or listening to the Quran during our daily affairs, while taking care of children, driving to work, and performing manual labor and chores, these interactions should not be seen as a substitute for the daily one-on-one with the Quran.

We'll also find that when we immerse ourselves in a calm setting, the sacredness of the Quran seeps into our consciousness. Quiet and stillness heightens our sensitivity. When our environment is tranquil, we are less inhibited in expressing our emotions, allowing the words of God, if we are so inclined, to wring our hearts dry and draw out our tears. The most genuine prayers will flow from our tongues without even having to calculate what it is we should be praying for.

Part of creating an environment conducive to benefiting from the Quran is selecting the right time to recite. We're conditioned to view our time with the Quran as secondary to our studies, jobs, and our leisure time. Reciting the Quran is reserved only for our spare time—that is, any time left over after working, eating, scrolling through endless media feeds, and making sure we catch up on our favorite television series. Maybe you play your favorite Quran recitation while driving, with your mind swinging between the road (where it should be), your daily tasks, and maybe every so often how beautiful that ayah that just played is. Or perhaps you complete your daily portion of recitation while commuting on the bus or train, trying with all your might to keep your eyes on the page despite the blur of passing bodies in the peripheries.

Some of us might delay our recitation until we're lying in our beds at the end of the day; while the quiet environment may be appropriate, your fatigued mind no longer has the capacity to engage with anything on a substantial level. Listening to the Quran while occupied with a physical or mental task is acceptable and helps us reap some benefits, but it should not be the basis of our primary conversation with the Quran. Give the Quran a time of day when your heart is active, your mind is fresh, and you can be focused on the meanings of God's words.

Don't forget, as well, to make wudu and brush your teeth before reciting. Aside from any technical rulings that may be relevant here, this is an effective practical step to prepare yourself both physically and psychologically to recite God's scripture. Cleanse your body to hold His book, freshen your breath to recite His words, and build within yourself a sense of respect and honor for the source of humanity's guidance.

2. ASK GOD FOR HELP

After you've freshened up, grabbed your Quran, and found a place to sit and recite in peace, you need to do one more thing before starting: recognize your weakness, realize God's power, and ask Him for help with a yearning heart. Remind yourself of how much you want this, and tell Allah. Ask Him to open the doors of understanding for you. Ask Him to allow His light to illuminate our dark hearts—the darkness is, after all, a result of our distance from Him and His majestic book.

Remember that He is the One who, when you were just a lump of flesh engulfed in darkness, nourished you and formed you into a perfect human being—and you had nothing to do with it. Then He brought you into the world, safe and sound, and gave you your faculties and capacities to interact with everything around you—and you had nothing to do with it. God taught you to walk and talk, and planned every step you took to be for your own ultimate benefit—and you had nothing to do with it. Do you really think, now, that you can unlock the secrets of His glorious scripture on your own? Given our endless debt to Him, let us begin our call for help with a plea for forgiveness.

لَوْلَا تَسْتَغْفِرُونَ ٱللَّهَ لَعَلَّكُمْ تُرْحَمُونَ ۝

"If only you sought Allah's forgiveness so you may be shown mercy!" [27:46]

The Quran is the source of the heart's life and sustenance. Its effect is universal, but its most precious jewels are rare and not exposed to everyone. It is only Allah who can assist us in our search for them. Our dire need for His help is clear. Even the Prophet ﷺ himself constantly sought help from Allah in internalizing and understanding the meanings of the Quran. He ﷺ said, **"When anyone is stricken with worry or grief, they should say, "O Allah, I am your servant, the child of your male and female servant. My fate is in your hands, your decree for me is inevitable, and your judgment of me is fair. I ask you by every name that you have, with which you named yourself, or which you revealed in your scripture, or which you taught to anyone of you creation, or which you have kept privy to yourself in your exclusive knowledge of the unseen: please make the Quran the spring of my heart, the light of my sight, the reliever of my grief, and the remover of my worries."** The Prophet ﷺ continued saying, **"[Whoever said this] Allah will relieve their worry and replace their grief with happiness."** The Companions asked, **"Messenger of Allah, should we learn these words?"** He ﷺ said, **"Yes, whoever hears them should learn them."**[50]

3. SEEK PROTECTION

The final step, after setting the scene and begging for help, is to ask for God's protection from Satan. His tireless efforts against us will not end once we have the Quran in our hands—on the contrary, his hostility will only intensify. The devil knows well the Quran's

power to heal and guide, and so he will put in twice the effort to divert you from truly benefitting from it. He is relentless and spiteful, and so our only solution is to ask for help and
protection from the One in whose hand lies all power and control.

$$\text{فَإِذَا قَرَأْتَ ٱلْقُرْءَانَ فَٱسْتَعِذْ بِٱللَّهِ مِنَ ٱلشَّيْطَٰنِ ٱلرَّجِيمِ ۝ إِنَّهُۥ لَيْسَ لَهُۥ}$$
$$\text{سُلْطَٰنٌ عَلَى ٱلَّذِينَ ءَامَنُوا۟ وَعَلَىٰ رَبِّهِمْ يَتَوَكَّلُونَ ۝}$$

*When you recite the Quran, seek refuge with Allah
from Satan, the accursed. He certainly has no
authority over those who believe and put their trust in
their Lord.* [16:98-99]

4. TAKE YOUR TIME

Our recitation should be unhurried and relaxed. This allows us to properly pronounce each
letter and beautify our recitation with a smooth and harmonious flow. Allah tells the Prophet ﷺ:

$$\text{وَرَتِّلِ ٱلْقُرْءَانَ تَرْتِيلًا ۝}$$

Recite the Quran in a measured way. [74:3]

Let us remember, as Ibn Mas'ood said, to not make our primary goal reaching the end of the
surah. Our excitement to complete a recitation of the entire Quran should not cause us to
speed up our recitation, for how many times have we completed reciting the Quran before,
and what has it benefited us?

The Prophet's recitation was gentle and thoughtful, to the point that someone listening
would be able to make out every single letter in each word that he pronounced. His wife,
Umm Salamah, described his recitation as "deliberately clear, with each letter distinct from
the next."[51] Hafsah said that, "he would recite a surah so slowly and measured that it would
seem longer than a surah of greater length."[52]

Some of us believe that failing to complete the entire Quran in a month is tantamount
to sin. While we should indeed occupy ourselves with the Quran and recite on a consistent
schedule, making sure that a single day does not pass without reciting the Quran therein,
there is no mandate to complete the entire recitation of the Quran in any specific time frame.
Even the Companions, who dedicated their lives to the Quran, differed in how long it took
them to finish reciting it in its entirety.

Abu Dawud reported that the strongest among the Companions of the Messenger of Allah
ﷺ would recite the Quran in seven days, while others would recite it in a month, others in
two months, and others in even longer periods than that.[53] This is obviously not a license

to drag out your completion of the Quran, but rather a reminder to set sustainable goals. There is tremendous benefit in reading daily and completing readings of the entire Quran periodically, but there is no deadline for that completion. When you are not forcing yourself to meet some self-imposed quota, the quality of the time spent reciting the Quran will make you naturally want to increase your daily amount, instead of burdening you.

5. MAINTAIN MINDFULNESS

When you read any worthwhile book, you channel your mental energy to understanding and analyzing the author's words. If at any time you don't understand something, you backtrack in an effort to properly comprehend it. Despite the Quran's wisdom and unparalleled depth, we fail to put in the same effort to interact with and unlock its meaning. It is certainly more deserving of our labor and toil than any other book.

We should bring all our skills of attention, analysis, and drawing connections to bear on our reading of the Quran. Compare how you highlight and annotate your textbooks, taking notes on what you will need and reading any supplementary material that will add to your understanding of the subject. Do you have a notebook for your thoughts on the Quran?

Read the Quran with a present, inquisitive mind. If you find yourself growing distracted, you can backtrack to reread the verses that slipped from your understanding. Every single word was chosen by God Himself in His letter to mankind, and so every single word deserves our attention.

We might find it difficult to apply this at first because of preexisting habits. We have gotten quite comfortable with a shallow interaction with the Quran, focusing on the sounds of the words rather than their meanings. For those who memorize large portions of the Quran, they may have grown accustomed to reciting solely for the sake of memorization and review, paying little or no attention to the meanings. This new mindfulness habit with the Quran requires persistent effort and consistency, but with Allah's permission and help, it can be achieved easily. It helps to remember that Allah says,

وَإِذَا قُرِئَ ٱلْقُرْءَانُ فَٱسْتَمِعُوا لَهُۥ وَأَنصِتُوا لَعَلَّكُمْ تُرْحَمُونَ ۝

When the Quran is recited, listen to it attentively and be silent,
so you may be shown mercy. [7:204]

Oftentimes we find ourselves sleepy or bored when we begin our recitation, unable to focus on what we are reciting. What should we do then, if we find it so difficult to recite mindfully after trying so hard to change? Renew your intention, refresh your energy, and then return to the task a short time later. Come back when you are better rested and give the Quran the best of your daily energy. Consider when the Prophet ﷺ said, **"If you stand to recite during the night, but find the Quran incomprehensible when you recite, not realizing what you are saying, then lie down."**[54] Being able to focus and be present without drifting off when reciting the Quran is a must if we wish to benefit from the Quran.

6. BE SHY IN FRONT OF ALLAH

When your text message alert goes off, you instantly reach for your phone to check who messaged you. Even when it is from someone you don't particularly care for, you pause to read every single word in the message. For this one message, that will likely now turn into a conversation, you've devoted a good portion of your mind's energy and put your life on hold. So how can you treat the message from your Creator casually?

Think about the last class or lecture you attended where someone in the room was making too much noise or distracting you. You might have ignored it the first time, mustering all of your brain power to drown out the noise and focus on what the instructor was saying. The next time, you might become bothered and try once more to stay attentive. But the third time you'll surely gesture to your classmate or even move your seat away from the distraction and closer to the speaker. We invest all of this interest and effort for information that we deem valuable and essential for our success, but when we read the Quran, we allow our mind to roam free and get snagged by any distraction that arises. We should feel a shyness in front of Allah when we read the Quran, knowing that how we handle distractions is a reflection on our mindfulness and respect for God's words.

7. ACCEPT LIMITATIONS

Sometimes when we attempt to contemplate over the Quran, we find ourselves engrossed in trying to force deep meanings out of every single word, ultimately making the process of reflection quite arduous and exhausting. It isn't long until we burn out and revert back to our previous, easier habit of reciting with no reflection at all. How then can we find that balance between reflecting with substance and moving forward in our recitation smoothly and naturally?

One of the easiest ways to achieve both goals simultaneously is to pay attention to the general theme of the verses in a given passage to the best of our abilities. Then we can apply this top-down understanding when we come across phrases we don't understand, and try to glean general meanings through context; this is of the most engaging and productive ways of learning. The Messenger of Allah ﷺ himself actually alluded to this when he said, **"The Quran did not come down with some parts contradicting others; rather every part affirms the others. Act upon whatever you know of it, and defer whatever you do not know to those who know it."**[55]

To actively engage with the Quran by employing what you do know to shed light on what you don't makes reflecting on the Quran achievable and enjoyable for all. Shaykh Abdul-Rahman al-Sa'di affirms this in his introduction to his famous commentary on the Quran. He says, "Make the meaning your goal, and the word your means to achieve it."[56]

8. KNOW THE VALUE OF TAFSEER

Tafseer is the science of explaining the Quran and deriving its rulings. While the books of *tafseer* are an indispensable resource, they are not a prerequisite in the heart's conversation with the Quran. Looking up words that we don't know while reading is an obvious way to enhance our understanding of the Quran. Allah has even blessed us in our times with physical Quran's that have the definitions of the words printed on the margins, and apps that allow us to access all of the linguistic properties of any word in the Quran by literally pointing our fingers at it. This helps us deepen our understanding of our recitation while not interrupting the recitation itself. We can't use a lack of understanding or lack of access as an excuse anymore, as these tools are tailored to help us focus and engage with the Quran.

⇒ Which Tafseer is the best? ⇐

Every Quran teacher is asked the same question by students who search for the sweetness of understanding the Quran: "What's the best tafseer to read?" There are almost as many tafseer books as scholars in our history, each approaching the verses from a different angle. With each title more ornate than the next, it can be difficult to choose where to begin.

Imam Hasan al-Banna was once asked this question, and his response was straightforward. When he was asked what the best commentary on the Quran was and the best way to understand God's book al-Banna responded with one word:
"Your heart."

He explained, "The heart of the believer is his best source of commentary for the Quran, and the best tool for understanding it deeply is to recite with insightful contemplation and submissive humility. He should be striving to for inspiration and accuracy, maintaining control of his own mind throughout the whole recitation. He should relate the verses to what he knows of the Prophet's life story, taking note of the reasons why particular surahs were revealed and tying each to its proper context. That is the best aid to understanding the Quran correctly.
(continued on next page)

⟫ *Which Tafseer is the best?* ⟪

Imam al-Banna continued, "When you read the books of tafseer after mastering that technique, it should be for the purpose of understanding a specific word that you could not figure out on your own, or to unpack the meaning of a phrase, or to increase in knowledge that can help one correctly understand the book of Allah. Reading tafseer is a supplementary aid to understanding. This understanding will gradually become a glowing light, emanating from deep within our hearts…

Whoever follows this process will no doubt find the effects of it within himself after some time. It will become a gift, and this level of comprehension will be second nature, a light that illuminates in this world and the next, if Allah wills."

Now this does not mean that we have nothing to benefit from the books of tafseer, wherein the most qualified scholars of our religion explain and elaborate the meanings of each ayah. Reading tafseer can take one's understanding to the next level, and is absolutely essential for understanding the legislative meanings of the Quran.[49] This is a level of interpretation that requires expertise, and we should extract the benefits of this knowledge. For our daily reading, however, tafseer is not essential. We can extract unique personal reflections on how God's words relate to our lives on a personal level, while still remaining within the bounds set by the Prophet ﷺ, and by the Quran itself.

The time we dedicate to studying the Quran—whether by reading books of tafseer, listening to lectures, learning tajweed (the art of recitation), or actually learning Arabic to better understand the Quran—must not take away from the time we dedicate to reciting the Quran. Our objective cannot only be to enhance our understanding of the Quran, but to awaken our sleeping hearts and energize our soul. This requires a raw one-on-one meeting with the Quran that is stripped of the involvement of anyone else. We must lay our emotions and vulnerabilities on the table for God's words to wash them away. Using another human being's words as the only lens in understanding the Quran will only keep us crippled. We have to learn to interact with God's words on our own, using tafseer as one of several tools. The reflections we take from the Quran—they are not tafseer or definitive principles—but they are the product of our soul's very own interaction with the revelation.

9. TALK TO ALLAH

The Quran is God's direct communication to us, both individually and collectively. In this letter addressed to each one of us, God communicates with us in different styles: rhetorical questions, promises and threats, commands and prohibitions, analogies and reminders. Each ayah calls for a response from our hearts. When God poses a question, it is for us to consider the implications of our response. God's mentions of reward incites us to good deeds, and his threats should drive us away from sin. When He tells us about His power and might, we should humble ourselves voluntarily, before we are forced to do so by more painful means. When he points out His grand blessings and compassionate care for us, it is to foster our love for Him. We should memorize the prayers that He taught us in the Quran, uttering them in our times of desperation.

◆◆◆

I prayed with the Prophet ﷺ one night, and he began by reciting Surah al-Baqarah. I said, "He will bow after one hundred verses," but when he passed them, I said, "He will finish this rak'ah with it." When he finished it, I said, "Now he will bow," but he then began to recite Surah al-Nisā'. He recited it all and then began to recite Surah Āli 'Imrān, reciting it entirely. He recited gently and slowly. When he came across an ayah of glorification, he would glorify; when he came across an ayah of supplication, he would supplicate; and when he came across an ayah of seeking refuge, he would seek refuge.[57]

Huthayfah ibn al-Yaman

Abdullah bin Sā'ib reports about Umar bin al-Khattab that he came late to the 'Ishā' prayer one night. He says, "The prayer began, and when he entered he began to pray behind me. I recited Surah al-Dhāriyāt, and when I reached this ayah:

وَفِي ٱلسَّمَآءِ رِزْقُكُمْ وَمَا تُوعَدُونَ ۝

In the heaven is your sustenance and whatever you are promised. [51:22]

He exclaimed, 'I testify!' with his voice filling the mosque."[58]

Abdullah bin Mas'ood once heard a man reciting,

هَلْ أَتَىٰ عَلَى ٱلْإِنسَٰنِ حِينٌ مِّنَ ٱلدَّهْرِ لَمْ يَكُن شَيْـًٔا مَّذْكُورًا ۝

Was there not a period of time when each human was nothing worth mentioning? [76:1]

Upon hearing the verse, Ibn Mas'ood cried, "Yes—by my Lord! You gave him the faculties of hearing and vision, and gave him life and death!"[59]

Abu 'Umārah al-Koofi narrates that he heard Ali once recite this ayah in prayer:

سَبِّحِ اسْمَ رَبِّكَ ٱلْأَعْلَى ۝

Glorify the Name of your Lord,
the Most High [87:1]

Then he said, "Glorified is my Lord, the Most High!"[60] See how the early Muslims interacted with the Quran through spontaneous exclamations of glorification and fear. What is stopping us from interacting with the Quran in such a visceral and direct way? Talking to Allah during your recitation will keep your mind active during recitation and accustom your heart to responding more spontaneously to God.

This technique might seem forced at first, but one way to help generate these reactions sincerely is to realize that Allah, the Creator of the world and everything in it, addressed this letter to you personally. The prolific thinker, poet, and literary genius Muhammad Iqbal says to emphasize this,

> I had decided to start reciting the Quran after the morning prayer every day. When my father saw me, he asked, "What are you doing?" I responded, "I am reciting the Quran." He continued to ask me this every day for three years, and I would reply with the same answer. Then one day I said to him, "What is it with you, father? You ask me the same question every day, and I always respond to you with the same answer, but you never fail to ask me the same question every day." He said, "I only want to remind you, my son, to recite the Quran as it was revealed to you." It was only from that day onwards that I began to make an attempt to understand the Quran, and have since gained so much of its insights and have been able to compose my words.[61]

10. LEAN INTO VERSES

Staying attentive while reciting the Quran is something that we can all achieve with enough mental application and self control. But to have a heart that responds emotionally during recitation is something that requires training and a substantial relationship with God. In order to allow the Quran's light into our dark chests, we must have a daily routine of meaningful, slow-paced, and mindful recitation, along with total surrender to God, begging Him to open our hearts to His words. This is why fear was discussed in the previous chapter as a prerequisite key to accessing the Quran; fear compels us to realize our need for Allah and His guidance.

After acknowledging our brokenness and need for God's help, we will find the Quran to have more of an impact when we recite it. The first time you come across an ayah, tasting the richness of it—not only understanding it on an intellectual level, but internalizing it - you will begin to realize what you have been missing out on for so long. It might just be one verse out of many that touches you this way. You will begin to understand its value, and why God reserved its delight for so few people.

When this moment comes to you, don't let it go. Lean into your interaction with the verse. Take hold of it with every ounce of strength, for these are the rare moments that have the potential to completely change our lives. The feeling you've just experienced is the light of that ayah penetrating your heart and alleviating the darkness—the physical manifestation of the metaphysical. Though iman usually grows through gradual processes, you've experienced an instantaneous lift that only God can provide.

Such inspiration is rare in the beginning, but don't let that deter you from striving. After all, to experience these moments of deep spiritual insight is not our end goal; our goal is God's pleasure and Paradise, and this is just one of the many ways in which He makes the journey enjoyable for us. Too many make the mistake of investing too much time and energy into seeking spiritual highs, compromising the ultimate objective. The beautiful sights on the road are there to keep us moving forward, not to stop us from reaching our destination. For as you keep on, the views grow more beautiful, and the journey's end is more worthy.

Don't be stingy in your recitation. When you find a verse that increases your iman, dwell on it. Ibn al-Qayyim says,

> If only people knew what came with reciting the Quran with deep reflection, they would busy themselves with it over everything else. When they come across that ayah that they are in desperate need of, they would repeat it hundreds of times or for a whole night's duration. Reading a single ayah with deep contemplation and understanding is better than reciting the entire Quran without. This is more beneficial to the heart and more conducive to increasing your faith and tasting its sweetness. This was the norm for the earlier generations; they would often repeat one ayah until the morning came.[62]

Hamzah bin Abdullah bin Zubayr narrates that his grandmother Asma', the daughter of Abu Bakr and sister of Aisha, once sent him to the market. She began reciting Surah al-Toor, and by the time he had left she reached the verse:

$$\text{فَمَنَّ ٱللَّهُ عَلَيْنَا وَوَقَىٰنَا عَذَابَ ٱلسَّمُومِ ۝}$$

*So Allah has graced us and protected us from the
torment of (Hell's) scorching heat.* [52:27]

He narrates, "I left to the market, and when I came back, she was still repeating, "and protected us from the torment of (Hell's) scorching heat."[63]

Abdullah bin Mas'ood would often spend the night repeating the ayah: "My Lord! Increase
me in knowledge" [20:114] until the morning came.[64] Umar bin al-Khattab, as well, would
repeat Surah al-Fatihah until the morning without reciting anything else.[65] This practice of
repeating a single ayah over develops an ability of reflection that we would not otherwise
have. Let the meanings sink deeply within, translating into movements of prostration and
expressions of tears and earnest supplication. God says in praise of those who were devoted
to worshipping Him,

$$\text{ٱلَّذِينَ أُوتُوا ٱلْعِلْمَ مِن قَبْلِهِۦ إِذَا يُتْلَىٰ عَلَيْهِمْ يَخِرُّونَ لِلْأَذْقَانِ سُجَّدًا ۝}$$
$$\text{وَيَقُولُونَ سُبْحَٰنَ رَبِّنَآ إِن كَانَ وَعْدُ رَبِّنَا لَمَفْعُولًا ۝ وَيَخِرُّونَ لِلْأَذْقَانِ}$$
$$\text{يَبْكُونَ وَيَزِيدُهُمْ خُشُوعًا ۝}$$

*Indeed, when it is recited to those who were gifted with
knowledge before it (was revealed), they fall upon their
faces in prostration, and say, 'Glory be to our Lord!
Surely the promise of our Lord has been fulfilled.' And
they fall down upon their faces weeping, and it increases
them in humility."* [17:107-109]

Read with a Theme

A powerful technique of approaching the Quran is to seek a spiritual theme during your
recitation. Notice how God says,

$$\text{لَّقَدْ كَانَ فِي يُوسُفَ وَإِخْوَتِهِۦٓ ءَايَٰتٌ لِّلسَّآئِلِينَ ۝}$$

*There are lessons in the story of Joseph and his brothers
for all who seek them.* [12:7]

"Those who seek," as defined by Shaykh Abdul-Rahman al-Sa'di, are those who seek
to benefit from the verses and stories in the Quran. Benefitting to this degree requires
a certain level of focus and attention, as we have discussed above. We can apply this
seeking approach to our reading of the Quran, searching for the spiritual implications
of the verses we recite as well as seeking to strengthen a specific aspect of our iman.

Challenge yourself with a specific spiritual lens while reading the Quran. Embark
on your recitation with a theme in mind, searching for answers that will increase
a particular aspect of your iman. In this chapter, we will suggest examples of this

theme-based reading of the Quran. Focusing on a theme during recitation will open up your mind to reflection, while also drawing your attention to the multiple themes and angles from which any ayah can be approached. This focus does not take away from all of the other aspects that the verses address; rather, the opposite is true as we make new connections between ideas and spiritual meanings. This method of reading engages a higher level of analysis in our recitation. We learn reflective thinking. It makes the sweetness of faith more potent. Relating the verses you read to your life struggles and experiences will evoke nearness, familiarity, and comforting companionship with God.

Test out one of the lenses suggested in the upcoming pages and complete a reading of the entire Quran with it. Pick up on phrases, tones, and meanings that are recurring through different passages, and which might be relevant to your current experiences. For example, when you find yourself in a state of concern for the worsening conditions of the Muslims around the world, you should bring that to the forefront of your mind when reciting. With that lens, you will notice a common pattern in the stories of past believers to whom Allah gave victory after being tested with similar trials. Similarly, when you are enduring a personal struggle of any sort, look for both diagnosis and treatment in the Quran. When we learn about the importance of fear, we can read the Quran with the lens of fear, seeking to increase our sensitivity, humility, and awe.

The following are suggested themes to keep in mind while reading the Quran. You can journey with one of these themes as your lens, or adjust the lens to fit the needs of your heart at the moment.

⇒ *Read with a Theme* ⇐

Know God as One
Recognize Allah's Blessings
God's Mercy
Righteousness for our benefit
Your Dependency on God
God's Nearness
God's Signals
Divine Patterns
Understanding Trials
Sincerity
Success and Failure
Victory
Guidance
Gratitude

◄ KNOWING GOD AS THE ONE ►

During your next voyage from Surah al-Fatihah to Surah al-Nas, pay close attention to the verses that mention God's oneness. This topic is addressed extensively in the Quran. God repeatedly reminds us that all of the universe points to the necessary existence of a single, non-contingent Creator (*al-Wahid*). The world around us testifies to the fact that Allah is One, without any partners, a testimony that God encourages us repeatedly to pick up on. He says,

أَمْ خُلِقُوا مِنْ غَيْرِ شَىْءٍ أَمْ هُمُ ٱلْخَٰلِقُونَ ۝

Or were they created by nothing, or are they (their own) creators? [52:35]

Pay close attention to those verses wherein God disproves those who oppose the simple and natural theology of Islam. He often challenges the deniers and polytheists rationally:

لَوْ كَانَ فِيهِمَآ ءَالِهَةٌ إِلَّا ٱللَّهُ لَفَسَدَتَا

Had there been other gods besides Allah in the heavens or the earth, both (realms) would have surely been corrupted. [21:22]

To those who deify other human beings, God says,

مَّا ٱلْمَسِيحُ ٱبْنُ مَرْيَمَ إِلَّا رَسُولٌ قَدْ خَلَتْ مِن قَبْلِهِ ٱلرُّسُلُ
وَأُمُّهُ صِدِّيقَةٌ كَانَا يَأْكُلَانِ ٱلطَّعَامَ ٱنظُرْ كَيْفَ نُبَيِّنُ لَهُمُ
ٱلْءَايَٰتِ ثُمَّ ٱنظُرْ أَنَّىٰ يُؤْفَكُونَ ۝

The Messiah, son of Mary, was no more than a messenger. (Many) messengers had (come and) gone before him. His mother was a woman of truth. They both ate food. See how We make the signs clear to them, yet see how they are deluded (from the truth)! [5:75]

◄ ALLAH'S BLESSINGS ►

What is unique about the Quran—and what makes it so valuable—is that in it, God teaches us about Himself. He informs us about how He dealt with past nations, reminds us of the nature of this world and our place in it, and introduces us to His wonderful names and attributes. One attribute that is mentioned and alluded to often is God's generosity and blessings.

The Quran directs our attention to notice the effects of God's blessings and how they manifest in ourselves and the world around us. If we are truthful in reflecting on the minute details of how every constant is fine-tuned to facilitate life, and then further on the plethora of gifts we have received from God in our lives without even asking, we would surely realize that His blessings are overwhelmingly uncountable. It is this thought that should accompany our recitation.

We would notice that these blessings are not only incalculable in their number, but also invaluable in their quality and importance to our lives. Consider your five senses, as well as your capacity for rational thought, and how difficult life is for those of us who have lost or become handicapped in any of these. God says,

$$قُلْ هُوَ ٱلَّذِىٓ أَنشَأَكُمْ وَجَعَلَ لَكُمُ ٱلسَّمْعَ وَٱلْأَبْصَٰرَ وَٱلْأَفْـِٔدَةَ قَلِيلًا مَّا تَشْكُرُونَ ۞$$

Say, (O Prophet,) "He is the One Who brought you into
being and gave you hearing, sight, and intellect. (Yet)
you hardly give any thanks." [67:23]

Consider the cycles of nature that make life easy for us to navigate. Imagine if there were no solid substances to build shelter from. Imagine if there were no invisible layers of gas above our planet to filter the sun's rays for us. Imagine if the times of sunrise and sunset were completely random and unpredictable, or if there was no alteration in time at all:

$$يُولِجُ ٱلَّيْلَ فِى ٱلنَّهَارِ وَيُولِجُ ٱلنَّهَارَ فِى ٱلَّيْلِ وَهُوَ عَلِيمٌۢ بِذَاتِ ٱلصُّدُورِ ۞$$

He merges the night into day and the day into night. And He
knows best what is (hidden) in the heart. [6:57]

One of God's greatest blessings is that of protection. Were the forces of this world left unattended, the chances of us living to an old age would be impossible. Think about the last time you had a "close call." What do you think it was that diverted harm away? Surely it was God, who has been protecting and safeguarding your wellbeing since before your very existence. This is an example of one of many blessings that we only notice when we lose it.

Allah placed His angels as guards over us for our protection, not because He needed to, but rather as a sign of honor to us:

وَإِنَّ عَلَيْكُمْ لَحَفِظِينَ ۝

And assigned over you are guards [82:10]

He also subjected the earth to human life, customizing it for us and creating the ideal environment for civilization:

وَسَخَّرَ لَكُم مَّا فِى ٱلسَّمَـٰوَٰتِ وَمَا فِى ٱلْأَرْضِ جَمِيعًا مِّنْهُ إِنَّ فِى ذَٰلِكَ لَـَٔايَـٰتٍ لِّقَوْمٍ يَتَفَكَّرُونَ ۝

He has subjected all that is in the heavens and the earth for your benefit, as a gift from Him. There truly are signs in this for those who reflect. [45:13]

Reading the Quran with the lens of blessings, we cannot but realize that the most valuable of God's blessings upon us is His guidance. There are so many paths that a human can take in life to try to fill a void. Some choose to fill it with lowly and temporary pleasures, some with mythical and meaningless rituals, and some pay absolutely no mind to the empty feeling at all, eating, sleeping, and working until they die, failing to distinguish themselves from the animals. The fact that we find ourselves on the one path that leads to God is such an overwhelming solace. We would never have found this path on our own.

وَلَوْلَا فَضْلُ ٱللَّهِ عَلَيْكُمْ وَرَحْمَتُهُۥ مَا زَكَىٰ مِنكُم مِّنْ أَحَدٍ أَبَدًا وَلَـٰكِنَّ ٱللَّهَ يُزَكِّى مَن يَشَآءُ

Had it not been for Allah's grace and mercy upon you, none of you would have ever been purified. But Allah purifies whoever He wills. [24:21]

Take note of these subtle yet impactful indications in Allah's book, reading each ayah through the lens of someone who is in awe of God's bewildering blessings, especially the blessing of guidance.

وَجَـٰهِدُوا۟ فِى ٱللَّهِ حَقَّ جِهَادِهِۦ هُوَ ٱجْتَبَىٰكُمْ وَمَا جَعَلَ عَلَيْكُمْ فِى ٱلدِّينِ مِنْ حَرَجٍ

Strive hard for God as is His due: He has chosen you and placed no hardship in your religion, the faith of your forefather Abraham. [22:78]

◀ GOD'S MERCY ▶

God's uniquely boundless mercy is hard to overlook when reading the Quran. God points out the many ways His mercy comes to us, directing us to reflect on its manifestations in the natural world in order to understand its parallels in the spiritual. When speaking about rain, for example, God says,

فَٱنظُرْ إِلَىٰٓ ءَاثَٰرِ رَحْمَتِ ٱللَّهِ كَيْفَ يُحْىِ ٱلْأَرْضَ بَعْدَ مَوْتِهَآ

See then the impact of Allah's mercy: how He gives life to the
earth after its death! [30:50]

Giving life to the land's vegetation after it was nothing but lifeless soil and seeds is not only a point for us to reflect on God's ability to raise us from the dead (which is addressed in the rest of the ayah). God says that this action is a result of His mercy, leading us to make a connection here between His divine compassion and the potential for growth, revival, and transformation. As if to say, perhaps, that even when we feel that our souls are dead, our hearts are rock solid, and our chance to change is lost, remember that just as God gives life through His mercy to the dry and lifeless earth, He can very well awaken your soul and revive your heart. No sin is too big to be forgiven, no heart is too dark to be cleansed, and no one should ever give up on attaining God's mercy. Relate this as well to the verse,

قُلْ يَٰعِبَادِىَ ٱلَّذِينَ أَسْرَفُوا عَلَىٰٓ أَنفُسِهِمْ لَا تَقْنَطُوا مِن رَّحْمَةِ ٱللَّهِ إِنَّ
ٱللَّهَ يَغْفِرُ ٱلذُّنُوبَ جَمِيعًا إِنَّهُۥ هُوَ ٱلْغَفُورُ ٱلرَّحِيمُ ۞

Say, (O Prophet, that Allah says,) "O My servants who have
exceeded the limits against their souls! Do not lose hope
in Allah's mercy, for Allah certainly forgives all sins. He is
indeed the All-Forgiving, Most Merciful. [39:53]

Of the greatest and unparalleled forms of God's mercy is His sending of Muhammad as His Prophet and Messenger. A brief glance at his life story, characteristics, and the exceptional compassion with which he treated both his friends and his enemies will instantly help us understand why God called him, "a mercy to all creation" [21:107]. He was a comforting, guiding presence for those who accompanied him, and his tradition and teachings are a means of salvation for those after him.

◁ RIGHTEOUSNESS IS FOR YOUR OWN BENEFIT ▷

إِن تَكْفُرُوا فَإِنَّ ٱللَّهَ غَنِيٌّ عَنكُمْ

If you disbelieve, then (know that) Allah is truly not in need of you... [39:7]

Allah is free of all dependencies. He does not need your prayer, your charity, nor any of your worship or righteous acts. He is completely independent, while all else is completely dependent upon Him. He is unaffected by our sins and does not benefit from our righteousness.

Our worship of Him is for our own good. If you fail in this, the only one who suffers is you. This theme is alluded to throughout the Quran. God says, for example:

قُلِ ٱللَّهَ أَعْبُدُ مُخْلِصًا لَّهُ دِينِي ۝ فَٱعْبُدُوا مَا شِئْتُم مِّن دُونِهِۦ قُلْ إِنَّ ٱلْخَـٰسِرِينَ ٱلَّذِينَ خَسِرُوٓا أَنفُسَهُمْ وَأَهْلِيهِمْ يَوْمَ ٱلْقِيَـٰمَةِ أَلَا ذَٰلِكَ هُوَ ٱلْخُسْرَانُ ٱلْمُبِينُ ۝

Say, "It is Allah that I worship, being sincere in my devotion to Him." Say, "Worship then whatever you want instead of Him." Say, "The losers are those who will lose themselves and their families on Judgment Day. That is indeed the clearest loss." [39:14-15]

We strive for excellence so that we can benefit ourselves, not God. We refrain from wrongdoing out of fear of harming ourselves, not God:

إِنْ أَحْسَنتُمْ أَحْسَنتُمْ لِأَنفُسِكُمْ وَإِنْ أَسَأْتُمْ فَلَهَا

If you act rightly, it is for your own good, but if you do wrong, it is to your own loss. [17:7]

Even someone who strives or fights "for Allah's sake," only does so for his own good:

وَمَن جَـٰهَدَ فَإِنَّمَا يُجَـٰهِدُ لِنَفْسِهِۦٓ إِنَّ ٱللَّهَ لَغَنِيٌّ عَنِ ٱلْعَـٰلَمِينَ ۝

And whoever strives (in Allah's cause), only does so for their own good. Surely Allah is not in need of (any of) His creation. [19:6]

While on the surface level, we would believe that withholding help from someone in need—whether it be monetary, physical, or emotional support—would be harmful to that person or cause, God informs us of the unseen reality:

$$وَمَن يَبْخَلْ فَإِنَّمَا يَبْخَلُ عَن نَّفْسِهِۦ ۚ وَٱللَّهُ ٱلْغَنِىُّ وَأَنتُمُ ٱلْفُقَرَآءُ ۚ وَإِن تَتَوَلَّوْاْ يَسْتَبْدِلْ قَوْمًا غَيْرَكُمْ ثُمَّ لَا يَكُونُوٓاْ أَمْثَـٰلَكُم ۝$$

Whoever is grudging is so only towards himself: God
is the source of wealth and you are the needy ones. He
will substitute other people for you if you turn away,
and they will not be like you. [47:38]

Just as you would invest for your future financially in order to ensure your own well-being, invest in the only guaranteed return through good, sincere deeds. You are the primary beneficiary, and in fact it will be the only thing of benefit to you:

$$لَن تَنفَعَكُمْ أَرْحَامُكُمْ وَلَآ أَوْلَـٰدُكُمْ ۚ يَوْمَ ٱلْقِيَـٰمَةِ يَفْصِلُ بَيْنَكُمْ ۚ وَٱللَّهُ بِمَا تَعْمَلُونَ بَصِيرٌ ۝$$

Neither your relatives nor children will benefit you on
Judgment Day—He will decide between you (all). For Allah is
All-Seeing of what you do. [60:3]

❧ YOUR DEPENDENCY ON GOD ❧

No matter our financial status or health conditions, we depend on God in times of ease and difficulty. Without His help and strength, we are nothing but hollow shells, worthless and incompetent. This is the true meaning of the phrase "lā ḥawla walā quwwata illā billāh" (there is no source of power or might other than God). It is imperative for us to dedicate at least one complete journey through the Quran with this as our lens: our poverty and dependence on Allah.

$$قُلْ أَرَءَيْتُمْ إِنْ أَخَذَ ٱللَّهُ سَمْعَكُمْ وَأَبْصَـٰرَكُمْ وَخَتَمَ عَلَىٰ قُلُوبِكُم مَّنْ إِلَـٰهٌ غَيْرُ ٱللَّهِ يَأْتِيكُم بِهِ$$

Ask (them, O Prophet), "Imagine if Allah were to take away
your hearing or sight, or seal your hearts—who else other
than Allah could restore it?" [6:46]

The Quran overflows with reminders for us to internalize this dependency and flee to Allah with urgency. God shows us, ayah by ayah, how desperate our need for Him. He is constantly providing for us:

أَمَّنْ هَٰذَا ٱلَّذِي يَرْزُقُكُمْ إِنْ أَمْسَكَ رِزْقَهُۥ

Or who is it that will provide for you if He withholds His provision? [67:21]

We are dependent on Allah even for the stability of our iman, to protect us from falling into sin and unbelief. In his cry for rescue from the women who plotted against him, Joseph confided to His Lord:

وَإِلَّا تَصْرِفْ عَنِّي كَيْدَهُنَّ أَصْبُ إِلَيْهِنَّ وَأَكُن مِّنَ ٱلْجَٰهِلِينَ ۝

"If You do not turn their cunning away from me, I might yield to them and fall into ignorance." [12:33]

We even need God's inspiration to carry out good deeds. Allah says about the Prophets,

وَأَوْحَيْنَآ إِلَيْهِمْ فِعْلَ ٱلْخَيْرَٰتِ وَإِقَامَ ٱلصَّلَوٰةِ وَإِيتَآءَ ٱلزَّكَوٰةِ

We inspired them to do good deeds, establish prayer, and pay alms-tax. [21:73]

Knowledge, as well, ultimately stems from God and God alone. Even the angels recognized this when they said:

سُبْحَٰنَكَ لَا عِلْمَ لَنَآ إِلَّا مَا عَلَّمْتَنَآ

"Glory be to You! We have no knowledge except what You have taught us." [2:32]

This dependence on God for knowledge was, in fact, the introductory theme to the revelation. When Prophet Muhammad ﷺ was in seclusion in the cave, contemplating the pain of his people and his own spiritual journey, God sent the angel Gabriel to him with a humbling but powerful reminder of our reliance on God's knowledge:

ٱقْرَأْ بِٱسْمِ رَبِّكَ ٱلَّذِي خَلَقَ ۝ خَلَقَ ٱلْإِنسَٰنَ مِنْ عَلَقٍ ۝ ٱقْرَأْ وَرَبُّكَ ٱلْأَكْرَمُ ۝ ٱلَّذِي عَلَّمَ بِٱلْقَلَمِ ۝ عَلَّمَ ٱلْإِنسَٰنَ مَا لَمْ يَعْلَمْ ۝

Read, in the Name of your Lord who created—created humans from a clinging clot. Read! And your Lord is the Most Generous, Who taught by the pen—taught humanity what they knew not. [96:1-4]

See how we depend on Allah for guidance, success, victory, purification, knowledge, and repentance. Nothing is possible without Him, and there is no source of power or might but Him. Read the Quran with this lens to become keenly aware of our nuclear and existential need for God.

⟨ GOD'S NEARNESS ⟩

God describes Himself as being close to us. So not only does He see what we do, hear what we say, and know every little detail of what takes place behind the scenes, but He is close to us, accompanying every one of His creation at every single moment. Not a single speck of dust escapes His knowledge—no tear falls unnoticed, no pain goes unrecognized. He knows what you feel and wants you to turn to Him at every moment.

Consider the implications of this ayah:

$$وَعِندَهُۥ مَفَاتِحُ ٱلْغَيْبِ لَا يَعْلَمُهَآ إِلَّا هُوَ وَيَعْلَمُ مَا فِى ٱلْبَرِّ وَٱلْبَحْرِ وَمَا$$
$$تَسْقُطُ مِن وَرَقَةٍ إِلَّا يَعْلَمُهَا وَلَا حَبَّةٍ فِى ظُلُمَٰتِ ٱلْأَرْضِ وَلَا رَطْبٍ وَلَا يَابِسٍ$$
$$إِلَّا فِى كِتَٰبٍ مُّبِينٍ ۝$$

He has the keys to the unseen: no one knows them but Him. He knows all that is in the land and sea. No leaf falls without His knowledge, nor is there a single grain in the darkness of the earth, or anything, fresh or withered, that is not written in a clear Record. [6:59]

God is nearer to us than anything—what we can and can't see. He hears every breath, feels every pulse, and knows what your soul urges you to do at every moment:

$$وَلَقَدْ خَلَقْنَا ٱلْإِنسَٰنَ وَنَعْلَمُ مَا تُوَسْوِسُ بِهِۦ نَفْسُهُۥ وَنَحْنُ أَقْرَبُ إِلَيْهِ مِنْ$$
$$حَبْلِ ٱلْوَرِيدِ ۝$$

Indeed, We created humankind and know what their souls whisper to them, and We are closer to them than (their) jugular vein. [50:16]

He sees when we frown, hears every sound, and knows every thought we keep hidden deep down:

$$يَعْلَمُ خَآئِنَةَ ٱلْأَعْيُنِ وَمَا تُخْفِى ٱلصُّدُورُ ۝$$

Allah (even) knows the sly glances of the eyes and whatever the hearts conceal. [40:19]

But there is still more to this. We should not only find immense comfort and security in God's proximity, but it should also bring us to rectify our hearts and limbs. Knowing that our Ultimate Judge is so intimately acquainted with our every thought and action should yield complete compliance with His commands. In Surah al-Mujādilah, we are told that when the Day of Judgment comes, some will be shocked by their records:

يَوْمَ يَبْعَثُهُمُ ٱللَّهُ جَمِيعًا فَيُنَبِّئُهُم بِمَا عَمِلُوٓا۟ أَحْصَىٰهُ ٱللَّهُ وَنَسُوهُ وَٱللَّهُ عَلَىٰ كُلِّ شَىْءٍ شَهِيدٌ ۝

On the Day Allah resurrects them all together, He will then
inform them of what they have done. Allah has kept account
of it all, while they have forgotten it. For Allah is a Witness
over all things. [58:6]

God is so intricately aware of us and our deeds that He will remind us of the sins we have forgotten. The more aware we are of His proximity now, the less grief we will find on that day. Be aware of His oversight today to spare yourself dismay tomorrow. The very next verse draws our attention to this:

أَلَمْ تَرَ أَنَّ ٱللَّهَ يَعْلَمُ مَا فِى ٱلسَّمَٰوَٰتِ وَمَا فِى ٱلْأَرْضِ مَا يَكُونُ مِن نَّجْوَىٰ ثَلَٰثَةٍ إِلَّا هُوَ رَابِعُهُمْ وَلَا خَمْسَةٍ إِلَّا هُوَ سَادِسُهُمْ وَلَآ أَدْنَىٰ مِن ذَٰلِكَ وَلَآ أَكْثَرَ إِلَّا هُوَ مَعَهُمْ أَيْنَ مَا كَانُوا۟ ثُمَّ يُنَبِّئُهُم بِمَا عَمِلُوا۟ يَوْمَ ٱلْقِيَٰمَةِ إِنَّ ٱللَّهَ بِكُلِّ شَىْءٍ عَلِيمٌ ۝

Do you not see that Allah knows whatever is in the heavens
and whatever is on the earth? If three converse privately, He is
their fourth. If five, He is their sixth. Whether fewer or more,
He is with them wherever they may be. Then, on the Day
of Judgment, He will inform them of what they have done.
Surely Allah has (perfect) knowledge of all things. [58:7]

Paying close attention and pondering over these verses will lead to a feeling of shyness that will prevent us from sinning in front of Allah. Knowing that the camera is rolling on our hearts at all times forces us to keep them clean. We will also turn to God immediately in every circumstance, knowing that no one is closer to us than He is. We will find it easy to put down our masks and be genuine in our conversations with Him, knowing that His response is never delayed. We will actualize the meanings of the verse we hear so often:

وَإِذَا سَأَلَكَ عِبَادِى عَنِّى فَإِنِّى قَرِيبٌ أُجِيبُ دَعْوَةَ ٱلدَّاعِ إِذَا دَعَانِ

$$\text{فَلْيَسْتَجِيبُوا لِى وَلْيُؤْمِنُوا بِى لَعَلَّهُمْ يَرْشُدُونَ} ۝$$

When My servants ask you (O Prophet) about Me: I am truly
near. I respond to one's prayer when they call upon Me. So
let them respond (with obedience) to Me and believe in Me,
perhaps they will be guided (to the Right Way). [2:186]

◖ GOD'S SIGNALS ◗

God is incomparable to any of His creation. He is beyond our comprehension, for human minds are only equipped to comprehend what we experience. We can only know about Him what He tells us about Himself. Some of His divine qualities can be seen through His creation, as He says,

$$\text{وَيُرِيكُمْ ءَايَتِهِۦ فَأَىَّ ءَايَتِ اللَّهِ تُنكِرُونَ} ۝$$

And He shows you His signs. Now which of Allah's signs will
you deny? [40:81]

He surrounded us with signs, whose primary function is to teach and remind us of God. He makes this clear when He says,

$$\text{وَيُبَيِّنُ ءَايَتِهِۦ لِلنَّاسِ لَعَلَّهُمْ يَتَذَكَّرُونَ} ۝$$

He makes His revelations clear to the people so perhaps they
will be mindful. [2:221]

Every iota of God's creation contains a sign that points us to Him. Every moment contains a lesson that teaches us about Him. He has made it easy for us to know Him in this way, and so our duty is to actually reflect. This is a consistent theme and reminder throughout the Quran. Allah says,

$$\text{إِنَّ فِى السَّمَوَتِ وَالْأَرْضِ لَءَايَتٍ لِلْمُؤْمِنِينَ} ۝ \text{وَفِى خَلْقِكُمْ وَمَا يَبُثُّ}$$
$$\text{مِن دَآبَّةٍ ءَايَتٌ لِقَوْمٍ يُوقِنُونَ} ۝ \text{وَاخْتِلَفِ الَّيْلِ وَالنَّهَارِ وَمَآ أَنزَلَ اللَّهُ مِنَ}$$
$$\text{السَّمَآءِ مِن رِّزْقٍ فَأَحْيَا بِهِ الْأَرْضَ بَعْدَ مَوْتِهَا وَتَصْرِيفِ الرِّيَحِ ءَايَتٌ لِقَوْمٍ}$$
$$\text{يَعْقِلُونَ} ۝ \text{تِلْكَ ءَايَتُ اللَّهِ نَتْلُوهَا عَلَيْكَ بِالْحَقِّ فَبِأَىِّ حَدِيثٍ بَعْدَ اللَّهِ}$$
$$\text{وَءَايَتِهِۦ يُؤْمِنُونَ} ۝$$

In (the creation of) the heavens and the earth are signs for the
believers. And in your own creation, and whatever living beings

*He dispersed, are signs for people of sure faith. And in the
alternation of the day and the night, the provision sent down
from the skies by Allah—reviving the earth after its death—and
the shifting of the winds, are signs for people of understanding.
These are Allah's revelations which We recite to you (O Prophet)
in truth. So what message will they believe in after (denying)
Allah and His revelations?* [45:3-6]

Even the most seemingly horrible events contain divine justice and wisdom. They do not
come without warning, and can be a source of punishment, purification, or reward for the
patient. These frightful scenes are warnings and lessons for the onlookers. Even the simplest
display of God's might should instill in us a fear of Him that propels us to Him:

وَمِنْ ءَايَٰتِهِۦ يُرِيكُمُ ٱلْبَرْقَ خَوْفًا وَطَمَعًا

*And one of His signs is that He shows you lightning, inspiring
(you with) hope and fear.* [30:24]

The stories of nations and civilization who were obliterated even after achieving such high
levels of advancement should give us pause:

وَلَقَدْ مَكَّنَّٰهُمْ فِيمَآ إِن مَّكَّنَّٰكُمْ فِيهِ وَجَعَلْنَا لَهُمْ سَمْعًا وَأَبْصَٰرًا وَأَفْـِٔدَةً
فَمَآ أَغْنَىٰ عَنْهُمْ سَمْعُهُمْ وَلَآ أَبْصَٰرُهُمْ وَلَآ أَفْـِٔدَتُهُم مِّن شَىْءٍ إِذْ كَانُوا۟
يَجْحَدُونَ بِـَٔايَٰتِ ٱللَّهِ وَحَاقَ بِهِم مَّا كَانُوا۟ بِهِۦ يَسْتَهْزِءُونَ ۝ وَلَقَدْ أَهْلَكْنَا مَا
حَوْلَكُم مِّنَ ٱلْقُرَىٰ وَصَرَّفْنَا ٱلْءَايَٰتِ لَعَلَّهُمْ يَرْجِعُونَ ۝

*Indeed, We had established them in a way We have not
established you. And We gave them hearing, sight, and
intellect. But neither their hearing, sight, nor intellect were
of any benefit to them whatsoever, since they persisted in
denying Allah's signs. And (so) they were overwhelmed
by what they used to ridicule. We certainly destroyed the
societies around you after having diversified the signs so
perhaps they would return (to the Right Path).* [46:26-27]

Notice that last sentence. Allah sends signs in so many different forms, but after an insistent
denial of the truth He makes the deniers themselves a sign for others. May He spare us of
this end.

Perhaps the most potent of these examples is that of the Pharaoh. Even after millenia have
passed, the bodies of the Pharaohs are still preserved in their physical form. Some marvel at
this as an indication of the ancient Egyptians' scientific sophistication, but the Muslim should

recognize the signal of God's overwhelming power and all-encompassing capability. Even before the modern archaeological excavations discoveries of the process of mummification, God sent down in His Quran that he said to the Pharaoh,

$$فَٱلْيَوْمَ نُنَجِّيكَ بِبَدَنِكَ لِتَكُونَ لِمَنْ خَلْفَكَ ءَايَةً وَإِنَّ كَثِيرًا مِّنَ ٱلنَّاسِ عَنْ ءَايَٰتِنَا لَغَٰفِلُونَ ۝$$

*Today We will preserve your corpse so that you may become
an example for those who come after you. And surely most
people are heedless of Our examples!* [10:92]

Now it is our duty to react to these signals. Paying attention is imperative; we cannot afford to turn away and risk punishment ourselves. God says,

$$وَمَنْ أَظْلَمُ مِمَّن ذُكِّرَ بِـَٔايَٰتِ رَبِّهِۦ ثُمَّ أَعْرَضَ عَنْهَآ$$

*And who does more wrong than the one who is reminded of
Allah's revelations then turns away from them?* [32:22]

◖ THE DIVINE PATTERNS ◗

God designed life on earth to follow certain laws and patterns, around which we humans live our lives. For example, we can count on the consistency of gravity as a physical force, we can predict when and where celestial bodies will rise and set, and we accept the phenomenon that history indeed repeats itself. God has set the course of certain things in certain ways:

$$فَلَن تَجِدَ لِسُنَّتِ ٱللَّهِ تَبْدِيلًا وَلَن تَجِدَ لِسُنَّتِ ٱللَّهِ تَحْوِيلًا ۝$$

*You will find no change in the way of Allah, nor will you find
it diverted.* [35:43]

We build our societies and structure our lives on these universal laws. Most of them share one basic principle that every action has a reaction. We can use this realization to build confidence in some common themes found throughout the Quran: good yields good, and bad yields bad; seeking guidance achieves it, while neglecting it renders one lost; wholesome and holistic efforts bring about happiness, while corrupt and short-sighted efforts end in waste. Things are made easy or difficult, tranquil or anxiety-inducing, due to certain divine laws. All of these situations are the result of a prerequisite cause.

Any pain, difficulty, or discomfort that we feel is a result of something we did or neglected to do. It is nothing more than the harvest of the seeds we planted ourselves. Allah says,

أَوَلَمَّآ أَصَٰبَتْكُم مُّصِيبَةٌ قَدْ أَصَبْتُم مِّثْلَيْهَا قُلْتُمْ أَنَّىٰ هَٰذَا قُلْ هُوَ مِنْ عِندِ أَنفُسِكُمْ إِنَّ ٱللَّهَ عَلَىٰ كُلِّ شَىْءٍ قَدِيرٌ ۝

Why do you [believers] say, when a calamity befalls you,
even after you have inflicted twice as much damage [on your
enemy], 'How did this happen?'? [Prophet], say, 'You brought
it upon yourselves.' God has power over everything. [3:165]

We may believe that we don't deserve the tests that come to us, or didn't do anything wrong to deserve such pain. But God never does even the slightest bit of injustice to anyone:

ذَٰلِكَ بِمَا قَدَّمَتْ أَيْدِيكُمْ وَأَنَّ ٱللَّهَ لَيْسَ بِظَلَّامٍ لِّلْعَبِيدِ ۝

That is on account of what you stored up for yourselves with
your own hands: God is never unjust to His servants. [3:182]

We are the ones who have committed wrong, and our first victims are ourselves:

إِنَّ ٱللَّهَ لَا يَظْلِمُ ٱلنَّاسَ شَيْئًا وَلَٰكِنَّ ٱلنَّاسَ أَنفُسَهُمْ يَظْلِمُونَ ۝

Indeed, Allah does not wrong people in the least, but it is
people who wrong themselves. [10:44]

This theme is especially clear when reading the passages in the Quran on the rise and fall of previous nations. The Children of Israel are the most commonly mentioned, and this is not unintentional. Consider how God honored them and allowed them to flourish on earth after the atrocities that the Pharaoh committed against them:

وَأَوْرَثْنَا ٱلْقَوْمَ ٱلَّذِينَ كَانُوا يُسْتَضْعَفُونَ مَشَٰرِقَ ٱلْأَرْضِ وَمَغَٰرِبَهَا ٱلَّتِي بَٰرَكْنَا فِيهَا وَتَمَّتْ كَلِمَتُ رَبِّكَ ٱلْحُسْنَىٰ عَلَىٰ بَنِي إِسْرَٰءِيلَ بِمَا صَبَرُوا وَدَمَّرْنَا مَا كَانَ يَصْنَعُ فِرْعَوْنُ وَقَوْمُهُۥ وَمَا كَانُوا يَعْرِشُونَ ۝

And (so) We made the oppressed people successors of the
eastern and western lands, which We had showered with
blessings. (In this way) the noble Word of your Lord was
fulfilled for the Children of Israel for what they had endured.
And We destroyed what Pharaoh and his people constructed
and what they established. [7:137]

God also says, making His favor upon them clear:

وَلَقَدِ ٱخْتَرْنَٰهُمْ عَلَىٰ عِلْمٍ عَلَى ٱلْعَٰلَمِينَ ۝

And indeed, We chose the Israelites knowingly above the
others. [44:32]

But when they failed to uphold this blessing and went overboard in their crimes and transgression, they began to harvest the most bitter of fruits:

فَبِظُلْمٍ مِّنَ ٱلَّذِينَ هَادُوا حَرَّمْنَا عَلَيْهِمْ طَيِّبَٰتٍ أُحِلَّتْ لَهُمْ وَبِصَدِّهِمْ عَن
سَبِيلِ ٱللَّهِ كَثِيرًا ۞

We forbade the Jews certain foods that had been lawful to
them for their wrongdoing, and for hindering many from the
Way of Allah [4:160]

God states further,

ذَٰلِكَ جَزَيْنَٰهُم بِبَغْيِهِمْ وَإِنَّا لَصَٰدِقُونَ ۞

In this way We rewarded them for their violations. And We
are certainly truthful. [6:146]

These stories that God chooses carefully to place in His final scripture are not merely historical accounts for us to muse over. These stories are meant to serve as reminders and warnings lest we fall into the same violations. They help us diagnose our own spiritual missteps and prevent us from walking further down the already trodden path of destruction. The Prophet ﷺ went as far as to warn us: **"You will inevitably follow those before you step by step, inch by inch. Even if they went into a lizard's hole, you would follow them."** The Companions present asked, **"Messenger of Allah, do you mean the Jews and the Christians?"** He responded, **"Who else?"**[66]

The Quran is full of verses that fit into the theme that our pleasure and pain are consequences of our own actions. God says,

وَلَوْ أَنَّا كَتَبْنَا عَلَيْهِمْ أَنِ ٱقْتُلُوا أَنفُسَكُمْ أَوِ ٱخْرُجُوا مِن دِيَٰرِكُم مَّا فَعَلُوهُ
إِلَّا قَلِيلٌ مِّنْهُمْ وَلَوْ أَنَّهُمْ فَعَلُوا مَا يُوعَظُونَ بِهِۦ لَكَانَ خَيْرًا لَّهُمْ وَأَشَدَّ تَثْبِيتًا
۞ وَإِذًا لَّءَاتَيْنَٰهُم مِّن لَّدُنَّآ أَجْرًا عَظِيمًا ۞ وَلَهَدَيْنَٰهُمْ صِرَٰطًا مُّسْتَقِيمًا ۞

If We had commanded them to sacrifice themselves or
abandon their homes, none would have obeyed except for a
few. Had they done what they were advised to do, it would
have certainly been far better for them and more reassuring,
and We would have granted them a great reward by Our
grace and guided them to the Straight Path. [4:66-68]

Consider the magnified reward that God promises to those who spend for His sake:

مَّثَلُ ٱلَّذِينَ يُنفِقُونَ أَمْوَٰلَهُمْ فِى سَبِيلِ ٱللَّهِ كَمَثَلِ حَبَّةٍ أَنۢبَتَتْ سَبْعَ سَنَابِلَ فِى
كُلِّ سُنۢبُلَةٍ مِّا۟ئَةُ حَبَّةٍ وَٱللَّهُ يُضَٰعِفُ لِمَن يَشَآءُ وَٱللَّهُ وَٰسِعٌ عَلِيمٌ ۝

The example of those who spend their wealth in the cause of
Allah is that of a grain that sprouts into seven ears, each bearing
one hundred grains. And Allah multiplies (the reward even
more) to whoever He wills. For Allah is All-Bountiful, All-
Knowing. [2:261]

All of this reward is tied to the effort that we put forth. Without our initiative, we can gain no reward, opportunities, or progress. You cannot harvest fruits you don't plant.

Coming to God requires an initiative on our part as well. The Prophet ﷺ said that Allah says, **"Human being, stand up for me, and I will walk to you. Walk to me, and I will run to you."**[67] The Quran makes this concept very clear, showing us the results of both compliance and rejection:

وَلَوْ أَنَّ أَهْلَ ٱلْقُرَىٰٓ ءَامَنُوا۟ وَٱتَّقَوْا۟ لَفَتَحْنَا عَلَيْهِم بَرَكَٰتٍ مِّنَ ٱلسَّمَآءِ وَٱلْأَرْضِ
وَلَٰكِن كَذَّبُوا۟ فَأَخَذْنَٰهُم بِمَا كَانُوا۟ يَكْسِبُونَ ۝

Had the people of those societies been faithful and mindful (of
Allah), We would have overwhelmed them with blessings from
heaven and earth. But they disbelieved, so We seized them for
what they used to commit. [7:96]

God also says,

مَّنْ عَمِلَ صَٰلِحًا فَلِنَفْسِهِۦ وَمَنْ أَسَآءَ فَعَلَيْهَا وَمَا رَبُّكَ بِظَلَّٰمٍ لِّلْعَبِيدِ ۝

Whoever does good does it for his own soul and whoever does
evil does it against his own soul: your Lord is never unjust to
His creatures. [41:46]

◈ UNDERSTANDING TRIALS ◈

Pain and suffering in this life for the wrongdoers can be punishment, reminder, or both:

وَلَنُذِيقَنَّهُم مِّنَ ٱلْعَذَابِ ٱلْأَدْنَىٰ دُونَ ٱلْعَذَابِ ٱلْأَكْبَرِ لَعَلَّهُمْ يَرْجِعُونَ ۝

We will certainly make them taste some of the minor torment

(in this life) before the major torment (of the Hereafter), so
perhaps they will return (to the Right Path). [32:21]

For the believer, pain is how God tests them, reminds them of the insignificance of this world, purifies them of sins, and raises them closer to Him. God tests His servants in order to refine their humility, brokenness, repentance, and servitude to Him. As these qualities become more firmly established in the hearts of the believers, their trials often intensify in order to raise them further up. This is how those who are most devoted to God reach their lofty stations.

Sa'd bin Abi Waqqas once asked the Prophet ﷺ, "Messenger of Allah, who are the ones with the most severe trials?" He responded, "The Prophets, then the righteous, and then those people who resemble them in successive order. A man is tested according to his religious commitment. If his religion is solid, then he will increase in his trials, and if his religion is flimsy, it will be made lighter for him. Trials will continue for a servant until he walks on the surface of the earth without any wrongdoings."[68]

There are certain things that we gain from being tested that we could not gain by any other means. The stations that some of us reach through enduring pain patiently could not be reached otherwise. Without our trials, we could have remained heedless and immature—only God knows. Though the taste is bitter, enduring difficulty comes with much good for the believers and certainly increases our faith. In the end, this world is not of so much value anyway. God tells us about two instances wherein this phenomenon was experienced by the Companions:

$$\text{ٱلَّذِينَ قَالَ لَهُمُ ٱلنَّاسُ إِنَّ ٱلنَّاسَ قَدْ جَمَعُواْ لَكُمْ فَٱخْشَوْهُمْ فَزَادَهُمْ إِيمَٰنًا}$$
$$\text{وَقَالُواْ حَسْبُنَا ٱللَّهُ وَنِعْمَ ٱلْوَكِيلُ ۝}$$

Those whose faith only increased when people said, 'Fear
your enemy: they have amassed a great army against you,'
and who replied, 'God is enough for us: He is the best
protector.' [3:173]

Even when the believers were surrounded and under siege by the largest army they had ever seen, during the Battle of the Trench, they stood firm, and so Allah rewarded them unimaginably:

$$\text{وَلَمَّا رَءَا ٱلْمُؤْمِنُونَ ٱلْأَحْزَابَ قَالُوا هَٰذَا مَا وَعَدَنَا ٱللَّهُ وَرَسُولُهُۥ وَصَدَقَ ٱللَّهُ}$$
$$\text{وَرَسُولُهُۥ وَمَا زَادَهُمْ إِلَّآ إِيمَٰنًا وَتَسْلِيمًا ۝}$$

When the believers saw the enemy alliance, they said, "This is
what Allah and His Messenger had promised us. The promise
of Allah and His Messenger has come true." And this only
increased them in faith and submission. [33:22]

Sometimes a gift can lie in the absence of something we wished for. Sometimes a blessing can be disguised as a calamity. God constantly reminds us that there is more to the world than the apparent realities at its surface:

وَعَسَىٰ أَن تَكْرَهُوا شَيْئًا وَهُوَ خَيْرٌ لَّكُمْ وَعَسَىٰ أَن تُحِبُّوا شَيْئًا وَهُوَ شَرٌّ لَّكُمْ وَٱللَّهُ يَعْلَمُ وَأَنتُمْ لَا تَعْلَمُونَ ۝

Perhaps you dislike something which is good for you and like something which is bad for you. Allah knows and you do not know. [2:216]

These reminders are for us to be humble and aware that our understanding is shallow, imperfect and incomplete. Tests and calamities should inspire a swift return to God, pleading with humility for forgiveness and protection.

فَلَوْلَآ إِذْ جَآءَهُم بَأْسُنَا تَضَرَّعُوا

If only they had learned humility when suffering came from Us! [6:43]

Just as frequently as we see the believers being tried with oppression and subjugation, we also see those who reject truth being showered in what they consider to be blessings. This does not mean that God is not punishing them for their evil. What seems like a gift from God at face value may very well be a form of punishment and disgrace. It is just one of the many ways by which God subtly leads the disbelievers towards a more tragic end. God tells us to remember when seeing them in their luxury:

فَذَرْنِي وَمَن يُكَذِّبُ بِهَٰذَا ٱلْحَدِيثِ سَنَسْتَدْرِجُهُم مِّنْ حَيْثُ لَا يَعْلَمُونَ ۝

So leave to Me those who reject this message. We will gradually draw them to destruction in ways they cannot comprehend. [68:44]

These apparent blessings should also serve as a means to humble the disbelievers and prompt them to reflect. If they were truthful with their own hearts, they would realize that they do not deserve what God has blessed them with in this life. They would seek out His guidance and mercy, and this is why God says as a warning to His servants:

أَوَلَا يَرَوْنَ أَنَّهُمْ يُفْتَنُونَ فِي كُلِّ عَامٍ مَّرَّةً أَوْ مَرَّتَيْنِ ثُمَّ لَا يَتُوبُونَ وَلَا هُمْ يَذَّكَّرُونَ ۝

Do they not see that they are tried once or twice every year?
Yet they neither repent nor do they learn a lesson. [9:126]

Whenever they encounter a wake up call, their conscience calls out to them that there is a greater truth. Some respond, changing their lifestyle and direction to align with the right path. But others drown the call with the clamour of their own egos and passions. They continue on blindly, submerging themselves deeper into a poisonous oblivion. Perhaps if they were to reflect over God's verses, they would have been spared:

وَلَقَدْ أَرْسَلْنَآ إِلَىٰٓ أُمَمٍ مِّن قَبْلِكَ فَأَخَذْنَٰهُم بِٱلْبَأْسَآءِ وَٱلضَّرَّآءِ لَعَلَّهُمْ يَتَضَرَّعُونَ ۝
فَلَوْلَآ إِذْ جَآءَهُم بَأْسُنَا تَضَرَّعُوا وَلَٰكِن قَسَتْ قُلُوبُهُمْ وَزَيَّنَ لَهُمُ ٱلشَّيْطَٰنُ مَا
كَانُوا يَعْمَلُونَ ۝ فَلَمَّا نَسُوا مَا ذُكِّرُوا بِهِۦ فَتَحْنَا عَلَيْهِمْ أَبْوَٰبَ كُلِّ شَىْءٍ حَتَّىٰٓ
إِذَا فَرِحُوا بِمَآ أُوتُوٓا أَخَذْنَٰهُم بَغْتَةً فَإِذَا هُم مُّبْلِسُونَ ۝

We sent messengers before you [Prophet] to many communities
and afflicted their people with suffering and hardships, so that
they could learn humility. If only they had learned humility
when suffering came from Us! But no, their hearts became
hard and Satan made their foul deeds alluring to them. When
they became oblivious to warnings, We showered them with
everything they desired. But just as they became prideful of
what they were given, We seized them by surprise, then they
instantly fell into despair! [6:42-44]

An individual's abundance of wealth and high status can actually prevent them from much good, even if it is not obvious at first glance. God says,

أَيَحْسَبُونَ أَنَّمَا نُمِدُّهُم بِهِۦ مِن مَّالٍ وَبَنِينَ ۝ نُسَارِعُ لَهُمْ فِى ٱلْخَيْرَٰتِ بَل
لَّا يَشْعُرُونَ ۝

Do they think, since We provide them with wealth and
children, that We hasten to (honour) them (with) all kinds of
good? No! They are not aware. [23:55-56]

Too much material wealth and ease can be dangerous. Too much comfort hinders our ability to empathize with pain. Too much ease makes us fragile at the first taste of hardship.

The "good" that the evil-doers seem to be blessed with is nothing more than a temporary distraction from their eventual destiny. But still, Allah never closes the door of repentance; there is always a chance for them to return. When their glass house shatters, they should take it as a sign from God to begin their journey back. This is one of the wisdoms behind suffering:

ظَهَرَ ٱلْفَسَادُ فِى ٱلْبَرِّ وَٱلْبَحْرِ بِمَا كَسَبَتْ أَيْدِى ٱلنَّاسِ لِيُذِيقَهُم بَعْضَ ٱلَّذِى
عَمِلُوا لَعَلَّهُمْ يَرْجِعُونَ ۝

Corruption has spread on land and sea as a result of what
people's hands have done, so that Allah may cause them to
taste the consequences of some of their deeds and perhaps
they might return. [30:41]

Not every blessing that Allah grants a person in this world is a sign of honor. Blessings are tests that call for the one being blessed to show the proper form of gratitude. We must use what God gave us in service of Him; this is how we pass the test and rise in rank. Otherwise, the blessing will serve as evidence of our ingratitude on the Day of Judgment. On that Day, many people will wish they had never received the blessing in the first place. What appeared to be a blessing only reaped grief and loss in the end.

Just as being blessed with something in this world requires gratitude, being deprived of something in this world calls for patience. Allah makes this clear throughout the Quran. Every moment in life, both the highs and the lows, are tests.

وَنَبْلُوكُم بِٱلشَّرِّ وَٱلْخَيْرِ فِتْنَةً وَإِلَيْنَا تُرْجَعُونَ ۝

And We test you with good and evil as a trial, then to Us you
will be returned. [21:35]

وَهُوَ ٱلَّذِى جَعَلَكُمْ خَلَـٰٓئِفَ ٱلْأَرْضِ وَرَفَعَ بَعْضَكُمْ فَوْقَ بَعْضٍ دَرَجَـٰتٍ
لِّيَبْلُوَكُمْ فِى مَآ ءَاتَىٰكُمْ إِنَّ رَبَّكَ سَرِيعُ ٱلْعِقَابِ وَإِنَّهُ لَغَفُورٌ رَّحِيمٌ ۝

He is the One Who has placed you as successors on earth and
elevated some of you in rank over others, so He may test you with
what He has given you. Surely your Lord is swift in punishment,
but He is certainly All-Forgiving, Most Merciful. [6:165]

To think that God blesses the rich, but does not care about those for whom He destined poverty is a deeply flawed way of thinking. We may even hold this belief at a subconscious level; many of us associate doing well, financially and otherwise, as a sign of God's approval. The truth is, however, that each is being tested in their own way:

فَأَمَّا ٱلْإِنسَـٰنُ إِذَا مَا ٱبْتَلَىٰهُ رَبُّهُ فَأَكْرَمَهُ وَنَعَّمَهُ فَيَقُولُ رَبِّى أَكْرَمَنِ ۝ وَأَمَّآ إِذَا
مَا ٱبْتَلَىٰهُ فَقَدَرَ عَلَيْهِ رِزْقَهُ فَيَقُولُ رَبِّى أَهَـٰنَنِ ۝ كَلَّا بَل لَّا تُكْرِمُونَ ٱلْيَتِيمَ ۝

[The nature of] man is that, when his Lord tries him through
honour and blessings, he says, 'My Lord has honoured me,'

but when He tries him through the restriction of his provision,
he says, 'My Lord has humiliated me.' Absolutely not! You
[people] do not honor orphans. [89:15-17]

Our reactions to these tests shape our character and relationship with God and determine where we end up in the afterlife. They also have more immediate effects in this life as well. God promises, for example, that when we are grateful, He will give us more:

وَإِذْ تَأَذَّنَ رَبُّكُمْ لَئِن شَكَرْتُمْ لَأَزِيدَنَّكُمْ

And (remember) when your Lord proclaimed, "If you are
grateful, I will certainly give you more…" [14:7]

He also emphasizes the virtue of patience by telling us that its reward is limitless—meaning not limited to the next life alone:

إِنَّمَا يُوَفَّى ٱلصَّٰبِرُونَ أَجْرَهُم بِغَيْرِ حِسَابٍ ۝

Only those who endure patiently will be given their reward
without limit. [39:10]

To Allah, this world and everything in it is not worth so much as the wing of a fly. The limited pain that we might feel in this life is negligible compared to the eternal bliss and freedom of Paradise. To put things into perspective, Jabir narrates that the Messenger of Allah ﷺ said, **"When the people who were tested severely receive their reward on the Day of Judgment, the people who had it easy will wish that their skin was torn apart by scissors in this life."**[69]

The Quran is full of verses that fit into this theme; hardly any surah is free of its mention. It is important that we keep our ears attentive and hearts awake to catch these meanings when we pass them, allowing them to become part of our character and worldview.

◁(SINCERITY)▷

The heart is the center of our connection to God. Our rank with God is determined by the level of sincerity and goodness within the heart. To grant us a fair chance, He filled his book with verses that make this clear to us, helping us reflect on our inner state as we recite.

Some verses are straightforward and clear. For example, God says,

إِن يَعْلَمِ ٱللَّهُ فِى قُلُوبِكُمْ خَيْرًا يُؤْتِكُمْ خَيْرًا مِّمَّآ أُخِذَ مِنكُمْ وَيَغْفِرْ لَكُمْ

If Allah finds goodness in your hearts, He will give you better
than what has been taken from you, and forgive you. [8:70]

Sincerity yields beauty and great benefit in this life, through its tangible and intangible effects:

فَعَلِمَ مَا فِى قُلُوبِهِمْ فَأَنزَلَ ٱلسَّكِينَةَ عَلَيْهِمْ وَأَثَٰبَهُمْ فَتْحًا قَرِيبًا ۝

He knew what was in their hearts, so He sent down serenity upon them and rewarded them with a victory at hand. [48:18]

And in order to shift our focus inwards, Allah says:

لَّا يُؤَاخِذُكُمُ ٱللَّهُ بِٱللَّغْوِ فِىٓ أَيْمَٰنِكُمْ وَلَٰكِن يُؤَاخِذُكُم بِمَا كَسَبَتْ قُلُوبُكُمْ

Allah will not hold you accountable for unintentional oaths, but for what you intended in your hearts. [2:225]

With His knowledge of our hearts, God only grants us what we ourselves yearn for, good or evil. He says:

فِى قُلُوبِهِم مَّرَضٌ فَزَادَهُمُ ٱللَّهُ مَرَضًا

There is a disease in their hearts, and Allah increases them in their disease. [2:10]

Some might be so bold to claim that they do not believe in Islam because God did not guide them, and so they will continue to follow their desires until guidance comes. But the truth is they did not want guidance in the first place. They made no effort to rectify their hearts. God saw in their hearts aversion and rejection, and only facilitated them towards what they desired:

وَلَوْ عَلِمَ ٱللَّهُ فِيهِمْ خَيْرًا لَّأَسْمَعَهُمْ

Had Allah known any goodness in them, He would have certainly made them hear. [8:23]

God knows well that if the unbelievers had the exact opportunities that He afforded to the believers to come near to Him, they would not have taken advantage of that.

وَلَوْ أَسْمَعَهُمْ لَتَوَلَّوا وَّهُم مُّعْرِضُونَ ۝

(But) even if He had made them hear, they would have surely turned away heedlessly. [8:23]

The inverse is true for those whom God guides. He guides those who genuinely want to be near Him. When people criticized the fact that most of his followers were poor and weak, Prophet Noah responded:

وَلَآ أَقُولُ لَكُمْ عِندِى خَزَآئِنُ ٱللَّهِ وَلَآ أَعْلَمُ ٱلْغَيْبَ وَلَآ أَقُولُ إِنِّى مَلَكٌ وَلَآ أَقُولُ لِلَّذِينَ تَزْدَرِىٓ أَعْيُنُكُمْ لَن يُؤْتِيَهُمُ ٱللَّهُ خَيْرًا ٱللَّهُ أَعْلَمُ بِمَا فِىٓ أَنفُسِهِمْ إِنِّىٓ إِذًا لَّمِنَ ٱلظَّٰلِمِينَ ۝

I do not say to you that I possess Allah's treasuries or
know the unseen, nor do I claim to be an angel, nor do I
say that Allah will never grant goodness to those you look
down upon. Allah knows best what is within them. If I
did, then I would truly be one of the wrongdoers. [11:31]

Prophet Noah points out to his people that God does not honor with His guidance whomever *we* determine to be worthy. Allah is the supreme judge—He chooses those whose hearts are worthy of being with Him. It all starts from within. The more attention we give to purifying our core, the more doors God will open for us to come closer to Him. The destinies are chosen by the All-Knowing, who does nothing without full knowledge and nuanced wisdom:

وَلَقَدِ ٱخْتَرْنَٰهُمْ عَلَىٰ عِلْمٍ عَلَى ٱلْعَٰلَمِينَ ۝

And indeed, We chose them knowingly above all others.
[44:32]

Now we can understand why Abu Bakr was granted such a high rank in our religion, as those around him said, "Abu Bakr did not surpass you with his abundant prayer or fasts; rather there was something lodged deep in his heart."

God dedicated much of His scripture to the internal dimension of our heart. He makes clear to us that His pleasure and punishment are only earned through the contents and actions of our hearts. How can we pass these verses casually, without giving our internal states a second thought?

وَٱعْلَمُوٓا۟ أَنَّ ٱللَّهَ يَعْلَمُ مَا فِىٓ أَنفُسِكُمْ فَٱحْذَرُوهُ

Know that Allah is aware of what is in your hearts, so
beware of Him. [2:235]

◄ SUCCESS AND FAILURE ►

Definitions of success and failure are loaded with implications that change with time and place. When we use the Quran as our lens for understanding the world around us, we see that success is related to guidance, accuracy, and reaching the goals that you set for yourself. This is why the Prophet ﷺ instructed us to, **"Ask God, the Exalted, for guidance and accuracy. With guidance, think about being guided on a journey, and with accuracy, think about when you aim with your arrow."**[70]

God not only defines these concepts for us in the Quran, but also makes clear to us how to earn God's assistance along the way. Success is only earned through His help, and whoever is left to fend for themselves will be left weak and vulnerable to ego and whim. The outcome is indeed determined by God, but at the same time it all starts with us, as discussed earlier. By lowering ourselves for God, we achieve His divine assistance towards success, and by relying on our own limited capacity, we guarantee our own failure.

Notice the precise wording of the Prophet's prayers. He taught us, for example, to say every morning and every evening, **"Living, Sustaining God! I seek assistance in your mercy, Rectify all of my affairs and do not leave me on my own for the blink of an eye!"**[71] In the ultimate display of humility and reliance upon God, he also said, **"If you leave me to myself, you will leave me to weakness, vulnerability, sin, and wrongdoing. I only every trust in your mercy!"**[72]

We sometimes find ourselves swinging between success and failure many times in the same day. We might go from genuinely relying upon Allah, to then being self-impressed and deluded into attributing any part of success to ourselves, thus leading us back to failure. This is the nature of how and when God distributes success, and we can see it manifest clearly all throughout history.

We shouldn't be surprised by how salient this concept is in the life of our Prophet ﷺ and his Companions. When the believers showed up to fight against their enemies despite their impossible chances of victory, God aided them to triumph by sending angels to fight alongside them. He says about this incident,

$$ وَلَقَدْ نَصَرَكُمُ ٱللَّهُ بِبَدْرٍ وَأَنتُمْ أَذِلَّةٌ $$

Indeed, Allah made you victorious at Badr when you were outnumbered. [3:123]

They looked past the apparent odds and relied on God for their success while doing their part, and so He gave it to them. This becomes even clearer when we learn that the Prophet ﷺ had spent the night before the battle begging His Lord for help. Allah then said, to prove that his cries were not unheard nor unanswered:

$$إِذْ تَسْتَغِيثُونَ رَبَّكُمْ فَٱسْتَجَابَ لَكُمْ أَنِّي مُمِدُّكُم بِأَلْفٍ مِّنَ
ٱلْمَلَـٰئِكَةِ مُرْدِفِينَ ۝$$

*When you cried out to your Lord for help, He answered, "I
will reinforce you with a thousand angels—followed by many
others." [8:9]*

The same lesson can be learned from when the women in Egypt were coercing Prophet
Joseph to commit what he knew was a sin. He knew that he would not be able to overcome
his own human inclinations, nor the clever traps of seduction that were being plotted against
him, and so he cried out,

$$وَإِلَّا تَصْرِفْ عَنِّي كَيْدَهُنَّ أَصْبُ إِلَيْهِنَّ وَأَكُن مِّنَ ٱلْجَـٰهِلِينَ ۝$$

*"If You do not turn their cunning away from me, I might yield
to them and fall into ignorance." [12:33]*

Allah responded to Joseph's prayer immediately:

$$فَٱسْتَجَابَ لَهُۥ رَبُّهُۥ فَصَرَفَ عَنْهُ كَيْدَهُنَّ إِنَّهُۥ هُوَ ٱلسَّمِيعُ ٱلْعَلِيمُ ۝$$

*So his Lord responded to him, turning their cunning away
from him. Surely He is the All-Hearing, All-Knowing. [12:34]*

There is a well-documented story about the three Companions who stayed behind during
one of the battles without any valid excuse. This was a grave offense; conscription for battle
was mandatory at that time, as the Muslims needed all hands on deck in every major battle.
When the Prophet ﷺ returned, all of the hypocrites who made up excuses were excused
immediately, but the Prophet ﷺ delayed the pardoning of these three sincere Companions
in order to show them the enormity of their action, as well as to distinguish them from the
rest of the hypocrites. The uncertainty of their fate made this period more strenuous for them
than any physical battle could have been, and the shunning and coldness of the Prophet ﷺ
towards them was more painful than any wound they could have incurred. But through their
anguish and by submitting whole-heartedly to Allah, they earned His redemption:

$$وَعَلَى ٱلثَّلَـٰثَةِ ٱلَّذِينَ خُلِّفُوا۟ حَتَّىٰٓ إِذَا ضَاقَتْ عَلَيْهِمُ ٱلْأَرْضُ بِمَا رَحُبَتْ وَضَاقَتْ
عَلَيْهِمْ أَنفُسُهُمْ وَظَنُّوٓا۟ أَن لَّا مَلْجَأَ مِنَ ٱللَّهِ إِلَّآ إِلَيْهِ ثُمَّ تَابَ عَلَيْهِمْ لِيَتُوبُوٓا۟
إِنَّ ٱللَّهَ هُوَ ٱلتَّوَّابُ ٱلرَّحِيمُ ۝$$

*And (Allah has also turned in mercy to) the three who had
remained behind, (whose guilt distressed them) until the earth,*

despite its vastness, seemed to close in on them, and their
souls were torn in anguish. They knew there was no refuge
from Allah except in Him. Then He turned to them in mercy
so that they might repent. Surely Allah is the Acceptor of
Repentance, Most Merciful. [9:118]

Not every story is one of triumph and redemption. Allah also teaches us through His disciplining and development of the Companions that relying on and being impressed with yourself leads to nothing but failure. This is the quickest way to forfeit God's help. He says:

وَيَوْمَ حُنَيْنٍ إِذْ أَعْجَبَتْكُمْ كَثْرَتُكُمْ فَلَمْ تُغْنِ عَنكُمْ شَيْئًا وَضَاقَتْ عَلَيْكُمُ ٱلْأَرْضُ بِمَا رَحُبَتْ ثُمَّ وَلَّيْتُم مُّدْبِرِينَ ۝

At the Battle of ⸢unain when you took pride in your great
numbers, they proved of no advantage to you. The earth,
despite its vastness, seemed to close in on you, so you turned
back in retreat. [9:25]

⸢ VICTORY ⸣

God speaks about victory often in His scripture:

وَمَا ٱلنَّصْرُ إِلَّا مِنْ عِندِ ٱللَّهِ

And victory comes only from Allah [3:126]

إِن يَنصُرْكُمُ ٱللَّهُ فَلَا غَالِبَ لَكُمْ

If Allah helps you, none can defeat you. [3:160]

Reading the verses that promise victory can indeed empower us, but can also result in some sitting idly in their homes waiting for God's triumph. This would obviously be a misunderstanding of the verses, as it fails to take into consideration the bigger picture.

It is without question that victory comes from God. He determines who rises and who falls. But just as universal and constant as this concept is, so is the precept of exerting the work ourselves to achieve results. The Quran makes this clear in many places. For example, God gives us a formula:

وَلَيَنصُرَنَّ ٱللَّهُ مَن يَنصُرُهُۥ

Allah will certainly help those who stand up for Him. [23:40]

يَـٰٓأَيُّهَا ٱلَّذِينَ ءَامَنُوٓاْ إِن تَنصُرُواْ ٱللَّهَ يَنصُرْكُمْ وَيُثَبِّتْ أَقْدَامَكُمْ ۝

Believers! If you stand up for Allah, He will help you and
make your stance firm. [47:7]

Stand up for Allah, and not only will He help you rise in your stance above others, but also make your foothold firm and unshakeable. Put Allah first in your life, and He will put you first before others. Make Him your priority, and He will prioritize your success.

In addition to relying on God, there is another condition that God makes clear to us. He promises:

وَعَدَ ٱللَّهُ ٱلَّذِينَ ءَامَنُواْ مِنكُمْ وَعَمِلُواْ ٱلصَّـٰلِحَـٰتِ لَيَسْتَخْلِفَنَّهُمْ فِى ٱلْأَرْضِ
كَمَا ٱسْتَخْلَفَ ٱلَّذِينَ مِن قَبْلِهِمْ وَلَيُمَكِّنَنَّ لَهُمْ دِينَهُمُ ٱلَّذِى ٱرْتَضَىٰ لَهُمْ
وَلَيُبَدِّلَنَّهُم مِّنۢ بَعْدِ خَوْفِهِمْ أَمْنٗا يَعْبُدُونَنِى لَا يُشْرِكُونَ بِى شَيْـًٔا

Allah has promised those of you who believe and do good that
He will certainly make them successors in the land, as He did
with those before them; and will surely establish for them their
faith which He has chosen for them; and will indeed change
their fear into security—(provided that) they worship Me,
associating nothing with Me. [24:55]

Notice that the condition is that we don't associate anything as a partner with Allah. The verse didn't say "anyone." Our devotion to God is not just free of being partially directed towards other people, but other things as well, such as wealth, influence, and power. The Arabic wording (*shay'a*) indicates that our devotion is undivided, completely reserved for God.

What is required for victory is that we turn to God so completely, sincerely, and whole-heartedly that we shed our attachments to anyone or anything else. Every action, even the most mundane, are to be acts of devotion to God. This is what is meant in the verse,

قُلْ إِنَّ صَلَاتِى وَنُسُكِى وَمَحْيَاىَ وَمَمَاتِى لِلَّهِ رَبِّ ٱلْعَـٰلَمِينَ ۝ لَا شَرِيكَ
لَهُۥ وَبِذَٰلِكَ أُمِرْتُ

Say, "Surely my prayer, my worship, my life, and my death are
all for Allah—Lord of all worlds. He has no partner. This is
what I am commanded..." [6:162-163]

The result of this absolute devotion to the truth and holistic approach to submitting to God is not something we can afford to miss out on. God guarantees this:

وَمَن يُسْلِمْ وَجْهَهُۥ إِلَى ٱللَّهِ وَهُوَ مُحْسِنٌ فَقَدِ ٱسْتَمْسَكَ بِٱلْعُرْوَةِ ٱلْوُثْقَىٰ

Whoever fully submits themselves to Allah and is a good-doer,
they have certainly grasped the firmest hand-hold. [31:22]

Victory comes only with this comprehensive submission and active devotion to God, but it also requires necessary efforts and preparation on our part. This is why God commanded the believers, who were engaged in many battles against their enemies:

وَأَعِدُّوا لَهُم مَّا ٱسْتَطَعْتُم مِّن قُوَّةٍ وَمِن رِّبَاطِ ٱلْخَيْلِ

Prepare against them what you can of power and cavalry...
[8:60]

God commands us to put forth our best efforts to reach our goals, but to ultimately rely on Him for the outcome. With this strategy, we can expect victory from the Divine. With God's assistance, we can be an unstoppable force. For when God Helps us, no one can defeat us. God is all we have and all we need:

أَلَيْسَ ٱللَّهُ بِكَافٍ عَبْدَهُۥ

Is Allah not sufficient for His servant? [39:36]

⟨ LENS OF GUIDANCE ⟩

Guidance is a blessing and gift that God gives to whomever He wishes. In the Quran, Allah informs us:

إِنَّ عَلَيْنَا لَلْهُدَىٰ ۝

It is certainly upon Us (alone) to show guidance. [92:12]

Upon reflecting on how they reached their blissful end, the people in Paradise will acknowledge:

ٱلْحَمْدُ لِلَّهِ ٱلَّذِى هَدَىٰنَا لِهَٰذَا وَمَا كُنَّا لِنَهْتَدِىَ لَوْلَا أَنْ هَدَىٰنَا ٱللَّهُ

"Praise be to Allah for guiding us to this. We would have never
been guided if Allah had not guided us." [7:43]

But this aspect of guidance doesn't mean that God dishes it out arbitrarily without any wisdom and justice. God guides those who want to be guided. This means that our task is to make sure we truly desire it and tame our desires so that our hearts can be viable and receptive. We must first defeat our egos before we can expect to receive guidance, as He says,

$$فَمَنْ أَسْلَمَ فَأُولَٰئِكَ تَحَرَّوْا رَشَدًا ۝$$

Whoever submits, it is they who have attained Right Guidance. [72:14]

The Prophet ﷺ also informs us that God said, **"My servant, you are all lost except for whomever I guide, so seek guidance of Me."**[73] This is the crude reality of how life works—anyone who neglects or rejects God guidance is indeed lost. The *hadith qudsi* then refers to the most practical step to gaining guidance (in God's words): **"So seek guidance from me, and I will guide you."**[74]

The reason for people veering away from the truth lies in one of two causes: ignorance or passion. God says,

$$إِنَّا عَرَضْنَا ٱلْأَمَانَةَ عَلَى ٱلسَّمَٰوَٰتِ وَٱلْأَرْضِ وَٱلْجِبَالِ فَأَبَيْنَ أَن يَحْمِلْنَهَا وَأَشْفَقْنَ مِنْهَا وَحَمَلَهَا ٱلْإِنسَٰنُ إِنَّهُ كَانَ ظَلُومًا جَهُولًا ۝$$

Indeed, We offered the trust to the heavens and the earth and the mountains, but they (all) declined to bear it, being fearful of it. But humanity assumed it; they are truly wrongful and ignorant. [33:72]

This verse makes clear that the reason any given human fails to uphold their duty and carry out their purpose is due to either wrongdoing based on desire or willful ignorance.

In the Quran, Allah also attributes the rejection of the unbelievers to the fact that they genuinely do not want to believe. This is not due to any valid doubts or misunderstandings, but rather a refusal to change their ways. God shows us that,

$$بَلْ يُرِيدُ ٱلْإِنسَٰنُ لِيَفْجُرَ أَمَامَهُ ۝ يَسْـَٔلُ أَيَّانَ يَوْمُ ٱلْقِيَٰمَةِ ۝$$

Still people want to deny what is yet to come, asking, "When is this Day of Judgment?" [75:5-6]

The reason they ask questions in the first place is to poke superficial holes in the religion. If someone asks seeking the truth, they will find themselves bound to surrender to it. But when one asks in order to mock and undermine, they prove that their objective was never to find the truth in the first place. They are lost because they refuse to accept truth as truth, attempting instead to fit it into their own distorted world view:

$$ٱلَّذِينَ يَصُدُّونَ عَن سَبِيلِ ٱللَّهِ وَيَبْغُونَهَا عِوَجًا وَهُم بِٱلْءَاخِرَةِ كَٰفِرُونَ ۝$$

Those who hindered (others) from Allah's Way, strived to
make it crooked, and disbelieved in the Hereafter. [7:45]

When someone is hell-bent on their own flawed judgment and preferences, there is no
hope of convincing them of the truth:

وَلَئِنْ أَتَيْتَ ٱلَّذِينَ أُوتُوا ٱلْكِتَـٰبَ بِكُلِّ ءَايَةٍ مَّا تَبِعُوا قِبْلَتَكَ

Even if you were to bring every proof to the People of the
Book, they would not accept your direction... [2:145]

When the root of someone's unbelief is ignorance rather than subversive motives, it is an
easier challenge to tackle. Those who are sincerely committed to teaching and spreading the
truth of Islam will find that the Quran gives us many examples of people who were unbelievers because of a lack of information, and when the truth was made clear to them in a way
that won over both their hearts and minds, they submitted without hesitation.

Consider the magicians who performed for the Pharaoh when He challenged Moses.
Pharoah insisted that his court magicians were able to replicate any "sign" that Moses
claimed came from God. These sorcerers may have also thought that Moses was a fraud as the
Pharaoh claimed, but they were literally brought to their knees when they saw God's power

فَأُلْقِيَ ٱلسَّحَرَةُ سَـٰجِدِينَ ۝ قَالُوٓا ءَامَنَّا بِرَبِّ ٱلْعَـٰلَمِينَ ۝ رَبِّ مُوسَىٰ
وَهَـٰرُونَ ۝

The magicians fell down, prostrating. They declared, "We (now)
believe in the Lord of all worlds—the Lord of Moses and Aaron."
[26:46-48]

The magicians and the Pharaoh witnessed the same miracle. But the magicians, who disbelieved out of ignorance, accepted the truth when their knowledge gap was filled. The Pharaoh,
on the other hand, disbelieved out of arrogance, and so nothing could bring him to believe.

There is a critical moment in the story of the Queen of Sheba. When she came to discuss
whether or not her kingdom would accept God's religion with Solomon, she experienced the
ultimate astonishment at the wonders that God gave him:

وَصَدَّهَا مَا كَانَت تَّعْبُدُ مِن دُونِ ٱللَّهِ إِنَّهَا كَانَتْ مِن قَوْمٍ كَـٰفِرِينَ ۝ قِيلَ
لَهَا ٱدْخُلِي ٱلصَّرْحَ فَلَمَّا رَأَتْهُ حَسِبَتْهُ لُجَّةً وَكَشَفَتْ عَن سَاقَيْهَا قَالَ إِنَّهُۥ
صَرْحٌ مُّمَرَّدٌ مِّن قَوَارِيرَ قَالَتْ رَبِّ إِنِّي ظَلَمْتُ نَفْسِى وَأَسْلَمْتُ مَعَ سُلَيْمَـٰنَ
لِلَّهِ رَبِّ ٱلْعَـٰلَمِينَ ۝

But she had been hindered by what she used to worship

*instead of Allah, for she was indeed from a disbelieving
people. Then she was told, "Enter the palace." But when she
saw the hall, she thought it was a body of water, so she bared
her legs. Solomon said. "It is just a palace paved with crystal."
(At last) she declared, "My Lord! I have certainly wronged
my soul. Now I (fully) submit myself along with Solomon to
Allah, the Lord of all worlds."* [27:43-44]

Notice how God points out where she came from. She didn't believe in God's message previously only because it wasn't yet available to her. She was prevented from the true faith by her environment, much like the majority of people around the world who have not heard about Islam, or have only seen misrepresentations of it. If we pay close attention to the Quran and reflect on other instances like this one, we will see that there are many things that come between people and God's religion, and we will learn how to interact with them in a way that is compassionate, considerate, and conducive to faith.

◁(WISDOM AND GRATITUDE)▷

The beginning of Surah Luqman makes a clear connection between gratitude and wisdom:

$$ وَلَقَدْ ءَاتَيْنَا لُقْمَٰنَ ٱلْحِكْمَةَ أَنِ ٱشْكُرْ لِلَّهِ $$

*Indeed, We blessed Luqmân with wisdom, (saying), "Be
grateful to Allah...* [31:12]

Expressing gratitude is the surest way to avoid God's punishment:

$$ مَّا يَفْعَلُ ٱللَّهُ بِعَذَابِكُمْ إِن شَكَرْتُمْ وَءَامَنتُمْ $$

Why should Allah punish you if you are grateful and faithful? [4:147]

The blessings we receive are tests of our gratitude. Prophet Solomon, whom God blessed with worldly luxuries that would never again be witnessed, said:

$$ قَالَ هَٰذَا مِن فَضْلِ رَبِّي لِيَبْلُوَنِ ءَأَشْكُرُ أَمْ أَكْفُرُ $$

*"This is by the grace of my Lord to test me whether I am
grateful or ungrateful."* [27:40]

And the more grateful we are for what God already gave us, the more He will give us!

$$ لَئِن شَكَرْتُمْ لَأَزِيدَنَّكُمْ $$

If you are grateful, I will certainly give you more. [14:7]

Because gratitude is the key to everything good in this world and the next, Satan works tirelessly day and night to strip us of this mindset. He swore to God directly after he was cursed for disobeying God's command to bow to Adam that he would come to us, Adam's children, from every angle to divert us from gratitude.

قَالَ فَبِمَا أَغْوَيْتَنِي لَأَقْعُدَنَّ لَهُمْ صِرَاطَكَ الْمُسْتَقِيمَ ۝ ثُمَّ لَآتِيَنَّهُم مِّن بَيْنِ أَيْدِيهِمْ وَمِنْ خَلْفِهِمْ وَعَنْ أَيْمَانِهِمْ وَعَن شَمَائِلِهِمْ ۖ وَلَا تَجِدُ أَكْثَرَهُمْ شَاكِرِينَ ۝

He said, "For leaving me to stray I will lie in ambush for them on Your Straight Path. I will approach them from their front, their back, their right, their left, and then You will find most of them ungrateful." [7:16-17]

Gratitude seems like one of those abstract concepts that we always talk about without any concrete ideas of how to actualize it. Allah teaches us in the Quran that gratitude is more than just saying "thank you"; gratitude is best expressed through action:

اعْمَلُوٓا ءَالَ دَاوُودَ شُكْرًا

"Work gratefully, O family of David!" [34:13]

There is perhaps no scene in the life of the Prophet ﷺ that exemplifies this concept better than the night when Aishah found him praying with intense focus and humbling brokenness. She noticed his distress; he had been standing so long in prayer that his feet swelled up. When he finished, she asked, **"Why do you do this, Messenger of Allah, when Allah has already forgiven you?"** He responded, **"Shouldn't I, then, be a grateful servant?"**[75]

Gratitude for individual blessings comes first by acknowledging them, one by one, and praising God for each and every one. Then we must use the blessing as a means to come closer to Allah, making sure not to use it in sin, being keen to use it only for what pleases God. The most salient example would be our eyesight. To use this priceless gift to look at what God forbadewould be a gross form of ingratitude. Instead we should be using our senses to read and learn more about God and His religion. We can take it even one step further by using what Allah gave us to benefit others, keeping in mind all the while that you would be of no help to anyone had Allah not given you the opportunity. We should give charity, for example, with an appreciation for those to whom we give as opposed to feeling above them. Allah says about those who give ungratefully:

يَـٰٓأَيُّهَا ٱلَّذِينَ ءَامَنُوا لَا تُبْطِلُوا صَدَقَـٰتِكُم بِٱلْمَنِّ وَٱلْأَذَىٰ كَٱلَّذِى

يُنفِقُ مَالَهُۥ رِئَآءَ ٱلنَّاسِ وَلَا يُؤْمِنُ بِٱللَّهِ وَٱلْيَوْمِ ٱلْءَاخِرِ فَمَثَلُهُۥ

كَمَثَلِ صَفْوَانٍ عَلَيْهِ تُرَابٌ فَأَصَابَهُۥ وَابِلٌ فَتَرَكَهُۥ صَلْدًا لَّا يَقْدِرُونَ

عَلَىٰ شَىْءٍ مِّمَّا كَسَبُوا وَٱللَّهُ لَا يَهْدِى ٱلْقَوْمَ ٱلْكَـٰفِرِينَ ۝

*Believers! Do not waste your charity with reminders (of
your generosity) or hurtful words, like those who donate
their wealth just to show off and do not believe in Allah
or the Last Day. Their example is that of a hard barren
rock covered with a thin layer of soil hit by a strong rain—
leaving it just a bare stone. Such people are unable to
preserve the reward of their charity. Allah does not guide
(such) disbelieving people.* [2:264]

Gratitude is a theme that is hard to miss when reading the Quran. We should take a
moment to reflect every time we come across a verse that mentions it, looking at what specific aspect of gratitude God is addressing. We can try to connect different verses together
to help form a clearer and more holistic image of what it means to be grateful, all the while
putting the insights gained into practice.

Depth over Distance

Acknowledging the importance of interacting with and reflecting upon the Quran brings
up questions of consistency and priorities. How can we make sure that we are spending
quality time with the Quran while also reading enough to complete it entirely multiple times
throughout the year and to review the portions we have memorized? This question is critical
and a natural challenge that comes along with setting our sights on depth rather than distance.

Our primary goal with the Quran must be to reflect on its meanings and act upon its
instructions in order to give life to our hearts and bring light to our lives of darkness. There
is truly no replacement, even within the field of worship and knowledge, for the role it plays
in our lives. It is, as Allah calls it,

كِتَـٰبٌ أَنزَلْنَـٰهُ إِلَيْكَ مُبَـٰرَكٌ لِّيَدَّبَّرُوٓا ءَايَـٰتِهِۦ وَلِيَتَذَكَّرَ أُولُوا ٱلْأَلْبَـٰبِ ۝

*A blessed Book which We have revealed to you so that they
may contemplate its verses, and people of reason may be
mindful.* [38:28]

Think about the last time you wanted to finish the Quran in a specific amount of time.

You recited it quickly, tiring your tongue and your vocal chords in trying to reach that goal. But let us ask ourselves what was the benefit from that? Did we change during that recitation? The recitation of the tongue without any engagement of the mind is nothing more than lifting a barbell with no weights attached—you can probably do a lot of reps, but you're getting little out of it.

> Failing to reflect over the Quran when we recite is a liability to our spiritual well-being. Those hours that we spent reciting without depth can end up being a source of regret and an evidence against us on the Day of Judgment. The least we can do when we recite is to involve our intellect by understanding what we recite, even if it's just a general overview of the passage. Read the translation before recitation if language is a barrier. This will clear the way for more meanings and reflections to start flowing through your mind. With the help of Allah, the Ultimate Facilitator, the doors of understanding will open, and we will gradually ascend in our relationship with the Quran.

Do not become frustrated by the initial lack of insightful reflections. You might start off with thoughts that don't diverge much from any basic translation, but this is actually helping you build a foundation for more impactful meanings. As you pass by the same verses over and over, noticing the consistent themes through the diverse rhetorical styles, their meanings will settle within you. With time and Allah's grace, you will come to know what truly contemplating over the Quran's meanings feels like, its meanings coming to life all throughout your daily activities. You will dream about the pictures the verses paint and the stories they tell. When their treasures surface, you will stand in awe of their beauty and develop an obsession and hunger to dig deeper into the revelation. This is what it means for the Quran to be in our hearts, and such an experience is reserved only for those whom Allah chooses:

بَلْ هُوَ ءَايَتٌ بَيِّنَتٌ فِى صُدُورِ ٱلَّذِينَ أُوتُوا ٱلْعِلْمَ

This is (a set of) clear revelations in the hearts of those gifted with knowledge. [29:49]

With enough practice, we will start to find ourselves able to engage with the verses in a meaningful way without having to interrupt our flow of reading or recitation. The verses will spark thoughts that will flow more easily through our minds and be retained after our recitation. Our reflections will be more organic, and our recitation more productive.

To make the timeline more clear, imagine visiting an illustrious palace for the first time. You know there are endless treasures and precious objects inside, so after you take that first step to enter, you stop. You marvel at the chandeliers, the grand entryways, the tapestries, trying to soak in every luxurious detail. You tread lightly and quietly, lest you blunder past a marvel without noticing. You might not understand the meaning of every artwork or the history behind every artifact,, but why should that hinder your appreciation for them? Perhaps the next time you visit, you'll have learned a bit more to dive deeper than this initial, surface-level reverence.

The palace of the Quran is open for you to visit as often as you like. Every time you enter its halls, you're guaranteed to find a new spectacle to obsess over. Even when you are outside of the palace, you can't seem to stop thinking or speaking about it to others. As you begin to learn the true value of what is inside, you will want to spend more time exploring its limitless dimensions, and you will invite others to explore it with you.

There will inevitably come moments of confusion and lack of understanding in our journey through the Quran. When we reach an ayah that we can't seem to figure out, we must first begin our search for its meaning by humbling ourselves to Allah, who sent that ayah down to us, begging him to bless us with an accurate understanding. Only after that should we search through the dictionaries and books of commentary. The Prophet ﷺ once heard some people debating over the meanings of some verses, so he said to them, **"This is certainly what caused the destruction of those before you. They would cite the Book of Allah against one another, while the Book of Allah descended to affirm itself. So do not reject part of it with another part. Speak what you know of it, and leave what you do not know of it to the one who knows it."**[76]

Ibn al-Qayyim points out that nothing helps our hearts more than reciting the Quran with reflection and contemplation. It encompasses every stage of one's journey through life, addresses all circumstances universally, and maps out for us clearly the road to Allah. The Quran teaches us to be grateful for God's gifts and patient through His tests, and contains all of the necessary nutrients to keep our hearts healthy. If people only knew the power of reciting the Quran with reflection, they would choose it over any other activity. Reciting just one ayah with meaningful engagement and understanding is better than reading the entire Quran without reflection. This reflective mode of recitation gives life to our hearts, cultivates our faith, and helps us taste the sweetness of faith.

Just imagine what might have been going through the mind of our Prophet ﷺ that night when he recited one single ayah, repeating it until the morning came:

إِن تُعَذِّبْهُمْ فَإِنَّهُمْ عِبَادُكَ وَإِن تَغْفِرْ لَهُمْ فَإِنَّكَ أَنتَ ٱلْعَزِيزُ ٱلْحَكِيمُ ۝

If You punish them, they belong to You after all. But if You forgive them, You are surely the Almighty, All-Wise. [5:118]

What made him stop there, instead of continuing on with the surah? What was he feeling as God's words flowed from his blessed mouth? What meanings coaxed those tears from his eyes until they soaked his beard?

A Contemporary Perspective

To complete our discussion on the Quran, we should understand the concept of reflection and contemplation through the words of someone who has experienced its wonders firsthand. Sayyid Qutb was a modern Muslim thinker, prolific author, and activist who was executed by the Egyptian government in the 1960's. His magnum opus is *In the Shade of the Qur'an*, a masterpiece of Quranic reflection, in which he wrote this account.

➣ *In the Shade of the Quran* ➢

Living in the shade of the Quran is a blessing. It is a blessing that no one but those who have actually tasted it can know. It is a blessing that brings joy and blessings to one's life, while purifying it. All praise is due to God, who has blessed me with a life in the shade of the Quran for some time. I have tasted therein delights that I never before knew of, which gave meaning and brought blessings to my life.

I live hearing God speak to me through this Quran. But since I am just a small and worthless soul, what a great and unmatched honor for me to receive! What high meaning is received through this revelation, and what an esteemed position it is for God to bless me with!

Living in the shade of the Quran, I see the waves of the world's ignorance from above, and I see the people's petty and trivial concerns. I see how impressed people are with such rudimentary knowledge, incipient understanding, and childish concerns; it is truly as I am an adult watching children play all around. The attempts are childish, and the expressions are childish, and so I am astonished... What is with these people? Why are they stuck in this toxic wasteland? Why don't they hear the heavenly majestic call, the call to give meaning and blessing and purity to their lives?

Living in the shade of the Quran, I feel the beautiful harmony of human motion as God intended it, and the harmony of this universe that God created. Then I look and see the human race diverging from the nature of the world around them. I see the clash between these corrupt and wicked ideas that they are fed and the natural disposition upon which God created them. I ask myself: Who is this blasted devil that they are following into the pit of Hell?

In the shade of the Quran, I learned that there is no room for random coincidence or incidental events:

إِنَّا كُلَّ شَيْءٍ خَلَقْنَٰهُ بِقَدَرٍ ۝

Indeed, We have created everything, perfectly preordained.
[54:49]

وَخَلَقَ كُلَّ شَيْءٍ فَقَدَّرَهُۥ تَقْدِيرًا ۝

He has created everything, ordaining it precisely. [25:2]

Everything is for a wisdom, but the wisdom of the deep unseen realm may not be detectable to the human's imperfect perception:

وَعَسَىٰٓ أَن تَكْرَهُوا شَيْـًٔا وَهُوَ خَيْرٌ لَّكُمْ وَعَسَىٰٓ أَن تُحِبُّوا
شَيْـًٔا وَهُوَ شَرٌّ لَّكُمْ وَٱللَّهُ يَعْلَمُ وَأَنتُمْ لَا تَعْلَمُونَ ۝

Perhaps you dislike something which is good for you and
like something which is bad for you. Allah knows and you
do not know. [2:216]

Living in the shade of the Quran, my soul is calm, my heart is at peace, and my core is firm. I see the divine hand at work in every event and every moment. I live under God's care and supervision. I see His attributes come to life and notice His actions manifest in this world.

أَمَّن يُجِيبُ ٱلْمُضْطَرَّ إِذَا دَعَاهُ

Who responds to the distressed when they cry to Him?
[27:62]

وَهُوَ ٱلْقَاهِرُ فَوْقَ عِبَادِهِۦ وَهُوَ ٱلْحَكِيمُ ٱلْخَبِيرُ ۝

He reigns supreme over His creation. And He is the All-
Wise, All-Aware. [6:18]

فَعَّالٌ لِّمَا يُرِيدُ ۝

The Doer of whatever He wills. [85:16]

وَمَن يُهِنِ ٱللَّهُ فَمَا لَهُۥ مِن مُّكْرِمٍ

And whoever Allah disgraces, none can honour. [22:18]

This world is not dictated by limited and incidental systems. Behind the patterns of our world is a divine will that manages it. God creates as He wills and chooses, and I've learned of the Quran has made clear, God's way of doing things is applicable in any place, time, and stage of human development. After spending some time in the shade of the Quran, I reached a point of certainty that there is nothing good on this earth, nor any source of peace, comfort, honor, blessing, or purity for the human being, nor nothing more in synchrony with the universe, than to wholeheartedly return to Allah.

There is really only one way to return to Allah, as living in the shade of the Quran has made clear to me: it is to dedicate your whole life to Allah. He gave you a map and instructions on how to do so in His scripture. This means to let the Quran dictate our every move. The Human being, who was created by God, will never unlock the door to their inner dimensions with anything other than a key from God Himself. Nothing can cure the illnesses in the bodies and souls save the medicine from God Himself. And he has certainly given us the key to all door, and the cure for all maladies:

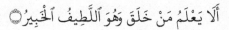

We send down the Quran as a healing and mercy for the
believers [17:82]

Despite all of this, the human race is not concerned about its own well being and humanity. Many are not interested in securing their own happiness and protecting themselves from punishment. They know that the best repair for a broken device would be done by the device's inventor, but they don't want to apply this rule when it comes to their own selves. They are not interested in returning to the One who created them in order to find the best way to repair their hearts and souls. They are dealing with incredibly nuanced and delicate devices, their own hearts and souls, whose inner workings no one can know but their inventor.

أَلَا يَعْلَمُ مَنْ خَلَقَ وَهُوَ ٱللَّطِيفُ ٱلْخَبِيرُ ۝

How could He not know His Own creation? For He (alone)
is the Most Subtle, All-Aware. [67:14]

This is where the misery of the confused and lost human being stems from. People will never find righteousness, guidance, comfort, or happiness until they submit their human nature to its grand Creator, just as any broken device would be brought back to its maker.

....

ENDNOTES

1. Ibn Abu Shaybah in *al-Musannaf*, v. 6, p. 125, #30006; and Ibn Hibbān, v. 1, p. 329, #122); and al-Ṭabarāni, v. 22, p. 188. It is deemed Ḥasan by al-Arna'oot.
2. *Zād al-Muhājir ila Rabbih* (al-Risālah al-Tabookiyyah), p. 49-50
3. *Tahdheeb Madārij al-Sālikeen*, p. 293
4. Imam Ahmad in *al-Zuhd*, #192; al-Ḥākim, al-Mustadrak, v. 2, p. 479, #3652 (he deemed it Ṣaheeh, and al-Dhahabi concurs)
5. *Madārij al-Sālikeen*, v. 3, p. 146
6. *Miftāh Dār al-Sa'ādah*, v. 1, p. 553
7. Muslim v. 1, p. 512 #746
8. Muslim, v. 1, p. 536, #746
9. Ibn Abu Shaybah, v. 6, p. 152, #30268; and al-Tirmidhi, v. 5, p.402, #3297 (he graded the *hadith* as Ḥasan ghareeb); and al-Ḥākim, v. 2, p. 374, #30268, who graded it as authentic (al-Dhahabi agreed with him; al-Albāni also graded it as authentic in silsilat al-ṢaḤeeḤah, #955
10. Ibn Kathir; ibn Abi Hatim
11. Ibn Hishām, v. 2, p. 209; Ahmad, al-Musnad, v. 23, p. 51, #14704; and Abu Dawud, v. 1, p. 142, #198 (it was graded Ḥasan by al-Arna'oot)
12. Al-Ṭabari, *Muqaddamat al-Tafseer*, v. 1, p. 80
13. *Fadā'il al-Qur'an*, al-Firyāni, p. 241, #169
14. This is mentioned by al-Bayhaqi in Shu'ab al-Imān, v. 3, p. 346, #1805
15. Malik in *al-Muwatta'*, #695
16. Al-Qurtubi, al-Tafseer, v. 1, p. 40
17. ibid. (in this wording); al-Ājurry, Akhlāq Ahl al-Quran, #32 (in a similar wording)
18. Abu 'Ubayd, Fada'il al-Qur'an, p. 113
19. Ibn al-Mubārak, al-Jihād, p. 118
20. Abu 'Ubayd al-Qāsim bin Salām, *Fada'il-al-Qur'an*, p. 112
21. ibid., 132
22. ibid., 112
23. Muslim, v. 1, p. 203, #223
24. Mannā' al-Qattān, *Mabāhith fee 'Uloom al-Qur'an*, p. 186
25. Al-Bukhari, v. 9, p. 162, #7562
26. Abu Ubayd in *Fada'il al-Quran*, p. 130
27. Miftāh al-Sa'ādah, v. 1, pp. 203-204
28. Sa'eed bin Manṣoor, al-Tafseer, v. 2, p. 393, #127
29. 'Abdul-Razzāq, al-Muṣannaf, v. 3, p. 363, #5984
30. Ahmad, al-Musnad, v. 11, p. 104, #6546; it was graded Ṣaheeh by al-Arna'oot
31. Al-Ajiri, *Akhlaq al-Quran*, 1.
32. Abu 'Ubayd, Faḍā'il al-Qur'an, 157
33. Sunan al-Dārimi, v. 1, p. 339, #306
34. *Akhlaq Hamalat al-Quran*, #88.
35. Ibid, #90.
36. Al-Tirmidhi, v. 5, p. 175, #291 (He graded it as Ḥasan ṢaḤeeḤ; Imam al-Albāni graded it as authentic in al-Silsilah al-ṢaḤeeḤah, #3327)
37. Ibn Taymiyah, Fadā'il al-Qur'an,
38. This is narrated by Ahmad, v. 37, p. 82, #22397; and Abu Dawud, v. 6, p. 354, #4297 (in this wording). It was deemed Ḥasan by al-Arna'ooṬ.
39. Tafseer al-Qurtubi, v. 5, p. 290
40. Ibn Rajab, Dhayl Ṭabaqāt al-Ḥanābilah, v. 2, p. 156
41. al-Qāsim bin Salām, Faḍā'il al-Qur'an, p. 278
42. al-QurṬubi, al-Jāmi' li'AḤkām al-Qur'ān, v. 1, p. 30
43. Ahmad bin Ḥanbal, al-Zuhd, 1859

44. *Tahdheeb Madārij al-Sālikeen*

45. Fath al-Bāri, v. 9, p. 108-109

46. Ibn Mājah, v. 2, p. 362, #1337

47. *Ihya' Uloom ad-Deen*, v. 1, p. 442

48. Ibn Rajab, Dhayl Ṭabaqāt al-Ḥanābilah, v. 4, p. 519

49. Ibn Abu Shaybah, al-Muṣannaf, v. 6, p. 125, #30006; and Ibn Hibbān, v. 1, p. 329, #122); and al-Ṭabarāni, v. 22, p. 188. It is deemed Ḥasan by al-Arna'ooṬ.

50. Ahmad (3712) Ibn Hibban (972), deemed *sahih* by al-Arna'oot

51. Imam Aḥmad, v. 44, p. 147, #26526; and al-Tirmidhi, #2923 (he deemed it Ḥasan ṢaḤeeḤ ghareeb); and Abu Dawud, v. 2, p. 593, #1466; and al-Nasā'i, v. 2, p. 181, #1022

52. Muslim, v. 1, p. 507, #733

53. al-SuyuṬi, al-Itqān fee 'Uloom al-Qur'ān (v. 1, p. 362)

54. Muslim v. 1, p. 543 #787

55. Ahmad #6702, deemed hasan by al-Arna'oot

56. Tayseer al-Kareem al-RaḤmān, p. 3

57. Muslim v. 1, p. 536 #772

58. Abu 'Ubayd, Faḍā'il al-Qur'ān, p. 149

59. ibid., p. 150

60. ibid., p. 153

61. *Rawa'i Iqbal* by Abu Hasan al-Nadwi p. 39

62. Miftāh Dār al-Sa'ādah, v. 1, p. 553-554

63. Abu 'Ubayd, Faḍā'il al-Quran, p. 147

64. ibid

65. ibid

66. Bukhari #6928

67. Bukhari #7537, Muslim #2675

68. Ahmad, v. 3, p. 78, #1481

69. Narrated by al-Tirmidhi, v. 4, p 603, #2402

70. Ahmad, 2, 91, #664

71. al-Bazzār, v. 13, p, 49

72. Ahmad, v. 35, p. 520, #21666

73. Muslim #4802

74. Muslim, v. 4, p. 1994, #2577

75. al-Bukhari, v. 6, p. 135, #4837

76. Imam Ahmad, #6741

Prayer

To understand the role that *salah* (prayer) should play in awakening our faith
we need to understand its nature and how it connects us to God. Allah created
us for the purpose of worshipping Him:

اللَّهُ الَّذِى خَلَقَ سَبْعَ سَمَاوَاتٍ وَمِنَ الْأَرْضِ مِثْلَهُنَّ يَتَنَزَّلُ الْأَمْرُ بَيْنَهُنَّ
لِتَعْلَمُوا أَنَّ اللَّهَ عَلَى كُلِّ شَيْءٍ قَدِيرٌ وَأَنَّ اللَّهَ قَدْ أَحَاطَ بِكُلِّ شَيْءٍ عِلْمًا ۝

*Allah is the One Who created seven heavens (in layers),
and likewise for the earth. The (divine) command
descends between them so you may know that Allah
is Most Capable of everything and that Allah certainly
encompasses all things in knowledge.* [65:12]

He displays signs of His Names and Attributes in creation so that we may catch glimpses of
His infinite greatness, realizing our dependence on Him. Witnesses to these signs in creation,
we praise, thank, and ask of Him:

فَسُبْحَانَ اللَّهِ حِينَ تُمْسُونَ وَحِينَ تُصْبِحُونَ ۝ وَلَهُ الْحَمْدُ فِى السَّمَاوَاتِ
وَالْأَرْضِ وَعَشِيًّا وَحِينَ تُظْهِرُونَ ۝ يُخْرِجُ الْحَيَّ مِنَ الْمَيِّتِ وَيُخْرِجُ الْمَيِّتَ
مِنَ الْحَيِّ وَيُحْيِ الْأَرْضَ بَعْدَ مَوْتِهَا ۚ وَكَذَلِكَ تُخْرَجُونَ ۝

*So exalted is Allah when you reach the evening and when you
reach the morning. And to Him is [due all] praise throughout the
heavens and the earth. And (exalted is He) at night and when
you are at noon. He brings the living out of the dead and brings
the dead out of the living and brings to life the earth after its
lifelessness. And thus will you be brought out.* [30:17-19]

The verse shows that just as Allah is to be glorified *(tasbeeh)*, He is also to be praised *(tahmeed* or *hamd)*; this is another purpose of creation. To praise Allah is to declare your wonder, admiration and appreciation for His very being, and it comes by recognizing His names and attributes. He loves His creation to praise Him in a way that is befitting of Him. It is more general than gratitude, as gratitude is to show thanks for a favor. When we say Alhamdulillah — praise and thanks belong to Allah — we recognize His favor upon us over so many of His creation. To praise Allah means to acknowledge His absolute worthiness of being praised, even apart from all of His favors.

Gratitude, however, is just as essential in our relationship with Allah as glorification *(tasbeeh)* and praise *(tahmeed)*. Allah calls our attention to some of the most basic blessings from Him that we take for granted. These blessings are the architecture of our human experience—we hardly notice them although we benefit from them everyday.

وَاللَّهُ أَخْرَجَكُم مِّن بُطُونِ أُمَّهَاتِكُمْ لَا تَعْلَمُونَ شَيْئًا وَجَعَلَ لَكُمُ السَّمْعَ وَالْأَبْصَارَ وَالْأَفْئِدَةَ لَعَلَّكُمْ تَشْكُرُونَ ۝

And Allah brought you out of the wombs of your mothers
when you knew nothing, and gave you hearing, sight, and
intellect so perhaps you would be thankful. [16:78]

◆◆◆

Some Companions related that when Adam was made to witness his off-spring, he noticed discrepancies among them. Some were tested with poverty while others lived in comfort, and some were given prominence over others. He asked, "My Lord, why didn't you make them equals?" to which Allah responded, "I love to be thanked."[1]

Even Satan knows how important gratitude is for our faith. His major strategy in misguiding people is to deter them from thanking God:

قَالَ فَبِمَا أَغْوَيْتَنِي لَأَقْعُدَنَّ لَهُمْ صِرَاطَكَ الْمُسْتَقِيمَ ۝ ثُمَّ لَآتِيَنَّهُم مِّن بَيْنِ أَيْدِيهِمْ وَمِنْ خَلْفِهِمْ وَعَنْ أَيْمَانِهِمْ وَعَن شَمَائِلِهِمْ ۖ وَلَا تَجِدُ أَكْثَرَهُمْ شَاكِرِينَ ۝

He said, "For leaving me to stray I will lie in ambush for them
on Your Straight Path. I will approach them from their front,
their back, their right, their left, and then You will find most
of them ungrateful." [7:16-17]

The First Step is Gratitude

The first step in gratitude is to recognize a blessing as a blessing in the first place. It is upon us to acknowledge our blessings in secret and out loud, realizing what life would be without them and not feeling entitled to them. Remember that everything you have is a gift and a privilege, not some inherent right that is due to you just for being alive. A believer must express this basic level of gratitude to Allah in his heart through acknowledgment, with his tongue through praise, and with the limbs in humility and generosity toward those in need.

This is what we must do for each and every blessing. How then can we apply this to one of the most undeniably vital blessings that we have: the blessing of having God as our Lord and caretaker? We remind ourselves daily of this when we say in our prayers: "All praise is due to God, Lord of the Worlds!" But do we really mean it when we recite it? Does it come from our hearts or does it stop at our tongues? To answer this requires that we understand what Lordship (ruboobiyah) really means.

Who is Your Lord?

Let us look first at the meanings of lordship in Arabic. A *rabb*—a lord of something is the one who supports and sustains continuously. Allah gives continuous assistance to His slaves, supporting them with all they need to create meaningful lives.

$$\text{هُوَ الَّذِى يُسَيِّرُكُمْ فِى الْبَرِّ وَالْبَحْرِ}$$

It is He who enables you to travel on land and sea ... [10:22]

$$\text{وَأَنَّهُ هُوَ أَضْحَكَ وَأَبْكَىٰ ۝}$$

And it is He who makes [one] laugh and weep [53:43]

$$\text{وَالَّذِى هُوَ يُطْعِمُنِى وَيَسْقِينِ ۝}$$

And it is He who feeds me and gives me drink [26:79]

$$\text{وَهُوَ الَّذِى يَتَوَفَّاكُم بِاللَّيْلِ وَيَعْلَمُ مَا جَرَحْتُم بِالنَّهَارِ}$$
$$\text{ثُمَّ يَبْعَثُكُمْ فِيهِ}$$

*He is the One Who calls back your souls by night and knows
what you do by day, then revives you daily...* [6:60]

We should not misconstrue the ease and accessibility of a blessing to mean that it belongs to us or that we are entitled to it. When we experience loss of a blessing such as health or a beloved one, we assume that the blessing was the default. We forget that the very reason we feel pain and sorrow is because of the beauty of the blessing in the first place. God could have created us without deep feelings, with less attachment between family members, with bodies less strong and miraculous, but instead he blessed us with the enjoyment of our blessings for a time, as pathways to knowing Him. But each one of us is destined to pass through inevitable trials in our journey to the Hereafter, and therein lies the nature of our worldly test.

We are nothing without Allah's continuous support, as there is no ability or power except by Him. We have no inherent ability to see, hear, move, eat, drink, think, sleep or wake. The more we reflect, the more we find that our entire existence is tied to Allah, and if He were to leave us on our own for the blink of an eye, life would cease.

$$قُلْ أَرَأَيْتُمْ إِنْ أَصْبَحَ مَاؤُكُمْ غَوْرًا فَمَن يَأْتِيكُم بِمَاءٍ مَّعِينٍ ۝$$

Say, "Consider this: if your water were to sink [into the earth], then who could bring you flowing water?" [67:30]

Thankful for His Lordship

As we mentioned earlier, gratitude begins with recognizing the blessing and knowing its worth. The Quran helps us understand the worth of our blessings by inviting us to imagine life without sight, water, hearing, or safety. Through this exercise, we understand that we are unable to care for ourselves at the most basic level. We are utterly incompetent without our Lord's assistance and support, and we have no power at all to reach our objectives. Recognizing this incompetence is the most basic level of gratitude toward God as our Lord. This acknowledgment of our inherent inability to perform our own affairs, and our deep and infinite need for our Lord in every second, should overwhelm us.

••••

Prophet Musa asked his Lord, "How can I ever thank you, when the smallest blessing you have given me could never be repaid by anything that I do?' so the revelation came to him: 'Musa, now you have truly thanked me."[2] Musa's acknowledgement of his inability to thank Allah was in itself the essence of gratitude.

Acknowledging our Powerlessness

Ibn al-Jawzi said, "I figured out what is required from the creation: humility and recognition of their own flaw and inability."[3] In a word, it is gratitude that is required from us. Being grateful for God's Lordship is to remain humble and recognize our powerlessness. Any failing in these is a failure to be truly grateful.

The Quran makes clear that all creation, except for human beings and *jinn*, recognizes its deep need for Allah and its inability to exist without Him. All of creation is in a constant state of worship, humility and glorification of its Lord. As for us, we are often found in a state of disobedience and ingratitude to our Lord.

Think about the following verses from *Surah al-Nahl*. The verses warn those who commit sin that they have placed themselves on the path of punishment through their violations. Allah may choose not to act immediately, giving them a chance to repent and return. These verses remind us what our relationship with our Lord should look like, pointing out to us the endless signs of God's presence and the prostration of creation. Notice how the verses start by invoking a sense of fear:

أَفَأَمِنَ الَّذِينَ مَكَرُوا السَّيِّئَاتِ أَن يَخْسِفَ اللَّهُ بِهِمُ الْأَرْضَ أَوْ يَأْتِيَهُمُ الْعَذَابُ مِنْ حَيْثُ لَا يَشْعُرُونَ ۝ أَوْ يَأْخُذَهُمْ فِي تَقَلُّبِهِمْ فَمَا هُم بِمُعْجِزِينَ ۝ أَوْ يَأْخُذَهُمْ عَلَىٰ تَخَوُّفٍ فَإِنَّ رَبَّكُمْ لَرَءُوفٌ رَّحِيمٌ ۝

Do those who devise evil plots feel secure that Allah will not cause the earth to swallow them? Or that the torment will not come upon them in ways they cannot comprehend? Or that He will not seize them while they go about (their day), for then they will have no escape? Or that He will not destroy them gradually? But your Lord is truly Ever Gracious, Most Merciful. [16:45-47]

They are reminded of the reality of their existence and their complete dependence on Allah. Everything surrounding them is in a state of humble submission, even their own shadows:

أَوَلَمْ يَرَوْا إِلَىٰ مَا خَلَقَ اللَّهُ مِن شَيْءٍ يَتَفَيَّؤُا ظِلَالُهُ عَنِ الْيَمِينِ وَالشَّمَائِلِ سُجَّدًا لِّلَّهِ وَهُمْ دَاخِرُونَ ۝

Have they not considered how the shadows of everything Allah has created incline to the right and the left prostrating to Allah in all humility? [16:48]

Prostration is the ultimate form of humility and submission, and a physical translation of one's inner devotion to God. Prostration is the tangible expression of our dependence, brokenness, and yearning for Him, Lord of the Worlds:

$$أَلَّا يَسْجُدُوا لِلَّهِ الَّذِي يُخْرِجُ الْخَبْءَ فِى السَّمَٰوَٰتِ وَالْأَرْضِ وَيَعْلَمُ مَا تُخْفُونَ وَمَا تُعْلِنُونَ ۝$$

They do not prostrate to Allah, Who brings forth what is
hidden in the heavens and the earth, and knows what you
conceal and what you reveal. [27:25]

The Delusion of Independence

What distracted us from internalizing this relationship with our Lord? What made us forget the reality of our existence? How did we forget how small and weak we are? How did we fall into the illusion that we got to where we are today on our own, and that we are able to continue through our own resourcefulness?

Not me! I'm not like that, you may tell yourself. But isn't it enough that you don't feel the need for Allah constantly? Isn't it enough that we don't internalize the meanings of powerlessness and humility when we prostrate to our Lord who has infinite power over us? It's about time we wake up from this fantasy:

$$كَلَّا إِنَّ الْإِنسَٰنَ لَيَطْغَىٰ ۝ أَن رَّءَاهُ اسْتَغْنَىٰ ۝$$

Most certainly, one exceeds all bounds once they think they
are self-sufficient. [96:6-7]

It is self-deception to deny the bounty and help of your Lord and take credit for it yourself. It is the same deception of those before you who came and went. God tells us that when Qaroon was advised not to be so prideful and to ascribe his blessings to God, he replied:

$$إِنَّمَآ أُوتِيتُهُۥ عَلَىٰ عِلْمٍ عِندِى$$

I have been granted all this because of some
knowledge I have. [28:78]

How ignorant and foolish must a person be to deny the very help of God and take credit for it instead, gloating over others? Such a person is deluded to the highest degree and has stepped outside the realm of reality. This arrogance is a disease of the heart, the result of a deep denial and rejection of one's servitude and dependence on Allah. As we realize the roots of this disease, maybe we can begin to understand why the punishment for arrogance is so strong. It is a severing of the connection between the worshipper and his or her Lord:

$$يَا أَيُّهَا النَّاسُ إِنَّمَا بَغْيُكُمْ عَلَى أَنفُسِكُمْ ۖ مَّتَاعَ الْحَيَاةِ الدُّنْيَا$$

O humanity! Your transgression is only against your own souls.
There is only a brief enjoyment in this worldly life...[10:23]

Our Loving Lord

Allah the Exalted, wishes the best for us:

$$وَاللَّهُ يُرِيدُ أَن يَتُوبَ عَلَيْكُمْ$$

Allah wants to accept your repentance... [4:27]

$$وَاللَّهُ يَدْعُوا إِلَى الْجَنَّةِ وَالْمَغْفِرَةِ بِإِذْنِهِ ۖ$$

Allah invites (you) to Paradise and forgiveness by His grace [2:221]

The road to Paradise is a road of servitude, humility, and realization of one's insufficiency. God created us and the world around us in such a way to redirect those who verge off from this path. Our daily experiences remind us of our dependence on Him. For example, He created us without the ability to go more than a few days without sleep. We are unable to go too long without food or water, and we can last barely a single minute without air.

If these reminders fail, our Loving Master sends further signs and messages to remind us. He might temporarily take away our health, decrease our wealth, or send any one of the many tests that countless people have suffered in order to show how dependent on Him we really are. Then, the reality of our need for our Lord comes to light. False sources of power and security are exposed, and we realize that our previous calculations were false. We are pulled out of our heedless daze and reminded that we do not belong in this imperfect world:

$$وَمَا نُرِيهِم مِّنْ آيَةٍ إِلَّا هِيَ أَكْبَرُ مِنْ أُخْتِهَا ۖ وَأَخَذْنَاهُم بِالْعَذَابِ لَعَلَّهُمْ يَرْجِعُونَ ۞$$

Even though each sign We showed them was greater than the
previous one. We inflicted torment on them so that they might
return to the right path. [43:48]

Through this process of trials and difficulties, the connection between the earth and the heavens is established. This connection happens when an individual recognizes his or her state of need and seeks the One who holds the treasury of all things. Really, there is no weight to the human when he dismisses his need for connection to Allah.

$$\text{لَقَدْ خَلَقْنَا الْإِنسَانَ فِى أَحْسَنِ تَقْوِيمٍ ۝ ثُمَّ رَدَدْنَاهُ أَسْفَلَ سَافِلِينَ ۝}$$

We created humans in the best form, but We will reduce them
to the lowest of the low. [95:4-5]

When we accept the reality of our existence by returning broken, desperate, and humble to our Lord, we are actually right where we belong. We are servants to the Glorious Master, and only upon realizing this will He share with us the most precious gifts of nearness and divine affection. What else will you need after that?

$$\text{أَلَيْسَ اللَّهُ بِكَافٍ عَبْدَهُ}$$

Is Allah not sufficient for His servant? [39:36]

❖❖❖

It is mentioned that Moses once asked God, "My Lord, where can I find you?" God responded, "Find me among those whose hearts are broken for me. I come close to them by a wingspan everyday. Were it not for that, they would have despaired."[4]

Tests and trials might remind some people of their helplessness, but that by itself is not enough. Rather we need to direct those feelings of humility toward our Lord, who sent trials so that we could return to Him as servants. We find many verses that reprimand those who don't see the divine wisdom in earthly tests, not realizing what they were sent for:

$$\text{وَلَقَدْ أَخَذْنَاهُم بِالْعَذَابِ فَمَا اسْتَكَانُوا لِرَبِّهِمْ وَمَا يَتَضَرَّعُونَ ۝}$$

And We have already seized them with torment, but they
never humbled themselves to their Lord, nor did they submit.
[23:76]

What we must do, then, is come before Allah with feelings of poverty and need. We cannot direct those feelings to any else. It is only when we direct those feelings to God alone that we may enter the havens of worship.

Connecting Earth to the Heavens

Every human being affirmed Allah's Lordship in a previous stage of existence:

$$\text{وَإِذْ أَخَذَ رَبُّكَ مِنْ بَنِى آدَمَ مِن ظُهُورِهِمْ ذُرِّيَّتَهُمْ وَأَشْهَدَهُمْ عَلَىٰ أَنفُسِهِمْ}$$

أَلَسْتُ بِرَبِّكُمْ قَالُوا بَلَى شَهِدْنَا أَن تَقُولُوا يَوْمَ ٱلْقِيَمَةِ إِنَّا كُنَّا عَنْ هَذَا غَفِلِينَ ۝

*And remember when your Lord brought forth from the loins
of the children of Adam their descendants and had them
testify regarding themselves. Allah asked, "Am I not your
Lord?" They replied, "Yes, You are! We testify." He cautioned,
"Now you have no right to say on Judgment Day, 'We were
not aware of this.'"* [7:172]

During this great event, we stood before Allah and testified. When we said: 'Yes, we have testified," we affirmed His Lordship over us and all the realities entailed. There is no life or existence without Him, and He alone is our Caretaker. He raises us, gives us, and guides us. He is the Owner of the treasuries of creation: nothing is dealt from them except with His Permission and in the exact measure He has ordained. There is no other source of help or sustenance, for He is Lord of everything, and He is Sovereign over all things.

إِنَّا كُلَّ شَيْءٍ خَلَقْنَهُ بِقَدَرٍ ۝

Indeed, We have created everything, perfectly preordained.
[54:49]

وَإِن مِّن شَيْءٍ إِلَّا عِندَنَا خَزَآئِنُهُو وَمَا نُنَزِّلُهُۥٓ إِلَّا بِقَدَرٍ مَّعْلُومٍ ۝

*There is not any means (of sustenance) whose reserves We do
not hold, only bringing it forth in precise measure.* [15:21]

This is what our relationship with Allah must be founded upon. While Allah gave us the freedom to choose, He made it clear to us that our value is measured by the extent to which we worship Him, connecting to Him as the sustaining power.

God told us clearly that we would never be able to see Him here on earth:

لَّا تُدْرِكُهُ ٱلْأَبْصَارُ وَهُوَ يُدْرِكُ ٱلْأَبْصَارَ وَهُوَ ٱللَّطِيفُ ٱلْخَبِيرُ ۝

*Vision perceives Him not, but He perceives [all] vision; and
He is the Subtle, the Acquainted.* [6:103]

وَلَا يُحِيطُونَ بِهِۦ عِلْمًا

they cannot encompass Him in knowledge. [20:110]

He did, however, give us the chance to connect with him through the deeper meanings of worship. He gives the opportunity through worship to reconnect what was severed and bridge the gap between the earth and the heavens. Worship is a revival and renewing of the promise we made when He asked us: Am I not your Lord? This reaffirmation of our cosmic vow and fulfilling the very purpose for which we were created is the key to connecting with God.

The Relationship between Man and His Lord

To establish a worship relationship with Allah Exalted, you must acknowledge your power-lessness as you glorify Him. To connect with *Al-Qawiy*, the Most Strong, you must recognize your weakness. To connect with *Al-Qadir*, The Capable, you recognize your incompetence. To connect with *Al-Aleem*, The All-Knowing, you acknowledge your ignorance. It is a con-nection between a soul who has nothing and can change nothing with the One who is Perfect, who owns and has power over everything. Despite our weakness, He still reaches out to us to come close to Him, the Alive and Presiding, Close and Encompassing, Almighty and Wise.

Look at the progression of these verses. In the first verse, we are overwhelmed by the power and Lordship of Allah:

إِنَّ رَبَّكُمُ اللَّهُ الَّذِي خَلَقَ السَّمَاوَاتِ وَالْأَرْضَ فِي سِتَّةِ أَيَّامٍ ثُمَّ اسْتَوَىٰ عَلَى الْعَرْشِ يُغْشِي اللَّيْلَ النَّهَارَ يَطْلُبُهُ حَثِيثًا وَالشَّمْسَ وَالْقَمَرَ وَالنُّجُومَ مُسَخَّرَاتٍ بِأَمْرِهِ ۗ أَلَا لَهُ الْخَلْقُ وَالْأَمْرُ ۗ تَبَارَكَ اللَّهُ رَبُّ الْعَالَمِينَ ۝

Indeed your Lord is Allah Who created the heavens and the earth in six Days, then established Himself on the Throne. He makes the day and night overlap in rapid succession. He created the sun, the moon, and the stars—all subjected to His command. The creation and the command belong only to Him. Blessed is Allah, Lord of all worlds! [7:54]

The subsequent verses are an invitation to draw close to Him, calling upon Him with hum-bled spirit and the softest whispers:

ادْعُوا رَبَّكُمْ تَضَرُّعًا وَخُفْيَةً ۚ إِنَّهُ لَا يُحِبُّ الْمُعْتَدِينَ ۝ وَلَا تُفْسِدُوا فِي الْأَرْضِ بَعْدَ إِصْلَاحِهَا وَادْعُوهُ خَوْفًا وَطَمَعًا ۚ إِنَّ رَحْمَتَ اللَّهِ قَرِيبٌ مِّنَ الْمُحْسِنِينَ ۝

Call upon your Lord humbly and secretly. Surely He does not like the transgressors. Do not spread corruption in the land after it has been set in order. And call upon Him with hope and fear. Indeed, Allah's mercy is always close to the good-doers. [7:55-56]

This is the connection God wants from His servants. He wants us to call upon Him with sincere heartfelt pleas in which our feelings of need are laid bare. In our worship, we must learn to sit in deep humility, acknowledging our inability to fulfill our smallest needs. Only after this intense internal process are we ready to connect with God and come near to Him.

Prayer is Connection

Keeping these meanings of worship and humility in mind, we can now return to our starting point and better appreciate how important *salah* (prayer) is. Our Loving, Merciful Lord knows our weaknesses and how easily we forget Him, and so He mandated that we pray as a daily reminder of our original promise and a reestablishing of our connection with Him. As explained before, your value to Allah is based on your actualization of true worship and your steadfastness in upholding the purpose of your creation. When we neglect this relationship, we are set back in our life purpose and our hearts become hard.

If we were left to devise our own prayer schedules, we would be miserable and much more distant from God. The prescription of five daily prayers is an gentle mercy to ensure that we maintain our connection with God at a solid, consistent pace and are reminded of our purpose several times a day.

The Arabic word for prayer was carefully chosen by God to remind us of its very purpose. Salāh comes from the word Ṣilah, which means connection. Prayer is your connection to the Divine, your lifeline to the Heavens. Whenever we fall into a state of ignorance of our Lord and find ourselves distant and stuck deep in the ground, we use this rope to pull ourselves up towards our Lord.

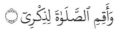

Establish prayer for My remembrance. [20:14]

Praying five times a day helps us stay focused on Him, fixing what has been torn and bringing close what has become distant, while extinguishing the fires of sin. Anas narrates that the Messenger of Allah ﷺ said, **"Allah has an angel that calls out at every prayer, 'Human Beings! Rise to the fires that you have lit against yourself, and put them out with prayer!"**[5]

Perhaps the most effective part of the prayer for extinguishing the flames of sin is the prostration *(sujud)*. Placing the most noble part of your body on the ground is the ultimate physical expression of humility to our Lord, the Most High. The Messenger of Allah ﷺ said, **"When a Muslim prays, his wrongdoings are raised onto his head. Whenever he prostrates, they fall off of him, and so he finishes his prayer with all of his wrongdoings fallen off of him."**[6]

What are most sins but a momentary heedlessness of purpose? We disobey the orders of the King because we are distracted from our position as His worshippers. Each sin is a breach of our contract with God and a breaking of our original pledge of servitude. And what is prostration but the essence of surrender? It is a holistic admission of our servitude and a return to worship.

$$\text{وَٱسْجُدْ وَٱقْتَرِب}$$

But prostrate and draw near [to Allah]. [96:19]

No Excuse

Every religious tradition has a form of prayer. The Prophet ﷺ even called prayer, **"the mainstay of the religion."**[7] We don't have to look far to see how universal the concept is—Allah tells us in the Quran that Jesus said:

$$\text{وَأَوْصَانِي بِالصَّلَاةِ وَالزَّكَاةِ مَا دُمْتُ حَيًّا}$$

And He bid me to establish prayer and give alms as long as I live. [19:31]

In Islam, no one is ever exempt from prayer; even a sick, bedridden person must pray by head gestures, and a traveler must pray while in transit. When the Prophet ﷺ and his Companions were in the heat of battle, Allah taught them to pray in a format that would guard them against attack. Even in moments of difficulty, we don't cease to be worshippers and are in more need of this connection than ever.

$$\text{حَٰفِظُوا عَلَى ٱلصَّلَوَٰتِ وَٱلصَّلَوٰةِ ٱلْوُسْطَىٰ وَقُومُوا لِلَّهِ قَٰنِتِينَ ۝ فَإِنْ خِفْتُمْ فَرِجَالًا أَوْ رُكْبَانًا فَإِذَآ أَمِنتُمْ فَٱذْكُرُوا ٱللَّهَ كَمَا عَلَّمَكُم مَّا لَمْ تَكُونُوا تَعْلَمُونَ ۝}$$

Observe the prayers—especially the middle prayer—and stand in true devotion to Allah. If you are in danger, pray on foot or while riding. Then when you are safe, remember Allah for teaching you what you did not know. [2:238-239]

The Method of Prayer

Salah is an astonishing display of gratitude to Allah. Reflect on the words of Allah to His Prophet ﷺ:

إِنَّآ أَعْطَيْنَٰكَ ٱلْكَوْثَرَ ۝ فَصَلِّ لِرَبِّكَ وَٱنْحَرْ ۝

*We have certainly granted you abundant goodness. So pray
and sacrifice to your Lord.* [108:1-2]

If you want to remember Allah, and pour out your heart to him, you should rush to pray:

قَدْ أَفْلَحَ مَن تَزَكَّىٰ ۝ وَذَكَرَ ٱسْمَ رَبِّهِۦ فَصَلَّىٰ ۝

*Successful indeed are those who purify themselves, remember
the Name of their Lord, and pray.* [87:14-15]

Someone might ask, why specifically salah though? Can't we turn towards Allah and call upon Him at any moment? That's true; it is possible to remind ourselves of Allah's favor and power at any moment. There is something about the method of prayer, however, its movements and spirit of obedience, that exemplifies our submission and makes it palpable.

If you reflect on the movements, words, and positions of salah, it becomes clear that it is the most appropriate way for servants to declare their devotion to Him. It contains such brilliant elements of brokenness, humility, surrender, and reverence. Every external action and movement therein facilitates these inner states for us.

The *takbeer,* raising your hands in declaration of Allah's Greatness, is the beginning of your communication. You then place the right hand over the left, in a reverent gesture of humility before your Lord, your gaze affixed to the ground. Then you proceed to the opening supplications, pronouncing words of praise and asking God for forgiveness and protection.

Surah al-Fatiha is the prayer's introduction wherein you restate your vow to the Lord of all the Worlds: "You alone we worship, and you alone we ask for help." The Prophet ﷺ informed us that after we recite each verse in *al-Fatiha*, God responds to us. After singling Him as our only object of worship and source of assistance, God says, "Let my servant have whatever He asks for." So we make our most important request: "Guide us to the straight path!" God opened the door for anything to be asked of Him, and then taught us to ask in this moment for proper guidance to Him.

Then you recite a few verses you have memorized of the Quran. Ideally you choose verses with impactful meanings that facilitate reflection. A natural reaction is to ask why we would recite God's own words in a conversation with Him. But is there anything better to show reverence and admiration? Are there any words more true to speak in the presence of our True Lord? Is there anything more effective in ridding us of our doubts and desires—the ultimate purpose of our prayer—or anything more appropriate to say before we fall on our knees in surrender to our Lord, Most High?

Before prostration, you bow in *ruku'.* You shift your center of balance forward towards the Kaaba and downwards towards the earth, catching yourself from falling completely to the floor with hands on your knees. In this reverent position, you declare most appropriately: "Glorified is my Magnificent Lord." Finally, to end each unit of prayer, you fall to our knees and put your face to the ground in the most humble state of worship, the sujud. In our *ruku'* and *sujud*, our praise is silent and our limbs are still; you murmur quietly, "Glorified is my Lord, the Most High." This whisper may not be heard by one praying next to you, but the Lord of the Heavens hears every syllable. With Allah, your brokenness is strength, and your humility is honor.

Go Back and Pray

To merely go through the motions of prayer without a presence of heart is a waste, but not entirely futile. We should still comply with the external dimensions of worship even if we cannot summon the spirit, for this is a form of submission to Allah. Do not give up on actions just because they are hollow—keep working to fill the empty shells of worship with substance, rather than discarding them altogether. Restoring life and awareness to our acts of worship is one of the most powerful methods for bringing life to the heart and awakening faith.

The deeper meanings of worship are embedded within the motions and words of prayer, therefore actions must be performed in a specific order and given their due right for prayer to be complete. You shouldn't take the postures of your prayer lightly. Each motion from the beginning to the end of prayer has been prescribed in an exact fashion. The Prophet of Allah ﷺ says, **"A man will walk away from his prayer and only a tenth of his prayer was written for him, a ninth, an eighth, a seventh, a sixth, a fifth, a fourth, a third, half."**[8] This is why the Prophet ﷺ once told a man, **"Go back and pray, for you have not prayed."**

The man went back and prayed as he did before and then came and greeted the Prophet ﷺ who again responded: "Go pray for you did not pray." This happened three times, so the man finally said: "By the one who sent you with the truth—I do not know how to do any better, so teach me!" The Prophet ﷺ then said: **"When you stand to pray, say 'Allahu Akbar,' then recite whatever is easy for you from the Quran. Then bow until your bowing is settled, then rise straight up. Then prostrate until your prostration is settled, then rise until you are sitting still. Do this throughout your entire prayer."**[9]

Establishing Salah

In the Quran, we are not only commanded to pray, but to "establish the prayer." The word "establish" helps us understand that prayer has a firm place in both our private and collective lives. It also reminds us that the prayer is not just a hollow demonstration, but a deep practice that we must perfect inside and out. While many Muslims perform the gestures of prayer correctly, many fall short in giving salah its full due.

One might ask, how can we be so certain that many Muslims perform the prayer superficially? Isn't prayer between God and the person praying? For sure, Allah alone knows the secrets of what we do, and He knows best as to the state and substance of everyone's prayers. But he has informed us about the effects of prayer on a person:

$$ وَأَقِمِ الصَّلَاةَ إِنَّ الصَّلَاةَ تَنْهَىٰ عَنِ الْفَحْشَاءِ وَالْمُنكَرِ $$

... establish prayer. Indeed, prayer prohibits immorality and wrongdoing. [29:45]

The believer should walk out of the prayer with stronger resolve to uphold all of his commitments, and the effects of his prayer should be obvious in all his actions. A sign that our prayers are sound and acceptable to Allah is that they renew our fear of disobeying Him, while making us more cautious and mindful. When one of the Companions said to the Prophet, "There is a man who prays at night, but steals the next day," he said, **"What you mentioned [of his praying at night] will prevent him."**[10]

Praying properly keeps us out of trouble. When we remember our weaknesses, dependencies, and desperate need for our Lord five times throughout the day, we are guaranteed to have fresh faith constantly running through our veins. We leave our prayer with greater dependence on and confidence in Allah. Our entire character and behavior reflects how successfully we performed our prayer.

True prayer has this effect, but the reverse doesn't not work here. You can't fake it to make it. Rather, if you were to try to make your limbs look humble in prayer to impress the people while your heart is heedless, you would be crossing into hypocrisy. The Prophet of Allah ﷺ said in a *hadith qudsi* that Allah said: **"I accept the prayer from the one who has humbled himself before my Magnitude, not from one who uses prayer to look down on My creation."**[11]

Created to Pray

The significance of prayer cannot be understated. We were created to be the worshipping slaves of Allah. Worship means humility and need before Allah, and *salah* (prayer) is the perfect expression of that.

We were created to work for God's cause and to call others to His religion, and prayer is the best preparation for this task. Why else would Prophet Abraham, after leaving his wife and child in the barren desert of Mecca, call out to God and beg:

$$\text{رَّبَّنَا إِنِّي أَسْكَنتُ مِن ذُرِّيَّتِي بِوَادٍ غَيْرِ ذِي زَرْعٍ عِندَ بَيْتِكَ الْمُحَرَّمِ}$$
$$\text{رَبَّنَا لِيُقِيمُوا الصَّلَاةَ}$$

Our Lord! I have settled some of my offspring in a barren
valley, near Your Sacred House, our Lord, so that they may
establish prayer. [14:37]

Prophet Abraham was less concerned with the provision of his family than for the conditionof their prayer. Prayer is the means through which man actualizes His purpose on earth, and Abraham's biggest fear was that they would neglect it. And so after he continues his soliloquy, Prophet Abraham requests a second time:

$$\text{رَبِّ اجْعَلْنِي مُقِيمَ الصَّلَاةِ وَمِن ذُرِّيَّتِي ۚ رَبَّنَا وَتَقَبَّلْ دُعَاءِ ۞ رَبَّنَا اغْفِرْ لِي}$$
$$\text{وَلِوَالِدَيَّ وَلِلْمُؤْمِنِينَ يَوْمَ يَقُومُ الْحِسَابُ ۞}$$

My Lord, make me an establisher of prayer, and [many] from
my descendants. Our Lord, accept my supplication. Our
Lord, forgive me and my parents and the believers the Day the
account is established. (14:40-41)

.... ✦✦✦ ....

The Prophet of Allah ﷺ says: "Five prayers have been ordained by Allah on his servants. Whoever perfects their wudu' and prays them on time, completing their bowing, prostration, and humble submission has a promise from Allah that He will forgive them. Whoever does not do this has no promise from Allah; if He wishes, He will forgive them, and if He wishes, He will punish them."[12]

....

Prayer is the most important thing in the life of a Muslim and should be our first priority. The Prophet ﷺ told Mu'ath bin Jabal: **"Should I tell you what the principle matter is, as well as its mainstay, and its pinnacle?"** Mu'adh replied, "Of course, Messenger of Allah!" He said, **"The principle of the matter is Islam, its mainstay is the prayer, and its pinnacle is jihad."**[13] Anything that distracts us from Salah has no good within it. God praises those who allow nothing to distract them from prayer:

$$\text{رِجَالٌ لَّا تُلْهِيهِمْ تِجَارَةٌ وَلَا بَيْعٌ عَن ذِكْرِ اللَّهِ وَإِقَامِ الصَّلَاةِ وَإِيتَاءِ الزَّكَاةِ ۙ}$$
$$\text{يَخَافُونَ يَوْمًا تَتَقَلَّبُ فِيهِ الْقُلُوبُ وَالْأَبْصَارُ ۞}$$

There are men who are not distracted—either by buying
or selling—from Allah's remembrance, or performing
prayer, or paying Zakah. [24:37]

One of the most important reasons that Allah would make believers victorious over others
is so that they establish prayer on earth:

الَّذِينَ إِن مَّكَّنَّاهُمْ فِي الْأَرْضِ أَقَامُوا الصَّلَاةَ وَآتَوُا الزَّكَاةَ وَأَمَرُوا
بِالْمَعْرُوفِ وَنَهَوْا عَنِ الْمُنكَرِ ۗ وَلِلَّهِ عَاقِبَةُ الْأُمُورِ ۝

[And they are] those who, if We give them authority in the
land, establish prayer and give zakah and enjoy what is
right and forbid what is wrong. And to Allah belongs the
outcome of [all] matters. [22:41]

Think of these connections when you hear the call to prayer, "Come to prayer! Come to
success!"

Ascension of the Heart

Life is a one-way journey to God. It is a string of days and nights and ends with our death:

يَا أَيُّهَا الْإِنسَانُ إِنَّكَ كَادِحٌ إِلَىٰ رَبِّكَ كَدْحًا فَمُلَاقِيهِ ۝

Humanity! Indeed, you are toiling tirelessly towards your
Lord, and will inevitably meet Him. [84:6]

وَأَنَّ إِلَىٰ رَبِّكَ الْمُنتَهَىٰ ۝

To your Lord is the ultimate return. [53:42]

We don't all reach the same level at the end of our journeys. Some are close to Allah, and
some are far. We should track our progress and assess which group we belong to by looking
at how well we kept our original promise to recognize and worship God. We've explored
how prayer is the best expression of this original promise when it is performed correctly in
its outer and inner aspects. In our journey, prayer is our ladder to the heavens and an ascension of the hearts to Allah. When we lower ourselves for Him, He raises us up towards Him:

وَاسْجُدْ وَاقْتَرِب ۝

Prostrate and draw near. [96:19]

Comfort us with it, Bilal!

When the time for prayer would come, the Prophet ﷺ would say to Bilal, who was in charge of calling the athan: **"Bilal, comfort us with salah."**[14] The Companion Huthayfah informed us that whenever something troubled the Messenger of Allah ﷺ, he would pray.

$$\text{وَاسْتَعِينُوا بِالصَّبْرِ وَالصَّلَاةِ}$$

And seek help through patience and prayer ... [2:45]

Prayer is meant to play a role of solace and rejuvenation in our lives. In this prayer connection, you find harmony in serving your purpose and being in synchronicity with the entire universe:

$$\text{وَلِلَّهِ يَسْجُدُ مَن فِي ٱلسَّمَوَتِ وَٱلْأَرْضِ طَوْعًا وَكَرْهًا}$$

Only to Allah do all in the heavens and the earth bow down—
willingly or unwillingly... [13:15]

When performed with servitude and humility, prayer is a return to our natural state. Our souls are in sync with the angels, and we are in elegant motion with the rest of the creation around us. We become protective of our one-on-one time with Him. When we practice prayer in this fashion, we begin to taste the same joy the Prophet ﷺ described when he said, **"Prayer was made to be my heart's delight."**[15]

Pleading in Prayer

We can observe how strong our relationship with Allah truly is by what we do when we encounter any difficulty in our lives. Did we run to Allah first for help? Did we plead with Him as desperately as we would plead with anyone else whom we thought had the power to influence our situation? Did we feel comforted knowing that our affairs are in His Hands, and He is with us every step of the way? The more we practice calling on Him and turning to Him in our prayers, the stronger our relationship will be.

Your conversation with God should be more than just asking Him for things. Asking Allah is important, but when you speak to Him, you should pour your heart out. When calling out to Allah, you should include all the gritty details: your worries, vulnerabilities, and unspeakable fears. He, our Exalted Lord, knows all of this but wants us to speak to Him and nurture a relationship with Him. Share with Allah all that you are going through on your journey to reach Him. Confide your insecurities and beg Him for His safety and affection.

This powerful relationship is a tradition of the prophets, as Allah tells us in the Quran.

Notice the personal details the prophets recounted in their supplications. When Prophet Noah felt so worn down to the point where he could not continue calling his people, He called upon Allah:

رَّبِّ إِنِّى دَعَوْتُ قَوْمِى لَيْلًا وَنَهَارًا ۝ فَلَمْ يَزِدْهُمْ دُعَآءِىٓ إِلَّا فِرَارًا ۝ وَإِنِّى كُلَّمَا دَعَوْتُهُمْ لِتَغْفِرَ لَهُمْ جَعَلُوٓا أَصَـٰبِعَهُمْ فِىٓ ءَاذَانِهِمْ وَٱسْتَغْشَوْا ثِيَابَهُمْ وَأَصَرُّوا وَٱسْتَكْبَرُوا ٱسْتِكْبَارًا ۝ ثُمَّ إِنِّى دَعَوْتُهُمْ جِهَارًا ۝ ثُمَّ إِنِّىٓ أَعْلَنتُ لَهُمْ وَأَسْرَرْتُ لَهُمْ إِسْرَارًا ۝ فَقُلْتُ ٱسْتَغْفِرُوا رَبَّكُمْ إِنَّهُۥ كَانَ غَفَّارًا ۝ يُرْسِلِ ٱلسَّمَآءَ عَلَيْكُم مِّدْرَارًا ۝ وَيُمْدِدْكُم بِأَمْوَٰلٍ وَبَنِينَ وَيَجْعَل لَّكُمْ جَنَّـٰتٍ وَيَجْعَل لَّكُمْ أَنْهَـٰرًا ۝

My Lord! I have surely called my people day and night, but my calls only made them run farther away. And whenever I invite them to be forgiven by You, they press their fingers into their ears, cover themselves with their clothes, persist (in denial), and act very arrogantly. Then I certainly called them openly, then I surely preached to them publicly and privately, saying, 'seek your Lord's forgiveness, He is truly Most Forgiving. He will shower you with abundant rain, supply you with wealth and children, and give you gardens as well as rivers." [71:5-12]

Our Lord tells us about Prophet Zachariah's desperate longing for a son, and how he called upon Allah to answer his wish:

ذِكْرُ رَحْمَتِ رَبِّكَ عَبْدَهُۥ زَكَرِيَّآ ۝ إِذْ نَادَىٰ رَبَّهُۥ نِدَآءً خَفِيًّا ۝ قَالَ رَبِّ إِنِّى وَهَنَ ٱلْعَظْمُ مِنِّى وَٱشْتَعَلَ ٱلرَّأْسُ شَيْبًا وَلَمْ أَكُنۢ بِدُعَآئِكَ رَبِّ شَقِيًّا ۝ وَإِنِّى خِفْتُ ٱلْمَوَٰلِىَ مِن وَرَآءِى وَكَانَتِ ٱمْرَأَتِى عَاقِرًا فَهَبْ لِى مِن لَّدُنكَ وَلِيًّا ۝ يَرِثُنِى وَيَرِثُ مِنْ ءَالِ يَعْقُوبَ وَٱجْعَلْهُ رَبِّ رَضِيًّا ۝

This is a reminder of your Lord's mercy to His servant Zachariah, when he cried out to his Lord privately, saying, "My Lord! Surely my bones have become brittle, and grey hair has spread across my head, but I have never been disappointed in my prayer to You, my Lord! And I am concerned about (the faith of) my relatives after me, since my wife is barren. So grant me, by Your grace, an heir, who will inherit (prophethood) from me and the family of Jacob, and make him, O Lord, pleasing (to You)!" [19:2-6]

Our Prophet Muhammad ﷺ also followed this tradition when he had found himself at an emotional rock bottom after visiting the City of Taif. His wife Khadijah and uncle Abu Talib had both recently passed away, and Quraysh intensified their campaign against him knowing that his main sources of psychological support and physical protection were no longer there. Taif's leaders not only rejected his message and appeal for asylum, but the citizens of Taif chased him through the streets and hurled insults at him, ordering their children to pelt him with stones as he headed back to Mecca disappointed and disheartened. With no one on earth to turn to, he turned to his Lord and said:

> Allah, I come to you to complain about my fragile strength, my meager means, and my worthlessness in the people's eyes. Most Merciful of All! You are the Lord of the oppressed, and you are my Lord. To whom will you leave me? To some stranger who will reject me? Or to an enemy who will decide my fate? If you are not angry with me, then I do not mind, but your security can surely encompass me. I seek refuge in the light of Your face by which all darkness is dispelled and both this life and the life to come are put in their right course against incurring your wrath or being the subject of your anger. To You I submit, until I earn Your pleasure. Everything is powerless without your support.

You have access to Allah at any moment, and frequently calling on Him and acknowledging His presence is the best way to strengthen your connection. However, calling on Allah from within your prayer has a special power, especially in prostration. The Prophet ﷺ told us: **"The closest a servant will ever be to his Lord is when he prostrates, so make a lot of duaa."**[16]

Calling Out is at the Heart of Prayer

Salah is how we express and affirm our relationship with Allah, bringing our limbs to life with the spirit of devotion. However salah is more than just movements; in fact, calling out to God in duaa, reaching for Him, and asking of Him is at the very heart of salah.

Aishah recounts one night when the Messenger of Allah ﷺ was with her. He asked her permission to spend the night in worship, and she said, "I love to be by your side, but I also love what brings you joy." She was reluctant to give up her right to his physical company, but she knew that the Messenger of Allah ﷺ relished his time with his Lord. He ﷺ stood up and purified himself and then began His prayer. Aishah says that he ﷺ couldn't stop crying, to the point that his beard, his clothes, and the floor beneath him were drenched in his tears. When Bilal came to call him for the prayer, he saw the state of the Prophet ﷺ and assumed they were tears of grief. He said, "Messenger of Allah, why do you cry when Allah has already forgiven you?" The Prophet ﷺ replied: **"Shouldn't I be a grateful servant?"** Tonight an ayah came down to me—doomed is whoever reads it without reflecting upon it!" He then recited:[17]

$$\text{إِنَّ فِي خَلْقِ السَّمَاوَاتِ وَالْأَرْضِ وَاخْتِلَافِ اللَّيْلِ وَالنَّهَارِ لَآيَاتٍ لِّأُولِي الْأَلْبَابِ}$$

Indeed, in the creation of the heavens and the earth and the alternation of the day and night there are signs for people of reason. [3:190]

Aishah also says about the Prophet's home life, highlighting his relationship to the prayer: "He was in the service of his family, but when the time for prayer came, he would leave to pray."[18]

Prayer and Self-Purification

We must engage in a continuous, nonstop process of purifying our hearts, so that our attachment to the world is loosened and our primary goal remains centered on God's pleasure:

$$\text{قُلْ إِنَّ صَلَاتِي وَنُسُكِي وَمَحْيَايَ وَمَمَاتِي لِلَّهِ رَبِّ الْعَالَمِينَ}$$

Say, "Surely my prayer, my worship, my life, and my death are all for Allah—Lord of all worlds. [6:162]

Without a process of purification, our sense of direction becomes skewed. We embark on this journey knowing that Allah is our final destination, but also recognizing that we cannot advance without His help. There is no source of power but Him, and we follow His instructions:

$$\text{وَاعْتَصِمُوا بِاللَّهِ هُوَ مَوْلَاكُمْ}$$

Hold fast to Allah. He is your Guardian. [22:78]

The endeavor of upholding prayer must be accompanied by a process of continuous self-purification. What is one of the greatest forms of purification? It is Zakah, the charity mandated in Islam—in fact, the word Zakah comes from the root word meaning to purify. Throughout the Quran, God connects upholding the prayer to paying Zakah. If we understand the meaning of Zakah in the broad sense of purification, we can understand why the two tenets of prayer and charity are always mentioned together:

$$\text{فَأَقِيمُوا الصَّلَاةَ وَآتُوا الزَّكَاةَ وَاعْتَصِمُوا بِاللَّهِ هُوَ مَوْلَاكُمْ فَنِعْمَ الْمَوْلَى وَنِعْمَ النَّصِيرُ}$$

So establish prayer, pay alms-tax, and hold fast to Allah. He is your Guardian. What an excellent Guardian, and what an excellent Helper! [22:78]

وَمَآ أُمِرُوٓا إِلَّا لِيَعْبُدُوا اللَّهَ مُخْلِصِينَ لَهُ الدِّينَ حُنَفَآءَ وَيُقِيمُوا الصَّلَوٰةَ وَيُؤْتُوا
الزَّكَوٰةَ وَذَٰلِكَ دِينُ الْقَيِّمَةِ ۝

They were only commanded to worship Allah with sincere devotion to Him in all uprightness, establish prayer, and pay Zakah. That is the upright Way. [98:5]

Prayer and Quran

Giving charity is undoubtedly one of the most potent forms of purifying ourselves from the evils within us. God says,

خُذْ مِنْ أَمْوَٰلِهِمْ صَدَقَةً تُطَهِّرُهُمْ وَتُزَكِّيهِم بِهَا

Take from their wealth (O Prophet) charity to purify and bless them... [9:103]

But charity alone is not enough; we have to take a holistic approach to cleanse our hearts and make them worthy of coming closer to the Knower of All Secrets. Among the most powerful methods of purification is what God Himself pointed us to: the Quran, about which He says,

قُلْ هُوَ لِلَّذِينَ ءَامَنُوا هُدًى وَشِفَآءٌ

It is a guide and a healing to the believers. [41:44]

The Quran gives us an insightful look into the diseases of the soul and tells us clearly how we can rid ourselves of them. It inspires hope in our hearts of a perfect Paradise that awaits those who beseech Him and warns us frighteningly of the fire that was made for those who neglect Him. The Quran is God's ultimate reminder of the worthlessness of this world in comparison to the next, and enlightens us with invaluable lessons on our own psychology and human tendencies. It is the light that extinguishes the darkness around us, and the spring that gives life to our suffering hearts.

أَوَمَن كَانَ مَيْتًا فَأَحْيَيْنَٰهُ وَجَعَلْنَا لَهُ نُورًا يَمْشِى بِهِۦ فِى النَّاسِ كَمَن مَّثَلُهُۥ
فِى الظُّلُمَٰتِ لَيْسَ بِخَارِجٍ مِّنْهَا

Can those who had been dead, to whom We gave life and a light with which they can walk among people, be compared to those in complete darkness from which they can never emerge? [6:122]

Nothing purifies our hearts like the Quran; it is a beautiful and comprehensive treatment, with Allah's permission. He tells us that He "sends down clear revelations to His servant to bring you out of darkness and into light." [57:9] The Messenger of Allah ﷺ also called the Quran **"a rope extended from the sky to the earth."**[19] It is to be ingrained in every aspect of our life and worship, and so we find that Allah connects the Quran to prayer, spending charity, and looking forward to God's pleasure and reward:

$$ إِنَّ ٱلَّذِينَ يَتْلُونَ كِتَـٰبَ ٱللَّهِ وَأَقَامُوا ٱلصَّلَوٰةَ وَأَنفَقُوا مِمَّا رَزَقْنَـٰهُمْ سِرًّا وَعَلَانِيَةً يَرْجُونَ تِجَـٰرَةً لَّن تَبُورَ ۝ $$

Surely those who recite the Book of Allah, establish prayer,
and donate from what We have provided for them secretly
and openly, hope for an exchange that will never result in loss
[35:29]

The Right Atmosphere

We've spoken extensively about the need to prepare ourselves internally for each new prayer. There are also some practical physical measures we can take in order to make sure we are upholding the prayer as it deserves and creating a suitable atmosphere for the prayer meeting. These include perfecting the ablution and the enunciation of the wordings in the prayer. It includes raising the call to prayer and calling out the *takbeer* (the opening of the prayer). It is also important to make sure there is nothing of immediate concern on our minds, such as food that is ready on the table or the urge to use the bathroom.

The Prophet ﷺ also gave us a helpful tip: he encouraged us to remember death in our prayer, setting the stage for a heart to engage humbly with its Lord. He ﷺ said, **"Remember death in your prayer, for someone who remembers death in their prayer is more likely to perfect it. Pray like someone who thinks he might not get the chance to pray again."**[20]

Don't Grow Weary of Prayer

We should be very careful to not belittle the importance of perfecting the prayer, both in its form and its meanings. It is the second pillar of Islam, the mainstay of our religion, and represents the emphasis of practical worship in our religion. Prayer is an act of worship that no one under any circumstance ever has an excuse to abandon. It is obligated while traveling just as it is at home, and it is obligated during illness and even war. Some of the last words of advice from our Prophet ﷺ were: **"The prayer! The prayer! And be mindful of Allah with what is under your ownership!"**[21]

We interact with prayer several times a day, so it is important to revive its meanings regularly in order not to forget its significance. The prayer is our direct connection to God, and is a physical display of our servitude to Him. It is an exhibition of humility, surrender, and reverence. When God introduced Himself to Moses, He mentioned the prayer in conjunction with His own name:

$$إِنَّنِى أَنَا ٱللَّهُ لَآ إِلَـٰهَ إِلَّآ أَنَا۠ فَٱعْبُدْنِى وَأَقِمِ ٱلصَّلَوٰةَ لِذِكْرِىٓ ۞$$

'It is truly I, Allah! There is nothing worthy of worship but Me.
So worship Me, and establish prayer for My remembrance.
[20:14]

God first mandated that we pray fifty times a day, which would have meant that every minute of our day would have been spent either in prayer or preparing for it. But then He lightened the load at the request of Prophet Muhammad ﷺ who was advised by Prophet Moses to ask for less. In the famous story of the night journey and ascension to the heavens, the Prophet ﷺ narrates:

> God inspired to me what He inspired, and then obligated fifty prayers every day and night for me. I went down to Moses, who asked, "What did your Lord prescribe for your nation?" I said: "Fifty prayers." He said: "Return to your Lord and ask Him for a reduction, for your people cannot handle that. Certainly, I have already put the Children of Israel to the test and attempted with them." I returned to my Lord and said: "My Lord, relieve my nation," and so He lowered it for me by five. I then returned to Moses and said: "He lowered it for me by five." He said: "Your nation will not be able to handle that, so return to your Lord and ask him for a reduction." I continued to go back and forth between my Lord, Blessed and Exalted, and Moses, until Allah said: "O Muhammad, they are now five prayers every day, and each prayer will be counted ten times over, so that is fifty prayers. Whoever intends a good deed and does not do it, it will be recorded as a good deed for him; if he does it, then it will be recorded for him ten times over. Whoever intends a bad deed and does not do it, then nothing will be recorded; if he does it, then only one bad deed will be recorded." I then descended until I again reached Moses and told him. He said: "Return to your Lord and ask Him for a reduction." I said: "I have already returned to my Lord, and now I feel shy from Him."[22]

The number of prayers was reduced, but their reward was not. The five prayers are supposed to have an effect that pervades the whole day. The Messenger of Allah ﷺ said, **"You burn and burn, but then when you pray the Fajr prayer, it washes it out. Then you burn and burn again, but when you pray the Dhuhr prayer, it washes it out. Then you burn and burn again, and when you pray the Asr prayer, it washes it out. You then burn and burn again,** and when you pray the Maghrib prayer, it washes it out. Then you burn and burn again, and when you pray the Isha prayer it washes it out. Then you sleep, and nothing is recorded against you until you wake up."[23] Anas bin Malik reports that the Messenger of Allah ﷺ said, "Allah has an angel that calls out at every prayer, 'Human being! Come to the fire that you started against yourself, and put it out with prayer!'"[24]

These *hadiths* highlight the vital importance of prayer to our spiritual well-being and salvation. It is also imperative to mention that the first thing we will be held accountable for on the Day of Resurrection is our prayer. The Messenger of Allah ﷺ said, "**The first thing for which the servant will be held accountable for on the Day of Resurrection is the prayer. His prayer will be investigated; if it is good, then he has succeeded, but if it is bad, then he has failed and lost out.**"[25] He also said, "**Prayer is the best matter, so let whoever is able to increase it do so.**"[26] Abu Hurayrah narrates that the Messenger of Allah ﷺ once passed by a grave and asked, "**Who is in this grave?**" When they told him, he said, "**This man would prefer to have two rakahs of prayer over anything else in this world.**"[27]

The Best Times of Day

Allah controls time and space, and He chose for us five specific times in the day during which prayer is mandatory. These are the brightest parts of our day, and we shouldn't take lightly praying at the beginning of a prayer's time. These prayers were fifty, but were then reduced to five with the reward of fifty—so one prayer is equivalent to ten. In order to show how much we value this opportunity, we must be keen on praying each prayer consistently within its due time. The Prophet ﷺ said, "**Allah obligated His servants with five prayers. Whoever perfects the ablution for them and prays them in their time, completing their bowing, prostration, and sense of humble submission has a vow from Allah that He will forgive them. Whoever does not do this has no vow from Allah; if He wishes, He will forgive them, and if He wishes, He will punish them.**"[28]

Allah's Prophet ﷺ was once asked, "What is the best action?" He replied, *"Praying on time."*[29] Nothing brings you closer to Allah than praying consistently on time. The Prophet ﷺ said that God said, "**My servant does not come closer to me with anything more beloved to me than what I have obligated for him.**"[30]

Praying in the Mosque

Mosques are the houses of Allah on this earth, places of peace and sanctuary. Mosques should facilitate a believer's connection with God. When we decorate and design our mosques, we should ask ourselves what simple elements help bring the meanings of surrender and focus into our prayers. We emphasize cleanliness and honor in our religion, but sometimes veer into elaborate designs and bright carpeting. A mosque can be beautiful, honored, and simple at the same time. We come to the mosque to shed our worldly attachments, not to indulge them. Consider the prophets and how they used to worship. Prophet Muhammad ﷺ said one night while prostrating: **"I say just as my brother David said: 'I cover my face with soil for my Master, and my Master deserves that our faces be covered in soil for Him."** [31]

Praying in Congregation

Some may question the importance of congregational prayers. Isn't it enough for a believer to work on expressing his devotion by himself in his prayers to Allah? Why should he strive to perform prayers in a group, since it can be more difficult to achieve concentration?

The answer, with the help of Allah, is that Salah in congregation announces the submission of the *ummah* in its entirety to Allah Exalted. We demonstrate our collective need for Him, and gather in a way that resembles the angels:

$$وَالصَّافَّاتِ صَفًّا ۝$$

By those [angels] lined up in rows [37:1]

Praying in congregation in a single space allows us to come together as a community several times a day; this is unprecedented and cannot be found in any other religious tradition. Our strength, brotherhood and unity emanates from our connection to Allah. Praying next to your brothers and sisters from all walks of life reminds us that we come from a single source, share a mission, and are fellow travelers to a single destination. Congregational prayer is a microcosm of the larger community, allowing for the differences and shortcomings of each individual to fall away by strengthening the whole. So many of the principles of Islam come to life in our congregational prayers: humility before others, graciousness, forebearance, tolerance, and equality. Abu Hurayrah narrates that the Messenger of Allah ﷺ said,

> A man's prayer in congregation is more than his prayer in his home or in his market by some twenty-odd degrees. That is because when you perform ablution, striving for perfection in doing so, and then come to the mosque with nothing driving you there but the prayer, and wanting nothing more than the prayer, then you rise by one rank and lose one sin with every single step towards the prayer until you enter the mosque. Then when you reach the mosque, you are in prayer for as long as you are waiting there. The angels pray for each of you for as long as you sit where you pray, saying, 'Allah, show him mercy! Allah, forgive him! Allah, accept his repentance!' as long as he does not do any harm or lose his state of ritual purity. [32]

Staying home to pray is highly discouraged for those who are able to make it to the mosque. Ibn Abbas narrates that the Prophet ﷺ said, **"Whoever hears the call to prayer and does not come to it has no prayer, except with a valid excuse."**[33] Ibn Umm Maktoom, a blind and elderly man, once asked the Prophet ﷺ for permission to pray in his own home. The Prophet ﷺ asked, **"Do you hear the call to prayer?"** He said, "Yes." The Prophet ﷺ said, **"I cannot find a concession for you."**[34]

To further emphasize the importance of praying in congregation and not being late in responding to the call to prayer, the Messenger of Allah ﷺ once said, **"I was about to appoint someone to lead the people in prayer, and then go out to those men who stay behind to order that their houses be burned over them with bundles of wood. If any of them knew that they would find a tender piece of meat, they would have come running!"**[35]

◆◆◆

"Whoever would like to meet Allah in the future as a Muslim must uphold these prayers when their call is made. Allah set for your Prophet ﷺ the paths to guidance, and prayers are some of those paths. If you were to stay behind and pray alone, you would be abandoning the practice of your Prophet, and if you abandon the practice of your Prophet, you will go astray. Any man who purifies himself, striving for perfection in doing so, and then heads out to the mosque, Allah will record a good deed for him, raise his rank, and remove a bad deed of his with every step. I remember when only those who were known hypocrites would miss the prayer, while another man would be brought on the shoulder of two others until he reached the prayer rows."[36] -Ibn Masood

Ibn 'Abbas also points out something that we usually miss despite how clear it actually is. He said, "Whoever hears the call 'come to success!' and does not respond has abandoned the way of Muhammad ﷺ." Is any call more clear in what it is calling us to? How can we bear ignoring that call or turning away from it?

The Prophet ﷺ also encouraged us specifically towards praying the Isha and Fajr prayers in congregation. Abu Hurayrah narrates that the Messenger of Allah ﷺ said, **"If the people knew what was in responding to the prayer call and the first row, and found that they were only able to draw lots for it, they would do so. If they knew what reward was in arriving early, they would race to it, and if they knew what was in the Isha and Fajr prayers, they would come to them, even crawling."**[37] After he prayed one morning, he asked if two specific people were in attendance. When those present said no, he said, **"These two prayers are the most burdensome prayers for the hypocrites. If you knew what lies within them, you would** even come crawling and on horseback."[38] This is why Ibn Umar said that if they would notice that a man was missing from the Isha or Fajr prayers, they would grow suspicious.

To shed some more light on some of the benefits of praying these prayers in congregation, the Prophet ﷺ said, **"Whoever prays the Isha prayer in congregation, it is as if he had prayed for half the night. Then whoever prays the morning prayer in congregation, it is as if he prayed the whole night."**[39] Specifically about the Fajr prayer, he said, **"Whoever prays the morning prayer in congregation is under the protection of Allah."**[40] Umar bin al-Khattab once noticed that a man named Sulayman was missing from the Fajr prayer. Umar went to the market that morning after the prayer, and when he passed by Suleyman's house he said to his mother, "I didn't see Sulayman this morning!" She said, "He spent the night praying, and so he couldn't stay awake for the Fajr prayer." Umar corrected this misplaced priority, saying, "I would prefer to attend the morning prayer in congregation over praying the entire night."[41]

An Allowance for Women

The prayer of a woman in her home is considered a source of great reward for her, even greater than the reward of praying in the mosque. This is an allowance of compassion and ease for her, not of exclusion. Imagine how much ease this brings the mother of a newborn child, an elderly woman who prefers the comfort of her home, or a single mother who cannot leave her children behind. The lifestyle of many women may not adapt as easily to the inconvenience of leaving the home every day to pray in the mosque, and so the obligation is lifted from her shoulders.

Attending the mosque is always an option for her; in fact, it is her right. Women should never be excluded from congregational prayers, and every mosque should be welcoming to those women who choose to attend the congregational prayers. However, no woman should feel pressured to attend on a daily basis, nor feel guilty for preferring the privacy of their homes for prayer. Prophet Muhammad ﷺ said: **"Do not prevent women from the mosques, though their homes are better for them."**[42]

The Importance of Voluntary Prayers

The initial decree of fifty prayers was brought down to only five, as we have discussed previously. The best way to thank God for relief from this burden is to strive to pray as many voluntary sunnah prayers as we can. These are prayers that are not mandatory, and while there is no sin for missing them, there is immense reward in carrying them out.

One virtue of the sunnah prayers is that they make up for any flaws in our mandatory prayers. Abu Hurayrah narrates that he heard the Messenger of Allah ﷺ say, **"The first** deed that a person will be held accountable for on the Day of Judgment is his prayer. If it is good, then he has succeeded and prospered, and if it is bad, then he has failed and lost out. If there are shortcomings in his mandatory prayers, then Allah will say, 'Look to see if my servant has any voluntary actions to complete what has fallen short of his obligation.' Then the rest of his deeds will be according to that."[43]

The voluntary prayers also further deepen our connection with our Lord. When we choose to pray more than the bare minimum we remember that prayer is more than just a duty. We build the foundations of our relationship with the mandatory acts, and then proceed to ascend towards God with every voluntary act after that. This formula is outlined for us in the famous *hadith*, wherein the Prophet ﷺ said that God said,

> My servant does not come closer to me with anything more beloved to me than what I have made obligatory for him. Then my servant continues to come closer to me with the voluntary actions until I love him. Then when I love him, I am the hearing with which he hears, the vision with which he sees, the hand with which he strikes, and the foot with which he walks. If he asks of me, I give him, and if he ever seeks my protection, I protect him.[42]

There are different levels of recommended prayers. Some are recommended at a basic level, but others are highly emphasized. With each extra prayer we add to our daily routine, we rise in rank in the sight of God. During the most grievous and painful year of the Prophet's life, God revealed the verse:

وَمِنَ ٱلَّيْلِ فَتَهَجَّدْ بِهِۦ نَافِلَةً لَّكَ عَسَىٰٓ أَن يَبْعَثَكَ رَبُّكَ مَقَامًا مَّحْمُودًا ۞

And rise at (the last) part of the night, offering additional prayers, so your Lord may raise you to a station of praise. [17:79]

May Allah, Exalted, make us and our families consistent in our prayers, forgive us and show us mercy, and help us in our attempt to fulfill our covenant with Him. In the words of Prophet Abraham,

رَبِّ ٱجْعَلْنِي مُقِيمَ ٱلصَّلَوٰةِ وَمِن ذُرِّيَّتِي رَبَّنَا وَتَقَبَّلْ دُعَآءِ ۞ رَبَّنَا ٱغْفِرْ لِي وَلِوَٰلِدَيَّ وَلِلْمُؤْمِنِينَ يَوْمَ يَقُومُ ٱلْحِسَابُ ۞

My Lord! Make me and my descendants keep up prayer. Our Lord! Accept my prayers. Our Lord! Forgive me, my parents, and the believers on the Day when the judgment will come to pass." [14:40-41]

....

ENDNOTES

1. Bayhaqi in *Shu'ab al-Iman* (6/253 #4128); al-Tabari (13/239)
2. Narrated by Ibn Abi Aldunya in *Ash-Shukr* (# 6)
3. Ṣayd al-Khāṭir, p. 56
4. Imam Ahmad, al-Zuhd, #391
5. al-Ṭabarāni in *al-Mu'jam al-Awsat* #9452, deemed *hasan* by al-Albani
6. al-Ṭabarāni in *al-Mu'jam al-Kabeer* v. 6, p. 250, deemed *hasan* by al-Albani
7. al-Bayhaqi, *Shu'ab al-Imān*, #2550
8. Narrated by Ahmad in *Al-Musnad* 31/189 # 18894
9. al-Bukhari, #757; Muslim, #397
10. Ahmad, #9776
11. Al-Bazar (11/105 #4723, 4755)
12. Ahmad, #22693
13. Ahmad, #22016
14. Narrated by Ahmad (38/178 #23088)
15. Ahmad, #12293
16. Muslim, #482
17. Ibn Hibban #620, deemed *sahih* by al-Arna'oot
18. Bukhari #676
19. Ahmad, #11104
20. al-Bayhaqi, al-Zuhd, #527
21. Ahmad, #585
22. Bukhari, #349; Muslim, #162
23. al-Ṭabarāni, *al-Mu'jam al-Awsat*, #2224
24. al-Ṭabarāni, *al-Mu'jam al-Awsat*, #9452
25. al-Tirmidhi, #413
26. al-Ṭabarāni, *al-Mu'jam al-Awsat*, #243, deemed *hasan* by al-Albani
27. al-Ṭabarāni, *al-Mu'jam al-Awsat*, #920, deemed *hasan* by al-Munthari and al-Albani
28. Ahmad, #22693
29. al-Bukhari, #7534
30. al-Bukhar, #6502
31. al-Ṭabarāni, al-Du'ā', #606
32. al-Bukhari, 477; Muslim, 649
33. Ibn Majah, 793; Abu Dawud, deemed *sahih* by al-Albani
34. Ahmad, #15490
35. Muslim, #651, Bukhari #644
36. Muslim, #654
37. al-Bukhari, #610; Muslim #437
38. Ahmad, #21265
39. Muslim, #656
40. Muslim #657; Abu Nu'aym #1467
41. Malik in *al-Muwatta'*, v. 1, p.131
42. Ahmad, #5468
43. Ahmad, #7902
44. al-Bukhari, #6502

Remembrance & Reflection

وَٱذْكُرُوا۟ ٱللَّهَ كَثِيرًا لَّعَلَّكُمْ تُفْلِحُونَ ۝

And remember Allah often so you may be successful. [62:10]

Abu al-Darda' narrates that the Messenger of Allah said, **"Should I not inform you of the best of all your deeds, the most pure of them with your King and the most uplifting of your ranks, something that is better for you than giving out gold and silver, and better for you than fighting against your enemy who strikes your necks and whose necks you strike? It is the remembrance of God."**[1] Abu Musa al-Ash'ari narrates that the Prophet said, **"The difference between one who makes remembrance of his Lord and one who does not make remembrance of his Lord is like the difference between the living and the dead."**[2]

Paradise is Built on Remembrance

Thikr, translated as remembrance or mentioning, is to think of God, feel reverence in the heart, and to mention His names and praises. How much we make *thikr* of our Lord is a reflection of how much we are centering Him in our life.

The Messenger of Allah said, **"On the night when I was taken on the Night Journey I met Abraham, God's beloved friend. He said, "Muhammad! Relay my greetings to your nation, and inform them that the soil in Paradise is pure, its water is fresh, and that it is full of fertile plains; its cultivation is through 'subhān Allāh,' 'al-ḥamdu lillāh,' lā ilāha illa Allāh,' and 'Allāhu Akbar."**[3] (The translation of these phrases is glory be to Allah, praise be to Allah, there is no God but Allah, and God is greatest.) Ibn al-Qayyim points out

thikr:

remembrance of God, mentioning His names and praises

ذكر

about this *hadith*, "The houses of Paradise are built through remembrance. Once you stop making remembrance, the angels stop building, and when you start again, the angels continue to build."[4]

To busy our hearts with too many trivialities is not only unhealthy, but also unbefitting. Our hearts are valuable and should not be wasted. The Companion Abu al-Darda' said, "Everything has a unique purpose, and the purpose of the heart is to remember God."[5] Ibn Taymiyyah also draws a handy comparison that helps us realize how vital *thikr* is: "Remembrance to the hearts is like water to fish; look at what happens to them when they come out of the water!"[6]

Remembrance is a Fortress

The Messenger of Allah ﷺ once mentioned that God gave Prophet Yahya (John) five instructions to act upon himself and to instruct the Children of Israel with. One of the five was, "**to remember God; the parable of this is like a man who is being chased quickly by an enemy, but soon reaches a formidable fortress and protects himself from them. Similarly, a person does not protect himself from Satan with anything better than the remembrance of God.**"[7]

Imam al-Ghazali makes an insightful remark about why the remembrance of God is so weighty and significant, despite how easy it is for the tongue and how little effort it requires compared to other acts of worship. He said, "Know well that what is actually impactful and beneficial is to make remembrance constantly and with a present heart. Remembrance with a heart that is preoccupied has very little effect, as the Prophet ﷺ said, '**Know that Allah does not answer a prayer from a heart that is inattentive and distracted.**"[8] Ibn al-Qayyim similarly points out in Madārij al-Sālikeen,

> The rewards that God attaches to certain phrases only applies to when the phrase is wholesome. For example, the Prophet ﷺ said, "Whoever says '*subhān Allāh wa bi hamdihi*' one hundred times in a day has his wrongdoings removed from him, even if they were like the foam of the sea." This does not apply to simply saying the phrase with the tongue. Whoever says this with his heart inattentive, without the synchrony of the heart and tongue, and not knowing its true value but still hoping for its reward, will have his sins removed according to what is in his heart.
>
> Deeds are not considered more virtuous by their form or their number, but rather by what is in the heart. Two actions, identical in form, might differ completely in their virtue. Two men standing in the same row, praying the same prayer, can be worlds apart in the virtue of that prayer.[9]

Awakening the Heart with Remembrance

Remembering God has such immense importance and value, but how can we leverage it to awaken our hearts and strengthen our iman? How can we remember Allah in the most correct and effective way? Ibn al-Qayyim explained it this way:

> The best remembrance is done with the tongue and the heart, but remembrance with the heart alone is better than with the tongue alone. Remembering God in your heart helps you to know Him, awakens your love for Him, has a profound impact on your daily life, and prevents you from falling short in your obedience and undermining the gravity of sins. Remembering God with your tongue alone does not produce any of this, and anything it does produce is negligible.[10]

The synchrony of the heart with the tongue while making remembrance (*thikr*) is a practice to which we may be unaccustomed. But this ability to engage in mindful remembrance is not according to innate talent; it does not matter how old or young you are, whether you speak Arabic or not, or how experienced you are in our practice of Islam. Good remembrance practices depend on the amount of faith in your heart, and as much as you try to force yourself to be attentive, you may still find yourself with your tongue in one place and your mind in another. Remembrance brings out the reality of our inner states of servitude to God, and only according to the quality of that state will our tongues and minds be in sync. Ibn al-Qayyim gave a great example to help us realize this: hearts are like pots, and the tongues are their ladles.

In the beginning we must focus on planting the concepts of fear, reverence, hope, love, and brokenness for Allah in our hearts through contemplation. We can contemplate over the Quran, God's miraculous revelation, or the world around us, God's miraculous creation. To draw our attention to the relationship between contemplation and remembrance, Allah says,

$$\text{إِنَّ فِي خَلْقِ السَّمَاوَاتِ وَالْأَرْضِ وَاخْتِلَافِ اللَّيْلِ وَالنَّهَارِ لَآيَاتٍ لِّأُولِي الْأَلْبَابِ}$$

$$\text{(١٩٠) الَّذِينَ يَذْكُرُونَ اللَّهَ قِيَامًا وَقُعُودًا وَعَلَىٰ جُنُوبِهِمْ وَيَتَفَكَّرُونَ فِي خَلْقِ}$$

$$\text{السَّمَاوَاتِ وَالْأَرْضِ رَبَّنَا مَا خَلَقْتَ هَٰذَا بَاطِلًا سُبْحَانَكَ فَقِنَا عَذَابَ النَّارِ (١٩١)}$$

Indeed, in the creation of the heavens and the earth and the alternation of the day and night there are signs for people of reason—those who remember Allah while standing, sitting, and lying on their sides, and reflect on the creation of the heavens and the earth (and pray), "Our Lord! You have not created this without purpose! Glory be to You! Protect us from the torment of the Fire." [3:190-191]

Allah encourages us in these powerful verses to study the universe we live in and contemplate the grandness of His creation. When this contemplation is paired with remembrance of Allah, it increases the hearts' senses of awe and yearning for Him. Notice how those people responding to Allah's signs say, "Glory be to You! Protect us from the torment of the Fire." In those verses, Allah paints an exemplary picture of how a constant state of reflection and remembrance looks, teaching us that one of them must not exist without the other.

> When the Prophet of Allah 🕌 asked Aishah's permission to step away from the bed in which they slept to pray, she told him, "I love to be by your side, but I also love what brings you joy." Aishah says that after he purified himself and began to pray, he couldn't stop crying, to the point that his beard, his clothes, and the floor beneath him were drenched in tears. Later when Bilal came to call him for the prayer, he saw the state of the Prophet 🕌 and assumed he wept tears of grief. He said, "Messenger of Allah, why do you cry when Allah has already forgiven you?" The Prophet 🕌 replied: "Shouldn't I, then, be a grateful servant?" Tonight an ayah came down to me—doomed is whoever reads it without reflecting upon it!" He then recited: "Indeed, in the creation of the heavens and the earth and the alternation of the day and night there are signs for people of reason." [3:190][11]

The great commentator on the Quran, Imam Al-Qurtubi, says in his explanation of the verses 190-200 at the end of Surah Aal-Imran, "It is recommended that whenever someone wakes up in the middle of the night, they should rub the sleepiness from their eyes and begin their worship with these ten verses just as the Messenger 🕌 did, combining the elements of action and reflection. Abdallah ibn Abbas stayed overnight in the home of his aunt Maimunah, the Prophet's wife, and there he observed, "The Messenger 🕌 got up at night and rubbed the sleepiness from his face. He recited the last ten verses of Surah Aal-Imran. Then he went to a water skin that was hanging up, made wudu, and prayed 13 rakahs."[12] We can see in this example how the worship of the Prophet 🕌 opened with remembrance and contemplation.

Connecting Remembrance to Contemplation

Just as remembrance supplies the heart with life and activity, reflection supplies it with certainty. Abu al-Darda' was once asked if contemplation is counted as a good deed. He said, "Yes; it certainly is." Abu al-Darda' is also quoted as saying, "To contemplate for a moment is better than praying an entire night."[13]

In order to get the complete benefit from these two acts of worship—remembrance and reflection—they must be done in tandem. Ibn al-Qayyim says,

> Reflection and remembrance are two states that produce various insights and the true essence of faith. The insights continue to come the more one reflects on his remembrance of God and uses his reflections for the remembrance of God, until eventually the heart is unlocked with the permission of the One who opens all doors."[14]

To add to this, al-Ḥasan al-Baṣri said, "The people of intellect never stop combining the remembrance of God with their reflection. Then when their hearts are asked to speak, they speak with wisdom."[15]

Begin with reflection, and then follow it with a word of remembrance that is appropriate. When we contemplate our sins and shortcomings with God, and then follow it up with asking God for forgiveness, that act of asking for forgiveness will have a stronger energy to it. It will have a sincerity that would not be found if we started with the words of remembrance first, and then reflected afterwards. The heart first feels its need for the forgiveness of Allah, and so it prompts the tongue to follow suit. Allah confirms this in the verse,

وَٱلَّذِينَ إِذَا فَعَلُوا فَٰحِشَةً أَوْ ظَلَمُوٓا أَنفُسَهُمْ ذَكَرُوا ٱللَّهَ فَٱسْتَغْفَرُوا لِذُنُوبِهِمْ وَمَن يَغْفِرُ ٱلذُّنُوبَ إِلَّا ٱللَّهُ وَلَمْ يُصِرُّوا عَلَىٰ مَا فَعَلُوا وَهُمْ يَعْلَمُونَ ۝

They are those who, upon committing an evil deed or
wronging themselves, remember Allah, then seek forgiveness
for their sins—and who forgives sins except Allah? And they
do not knowingly persist in sin. [3:135]

Note that the verse points out that they remember Allah and repent, rather than just mentioning their repentance alone. We also notice the same in the beginning of Surah al-Aʻla, where Allah commands us to remember Him and also to think and reflect on the nature of His creation:

سَبِّحِ ٱسْمَ رَبِّكَ ٱلْأَعْلَى ۝ ٱلَّذِى خَلَقَ فَسَوَّىٰ ۝ وَٱلَّذِى قَدَّرَ فَهَدَىٰ ۝ وَٱلَّذِىٓ أَخْرَجَ ٱلْمَرْعَىٰ ۝ فَجَعَلَهُۥ غُثَآءً أَحْوَىٰ ۝

Glorify the Name of your Lord, the Most High, Who created
and perfectly fashioned, and Who ordained precisely and
inspired accordingly, and Who brings forth the green pasture,
then reduces it to withered chaff. [87:1-5]

A similar passage occurs in Surah al-Wāqiʻah. After God mentions the diverse manifestations of His infinite power and how deeply the universe relies on Him, He commands us to glorify him through remembrance:

$$\text{أَفَرَءَيْتُمُ ٱلنَّارَ ٱلَّتِى تُورُونَ ﴿٧١﴾ ءَأَنتُمْ أَنشَأْتُمْ شَجَرَتَهَآ أَمْ نَحْنُ ٱلْمُنشِـُٔونَ ﴿٧٢﴾ نَحْنُ جَعَلْنَـٰهَا}$$
$$\text{تَذْكِرَةً وَمَتَـٰعًا لِّلْمُقْوِينَ ﴿٧٣﴾ فَسَبِّحْ بِٱسْمِ رَبِّكَ ٱلْعَظِيمِ ﴿٧٤﴾}$$

Have you considered the fire you kindle? Is it you who produce its trees, or is it We Who do so? We have made it a reminder and a provision for the travellers. So glorify the Name of your Lord, the Greatest. [56:71-74]

And then in Surah al-Zukhruf, God reminds us of His creations through which He facilitated and enhanced our lives, and then gives us a specific phrase to say when we utilize them:

$$\text{وَٱلَّذِى خَلَقَ ٱلْأَزْوَٰجَ كُلَّهَا وَجَعَلَ لَكُم مِّنَ ٱلْفُلْكِ وَٱلْأَنْعَـٰمِ مَا تَرْكَبُونَ ﴿١٢﴾ لِتَسْتَوُۥا}$$
$$\text{عَلَىٰ ظُهُورِهِۦ ثُمَّ تَذْكُرُوا نِعْمَةَ رَبِّكُمْ إِذَا ٱسْتَوَيْتُمْ عَلَيْهِ وَتَقُولُوا سُبْحَـٰنَ ٱلَّذِى سَخَّرَ}$$
$$\text{لَنَا هَـٰذَا وَمَا كُنَّا لَهُۥ مُقْرِنِينَ ﴿١٣﴾}$$

And He is the One Who created all things in pairs, and made for you ships and animals to ride so that you may sit firmly on their backs and remember your Lord's blessings once you are settled on them, saying, "Glory be to the One Who has subjected these for us, for we could have never done so!" [43:12-13]

Allah directs our attention to the necessity of remembering Him through His blessings. The pattern that He laid out for us is to contemplate on them first, and then praise and glorify Him for them afterwards. This glorification, without a doubt, will be a completely different experience than the ones that we just rattle off with our tongues while our hearts preoccupied with other things.

Prepping the Heart for the Reflection

Now that we see the importance of connecting remembrance to reflection, we will explore the different opportunities for reflection and contemplation in the upcoming section. Allah mentions such opportunities often in the Quran, repeatedly calling on us to reflect upon them in order to realize the concepts of servitude and certainty within our hearts. These opportunities will have profound effects on us, by Allah's will, if we just give them the attention they deserve. We should set aside a specific time to sit alone in order to prepare our hearts to take in the effects of reflection. Before we immerse ourselves in the exercises of reflection and remembrance, there are a few conditions that will help our heart engage more deeply.

◀(FEAR OF ALLAH)▶

A heart that is mindful and fearful of Allah will remember
Him more:

سَيَذَّكَّرُ مَن يَخْشَىٰ ۝

Those in awe will be mindful. [87:10]

The repentant heart that fears God will respond to the signs of the
heavens and earth:

أَفَلَمْ يَنظُرُوٓا۟ إِلَى ٱلسَّمَآءِ فَوْقَهُمْ كَيْفَ بَنَيْنَٰهَا وَزَيَّنَّٰهَا وَمَا لَهَا
مِن فُرُوجٍ ۝ وَٱلْأَرْضَ مَدَدْنَٰهَا وَأَلْقَيْنَا فِيهَا رَوَٰسِىَ وَأَنۢبَتْنَا فِيهَا
مِن كُلِّ زَوْجٍۭ بَهِيجٍ ۝ تَبْصِرَةً وَذِكْرَىٰ لِكُلِّ عَبْدٍ مُّنِيبٍ ۝

*Have they not then looked at the sky above them:
how We built it and adorned it, leaving it flawless?
As for the earth, We spread it out and placed upon
it firm mountains, and produced in it every type
of pleasant plant—a means of reflection and a
reminder to every repentant servant.* [50:6-8]

◀(UTILIZING THE QURAN)▶

The Quran softens the hearts and brings it to life, directing our
attention to where and how to reflect within the vast realm of creation. Reading the Quran itself combines acts of both reflection and
remembrance (*thikr*), as the act of contemplation of God's words is
the essence of reflection, and recitation is the best form of the *thikr*.

◀(A FOCUSED MIND)▶

It is also important to be of present mind during remembrance
and reflection, free of any preoccupation from any other matters.
Being attentive during any act of worship is one of the most powerful ways to maximize the impact and effect that is intended. Allah
made the ways to know Him clear when He said,

إِنَّ فِى ذَٰلِكَ لَذِكْرَىٰ لِمَن كَانَ لَهُۥ قَلْبٌ أَوْ أَلْقَى ٱلسَّمْعَ وَهُوَ شَهِيدٌ ۝

*Surely in this is a reminder for whoever has a heart and lends
an attentive ear.* [50:37]

Ibn al-Qayyim wrote,

> God's words are a reminder, but only those who meet the requirements actually
> benefit from it. Firstly, they must have hearts that are alive and attentive. Then
> they must direct their sense of hearing completely to the One who is speaking.
> After that their hearts and minds must be present during the experience. This is
> just like when something is right in front of you without you realizing that it was
> there. Perhaps your eyesight isn't strong, or you weren't focusing your gaze on that
> particular object, or maybe you were just lost in thought about something else—
> you still failed to realize what was in front of you. Think about how many things
> passed by you that you missed out on because your heart was too busy thinking
> about something else. Benefitting from God's reminders requires our hearts to be
> sound and present, and our attention to be fully invested.[16]

....

ENDNOTES

1. Ahmad, #21702; *Sahih* by Tirmithi; deemed *sahih* al-Albani
2. al-Bukhari, #6407
3. al-Tirmidhi, #3462
4. *al-Wābil al-Ṣayyib*, p. 161
5. Ibid, 81.
6. al-Wābil al-Ṣayyib, p. 85
7. Ahmad, #17170; al-Tirmidhi, #2863
8. Ihyā' 'Uloom al-Deen, v. 1, p. 301; the *hadith* is reported by al-Tirmidhi from Abu Hurayrah, #3479
9. *Tahthib Madarij as-Salikeen*, p. 188
10. al-Wābil al-Ṣayyib, p. 181
11. Ibn Hibban (2/386 #620) and Sahih al-Arna'ut
12. Bukhari (1/47 #183) and Muslim (1/526 #763); al-Jami' li Ahkam al-Quran li al-Qurtubi (4/197-200)
13. Ibn al-Mubārakh, al-Zuhd, p. 949
14. Tahdheeb Madārij al-Sālikeen, p. 237
15. *Ihya' Uloom ad-Din 5/6*
16. Tahdheeb Madārij al-Sālikeen, p. 568

Fields of Reflection

Thinking frequently about how God's Names manifest in ourselves and creation helps us to know Him better. The earth beneath our feet and the sky above our heads are full of traces that lead us to the divine attributes:

فَٱنظُرْ إِلَىٰٓ ءَاثَٰرِ رَحْمَتِ ٱللَّهِ كَيْفَ يُحْيِ ٱلْأَرْضَ بَعْدَ مَوْتِهَآ إِنَّ ذَٰلِكَ لَمُحْيِ ٱلْمَوْتَىٰ وَهُوَ عَلَىٰ كُلِّ شَىْءٍ قَدِيرٌ ۝

See then the imprints of Allah's mercy: how He gives life to the earth after its death! Surely That same God can raise the dead. For He is Most Capable of everything. [30:50]

God has made all that is in the sky and on the earth accessible for us to use. All of His plentiful and various creations were made to facilitate life on earth for us, and so that we could devote ourselves to worshipping Him. Every creature, resource, vista, and delicate balance in nature plays an important role in helping us come to know our Lord. They are all signs and indicators of His names and attributes.

In addition to its functionality in facilitating life, the natural world serves as a pointer to the divine, signs of His presence and constant intervention. We should see in the brilliant, fiery sun not only our source of energy and light, but a great illustration of His mercy, power, and His overseeing of time and creation.

In *Madārij al-Sālikeen*, Ibn al-Qayyim points out that when the creation around us and the systems in which they operate are contemplated, we will find that they all point to the different attributes of God and the essences of His beautiful names. And you don't have to look farther than within your own self, as God says, after pointing out that there are signs in the earth,

وَفِىٓ أَنفُسِكُمْ أَفَلَا تُبْصِرُونَ ۝

As there are within yourselves. Can you not see? [51:21]

Ibn al-Qayyim continues to show how all of the creation are signs of God's attributes, qualities, and names, while citing some lines of poetry to bring this idea to life:

Every moment points to the divine
And everything you see is a sign
Read the world around you
As a letter sent to you from your King.
The message etched in all that surrounds you:
God is Truth—Lord of everything!
It is clear if you look, and listen for the sound, too.
For even in silence, God's serenity rings.

There is nothing more clear, Ibn al-Qayyim asserts, than the divine imprints in creation that point to the Creator, teaching us the nature of His perfection and the meanings of His names. Allah repeatedly describes the believers in the Quran as those who ponder over His signs and come to the conclusion of His Oneness and perfection, and then prepare for the inevitable meeting with Him. For example,

وَمِنْ آيَاتِهِ أَنْ خَلَقَ لَكُم مِّنْ أَنفُسِكُمْ أَزْوَاجًا لِّتَسْكُنُوا إِلَيْهَا وَجَعَلَ بَيْنَكُم مَّوَدَّةً وَرَحْمَةً ۚ إِنَّ فِي ذَٰلِكَ لَآيَاتٍ لِّقَوْمٍ يَتَفَكَّرُونَ ۝

And one of His signs is that He created for you spouses from
among yourselves so that you may find comfort in them. And
He has placed between you compassion and mercy. Surely in
this are signs for people who reflect. [30:21]

We must be in a constant state of searching for and taking note of God's signs around us. He says in the Quran,

إِنَّ فِي خَلْقِ السَّمَوَاتِ وَالْأَرْضِ وَاخْتِلَافِ اللَّيْلِ وَالنَّهَارِ لَآيَاتٍ لِّأُولِي الْأَلْبَابِ ۝ الَّذِينَ يَذْكُرُونَ اللَّهَ قِيَامًا وَقُعُودًا وَعَلَىٰ جُنُوبِهِمْ وَيَتَفَكَّرُونَ فِي خَلْقِ السَّمَوَاتِ وَالْأَرْضِ رَبَّنَا مَا خَلَقْتَ هَٰذَا بَاطِلًا سُبْحَانَكَ فَقِنَا عَذَابَ النَّارِ ۝

Indeed, in the creation of the heavens and the earth and the
alternation of the day and night there are signs for people of reason:
those who remember Allah while standing, sitting, and lying on their
sides, and reflect on the creation of the heavens and the earth and say,
"Our Lord! You have not created this without purpose. Glory be to
You! Protect us from the torment of the Fire. [3:190-191]

Reflecting on the workings of the world around us leads us to certainty that God did not create all of this without any purpose or goal. What a failure it would be for us to let the signs of God pass by us without reflecting on them and using them as a way to better know our Lord! God says that His deniers will hear these words when they die,

$$\text{لَّقَدْ كُنتَ فِى غَفْلَةٍ مِّنْ هَـٰذَا فَكَشَفْنَا عَنكَ غِطَآءَكَ فَبَصَرُكَ ٱلْيَوْمَ حَدِيدٌ ۝}$$

"You were totally heedless of this. Now We have lifted this veil of yours, so Today your sight is sharp!" [50:22]

Let us sharpen our vision in this life and be keen to take note of Allah's signs before it's too late. We should be purposeful in searching for His attributes around us, so as not to be among those about whom God says,

$$\text{وَكَأَيِّن مِّنْ ءَايَةٍ فِى ٱلسَّمَـٰوَٰتِ وَٱلْأَرْضِ يَمُرُّونَ عَلَيْهَا وَهُمْ عَنْهَا مُعْرِضُونَ ۝}$$

How many signs in the heavens and the earth do they pass by with indifference! [12:105]

All creation is indicative of a Creator who has life, ability, knowledge, and a will. The perfection and mastery of the creation indicates the Creator's wisdom and deliberateness. The beauty and utility therein indicates His compassion, care, and grace. We can read in the Quran that God has all of these qualities, but to witness them come to life with your own eyes is an experience that gives definition and volume to your relationship with God. Each name of God listed in the Quran can be observed in our lives. Some of us will notice them, and some of us will not.

Ibn al-Qayyim draws our attention to the importance of reflecting on the manifestation of God's names and attributes. He writes,

> Coming closer to Allah through His names and attributes is extraordinary! You can do it while lying down on your bed, without any physical effort or exhaustion. You don't have to go to some far off land, or even leave your house at all.

$$\text{وَتَرَى ٱلْجِبَالَ تَحْسَبُهَا جَامِدَةً وَهِىَ تَمُرُّ مَرَّ ٱلسَّحَابِ}$$

Now you see the mountains, thinking they are firmly fixed, but they are travelling (just) like clouds. [27:88]

There is nothing impressive about someone who travels day and night, but ends up not covering any distance. What is really astonishing is someone who stands still and bears no signs of travel, yet makes strides in his journey. What a tremendous difference there is between someone who learns about God's names and attributes through experience and engagement, and someone who just learns their technical definitions.[1]

That being said, the foremost guide to correctly understanding the manifestations of God's names and attributes is the Quran, and thereafter the study of the life of the most pure human to ever walk the earth. Dr. Umar al-Ashqar says in his book *The Perfect Names of Allah*, "The safest way to know God is through the revelation through which He made these matters clear to us. This is a sound and secure path, for it was carved out by the All-Knowing One and His Messenger. No one knows God better than God Himself, and there is no human being who knows God better than His Messenger."[2]

Many Signs, One Attribute

There are two methods that we can follow in order to make reflecting on God's names easy for us. We can either focus on extracting one name or attribute in the many signs around us, or try to extract as many of them as we can in one single sign.

In the first method, we observe many different signs and aspects and come to one conclusion. There are many examples that Allah has already laid out for us in the Quran. For example, God says:

وَٱللَّهُ خَلَقَ كُلَّ دَآبَّةٍ مِّن مَّآءٍ فَمِنْهُم مَّن يَمْشِى عَلَى بَطْنِهِۦ وَمِنْهُم مَّن يَمْشِى
عَلَى رِجْلَيْنِ وَمِنْهُم مَّن يَمْشِى عَلَىٰٓ أَرْبَعٍ يَخْلُقُ ٱللَّهُ مَا يَشَآءُ إِنَّ ٱللَّهَ عَلَىٰ كُلِّ
شَىْءٍ قَدِيرٌ ۝

And Allah has created from water every living creature. Some
of them crawl on their bellies, some walk on two legs, and
some walk on four. Allah creates whatever He wills. Surely
Allah is Most Capable of everything. [24:45]

This verse points out many manifestations among creatures for just one of God's attributes: omnipotence. The following verse does the same, for example, with Allah's attribute of knowledge:

وَعِندَهُۥ مَفَاتِحُ ٱلْغَيْبِ لَا يَعْلَمُهَآ إِلَّا هُوَ وَيَعْلَمُ مَا فِى ٱلْبَرِّ وَٱلْبَحْرِ وَمَا

تَسْقُطُ مِن وَرَقَةٍ إِلَّا يَعْلَمُهَا وَلَا حَبَّةٍ فِي ظُلُمَتِ ٱلْأَرْضِ وَلَا رَطْبٍ وَلَا يَابِسٍ إِلَّا فِي كِتَبٍ مُّبِينٍ ۝

*With Him are the keys of the unseen—no one knows them
except Him. And He knows what is in the land and sea. Not
even a leaf falls without His knowledge, nor a grain in the
darkness of the earth or anything, green or dry—it is in a
Clear Record.* [6:59]

The following verse is an example of the same method for His ability to create:

وَلَقَدْ خَلَقْنَا ٱلْإِنسَٰنَ مِن سُلَٰلَةٍ مِّن طِينٍ ۝ ثُمَّ جَعَلْنَٰهُ نُطْفَةً فِي قَرَارٍ مَّكِينٍ ۝ ثُمَّ خَلَقْنَا ٱلنُّطْفَةَ عَلَقَةً فَخَلَقْنَا ٱلْعَلَقَةَ مُضْغَةً فَخَلَقْنَا ٱلْمُضْغَةَ عِظَٰمًا فَكَسَوْنَا ٱلْعِظَٰمَ لَحْمًا ثُمَّ أَنشَأْنَٰهُ خَلْقًا ءَاخَرَ فَتَبَارَكَ ٱللَّهُ أَحْسَنُ ٱلْخَٰلِقِينَ ۝

*And indeed, We created humankind from an extract of clay,
then placed each one as a sperm-drop in a secure place, then
We developed the drop into a clinging clot, then developed
the clot into a lump, then developed the lump into bones,
then clothed the bones with flesh, and then We brought it
into being as a new creation. So Blessed is Allah, the Best of
Creators.* [23:12-14]

One Sign, Many Attributes

God also teaches us to reflect on His attributes by mentioning one sign in which many attributes manifest. For example, He says,

فَلْيَنظُرِ ٱلْإِنسَٰنُ إِلَىٰ طَعَامِهِۦٓ ۝ أَنَّا صَبَبْنَا ٱلْمَآءَ صَبًّا ۝ ثُمَّ شَقَقْنَا ٱلْأَرْضَ شَقًّا ۝ فَأَنۢبَتْنَا فِيهَا حَبًّا ۝ وَعِنَبًا وَقَضْبًا ۝ وَزَيْتُونًا وَنَخْلًا ۝ وَحَدَآئِقَ غُلْبًا ۝ وَفَٰكِهَةً وَأَبًّا ۝ مَّتَٰعًا لَّكُمْ وَلِأَنْعَٰمِكُمْ ۝

*Let people then consider their food: how We pour down
rain in abundance and meticulously split the earth open,
causing grain to grow therein, as well as grapes and greens,
and olives and palm trees, and dense orchards, and fruit
and fodder—all as a means of benefit for you and your
animals.* [80:24-32]

Within the single object of food, God shows us how we can look at it from different angles in order to see His many attributes. We can see how He is the Ever-Living who gives life; the Maintainer of our crops and the water that irrigates them; the Compassionate one who made this food enjoyable and nutritious; The All-Encompassing One upon whom everything depends; and the Ever-Subtle, who is involved in every intricate detail of the world around us.

God says in another verse, showing us the abundance of the single blessing of water:

هُوَ ٱلَّذِىٓ أَنزَلَ مِنَ ٱلسَّمَآءِ مَآءً لَّكُم مِّنْهُ شَرَابٌ وَمِنْهُ شَجَرٌ فِيهِ تُسِيمُونَ ۞ يُنۢبِتُ لَكُم بِهِ ٱلزَّرْعَ وَٱلزَّيْتُونَ وَٱلنَّخِيلَ وَٱلْأَعْنَٰبَ وَمِن كُلِّ ٱلثَّمَرَٰتِ إِنَّ فِى ذَٰلِكَ لَءَايَةً لِّقَوْمٍ يَتَفَكَّرُونَ ۞

He is the One Who sends down rain from the sky, from which you drink and by which plants grow for your cattle to graze. With it He produces for you crops, olives, palm trees, grapevines, and every type of fruit. Surely there is a sign in this for those who reflect. [16:10-11]

He also directs our attention to reflecting on milk for the same purpose:

وَإِنَّ لَكُمْ فِى ٱلْأَنْعَٰمِ لَعِبْرَةً نُّسْقِيكُم مِّمَّا فِى بُطُونِهِ مِنۢ بَيْنِ فَرْثٍ وَدَمٍ لَّبَنًا خَالِصًا سَآئِغًا لِّلشَّٰرِبِينَ ۞

And there is certainly a lesson for you in cattle: We give you to drink of what is in their bellies, from between digested food and blood: pure milk, pleasant to drink. [16:66]

Not only did he describe to us the impossible process of how milk comes to us, but He pointed out both its purity and delightful taste. Such a gift could only have come from the Pure and All-Wise, the Source of All Good.

And even more astonishing than that...honey! Allah says:

وَأَوْحَىٰ رَبُّكَ إِلَى ٱلنَّحْلِ أَنِ ٱتَّخِذِى مِنَ ٱلْجِبَالِ بُيُوتًا وَمِنَ ٱلشَّجَرِ وَمِمَّا يَعْرِشُونَ ۞ ثُمَّ كُلِى مِن كُلِّ ٱلثَّمَرَٰتِ فَٱسْلُكِى سُبُلَ رَبِّكِ ذُلُلًا يَخْرُجُ مِنۢ بُطُونِهَا شَرَابٌ مُّخْتَلِفٌ أَلْوَٰنُهُۥ فِيهِ شِفَآءٌ لِّلنَّاسِ إِنَّ فِى ذَٰلِكَ لَءَايَةً لِّقَوْمٍ يَتَفَكَّرُونَ ۞

And your Lord inspired the bees: "Make homes in the mountains, the trees, and in what people construct, feed from any fruit, and follow the ways your Lord has made easy for you." From their bellies comes forth liquid of varying colours, in which there is healing for people. Surely in this is a sign for those who reflect. [16:68-69]

These two methods of reflection allow us to extract just some of God's names from his creation. We can look at anything around us and list the many names and attributes of God that it reflects. We can also use just one of those attributes as our lens to see everything that surrounds us. After developing a good sense for it, we can then see the effects in things that are less tangible, like sleep, illness, and death.

Guidelines for Reflection

In this process of reflection, we must constantly keep in mind the ayah that makes God's uniqueness clear to us:

$$\text{لَيْسَ كَمِثْلِهِ شَيْءٌ وَهُوَ ٱلسَّمِيعُ ٱلْبَصِيرُ ۝}$$

There is nothing like Him. He is the All-Hearing, All-Seeing.
[42:11]

God also tells us that we can never fully understand the true nature of His essence:

$$\text{وَلَا يُحِيطُونَ بِهِ عِلْمًا}$$

... but they cannot encompass Him in knowledge. [20:110]

Imam al-Sa'di, who wrote one of the most famous contemporary commentaries on the Quran, said therein about the first verse,

> This means that nothing is similar to Him, nor is any of His creation comparable to Him—not in His essence, His names, His attributes, nor His actions. All of His names are beautiful, and all of His attributes are perfect.

In this practice of reflection, it is important never to attempt to envision God's actual essence. The Messenger of Allah ﷺ actually forbade it, and instead instructed that we reflect on His creation. He said, "**Meditate on God's wonders, don't meditate on God Himself.**"[3] The Prophet ﷺ gave us the tools we need in order to defend ourselves against Satan's whispers. He said, "**Satan will come to one of you and say, 'Who created the sky? Who created the earth?' and you will say, 'God.' Then he will ask, 'Who created God?' Whoever experiences any of that must then say, 'I Believe in Allah and His Messengers.'**"[4] Abu Hurayrah also narrates that the Prophet ﷺ said, "**Satan comes to one of you and says, 'Who created this? Who created that?' until he says, 'Who created your Lord?' When it reaches there, ask God for protection and stop.**"[5]

The aforementioned hadiths teach important tactics for dispelling Satan's whispers: ask God for protection and busy your mind with other thoughts. It is a strategy for dealing with doubts and nagging whispers. The Messenger of Allah taught us powerful defenses for these thoughts, as mentioned in the previous hadiths and the following one: "People will soon reason with each other until one of these asks: 'this God created the creation, but who created God?' When they say that, you should say, 'God is One. God is the Independent One upon whom all depend. He does not beget, and was not begotten, and there is nothing equivalent to Him. (the words of Surah al-Ikhlas) Then spit on your left side three times and ask for protection from Satan."[6]

In the fields of creation and life, there are so many aspects to reflect upon. In the coming pages, we will explore different aspects that we may reflect upon as we learn to keep God's mention constantly in our mind and remember Him more often.

◄ Fields of Reflection ►

The Universe's Subservience
Counting Blessings
Life without Blessings
Thinking about our Past
Our dependence on God
End of Civilizations
The Days of God

◄ SUBSERVIENCE OF THE UNIVERSE ►

This universe that we live in glorifies God—every inch of the skies and the earth, the land and the sea, and the mountains and the plains is cognizant of Him:

تُسَبِّحُ لَهُ ٱلسَّمَـٰوَٰتُ ٱلسَّبْعُ وَٱلْأَرْضُ وَمَن فِيهِنَّ وَإِن مِّن شَىْءٍ إِلَّا يُسَبِّحُ بِحَمْدِهِۦ وَلَـٰكِن لَّا تَفْقَهُونَ تَسْبِيحَهُمْ إِنَّهُۥ كَانَ حَلِيمًا غَفُورًا ۝

The seven heavens, the earth, and all those in them glorify Him. There is not a single thing that does not glorify His praises—but you cannot comprehend their glorification. He is indeed Most Forbearing, All-Forgiving. [17:44]

أَلَمْ تَرَ أَنَّ ٱللَّهَ يَسْجُدُ لَهُۥ مَن فِى ٱلسَّمَـٰوَٰتِ وَمَن فِى ٱلْأَرْضِ وَٱلشَّمْسُ وَٱلْقَمَرُ وَٱلنُّجُومُ وَٱلْجِبَالُ وَٱلشَّجَرُ وَٱلدَّوَآبُّ وَكَثِيرٌ مِّنَ ٱلنَّاسِ وَكَثِيرٌ حَقَّ عَلَيْهِ ٱلْعَذَابُ وَمَن يُهِنِ ٱللَّهُ فَمَا لَهُۥ مِن مُّكْرِمٍ إِنَّ ٱللَّهَ يَفْعَلُ مَا يَشَآءُ ۝

Do you not see that to Allah bow down (in submission) all those in the heavens and all those on the earth, as well as the sun, the moon, the stars, the mountains, the trees, and (all) living beings, as well as many humans, while many are deserving of punishment. And whoever Allah disgraces, none can honour. Surely Allah does what He wills. [22:18]

We as Muslims also believe that humans are not the only creation to acknowledge Muhammad ﷺ as God's Messenger. He ﷺ said, "**There is nothing between the sky and the earth that does not know that I am the Messenger of Allah, except for the insubordinate among jinns and humans.**"[7]

The natural world has a sensitivity to God's oneness:

وَقَالُوا ٱتَّخَذَ ٱلرَّحْمَٰنُ وَلَدًا ۝ لَّقَدْ جِئْتُمْ شَيْئًا إِدًّا ۝ تَكَادُ ٱلسَّمَٰوَٰتُ يَتَفَطَّرْنَ مِنْهُ وَتَنشَقُّ ٱلْأَرْضُ وَتَخِرُّ ٱلْجِبَالُ هَدًّا ۝ أَن دَعَوْا لِلرَّحْمَٰنِ وَلَدًا ۝

They say, "The Most Compassionate has offspring." You have certainly made an outrageous claim! The heavens are about to burst because of it, the earth to split apart, and the mountains to crumble to pieces—all because they attribute children to the Most Compassionate. [19:88-91]

Even the formidable mountains would crumble because of the Quran:

لَوْ أَنزَلْنَا هَٰذَا ٱلْقُرْءَانَ عَلَىٰ جَبَلٍ لَّرَأَيْتَهُ خَٰشِعًا مُّتَصَدِّعًا مِّنْ خَشْيَةِ ٱللَّهِ وَتِلْكَ ٱلْأَمْثَٰلُ نَضْرِبُهَا لِلنَّاسِ لَعَلَّهُمْ يَتَفَكَّرُونَ ۝

Had We sent down this Quran upon a mountain, you would have certainly seen it humbled and torn apart in awe of Allah. We set forth such comparisons for people; perhaps they may reflect. [59:21]

Consider how the stones are affected by their awe of God and compare them to our unresponsive hearts:

وَإِنَّ مِنْهَا لَمَا يَشَّقَّقُ فَيَخْرُجُ مِنْهُ ٱلْمَآءُ وَإِنَّ مِنْهَا لَمَا يَهْبِطُ مِنْ خَشْيَةِ ٱللَّهِ

...others split, spilling water; while others are humbled in awe of Allah. [2:74]

Some mountains and birds even took part in worshipping God alongside one of the Prophets:

وَلَقَدْ ءَاتَيْنَا دَاوُۥدَ مِنَّا فَضْلًا يَٰجِبَالُ أَوِّبِي مَعَهُۥ وَٱلطَّيْرَ

Indeed, We granted David a privilege from Us. "O mountains! Echo his hymns! And the birds as well." [34:10]

God also says about David,

إِنَّا سَخَّرْنَا ٱلْجِبَالَ مَعَهُۥ يُسَبِّحْنَ بِٱلْعَشِيِّ وَٱلْإِشْرَاقِ

We truly subjected the mountains to hymn along with him in
the evening and after sunrise. [38:18]

This harmony exists for every believer, as the Prophet ﷺ described about those who chant the talbiyah during Hajj, **"There is no one who chants except that every rock, tree, and mud clot to his right and left chant along with him until the end of the earth on each side."**[8]

It is no wonder, then, that the very movements of our worship resemble the movements of nature. In Hajj, for example, our rotations around the Kaaba can be compared to how electrons revolve around the nucleus of an atom and how planets revolve around a star. Even the number of rotations around the Kaaba, as well as the number of laps between Safa and Marwah, equal the number of skies above us and layers of earth below.

Muslims feel a special bond with the flora and fauna around us. The Prophet ﷺ said, **"Every single Arabian horse is granted two prayers at every dawn: 'God, you gave me to whomever you gave me to own among the human beings and made me for him, so make me the most beloved part of his family and wealth to him.'"**[9] The natural world even helps us find more good and distance ourselves from evil. Abu Hurayrah narrates that the Messenger of Allah ﷺ said, **"When you hear the crowing of the rooster, ask God for His bounty, for it has seen an angel. When you hear the bray of a donkey, take refuge with God, for it has seen a demon."**[10]

The animals and objects around us even ask God to forgive people! The Messenger of Allah ﷺ said, **"Everything in the heavens and the earth seeks forgiveness for the scholar—even the fish in the sea!"**[11] Muslims share with the natural world their belief and fear of the Final Hour. The Prophet ﷺ said, **"Every single creature falls silent on Friday morning until the sun rises out of worry for the Final Hour, except for the jinn and the humans."**[12]

From these connections sprout feelings of both love and hate, mutual feelings between us and the universe. God tells us, for example, that the sky and earth do not mourn the death of an unbeliever:

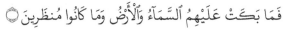

Neither heaven nor earth wept over them, nor was their fate
delayed. [44:29]

In contrast, the ground upon which the believer used to pray and the sky where his deeds would be lifted up to the heavens both grieve his passing, as Ali and Ibn 'Abbas are recorded to have said in *Tafseer al-Tabari*. We can even have a special, loving relationship with mountains! Anas said that the Messenger of Allah ﷺ once looked at Mount Uhud and said, **"Uhud is a mountain that loves us, and that we love."**[13]

Love requires that the lover does not offend or hurt the beloved. The Prophet ﷺ once climbed Mount Uhud while Abu Bakr, Umar, and Uthman were with him. It began to tremble, so he said, **"Stay still, Uhud! Upon you is a prophet, a paragon of truth, and two martyrs!"**[14] It was out of love for them that the mountain stopped shaking to ensure their safety. This love that nature has for the believers even extends to supporting them in battle. The Prophet ﷺ described how the trees and stones will call out to the Muslims during the apocalyptic battle at the end of times to expose the enemies hiding behind them. He even named the type of tree that would instead keep the enemies of the believers safe in alliance with them![15] We can see clearly how nature reciprocates with us based on our faith.

The Prophet ﷺ was so in touch with nature that he often drew out what we had in common with it. When he would see the new moon, he would say, **"God, bring it upon us with goodness and faith, with peace and Islam."** Then he would say, addressing the moon directly, **"My Lord and your Lord is Allah."**[16] He also prohibited us from cursing the forces of nature around us. Ibn 'Abbas says that a man once cursed the wind in the presence of the Prophet ﷺ, and so he said, **"Do not curse it, for it is instructed by its Lord."**[17]

We are prohibited from killing most creatures because of their recognition of God. Ibn Abbas narrates that the Prophet ﷺ forbade killing four creatures: the ant, the bee, the hoopoe bird, and the cuckoo bird.[18] Abu Hurayrah also narrates that the Messenger of Allah ﷺ said, **"An ant bit one of the prophets, and so he commanded that the whole colony of ants be burned. Then it was revealed to him: 'Is it because one ant bit you that you destroy one of the nations that glorify me?"**[19] The Prophet ﷺ also forbade killing frogs and said, **"Its croak is a glorification of God."**[20]

◁ NATURE'S WORSHIP ▷

Muhammad Ahmad al-Rashid writes in his book *al-Raqā'iq* that what brings all of the different parts of the universe together is servitude and worship of Allah. Everything on the face of the earth is in a synchrony of surrender, "from the tiny sprouts of grass to the tall lofty structures." Allah tells us this in the Quran:

$$\text{وَٱلنَّجْمُ وَٱلشَّجَرُ يَسْجُدَانِ ۝}$$

The stars and the trees bow down. [55:6]

Al-Rashid continues to say that we believers constantly see the world around us bowing down in servitude, and so it is a reminder for us to keep our hearts subservient to our Lord. This is how we enhance our physical prostration of our heads on the ground. He quotes the lines of poetry:

If you asked the green ground, or asked the running stream
Or the desert, so desolate, or the mountains towering
Ask the gardens, ask the roses, ask the petals, ask the dew
Ask the crickets of the night, ask the morning songbirds too
If you asked the wind around you, the ground below, or asked the sky
You'd hear everything say nothing but the praise of God so high.
The birds chirp His praise, while the cool cloud of shade
Sings of His glory under the tall tree, the crackle of the waves
Cry out His perfect names, as do the fish swimming through the salty sea
The glimmer of the rays, through the branches in the day
The tiny twinkle of the night, all chant for Him lovingly.

Everything in creation sings His glory, and so the universe is one vast symphony of His praise. The birds build studios in the trees to sing of His greatness for all to hear. In every wildlife call, every rustling leaf, ripple of water, and whistling wind we hear God's praise.

أَلَمْ تَرَ أَنَّ ٱللَّهَ يُسَبِّحُ لَهُۥ مَن فِى ٱلسَّمَـٰوَٰتِ وَٱلْأَرْضِ وَٱلطَّيْرُ صَـٰٓفَّـٰتٍ كُلٌّ قَدْ عَلِمَ صَلَاتَهُۥ وَتَسْبِيحَهُ

Do you not see that Allah is glorified by all those in the
heavens and the earth, even the birds as they soar? Each
(instinctively) knows their manner of prayer and glorification.
[24:41]

Train yourself to notice the signs of servitude around you, and your relationship with Allah will grow ever deeper. Dr. Malik Badri, a Muslim psychology expert, writes in his book *Contemplation: An Islamic Psychospiritual Study*, "Though the contemplating believers cannot decipher the glorification of God by the universe, they feel the harmony between their glorification and that of all other creatures. This feeling becomes deeper with the continuation of contemplation until they reach the peak of spirituality, feelings of pure bliss, and a spiritual delight that nothing in the material world can provide."[21]

◁ COUNTING BLESSINGS ▷

يَـٰٓأَيُّهَا ٱلنَّاسُ ٱذْكُرُوا نِعْمَتَ ٱللَّهِ عَلَيْكُمْ هَلْ مِنْ خَـٰلِقٍ غَيْرُ ٱللَّهِ يَرْزُقُكُم مِّنَ ٱلسَّمَآءِ وَٱلْأَرْضِ لَآ إِلَـٰهَ إِلَّا هُوَ فَأَنَّىٰ تُؤْفَكُونَ ۝

O humanity! Remember Allah's favours upon you. Is there
any creator other than Allah who provides for you from the
heavens and the earth? There is no god worthy of worship but
Him. How can you then be deluded? [35:3]

God instructs us to remember His favors in order for us to come to the inevitable conclusion that there is no ultimate Creator who sustains us but Him. When this reality settles in our minds and hearts, it is then easy for us to carry out our responsibilities.

This command to remember God's blessings can be found all throughout the Quran. The objective is for us to realize His endless grace, and subsequently work for Him in a spirit of gratitude. This exercise of reminding ourselves of God's gifts is important for us if we really wish to succeed in both this life and the next. This is why Prophet Hud said to his people,

أَوَعَجِبْتُمْ أَن جَآءَكُمْ ذِكْرٌ مِّن رَّبِّكُمْ عَلَىٰ رَجُلٍ مِّنكُمْ لِيُنذِرَكُمْ وَٱذْكُرُوٓا۟ إِذْ
جَعَلَكُمْ خُلَفَآءَ مِنۢ بَعْدِ قَوْمِ نُوحٍ وَزَادَكُمْ فِى ٱلْخَلْقِ بَصْۜطَةً فَٱذْكُرُوٓا۟ ءَالَآءَ
ٱللَّهِ لَعَلَّكُمْ تُفْلِحُونَ ۝

Do you find it astonishing that a reminder should come to
you from your Lord through one of your own so he may warn
you? Remember that He made you successors after the people
of Noah and increased you greatly in stature. So remember
Allah's favours, so you may be successful." [7:69]

Contemplation is not only an individual practice. Gatherings, with family and friends, in which we recount our blessings are a precious experience. Attempting as a family and as a group to count God's blessings in all of their different forms will help us comprehend that we can never fully encompass them!

وَإِن تَعُدُّوا۟ نِعْمَتَ ٱللَّهِ لَا تُحْصُوهَآ إِنَّ ٱلْإِنسَٰنَ لَظَلُومٌ كَفَّارٌ ۝

If you tried to count Allah's blessings, you would never be
able to number them. Indeed humankind is truly unfair,
ungrateful. [14:34]

Repeating this refrain to ourselves, "If you try to count Allah's blessings..." will remind us of our intrinsic failure to thank God. So we double our efforts, not only thanking Him in words but through action and work. Every blessing that God gives us has its own unique function which we must use in God's service.

إِنَّا خَلَقْنَا ٱلْإِنسَٰنَ مِن نُّطْفَةٍ أَمْشَاجٍ نَّبْتَلِيهِ فَجَعَلْنَٰهُ سَمِيعًۢا بَصِيرًا ۝ إِنَّا

هَدَيْنَـٰهُ ٱلسَّبِيلَ إِمَّا شَاكِرًا وَإِمَّا كَفُورًا ۝

*Indeed, We created humans from a drop of mixed fluids to
test them, so We made them hear and see. We then showed
them the Way, and so they are grateful or ungrateful.* [76:2-3]

The very essence of worship is gratitude:

بَلِ ٱللَّهَ فَٱعْبُدْ وَكُن مِّنَ ٱلشَّـٰكِرِينَ ۝

Rather, worship Allah and be one of the grateful. [39:66]

All of the blessings that God granted to us out of His generosity—big and small—require
our gratitude:

وَٱلْبُدْنَ جَعَلْنَـٰهَا لَكُم مِّن شَعَـٰٓئِرِ ٱللَّهِ لَكُمْ فِيهَا خَيْرٌ فَٱذْكُرُوا ٱسْمَ
ٱللَّهِ عَلَيْهَا صَوَآفَّ فَإِذَا وَجَبَتْ جُنُوبُهَا فَكُلُوا مِنْهَا وَأَطْعِمُوا ٱلْقَانِعَ وَٱلْمُعْتَرَّ
كَذَٰلِكَ سَخَّرْنَـٰهَا لَكُمْ لَعَلَّكُمْ تَشْكُرُونَ ۝

*We have made sacrificial camels [and cattle] among the symbols
of Allah, in which there is good for you. So pronounce the
Name of Allah over them when they are lined up [for sacrifice].
Once they have fallen on their sides, you may eat from their
meat, and feed the needy—those who do not beg, and those
who do. In this way We have subjected these [animals] to you so
that you may be grateful.* [22:36]

Consider all of the things that God subdued for our use and benefit. He reminds us,

وَعَلَّمْنَـٰهُ صَنْعَةَ لَبُوسٍ لَّكُمْ لِتُحْصِنَكُم مِّنۢ بَأْسِكُمْ فَهَلْ
أَنتُمْ شَـٰكِرُونَ ۝

*We taught him the art of making body armour to protect you
in battle. Will you then be grateful?* [21:80]

وَءَايَةٌ لَّهُمُ ٱلْأَرْضُ ٱلْمَيْتَةُ أَحْيَيْنَـٰهَا وَأَخْرَجْنَا مِنْهَا حَبًّا فَمِنْهُ يَأْكُلُونَ ۝
وَجَعَلْنَا فِيهَا جَنَّـٰتٍ مِّن نَّخِيلٍ وَأَعْنَـٰبٍ وَفَجَّرْنَا فِيهَا مِنَ ٱلْعُيُونِ ۝ لِيَأْكُلُوا
مِن ثَمَرِهِۦ وَمَا عَمِلَتْهُ أَيْدِيهِمْ أَفَلَا يَشْكُرُونَ ۝

*There is a sign for them in the dead earth: We give it life,
producing grain from it for them to eat. And We have placed
in it gardens of palm trees and grapevines, and caused springs*

to gush forth in it, so that they may eat from its fruit, which
they had no hand in making. Will they not then give thanks?
[36:33-35]

وَهُوَ ٱلَّذِى سَخَّرَ ٱلْبَحْرَ لِتَأْكُلُوا مِنْهُ لَحْمًا طَرِيًّا وَتَسْتَخْرِجُوا مِنْهُ حِلْيَةً
تَلْبَسُونَهَا وَتَرَى ٱلْفُلْكَ مَوَاخِرَ فِيهِ وَلِتَبْتَغُوا مِن فَضْلِهِۦ وَلَعَلَّكُمْ
تَشْكُرُونَ ۝

And He is the One Who has subjected the sea, so from it you
may eat tender seafood and extract ornaments to wear. And
you see the ships ploughing their way through it, so perhaps
you may seek His bounty and be grateful. [16:14]

Allah's grace is immeasurable. Because of our heedlessness and tendency to forget, we can
never truly realize the full extent of His generosity:

إِنَّ ٱللَّهَ لَذُو فَضْلٍ عَلَى ٱلنَّاسِ وَلَٰكِنَّ أَكْثَرَهُمْ لَا يَشْكُرُونَ ۝

Surely Allah is ever Bountiful to humanity, but most of them
are ungrateful. [10:60]

We must sit with ourselves from time to time and actually put in the effort to try to
count all of the different types of blessings. The more meticulously we look at every blessing,
turning it over in our mind, the more benefit we will get from the exercise. Every time we sit
for this activity, we should start where we last left off. Then end every session by glorifying
and praising God, with the thought of His blessings and grace fresh in our minds and hearts.

⟪ LIFE WITHOUT GOD'S BLESSINGS ⟫

Constantly receiving gifts without any interruption can make us insensitive to the One
who gives them to us. But if we were to imagine what life would be like if the most basic
blessings were taken from us, we can then realize their true value. We will constantly act
with gratitude out of fear of losing them.

God's repetitive reminders of His boundless blessings is a blessing in and of itself and
a form of His mercy. One way in which He reminds us is to mention those who have been
afflicted with illness and all types of weakness. The objective of this is to teach us the value
of good health and safety, then leading us to humble ourselves for His worship. Consider
the verse,

أَوَلَا يَرَوْنَ أَنَّهُمْ يُفْتَنُونَ فِى كُلِّ عَامٍ مَّرَّةً أَوْ مَرَّتَيْنِ ثُمَّ لَا يَتُوبُونَ وَلَا هُمْ
يَذَّكَّرُونَ ۝

Do they not see that they are tried once or twice every year?
Yet they neither repent nor do they learn a lesson. [9:126]

We have to always reflect on this idea, picturing our lives without the ability to see, hear, communicate, or walk. Think about how our situation could be changed completely if one body system or even one chemical was out of balance. Those of us who are safe from illness and disability might say we are fortunate, but that removes from the picture the One who gave these gifts to us and continues to protect us; let us instead say that we have been granted blessings.

The Quran is filled with verses that call us to imagine life without certain blessings. Allah says, for example,

أَفَرَءَيْتُمُ ٱلْمَآءَ ٱلَّذِى تَشْرَبُونَ ۝ ءَأَنتُمْ أَنزَلْتُمُوهُ مِنَ ٱلْمُزْنِ أَمْ نَحْنُ ٱلْمُنزِلُونَ ۝
لَوْ نَشَآءُ جَعَلْنَٰهُ أُجَاجًا فَلَوْلَا تَشْكُرُونَ ۝

Have you considered the water you drink? Is it you who
bring it down from the clouds, or is it We Who do so? If
We willed, We could make it salty. Will you not then give
thanks? [56:68-70]

قُلْ أَرَءَيْتُمْ إِنْ أَصْبَحَ مَآؤُكُمْ غَوْرًا فَمَن يَأْتِيكُم بِمَآءٍ مَّعِينٍ ۝

Say, "Consider this: if your water were to vanish, then who
could bring you flowing water?" [67:30]

Have you ever thought about what life would be like if the sun never set? How inconvenient it would be to endure twenty-four hours of complete daylight? This is not hard to imagine, and one only has to travel to northern Europe or Canada to experience it firsthand. For those of us who have never journeyed far enough to see it with our own eyes, God reminds us,

قُلْ أَرَءَيْتُمْ إِن جَعَلَ ٱللَّهُ عَلَيْكُمُ ٱلَّيْلَ سَرْمَدًا إِلَىٰ يَوْمِ ٱلْقِيَٰمَةِ مَنْ إِلَٰهٌ
غَيْرُ ٱللَّهِ يَأْتِيكُم بِضِيَآءٍ أَفَلَا تَسْمَعُونَ ۝ قُلْ أَرَءَيْتُمْ إِن جَعَلَ ٱللَّهُ
عَلَيْكُمُ ٱلنَّهَارَ سَرْمَدًا إِلَىٰ يَوْمِ ٱلْقِيَٰمَةِ مَنْ إِلَٰهٌ غَيْرُ ٱللَّهِ يَأْتِيكُم بِلَيْلٍ
تَسْكُنُونَ فِيهِ أَفَلَا تُبْصِرُونَ ۝ وَمِن رَّحْمَتِهِ جَعَلَ لَكُمُ ٱلَّيْلَ وَٱلنَّهَارَ
لِتَسْكُنُوا۟ فِيهِ وَلِتَبْتَغُوا۟ مِن فَضْلِهِ وَلَعَلَّكُمْ تَشْكُرُونَ ۝

*Say: "Imagine if Allah were to make the night perpetual for
you until the Day of Judgment, which god other than Allah
could bring you sunlight? Will you not then listen?" Ask:
"Imagine if Allah were to make the day perpetual for you until
the Day of Judgment, which god other than Allah could bring
you night to rest in? Will you not then see?" It is out of His
mercy that He has made for you the day and night so that
you may rest and seek His bounty, and so that you might be
grateful.* [28:71-73]

Not only should we remind others of these blessings to spread a culture of gratitude, but
you should also sit alone in solitude to reflect on your individual experience. You can focus
on your eyesight, for example; how difficult life would be without it, how God has blessed
you with it for so long, and what it would be like not to see the faces of your loved ones and
the beauty of creation. Then you can spend the next session reflecting over the blessing of
hearing, safety, or even being Muslim, walking through the same process, appreciating how
entrenched you are in God's bounty.

قُلْ أَرَءَيْتُمْ إِنْ أَخَذَ ٱللَّهُ سَمْعَكُمْ وَأَبْصَـٰرَكُمْ وَخَتَمَ عَلَىٰ قُلُوبِكُم مَّنْ إِلَـٰهٌ
غَيْرُ ٱللَّهِ يَأْتِيكُم بِهِ ٱنظُرْ كَيْفَ نُصَرِّفُ ٱلْءَايَـٰتِ ثُمَّ هُمْ يَصْدِفُونَ ۝

*Ask: "Imagine if Allah were to take away your hearing or
sight, or seal your hearts—who else other than Allah could
restore it?" See how We vary the signs, yet they still turn away.*
[6:46]

As we grasp some understanding of the extent of our blessings, and how helpless we would
be without them, we should pronounce words of humility and repentance: "there is no source
of power or strength but Allah." and "there is nothing worthy of worship but you—you are
perfect! I was certainly a wrongdoer."

﴾ THINKING ABOUT THE PAST ﴿

God addresses the believing Companions, who only a few years earlier had been pagans,
ignorant of God and His true religion:

كَذَٰلِكَ كُنتُم مِّن قَبْلُ فَمَنَّ ٱللَّهُ عَلَيْكُمْ فَتَبَيَّنُوٓا۟ إِنَّ ٱللَّهَ كَانَ بِمَا
تَعْمَلُونَ خَبِيرًا ۝

*You were initially like them then Allah blessed you. So be sure!
Indeed, Allah is All-Aware of what you do.* [4:94]

We are so quick to forget our pasts. We are so easily distracted from our previous trials, whether they be poverty, illnesses, sin, or even unbelief! Such a state of neglect prevents us from realizing the enormity of the blessings that flood our lives. In many verses throughout the Quran, God reminds the Israelites of their immense blessings with which He showered them so that they might return to Him, become humble to Him, and stop their rebellion and injustice. He says, for example,

يَـٰبَنِىٓ إِسۡرَٰٓءِيلَ ٱذۡكُرُوا۟ نِعۡمَتِىَ ٱلَّتِىٓ أَنۡعَمۡتُ عَلَيۡكُمۡ وَأَنِّى فَضَّلۡتُكُمۡ عَلَى ٱلۡعَـٰلَمِينَ ۝ وَٱتَّقُوا۟ يَوۡمًا لَّا تَجۡزِى نَفۡسٌ عَن نَّفۡسٍ شَيۡـًٔا وَلَا يُقۡبَلُ مِنۡهَا شَفَـٰعَةٌ وَلَا يُؤۡخَذُ مِنۡهَا عَدۡلٌ وَلَا هُمۡ يُنصَرُونَ ۝ وَإِذۡ نَجَّيۡنَـٰكُم مِّنۡ ءَالِ فِرۡعَوۡنَ يَسُومُونَكُمۡ سُوٓءَ ٱلۡعَذَابِ يُذَبِّحُونَ أَبۡنَآءَكُمۡ وَيَسۡتَحۡيُونَ نِسَآءَكُمۡ وَفِى ذَٰلِكُم بَلَآءٌ مِّن رَّبِّكُمۡ عَظِيمٌ ۝ وَإِذۡ فَرَقۡنَا بِكُمُ ٱلۡبَحۡرَ فَأَنجَيۡنَـٰكُمۡ وَأَغۡرَقۡنَآ ءَالَ فِرۡعَوۡنَ وَأَنتُمۡ تَنظُرُونَ ۝

O Children of Israel! Remember the favors that I granted you and how I honored you above all others. Beware of the Day on which no soul will be of help to another. No intercession will be accepted, no ransom taken, and no help will be given. We delivered you from the people of Pharaoh, who afflicted you with dreadful torment, slaughtering your sons and keeping your women. That was a severe test from your Lord. And We parted the sea, rescued you, and drowned Pharaoh's people before your very eyes. [2:47-50]

The verses continue to remind the Israelites of their past and how God blessed them with breathtaking blessings so that they would change their course from ingratitude to appreciation.

Remembering the past to appreciate God's blessings is such a powerful Quranic directive. Allah says,

وَٱذۡكُرُوهُ كَمَا هَدَىٰكُمۡ وَإِن كُنتُم مِّن قَبۡلِهِۦ لَمِنَ ٱلضَّآلِّينَ ۝

Praise Him for having guided you, for surely before this you were astray. [2:198]

In order for us to truly internalize the gift of guidance, we must remember our misguided past. Even the Messengers used this tool when preaching; God tells us that Prophet Shuaib said to his people,

وَٱذۡكُرُوٓا۟ إِذۡ كُنتُمۡ قَلِيلًا فَكَثَّرَكُمۡ وَٱنظُرُوا۟ كَيۡفَ كَانَ عَـٰقِبَةُ ٱلۡمُفۡسِدِينَ ۝

Remember when you were few, then He increased you in number. And consider the fate of the corruptors! [7:86]

Notice how God speaks to the Companions of the Prophet ﷺ who gave up everything they had and risked their lives to migrate to Medina; he says to them after they emerged victorious from the Battle of Badr against all odds:

وَٱذْكُرُوٓا۟ إِذْ أَنتُمْ قَلِيلٌ مُّسْتَضْعَفُونَ فِى ٱلْأَرْضِ تَخَافُونَ أَن يَتَخَطَّفَكُمُ ٱلنَّاسُ فَـَٔاوَىٰكُمْ وَأَيَّدَكُم بِنَصْرِهِۦ وَرَزَقَكُم مِّنَ ٱلطَّيِّبَٰتِ لَعَلَّكُمْ تَشْكُرُونَ ۝

Remember when you had been vastly outnumbered and oppressed in the land, constantly in fear of attacks by your enemy, then He sheltered you, strengthened you with His help, and provided you with good things so perhaps you would be thankful. [8:26]

Before the Messenger of Allah ﷺ arrived in Medina, the city's population was torn by tribal fervor and widespread social and economic corruption. It was only after the migration of the Muslims and a social upheaval of values and beliefs that the Medinan society became one of fraternity, justice, and generosity, and its believing people were henceforth called the Ansar, the Helpers. Reminding them of the catalyst for their righteousness, God says to the Companions,

وَٱذْكُرُوا۟ نِعْمَتَ ٱللَّهِ عَلَيْكُمْ إِذْ كُنتُمْ أَعْدَآءً فَأَلَّفَ بَيْنَ قُلُوبِكُمْ فَأَصْبَحْتُم بِنِعْمَتِهِۦٓ إِخْوَٰنًا وَكُنتُمْ عَلَىٰ شَفَا حُفْرَةٍ مِّنَ ٱلنَّارِ فَأَنقَذَكُم مِّنْهَا كَذَٰلِكَ يُبَيِّنُ ٱللَّهُ لَكُمْ ءَايَٰتِهِۦ لَعَلَّكُمْ تَهْتَدُونَ ۝

Remember Allah's favor upon you when you were enemies, then He united your hearts, so you—by His grace—became brothers. And you were at the brink of a fiery pit, but He saved you from it. This is how Allah makes His signs clear to you, so that you may be rightly guided. [3:103]

Perhaps the most frightening event in Muslim history after the persecution of the Muslims in Mecca was the Battle of Aḥzāb, wherein Quraysh gathered an alliance of tribes to lay seige to the entire city of Medina. The true colors of the tribes whose loyalty was based on material gain or political deception came to the surface when they turned their backs on their Muslim neighbors and aided the enemy alliance against them. The Muslims came together as a community to exchange ideas and distribute responsibilities based on their individual strengths, but the siege of 10,000 enemy soldiers and cavalry against the 3,000 Muslims lasted more than 30 days. Emotionally depleted, physically exhausted, and frighteningly outnumbered, the Muslims began to wonder what their fate—and that of their religion—would come to. It wasn't until God sent help from the heavens to assist His believers that they were able to defeat and drive away their attackers. Soon after their unlikely victory, God sent verses down to remind them of their weakness and human vulnerability:

يَـٰٓأَيُّهَا ٱلَّذِينَ ءَامَنُوا ٱذْكُرُوا نِعْمَةَ ٱللَّهِ عَلَيْكُمْ إِذْ جَآءَتْكُمْ جُنُودٌ فَأَرْسَلْنَا عَلَيْهِمْ رِيحًا وَجُنُودًا لَّمْ تَرَوْهَا وَكَانَ ٱللَّهُ بِمَا تَعْمَلُونَ بَصِيرًا ۝ إِذْ جَآءُوكُم مِّن فَوْقِكُمْ وَمِنْ أَسْفَلَ مِنكُمْ وَإِذْ زَاغَتِ ٱلْأَبْصَـٰرُ وَبَلَغَتِ ٱلْقُلُوبُ ٱلْحَنَاجِرَ وَتَظُنُّونَ بِٱللَّهِ ٱلظُّنُونَا۠ ۝ هُنَالِكَ ٱبْتُلِيَ ٱلْمُؤْمِنُونَ وَزُلْزِلُوا زِلْزَالًا شَدِيدًا ۝

O believers! Remember Allah's favour upon you when forces
came to you, so We sent against them a wind and forces
you could not see. And Allah is All-Seeing of what you do.
Remember when they came at you from east and west, when
your eyes grew wild in horror and your hearts jumped into
your throats, and you entertained those thoughts about Allah.
Then and there the believers were put to the test, and were
violently shaken. [33:9-11]

Let us each individually sit on our own and think about our past. Think about how engrossed in sin and lost we were, and how enslaved we were to our desires before God blessed us with guidance and direction. Think about the wrongs we committed and may not have been punished for yet. Think about those trials that you didn't think you would make it through and how God saved you and gave you even more blessings thereafter. Do not forget to say those words of humility and prayer that we mentioned before, that are befitting of your feelings of gratitude and appreciation, and which acknowledge your absolute dependence on God.

◖ OUR DEPENDENCE ON GOD ◗

Reflecting on how desperately and urgently we depend on God is the key to unlocking the true meaning of servitude. God says,

يَـٰٓأَيُّهَا ٱلنَّاسُ أَنتُمُ ٱلْفُقَرَآءُ إِلَى ٱللَّهِ وَٱللَّهُ هُوَ ٱلْغَنِيُّ ٱلْحَمِيدُ ۝ إِن يَشَأْ يُذْهِبْكُمْ وَيَأْتِ بِخَلْقٍ جَدِيدٍ ۝ وَمَا ذَٰلِكَ عَلَى ٱللَّهِ بِعَزِيزٍ ۝

O humanity! It is you who stand in need of Allah, and Allah

*is the Self-Sufficient, the Praiseworthy. If He willed, He could
eliminate you and produce a new creation. And that is not
difficult for Allah at all.* [35:15-17]

Our need for Allah is at the center of our identity. Our need does not decrease with any apparent physical strength or any amount of wealth; these are all secondary states of being to our contingent essence of existence.

No matter how many leaders and celebrities claim to have achieved riches from rags on their own accord, or how many athletes claim to have developed their skills through nothing but hard work, no one possesses any ability or independence apart from God. Everyone experiences moments in their lives through which they realize the limit of their perceived capacity and dire need for God's help.

Let us just consider one organ: the heart. How does it work? How many times does it beat, sending blood to every extremity each minute? What would happen if, for even just a couple of minutes, it stopped? Our hearts have been at work, night and day, since the moment God created us, without even a moment's rest. Who has been keeping it running all of this time?

Now think about your kidneys, and the vital role they play in keeping us alive. Your blood is constantly running through them in order to be cleansed of disease. Imagine if your kidneys just decided to take a day, or even just a few hours, off. What could you possibly do to get them to work again? Apply this line of thinking to every organ and body part: the brain, the nerves, the glands, the liver, and even your bone marrow and muscle tissue. How have all of these intricate and delicate components that are each uniquely vital to your wellbeing continued to operate seamlessly and simultaneously without any effort on your part? We move through our daily lives forgetting that there are hundreds of thousands of processes occurring within our bodies every single moment. If it is not us, then who keeps these systems running so smoothly day in and day out?

قُلْ مَن يَكْلَؤُكُم بِالَّيْلِ وَالنَّهَارِ مِنَ الرَّحْمَٰنِ

*Ask: "Who can defend you by day or by night against the
Most Compassionate?"* [21:42]

We must reflect on this reality often, remembering the countless diseases that can afflict any one of our fragile limbs. We will come to realize our dependence and need for Him. Despite all of the viruses and bacteria that we come in contact with every day, we still manage to live in good health and safety. If we were to calculate the chances of living for so long in light of all the possible diseases that threaten us each day, we would never predict that humans would live for so many years at a time. The reality we seem to observe is that good health is standard, and illness is exceptional. This is only possible by God's grace, and He tells us clearly how He does it:

$$وَيُرْسِلُ عَلَيْكُمْ حَفَظَةً$$

And He sends guardians over you. [6:61]

We owe every breath we take to Him. We are in constant need of His protection and continuous supervision in keeping us well. All of this is just in light of how He preserves our own bodies; there is still much to be said about how the massive earth stays intact, with all of its systems running regularly each day. We do not live in constant fear of earthquakes, volcanic eruptions, massive floods or fires. From a purely materialistic perspective, these horrors should occur much more often than they actually do, and it is beyond our capacity to accurately predict—let alone prevent—them. When we realize that it is He who keeps the world sound for us, we can begin to love Him through our dependence on Him.

We are even more desperately in need of God in matters of spiritual guidance. If we were left to our own devices, we wouldn't be able to stay upright and would be constantly ensnared in evil. God makes this clear to us when He says,

$$وَلَوْلَا فَضْلُ ٱللَّهِ عَلَيْكُمْ وَرَحْمَتُهُۥ مَا زَكَىٰ مِنكُم مِّنْ أَحَدٍ أَبَدًا وَلَٰكِنَّ$$
$$ٱللَّهَ يُزَكِّى مَن يَشَآءُ وَٱللَّهُ سَمِيعٌ عَلِيمٌ ۝$$

Had it not been for Allah's grace and mercy upon you, none
of you would have ever been purified. But Allah purifies
whoever He wills. And Allah is All-Hearing, All-Knowing.
[24:21]

None of us would be able to defend ourselves against our egos and passions that constantly prod us to give into our lowly nature and neglect our higher purpose. It is only through God's grace and mercy that we do not follow the herds of sinners.

Think about the people who worship cows, pieces of wood, or even abstract and arbitrary symbols. If we grew up in families and environments where this was normal, would we follow blindly? Why were those of us who were born Muslim placed in Muslim families? Did we do something to deserve such a blessing? It was purely a gift from God, Mighty and Majestic.

We can then go on to ponder how we continued to grow in faith, choosing to remain Muslim, despite the islamophobia and intellectual warfare against religion.

$$وَمَا كُنَّا لِنَهْتَدِىَ لَوْلَآ أَنْ هَدَىٰنَا ٱللَّهُ$$

We would have never been guided if Allah had not
guided us. [7:43]

Choosing guidance is one battle, but remaining firm upon guidance is a completely different one. Only He protects our hearts from veering towards falsehood.

The most righteous people on the planet always emphasized the fact that they had nothing to do with their righteousness. Prophet Abraham, even after having passed the heart-wrenching and harrowing tests that God gave him, pleaded God in his elderly years,

$$\text{وَإِذْ قَالَ إِبْرَٰهِيمُ رَبِّ ٱجْعَلْ هَٰذَا ٱلْبَلَدَ ءَامِنًا وَٱجْنُبْنِى وَبَنِىَّ أَن نَّعْبُدَ ٱلْأَصْنَامَ ۝}$$

Keep me and my children away from the worship of idols
[14:35]

When denouncing his people's false religion, Prophet Shuaib swore off ever returning to their ways, but made sure to highlight that his ultimate fate was in God's hands:

$$\text{قَدِ ٱفْتَرَيْنَا عَلَى ٱللَّهِ كَذِبًا إِنْ عُدْنَا فِى مِلَّتِكُم بَعْدَ إِذْ نَجَّىٰنَا ٱللَّهُ مِنْهَا وَمَا يَكُونُ لَنَآ أَن نَّعُودَ فِيهَآ إِلَّآ أَن يَشَآءَ ٱللَّهُ رَبُّنَا}$$

We would surely be fabricating a lie against Allah if we were to return to your faith after Allah has saved us from it. It does not befit us to return to it unless it is the Will of Allah, our Lord. [7:89]

An even more interesting example is when Prophet Joseph prayed to Allah, toward the end of his long story in the Quran:

$$\text{رَبِّ قَدْ ءَاتَيْتَنِى مِنَ ٱلْمُلْكِ وَعَلَّمْتَنِى مِن تَأْوِيلِ ٱلْأَحَادِيثِ فَاطِرَ ٱلسَّمَٰوَٰتِ وَٱلْأَرْضِ أَنتَ وَلِيِّۦ فِى ٱلدُّنْيَا وَٱلْءَاخِرَةِ تَوَفَّنِى مُسْلِمًا وَأَلْحِقْنِى بِٱلصَّٰلِحِينَ ۝}$$

My Lord! You have surely granted me authority and taught me the interpretation of dreams. Originator of the heavens and the earth! You are my Guardian in this world and the Hereafter. Allow me to die as one who submits and join me with the righteous. [12:101]

After having been separated from his family for years, kidnapped, enslaved, and accused of crimes he never committed, Prophet Joseph kept true to his faith in God and never gave up striving for excellence, even when he became entrusted with authority over the land of Egypt. But notice to whom he attributes his success; he acknowledges God as the sole dispenser of authority and knowledge. Then He points out that everything originated from God, and praises God as his Guardian throughout his perilous journey. Now even at the end of his course—after redemption, relief, and returning to his family—he still desperately pleads God to keep him in the state of submission and to raise him up to the level of the righteous, as if to deny himself of any claim to his own uprightness.

A student of the Companions once asked Umm Salamah, the Prophet's wife, about what the Prophet ﷺ used to pray for most frequently in his prayers. Her response is bone-chilling if we really reflect on it: **"Turner of the hearts, make my heart firm on your religion."**[22] The most flawless of all men would constantly ask God to make His heart firm. There is something to take note of even in the wording of his request: he calls God "the Turner of the hearts," alluding to the possibility that our course may be reversed at any moment. That man praying Fajr prayer in the first row of the mosque might become a slave of Satan by noon if God chooses to turn him astray. If so, there is nothing anyone can do to save him:

$$وَمَن يُرِدِ ٱللَّهُ فِتْنَتَهُۥ فَلَن تَمْلِكَ لَهُۥ مِنَ ٱللَّهِ شَيْـًٔا$$

Whoever Allah allows to be deluded, you can never be of any
help to them against Allah. [5:41]

We are incessantly in need of God's help and assistance. If we rely on ourselves for even a moment's time we are sure to slip and fall—literally and physically. Keeping this in mind helps affirm our absolute dependence, and we can then internalize the true meaning of "there is no source of power or might but God."

◖ THE END OF CIVILIZATIONS ◗

Some fields of reflection are less abstract than others. God often urges us throughout the Quran to reflect on history, both through learning the history that occurred and by actually observing the remains of past civilizations:

$$قَدْ خَلَتْ مِن قَبْلِكُمْ سُنَنٌ فَسِيرُوا فِي ٱلْأَرْضِ فَٱنظُرُوا كَيْفَ كَانَ$$
$$عَٰقِبَةُ ٱلْمُكَذِّبِينَ ۟$$

Similar situations came to pass before you, so travel
throughout the land and see the fate of the deniers. [3:137]

Seeing the dusty and withered remnants of what were once mighty and developed societies impacts how we understand the consequences of tyranny. God instructs us to pay special mind to the societies that were oppressive in their treatment of people. He also directs our focus towards the exemplars of patience and piety; Moses said to his people:

$$\text{إِنَّ ٱلْأَرْضَ لِلَّهِ يُورِثُهَا مَن يَشَآءُ مِنْ عِبَادِهِۦ وَٱلْعَٰقِبَةُ لِلْمُتَّقِينَ} \; \textcircled{\scriptsize ◌}$$

Indeed, the earth belongs to Allah. He grants it to whoever He chooses of His servants. The ultimate outcome belongs to the righteous. [7:128]

And God elsewhere repeats the same phrase in urging the Prophet ﷺ to endure the mistreatment from his own tribe with grace:

$$\text{فَٱصْبِرْ إِنَّ ٱلْعَٰقِبَةَ لِلْمُتَّقِينَ} \; \textcircled{\scriptsize ◌}$$

Surely the ultimate outcome belongs to the righteous. [11:49]

We must ponder over events in history to better understand the results of tyranny, extravagance, and corruption. We should study closely how these themes pan out in both individual biographies and societies, remembering that God is never unjust, but it is people who set themselves up for disappointment and destruction. He will take every tyrant to task, without exception, and His vengeance is one that will not fail:

$$\text{وَلَا يَحِيقُ ٱلْمَكْرُ ٱلسَّيِّئُ إِلَّا بِأَهْلِهِۦ فَهَلْ يَنظُرُونَ إِلَّا سُنَّتَ ٱلْأَوَّلِينَ فَلَن} \\ \text{تَجِدَ لِسُنَّتِ ٱللَّهِ تَبْدِيلًا وَلَن تَجِدَ لِسُنَّتِ ٱللَّهِ تَحْوِيلًا} \; \textcircled{\scriptsize ◌}$$

But evil plotting only backfires on those who plot. Are they awaiting anything but the fate of those before? You will find no change in the way of Allah, nor will you find it diverted. [35:43]

These frequent reminders all throughout the Quran should be actionable lessons to us and warnings to take a different path in order not to meet a similar ending. The way God deals with tyranny does not change with time and place, nor does His penalty miss a single offender. If we are as certain about these historical patterns as we are about our scientific observations, why then is it so difficult to learn from them? Why does history repeat itself so often without us deriving any benefit from it?

The Quran makes clear how the world's systems flawlessly operate and paints vivid pictures of how these formulas are carried out. If you want to know what the end result of ingratitude is, then read about the city of Sheba. If you want to learn a practical lesson on what happens to the conceited and arrogant, read the story of Qāroon. Why else would God so frequently repeat the stories of the Pharaoh and of cities like 'Ad and Thamud? The repetition is not superfluous; the patterns we learn from these stories help us avoid the same treacherous path of arrogance and self-deception. These are observational certainties that are impossible to ignore; all we can do is abide by the right formula and await the outcome:

قُل فَٱنتَظِرُوٓا۟ إِنِّى مَعَكُم مِّنَ ٱلْمُنتَظِرِينَ ۝

Say, "Keep waiting then! I too am waiting with you." [10:102]

Engaging in this type of reflection, collectively and individually, establishes certainty in our hearts of what it really means when God says,

وَٱللَّهُ غَالِبٌ عَلَىٰٓ أَمْرِهِۦ وَلَـٰكِنَّ أَكْثَرَ ٱلنَّاسِ لَا يَعْلَمُونَ ۝

Allah's Will always prevails, but most people do not know.
[12:21]

Falsehood is always self-destructive, and the barking of tyrants only scares those who are short-sighted. Those of us who take the afterlife into consideration easily trust our Lord and know that it is not our place to rush His decisions. Everything He does is with precise wisdom and perfect timing.

وَتِلْكَ ٱلْقُرَىٰٓ أَهْلَكْنَـٰهُمْ لَمَّا ظَلَمُوا۟ وَجَعَلْنَا لِمَهْلِكِهِم مَّوْعِدًا ۝

*We destroyed those societies when they persisted in wrong,
and We had set a time for their destruction.* [18:59]

The truth of this ayah can be witnessed clearly throughout history, both ancient and modern. Consider how communism began and bloomed to become a global phenomenon, and then shortly thereafter collapsed in on itself. Consider how many tyrants met with a belittled end. How many tyrants must fall to the same fate before we are confident in the inescapable consequence of injustice?

Pay close attention to how Allah changes the state of people and societies. You will see that He only removes a blessing from people as a result of their own neglect and ingratitude.

ذَٰلِكَ بِأَنَّ ٱللَّهَ لَمْ يَكُ مُغَيِّرًا نِّعْمَةً أَنْعَمَهَا عَلَىٰ قَوْمٍ حَتَّىٰ يُغَيِّرُوا۟ مَا بِأَنفُسِهِمْ

*This is because Allah would never discontinue His favour to a
people until they discontinue their faith.* [8:53]

Consider those who lost their riches after feeling so secure, those who found themselves ill despite taking great measures to live healthy, and those who reach the peaks of popularity but are soon torn down in people's eyes. Consider the tragic endings of those who toil to secure their children's wellbeing, working without rest to provide for them financially and secure their future, but forget to pay mind to their spiritual upbringing. Will their children be by their side when they reach old age? Will they pray for them—or will they even know how to? Learning these lessons from people who have already tasted their bitterness might spare us the pain of tasting it ourselves. We can then come to know the meaning of the verse,

$$وَهَلْ نُجَٰزِىٓ إِلَّا ٱلْكَفُورَ ۝$$

Would We ever punish anyone but the ungrateful? [34:17]

Become aware of the consequences of ingratitude and injustice, both on the scale of communities and on the individual level. Pondering over these consequences helps keep our hearts firm in faith while living under oppression and directs our energy toward working for God's sake. As we live in the dark shadows of tyrants, we know that their tyranny will end just like those before them. When we encounter falsehood, we will remember that it will never overcome the truth.

$$فَأَمَّا ٱلزَّبَدُ فَيَذْهَبُ جُفَآءً وَأَمَّا مَا يَنفَعُ ٱلنَّاسَ فَيَمْكُثُ فِى ٱلْأَرْضِ$$

The scum is then cast away, but what benefits people remains on the earth. [13:17]

We will remember that God is never ignorant of what the people do.

$$إِنَّ رَبَّكَ لَبِٱلْمِرْصَادِ ۝$$

Your Lord is truly vigilant. [89:14]

◁(THE DAYS OF GOD)▷

In our modern context, with blinding darkness and enemies attacking Muslims from every angle, it's even more important to reflect on God's displays of His power and the results of those who oppose Him and His religion. This is not the first time the believers were subjected to humiliation and subjugation. Instead of accepting the narrative of our weakness being due to our faith, and abandoning God for those whom He gave authority over us (politically, intellectually, or otherwise), let's ponder upon the times throughout history when those who chose God and His religion over everything else were mistreated for that decision, and were forced to taste the sweetness of faith through the bitterness of perseverance.

One of the most trying times in the history of believing people was when the Children of Israel were living in the shadow of Pharaoh's tyranny. Centuries after they were revered by means of Prophet Joseph, minister for the king of Egypt, the regime of the Pharaohs enslaved them for several generations. The Children of Israel were still upon the religion of their forefather Abraham, and were perhaps the largest, if not the only, community of believers on the face of the earth at that time. When they were on the verge of despairing in God's help, He sent them a messenger to revive their spirits and renew their conviction. God tells us how He did this:

$$وَلَقَدْ أَرْسَلْنَا مُوسَىٰ بِآيَاتِنَا أَنْ أَخْرِجْ قَوْمَكَ مِنَ الظُّلُمَاتِ إِلَى النُّورِ$$
$$وَذَكِّرْهُم بِأَيَّامِ اللَّهِ إِنَّ فِى ذَٰلِكَ لَآيَاتٍ لِّكُلِّ صَبَّارٍ شَكُورٍ ۝$$

Indeed, We sent Moses with Our signs; "Lead your people
out of darkness and into light, and remind them of Allah's
days." Surely in this are signs for whoever is steadfast,
grateful. [14:5]

Those were certainly dark days for the believers, and God instructed Moses to illuminate the hearts of his followers by reminding them of "Allah's days," the days in which Allah's Might towards the unbelievers and mercy for the faithful manifested clearly.

There are so many instances throughout history upon which we can ponder to see how God gave victory to His beloved servants through even the most basic worldly means, destroying the wrongdoers and their false beliefs despite their apparent power and fortitude. Consider, for example, how God flooded Noah's people, but saved him and the few believers who were with him. Reflect on how He obliterated Prophet Lot's people, leaving no chance for life in that locality thereafter, but gave life to the faith by saving Lot and his family. Think about the destruction of 'Ad and Thamud, the bitter end of Pharaoh, and the glorious victory God gave to the believers who suffered under them for years.

Perhaps the most salient, detailed and well-documented accounts of believers overcoming what seemed to be impossible chances of defeat are the triumphs within the story of our beloved Prophet Muhammad ﷺ. The believers emerged victorious at Badr, despite their small numbers and lack of resources, as well as overcoming the siege of their city by the surrounding tribes; it was Allah who sent to their enemies a blast of wind to break them and send them running back to their homes.

These are all inspiring instances of Allah's granting victory to one group of believers, but they are particular to just that group. We might also reflect on the bigger picture of how this faith started, how it grew, and what the wisdom might be behind our current state of weakness and incompetence. After being corrupted and tampered with by previous faith communities, Allah's religion sprouted anew in the barren desert among primitive shepherds, and blossomed quite literally, penetrating cultural geographical and cultural boundaries at unprecedented speed and scale. This rapid spread of faith was not through material means alone. Not only did the first community of believers defy inconceivable chances of failure, but our global family of faith across the earth is a testament to God's wisdom, ability, and dedication in supporting His believers.

These examples merit reflection so that we can learn how to engage with our current lamentable state. Reflecting on these displays of power and compassion must also be paired with words of prayer and supplication that tie these meanings together. After contemplating God's indisputable power and authority, and His wisdom and promise to empower us through our faith, we can say, "*Lā ilāha illa Allahu waḥdahu lā shareeka lahu, lahul-mulk, walahul-ḥamdu wahuwa ʿala kulli shay'in qadeer.*" ("there is nothing worthy of worship but God, without any partners. All authority and praise belongs to Him, and He is powerful over all things")

Broad Contemplation

It is possible, with God's help, to combine all of the above mentioned areas for reflection in one sweeping perspective, especially when reflecting on the physical world around us. We can look at the sun, for example, and reflect on its enormity and chemical makeup. We can think about how it was created, and the perfect nuances and intricacies of its structure. We can remember how clear of a proof it is for the existence of the One who created it, and think about His perfect names and most beautiful attributes that manifest therein. We can count all of the blessings that have reached us by means of the sun, with Allah's permission, considering what life would be like without its energy, light and warmth. We can contemplate the ways the sun will one day inflict suffering upon people, and how it is due to Allah's mercy that we are spared.

All of this would lead to knowing our Lord better. This line of thinking can be applied to anything around us, leaving us with endless possibilities and opportunities for reflection. Not only would we have a deeper connection with God, but it would be multifaceted and dynamic, with endless dimensions for exploration and discovery.

One More Method

Along with the aforementioned methods of connecting our words of prayer to deeper reflection, there is another method which we can use in tandem in order to engage both the heart and the tongue. It will help us develop a love for the practice of frequent remembrance. This is simply to educate ourselves about the virtues and benefits of remembrance itself.

How would you feel if your favorite celebrity mentioned your name? Consider how many times we send messages or tweets at celebrities who don't even bother to read what we have to say, let alone reply to your message out of the thousands of others that they receive. But here is God, Lord of the Creation, the King of the skies and earth who says:

فَٱذْكُرُونِي أَذْكُرْكُمْ

Mention me; I will mention you. [2:152]

And here you are, one out of several billion human beings on earth—one tiny decomposing speck in the ever-expanding universe—and God chose to say your name; all you had to do was say His. Allah. One of the most prominent masters of spirituality in Persia and Central Asia during the early centuries of Islam once said, "You ignorant, heedless human! If only you heard the scratching of the pen onto the Preserved Tablet when your name was written, you would die of joy!"[23]

It is also helpful to remember the benefits of specific types of prayers and remembrance. For example, before we ask God for forgiveness, let us remember what the Prophet ﷺ taught us about it: Al-Barâ' ibn Azib narrates that the Messenger of Allah ﷺ asked: "**What do you say about the joy of a man whose riding animal ran away from him, dragging its reins in a desolate land containing no food or drink for it, while upon it is his food and drink. He searches for it until it becomes too difficult for him, then it passes by the trunk of a tree, its reins catching onto it and he finds it entangled therein.**" We said: His joy **must be intense, O Messenger of Allah.**" He said: "**So then—by Allah!—Allah is more delighted by the repentance of His servant than this man is by his riding animal.**"[24]

We can also do the same for sending our prayers and peace to the Messenger of Allah ﷺ. He encouraged us to do so often, and even became overjoyed by the reward attached to it for us. The Companion Abu Talhah recounted how the Prophet ﷺ once came out looking noticeably cheerful. They asked him what had happened, as they could see the joy in his face, and he said, "**The angel just came to me and said, 'Muhammad, your Lord says, "Does it not please you that no one prays for blessings for you except that I will bless them ten times, and that no one sends peace upon you except that I will send peace upon them ten times?"**

By remembering the virtues of the words of remembrance while simultaneously giving it depth with contemplation, our hearts will slowly begin to synchronize with our tongues. With such volume and meaning, we can begin to find the delight and tranquility with which God described His remembrance:

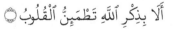

أَلَا بِذِكْرِ ٱللَّهِ تَطْمَئِنُّ ٱلْقُلُوبُ ۝

Only in the remembrance of Allah do hearts find comfort. [13:28]

A Concluding Word of Advice

Ibn al-Qayyim draws a comparison between those who begin remembering Allah on their tongues until their hearts are eventually present, and those who remain still and silent, not moving their tongues until they remember Allah in their hearts. For the former, the remembrance begins on their tongues and then moves to their hearts, while the latter moves from the heart to the tongue while keeping the heart engaged throughout. In the second case, the meaning settles into the heart then the words reflecting that meaning are spoken through the heart and pronounced by the tongue. He says, "The best and most beneficial remembrance is one wherein the heart matches the tongue, the prayers are those which the Prophet ﷺ taught us, and the one remembering is in touch with the meanings and objectives of the words."[25]

In order to benefit from this approach and maximize its potential, we have to fill our hearts with the meanings of these prayers. We have to understand the meanings behind many of the words of remembrance and supplications we are taught to recite. This will require us to reflect deeply on all of the areas mentioned in this chapter, leading us to connect reflection with the appropriate remembrance.

....

ENDNOTES

1. *Tareeq al-Hijratayn*, p. 215-216
2. P. 15
3. al-Ṭabarāni, *al-Muʻjam al-Awsat*, v. 6, p. 250, #6319; Sahih Al-Jamiʻ (2975)
4. Muslim, v. 1, p. 120, #134
5. Agreed upon; *Sahih al-Jamiʻ* (7993) and *as-Silsilah as-Sahihah* (117)
6. *Hasan* by Abu Dawud; *Sahih al-Jamiʻ* (8182)
7. Ahmad, v. 22, p. 236, #14333
8. Ibn Mājah, v. 4, p. 159, #2921; Tirmithi; deemed *sahih* by al-Albani
9. Ahmad, v. 35, p. 392, #21497; *Sahih al-Jamiʻ* (2414)
10. al-Bukhari, v. 4, p. 128, #3303; Muslim, v. 4, p. 2092, #2729
11. al-Tirmidhi, v. 5, p. 48, #2682
12. *Sahih*; Ahmad; An-Nasa'i; deemed *sahih* by al-Albani
13. al-Bukhari v. 4, p. 35, #2889; Muslim, v. 2, p. 1011, #1393
14. al-Bukhari, v. 5, p. 9, #3675
15. Muslim, v. 4, p. 2239, #2922
16. Ahmad, v. 3, p. 17, #1397; Tirmithi; al-Hakim; *as-Silsilah as-Sahihah* (1816)
17. Abu Dawud, v. 7, p. 270, #4908; *as-Silsilah as-Sahihah* (528)
18. Ahmad, v. 5, p. 192, #3066
19. Muslim, v. 4, p. 1759, #2241
20. al-Ṭabarāni, *al-Muʻjam al-Awsat*, v. 4, p. 104; deemed *sahih* by al-Albani
21. p. 58
22. al-Tirmidhi, v. 5, p. 423, #3522
23. Ḥilyat al-Awliyā', v. 10, p. 56
24. Muslim, #2746
25. al-Fawā'id, p. 247

Charity

Spending in charity is a central vein of our faith. The Quran and *hadith* urge us to spend in the way of God, freely and often. This spending enriches our life in a way no other form of investment can.

Our Creator Allah certainly knows best what is beneficial for us. Who better to teach us how to navigate the world than the One who created it? What better life hacks can we hope for than the ones offered in the Quran and sayings of the Prophet? This is why God asks the rhetorical question,

أَلَا يَعْلَمُ مَنْ خَلَقَ وَهُوَ ٱللَّطِيفُ ٱلْخَبِيرُ ۞

Doesn't the One who created know? He is the Most Subtle,
All-Aware. [67:14]

Spending in the way of God yields positive, multidimensional effects on every aspect of our livelihood and faith. It is the great multiplier, and in this aspect, spending for God appears to defy logic:

مَّثَلُ ٱلَّذِينَ يُنفِقُونَ أَمْوَلَهُمْ فِى سَبِيلِ ٱللَّهِ كَمَثَلِ حَبَّةٍ أَنبَتَتْ سَبْعَ سَنَابِلَ فِى
كُلِّ سُنْبُلَةٍ مِّائَةُ حَبَّةٍ وَٱللَّهُ يُضَعِفُ لِمَن يَشَآءُ

The example of those who spend their wealth in the cause of Allah is
that of a grain that sprouts into seven ears, each bearing one hundred
grains. And Allah further multiplies to whomever He wills. [2:261]

وَأَنفِقُوا فِى سَبِيلِ ٱللَّهِ وَلَا تُلْقُوا بِأَيْدِيكُمْ إِلَى ٱلتَّهْلُكَةِ

Spend in the cause of Allah and do not let your own hands
throw you into destruction. [2:195]

God does not need our money. Didn't it originate from Him in the first place? Doesn't He own us and everything around us? Why, then, is it so important that we share our wealth when He is the one who gave it to us in the first place? In order to answer these questions, we must first look within ourselves. Consider your deepest ambitions. Wealth, security, and prosperity is a high priority for almost every human being, pious or reckless. God tells us about ourselves:

$$وَتُحِبُّونَ ٱلْمَالَ حُبًّا جَمًّا ۝$$

You love wealth fervently. [89:20]

This burning desire for wealth is never extinguished, unlike other worldly passions. We are usually satisfied, albeit temporarily, when a craving is satiated. But when it comes to wealth, the more we get, the more we want. Accruing more wealth is like adding fuel to fire.

Our fascination with wealth is not exclusive to a particular time, place, or group. Prophet Muhammad ﷺ commented on this universal trait within us. He said, **"If a human being were given two valleys of riches, he would seek out a third. The human's appetite will only be fulfilled by soil, and Allah accepts the repentance of anyone who repents."**[1]

God created our souls with this intrinsic trait of selfishness, but instructed us to purify ourselves of it. One of the most effective ways to do so is to share what we have with others—the essence of spending for God's sake. Spending for the sake of God should generate a positive feedback loop; we spend, experience spiritual purification and material increase, and so we spend again. Allah makes the connection between giving and purifying often throughout His book. For example, He describes those who will be spared from the Hellfire as people who,

$$ٱلَّذِى يُؤْتِى مَالَهُۥ يَتَزَكَّىٰ ۝$$

who gives his wealth away as self-purification. [92:18]

When God instructs the Prophet ﷺ to take charity from the believers, there is a clear objective for that:

$$خُذْ مِنْ أَمْوَالِهِمْ صَدَقَةً تُطَهِّرُهُمْ وَتُزَكِّيهِم بِهَا$$

Take charity from their wealth to purify and bless them...
[9:103]

Helping the needy and supporting the Muslim community financially is essential. But even more important than helping others is the understanding that we require this spending in order to break free from our intrinsic greed and self-centeredness. God says,

$$وَأَنفِقُوا خَيْرًا لِّأَنفُسِكُمْ وَمَن يُوقَ شُحَّ نَفْسِهِۦ فَأُو۟لَٰٓئِكَ هُمُ ٱلْمُفْلِحُونَ ۝$$

*Spend in charity—that will be best for you. And whoever is
saved from the selfishness of their own souls, it is they who
are successful.* [64:16]

God teaches us about our selfish nature to alert us to the evil tendency within us, not to blame us. For example, He says,

$$وَأُحْضِرَتِ ٱلْأَنْفُسُ ٱلشُّحَّ$$

Humans are ever inclined to selfishness. [4:128]

This means (and God ultimately knows best) that the soul is held prisoner by our selfish nature. The true meanings of liberation and empowerment lie in freeing ourselves by means of persistent, intentional generosity.

Greed is the pathway to so much evil. It drives us to become overly invested and attached to this transient world. One of the students of Ali bin Abu Talib remembers hearing a man who was making tawaf (circling the Kaaba) saying, "God, protect me from my own greed!" and praying for nothing but that. Ali called out over the crowd to the man, not seeing who he was, advising him to pray for more than just that, and the man replied, "If I am protected from my own greed, then I will not steal, or fornicate, or commit many other sins." The man who spoke was none other than the Companion Abdul-Rahman bin 'Awf.[2]

The soul must journey upwards toward the heavens, even before it leaves this present life, and to do so it must shed the bulky attachments that weigh it down. Greed and selfishness are dead weights that prevent any form of spiritual ascension. When sharing becomes second nature for us, our souls become airborne. We are less dependent on wealth and lose some of our enthrallment for its perks. We are not exuberant when we receive it, nor depressed by its loss. We are humbly grateful, faithfully giving. Spending for the sake of God trains us in an abundance mindset that opens even more doors of goodness. That is what God alludes to in the following verse; after God informs us that every test that afflicts us was already written for us, He explains that we should not be so attached to material success that it affects our state of mind:

$$لِّكَيْلَا تَأْسَوْا عَلَىٰ مَا فَاتَكُمْ وَلَا تَفْرَحُوا بِمَآ ءَاتَىٰكُمْ$$

*So that you neither grieve over what you have missed nor
boast over what He has granted you.* [57:22]

This is the divine curriculum for self-purification. The Messenger of Allah ﷺ repeatedly emphasized the importance of giving. His task was to teach us how to effectively purify ourselves, as Allah says in the Quran:

كَمَآ أَرْسَلْنَا فِيكُمْ رَسُولًا مِّنكُمْ يَتْلُوا عَلَيْكُمْ ءَايَتِنَا وَيُزَكِّيكُمْ
وَيُعَلِّمُكُمُ ٱلْكِتَبَ وَٱلْحِكْمَةَ وَيُعَلِّمُكُم مَّا لَمْ تَكُونُوا تَعْلَمُونَ ۝

Since We have sent you a messenger from among yourselves—
reciting to you Our revelations, purifying you, teaching you
the Book and wisdom, and teaching you what you never
knew. [2:151]

The Prophet's methodology was not only to instruct, but to lead by example. Anas recounts, **"The Messenger was never asked for something in return for accepting Islam except that he gave it. A man once came, and he gave him a herd of sheep between two mountains. He went to his tribe and said: 'O my tribe! Accept Islam, for Muhammad certainly gives gifts and does not fear poverty.'** Anas continued on to say, "A man might accept Islam initially wanting only worldly benefit, but he would practice Islam until it was more dear to him than the world and all it held."[3]

The Prophet ﷺ was constantly shifting the perspective of those around him in order to understand the real nature of things. Aishah recounted that they once slaughtered a lamb and gave its meat away in charity. He asked Aishah, **"How much of it remains?"** She said, **"Only the shoulder remains."** He said, **"Rather, all of it remains except the shoulder."**[4] Through this illustration, the Prophet ﷺ taught Aishah and all the Muslims that when you give in charity, you lose nothing. Your real gain lies in whatever was given away.

⊰ Benefits of Charity ⊱	The Exponential Benefits of Charity

Best Investment
Shield from the Fire
Shade on Last Day
Cure for Sickness
Wards off Trials
Brings ease
Increases Sustenance
Extinguishes God's Anger

In addition to the purification effects, charity has many concrete beneficial aspects in this life and the next. There is really no better use of our money than for charity. Some of these benefits are recounted here.

⊰ CHARITY IS THE BEST INVESTMENT ⊱

The Prophet ﷺ said, **"Whoever spends anything good in charity— and God only accepts what is good—the Most Merciful accepts it with His right hand, even a single date! Then it grows in the palm of the Most Merciful until it becomes larger than a mountain, just as one of you would nurture his young horse or camel."**[5]

⊰ GIVING CHARITY SHIELDS FROM HELLFIRE ⊱

The Messenger of Allah ﷺ once said to Aishah, **"Veil yourself from the Hellfire, even with half of a date."**[6] The importance is not the amount of charity we give, but our mindset when giving it.

⊰ CHARITY IS A SHADE ON THE DAY OF JUDGMENT ⊱

The wealth we share will also come to shade us on the Day of Resurrection, when the sun will be brought just above our heads, causing some to drown in their sweat. The Messenger of Allah ﷺ said, **"Everyone will be in the shade of their charity until the people are judged."**[7]

⊰ CHARITY CURES SICKNESS ⊱

The benefits of charity are not only limited to the afterlife. Those who give charity frequently usually continue to do so because of the indisputable benefits they experience as a result. There is no blame in seeking these benefits, as the Prophet ﷺ even instructed us, **"Treat the ill among you through charity."**[8]

⊰ CHARITY WARDS OFF TRIALS AND DIFFICULTY ⊱

Another benefit of charity in this life is that it is a means of keeping difficult trials away. Through Prophet Zachariah, God gave five commands for the Children of Israel to live by. One of these addressed charity. When Zachariah stood in front of his people, he said, "I instruct you all to give charity. Imagine a man whose enemies capture him, tie his hands to his neck, and then bring him forward to execute him, but then the man says, 'Is there any way for me to ransom myself from you?' He then begins to give out his wealth in small, then big, amounts until he ransoms himself."[9] In his commentary on these words, Ibn al-Qayyim says,

> This is a claim that is proven through experience. We know it's true because it actually happens. Charity has far-reaching effects in preventing calamities, even for sinners and wrong-doers and even for unbelievers! When they give charity, God withholds trials from them. This is something that is commonly known and a widely accepted truth that everyone can relate to because of its universal experience.[10]

The metaphor is enlightening; charity is how we ransom ourselves from Hellfire. If we were to rely on our deeds alone, our sins would merit punishment, but the charity we give is what will ward off disaster. Some of the Companions taught their communities this lesson by saying, "Give charity with urgency, for it is a barrier that calamities cannot pass through."[11]

In the days of pre-Islamic ignorance, people attributed natural phenomena to supernatural events, neglecting God and His ultimate control over all things. The pagans in Arabia, for example, used to think that an eclipse was nature's way of mourning the death or celebrating the birth of someone great.

When the Prophet's son Ibrahim happened to have died just before an eclipse, this idea occurred again to new Muslims living with the Prophet ﷺ, and so he made a point to emphasize that such a belief was not in line with Islam. He stood up in front of his community and said, **"The sun and moon are just some of God's signs; they do not eclipse for the death or birth of anyone. When you see them, glorify God, call out to Him, pray, and give charity."**[12] The Prophet ﷺ used this opportunity to channel the fearful superstitions of his time into actionable awareness. Instead of the many superstitions that are false means of protection for our families and properties, the Prophet ﷺ instructed us to use charity as a means of protection from whatever we fear.

◄ CHARITY BRINGS EASE ►

It seems counterintuitive, but our lives become easier when we give. One reason why people are so averse to giving charity is the anticipated difficulty. It is painful for us to part with our wealth when we think of how hard we worked to earn it. We come up with a laundry list of financial responsibilities: debts, bills, groceries, tuition, childcare and all of the usual burdens that hover over us. This mindset, however, is not ideal for someone who truly believes in the Quran, as God promises ease and prosperity for those who share their wealth:

$$فَأَمَّا مَنْ أَعْطَىٰ وَٱتَّقَىٰ ۝ وَصَدَّقَ بِٱلْحُسْنَىٰ ۝ فَسَنُيَسِّرُهُۥ لِلْيُسْرَىٰ ۝$$

For the one who gives charity, stays cognizant, and believes in the finest reward, We will facilitate for them the Way of Ease. [92:5-7]

◄ CHARITY BRINGS MORE SUSTENANCE OUR WAY ►

The Prophet ﷺ made it clear that our worldly wealth grows when we give in charity. He told a story about a man in the desert who heard a voice commanding a cloud in the sky to rain water upon a specific man's garden. The rain poured down onto a rocky plain, and all of the water collected into just one flowing stream. He followed the stream to find a man directing the flow of water in different directions with a shovel. When he told the gardener what he heard from the sky, he asked why it might be that this blessing had come to him. The gardener informed him that he always measures his crops and gives a third of it in charity to the poor.[13]

◄ CHARITY EXTINGUISHES GOD'S ANGER ►

We learn through both scripture and experience that our sins can negatively affect our lives. Not only should we try to avoid committing them in the first place, but God also gave us the opportunity to mitigate the effects of our inevitable slip-ups with good deeds, especially charity. The Prophet ﷺ said, **"Good actions prevent bad incidents, charity in secret extinguishes the anger of your Lord, and maintaining family ties increases your lifespan."**[14]In another *hadith*, he compares the effects of sins to a raging fire. While Mu'ath ibn Jabal was traveling with the Prophet, he ﷺ turned to Mu'ath and said, **"Shall I tell you about the doors to goodness?"** Mu'ath replied, "Yes, Messenger of Allah!" He ﷺ said, **"Fasting is a shield, and charity extinguishes wrongdoings like water extinguishes fire."**[15]

After surveying these benefits of charity, we can see how charity cleanses our heart, increases our iman, and improves our life circumstances. Umar ibn Al-Khattab said, "I was told that good deeds will boast among each other, and charity will claim, "I am the best of all."[16]

How the Companions Practiced Charity

The Companions knew the value of spending for God's sake very well. They loved giving in charity and competed to see who could give most. Umar bin al-Khattab recounts the story of when the Messenger of Allah ﷺ once instructed them all to give in charity. Umar recalls that it was during a time when he had some wealth in his possession, and so he said to himself, "If there is any day that I beat Abu Bakr, it will be today."

So, Umar brought half of all that he owned to the Prophet ﷺ, and when the Prophet ﷺ asked him, "How much did you leave for your family?" he said with pride, "An equal amount." When Abu Bakr came forth with his charity, the Prophet ﷺ asked the same question, and he responded, "I left for them God and His Messenger." Umar was torn between admiration and disappointment and said, "I then knew that I would never beat him in anything."[17]

The Prophet ﷺ taught his Companions to give in charity with love. One of the students of Abdullah bin Umar used to see him frequently buying sugar and giving it to the poor.

Confused by this unusual form of giving, he said to him, "If you just bought food and gave it to them instead, it would be more beneficial for them." Ibn Umar said, "I know that, but I heard God say,

لَن تَنَالُوا ٱلْبِرَّ حَتَّىٰ تُنفِقُوا مِمَّا تُحِبُّونَ

You will never achieve righteousness until you donate what you cherish. [3:92]

He then remembered how much Abdullah bin Umar actually did love sugar![18]

This ayah had the same impact on many other Companions as well. A man named Abu Talhah was known to have the most date gardens among all of the Ansar, and his favorite garden was one named Bayruḥā'. It was located directly opposite the Prophet's mosque, and so the Messenger of Allah ﷺ would frequently enter it and drink some of the fresh water that was there.

After the above ayah was revealed, Abu Talhah went straight to the Prophet ﷺ and said, "Messenger of Allah, God says, 'You will never achieve righteousness until you donate what you cherish.' My most cherished property is Bayruḥā', and so it is now charity; I look forward to its reward and accumulation with God. Spend it, Messenger of Allah, wherever God shows you." The Messenger of Allah ﷺ told him, **"That is profitable wealth! Woah! That is profitable wealth!"**[19]

> Sa'd ibn Ubadah, a great Companion of the Ansar, would bring 800 of *Ahl as-Suffah*, the homeless people of the mosque, to his home every evening and serve them dinner.[20] Imagine the sacrifices this act of selflessness would entail; a daily routine designed around generosity and service. How do we compare in sharing our personal wealth, the spaces of our homes, and our leisure hours with those in need?

The Companions were so convinced that wealth given up for God's sake was a gain; it was not just an abstract concept to them. The more they spent, the more they felt their souls ascend and their iman grow. Abdullah bin Umar again proves this point perfectly when he was advised against being so open-handed, as those around him noticed that whenever he found himself impressed or delighted by anything he owned, he would give it up in charity for God's pleasure. Abdullah's student Nāfi' recalls that some slaves recognized this tendency, and so they would put in extra efforts to pray in the mosque, knowing that Abdullah would feel obligated to free them after seeing their commitment to righteousness. His peers warned him that these servants were only deceiving him so that they could be freed from servitude, and that perhaps they were taking advantage of his good will. Abdullah responded, "Whoever wishes to deceive us for Allah, we will gladly be deceived for Him!"[21]

How Charity Strengthens Iman

Giving charity is substantially tied to our relationship with Allah. It is one of the most rapid ways to ascend towards Him. This oft-neglected deed is an immediate method to give life to our hearts and awaken our faith. We've said before that to increase iman, we must reduce the competing loves that take up space in our heart, creating more space for faith to grow. Charity shrinks our love for wealth and ego while washing, softening, and widening our heart.

Allah informed us that He laid out two paths for us:

$$وَهَدَيْنَٰهُ ٱلنَّجْدَيْنِ ۝$$

Have we not shown them the two ways? [90:10]

This ayah alludes to the fact that we have the choice between two ways: the good or the bad. The path of good leads to God's pleasure and Paradise, while the latter leads to His wrath and punishment. But if it's this simple, then why are there so many who choose doom and destruction? God says in the next verse,

$$فَلَا ٱقْتَحَمَ ٱلْعَقَبَةَ ۝$$

If only they had attempted the challenging path [90:11]

The path of good is rewarding, but *challenging*. The hills are steep, and the trail is arduous. What are these difficulties that discourage so many from embarking?

$$وَمَآ أَدْرَىٰكَ مَا ٱلْعَقَبَةُ ۝ فَكُّ رَقَبَةٍ ۝ أَوْ إِطْعَٰمٌ فِى يَوْمٍ ذِى مَسْغَبَةٍ ۝ يَتِيمًا ذَا مَقْرَبَةٍ ۝ أَوْ مِسْكِينًا ذَا مَتْرَبَةٍ ۝$$

And what will make you realize what the challenging path is?
It is to free a slave; or to give food in times of famine, to an
orphaned relative, or to a poor person in distress. [90:12-16]

It is our own greed and selfishness that we must overcome, and it is only overcome by forcing ourselves to part with the wealth we hold so near and dear.

$$لَن تَنَالُوا۟ ٱلْبِرَّ حَتَّىٰ تُنفِقُوا۟ مِمَّا تُحِبُّونَ$$

You will never achieve righteousness until you donate what you
cherish. [3:92]

God's companionship is precious. His mercy and pleasure, and the delight that comes with a close relationship with him, is worth sacrificing for. The only way to obtain these is to give up what you presently love most; it's a high price to pay, but in return awaits a greater, more profound love that outweighs all previous love. God says,

فَـَٔاتِ ذَا ٱلْقُرْبَىٰ حَقَّهُۥ وَٱلْمِسْكِينَ وَٱبْنَ ٱلسَّبِيلِ ذَٰلِكَ خَيْرٌ لِّلَّذِينَ يُرِيدُونَ
وَجْهَ ٱللَّهِ وَأُوْلَـٰٓئِكَ هُمُ ٱلْمُفْلِحُونَ ۞

*So give your close relatives their due, as well as the poor
and the (needy) traveller. That is best for those who seek the
pleasure of Allah, and it is they who will be successful.* [30:38]

What does it say about us when we prefer the path of least resistance? How would that affect our generosity and giving for the sake of Allah? When someone chooses the path of least resistance, they have made cheap in their eyes the prize that lies at the end of the journey. They convince themselves that there will be other days for uphill battles, but in truth these opportunities to ascend toward God will not present themselves forever; there is no better day than the present for taking the challenging, uphill path.

وَمِنَ ٱلْأَعْرَابِ مَن يُؤْمِنُ بِٱللَّهِ وَٱلْيَوْمِ ٱلْءَاخِرِ وَيَتَّخِذُ مَا يُنفِقُ قُرُبَٰتٍ عِندَ
ٱللَّهِ وَصَلَوَٰتِ ٱلرَّسُولِ أَلَآ إِنَّهَا قُرْبَةٌ لَّهُمْ سَيُدْخِلُهُمُ ٱللَّهُ فِى رَحْمَتِهِۦٓ

*However, among the nomadic Arabs are those who believe in
Allah and the Last Day, and consider what they donate as a
means of coming closer to Allah and (receiving) the prayers of
the Messenger. It will certainly bring them closer. Allah will
admit them into His mercy.* [9:99]

It is very clear from this ayah that charity brings us closer to God. God tells us that He is close, but we are insistent on moving away from Him. To counteract our heedlessness and sin, we must constantly give charity, ensuring that we are always moving closer to Allah, not further away from him.

Even if you succeed in growing your faith and experiencing deep closeness with Allah for a time, you will not be able to maintain this state of closeness without a regimen of charity that counterbalances the inevitable accumulation of sin. Charity is purification from sins, and it is also maintenance for the heart.

Before It's Too Late

Some people only realize the importance of charity and its ability to prevent punishment after it's too late. They end up on the threshold of death, begging God to give them just a little more time to donate some money and do something good. God instructs us,

$$\text{وَأَنفِقُوا مِن مَّا رَزَقْنَٰكُم مِّن قَبْلِ أَن يَأْتِيَ أَحَدَكُمُ ٱلْمَوْتُ فَيَقُولَ رَبِّ لَوْلَآ}$$
$$\text{أَخَّرْتَنِي إِلَىٰ أَجَلٍ قَرِيبٍ فَأَصَّدَّقَ وَأَكُن مِّنَ ٱلصَّٰلِحِينَ ۞}$$

And donate from what We have provided for you before death
comes to one of you, and you cry, "My Lord! If only You
delayed me for a short while, I would give in charity and be
one of the righteous." [63:10]

God shows us in this ayah that the very first wish we will have when we see the Angel of Death is to have given more charity. In that moment, we will finally see reality for what it is. Spending countless hours and exhausting ourselves in the pursuit of wealth will prove fruitless if we don't invest it properly and spend it where it belongs—for the benefit of our own selves!

$$\text{حَتَّىٰٓ إِذَا جَآءَ أَحَدَهُمُ ٱلْمَوْتُ قَالَ رَبِّ ٱرْجِعُونِ ۞ لَعَلِّىٓ أَعْمَلُ صَٰلِحًا فِيمَا}$$
$$\text{تَرَكْتُ ۚ كَلَّآ}$$

When death approaches any of them, they cry, "My Lord! Let
me go back, so I may do good in what I left behind." Never!
[23:99-100]

Will we be the ones begging for a second chance? We will ignore all that went into pursuing wealth and will value only the amount that was spent in charity.

The Prophet ﷺ informs us that God says, **"People, how can you ever overpower me when I created you from this. And then I fashioned and proportioned you, and so you stroll about the earth pompously, dressed in two garments. You hoarded and withheld, and then when your soul reached your throat, you said, 'I will give charity!' What a time for charity!"**[22]

Charity plays a major role in our journey to God, and it saves us from His punishment. Rather than stipulating that we be perfect to earn His pleasure, God instructs us to make up for our sins with repentance and good deeds. The Prophet ﷺ said, **"Every human being is a sinner, and the best sinners are those who always repent."**[23] The successful one with God is one who makes up for lost time by following every sin with a good deed to erase it. Now is there anything better than charity to erase our sins with?

$$\text{وَٱلَّذِينَ صَبَرُوا ٱبْتِغَآءَ وَجْهِ رَبِّهِمْ وَأَقَامُوا ٱلصَّلَوٰةَ وَأَنفَقُوا مِمَّا رَزَقْنَٰهُمْ سِرًّا}$$

وَعَلَانِيَةً وَيَدْرَءُونَ بِالْحَسَنَةِ السَّيِّئَةَ أُوْلَـٰئِكَ لَهُمْ عُقْبَى ٱلدَّارِ

And those who endure patiently, seeking their Lord's pleasure,
establish prayer, donate from what We have provided for
them—secretly and openly—and respond to evil with good. It
is they who will have the ultimate abode. [13:22]

When Charity has no Benefit

Some people might object that the reality they experience is different. They don't see all of the benefits we spoke about. They complain that when they give charity, they see no positive effect on their lives and no relief from their financial hardship. The reality is that many of us might give once for every dozen opportunities that come our way. And before we do give, we check our bank accounts and calculate how much will be left after this donation. We are actually just like those whom God described when He said,

وَمِنَ ٱلْأَعْرَابِ مَن يَتَّخِذُ مَا يُنفِقُ مَغْرَمًا

And among the nomads are those who consider what they
donate to be a loss... [9:98]

Our fears over financial loss become our reality. Anyone who considers the money they give in charity to be any sort of loss to their wealth should actually expect nothing in return for it. The same goes for those of us who give on and off. God rebukes those who do this:

وَأَعْطَىٰ قَلِيلًا وَأَكْدَىٰٓ ۞

He paid a little, and then stopped... [53:34]

If we truly want to benefit from giving charity, we must make an effort to do so regularly until it becomes second nature. A one-time donation, no matter how large, doesn't have as much impact as smaller, consistent donations—neither on the donor nor the recipient. We must learn to give charity no matter what our financial circumstances may be, in order to be one of those whom God praises:

ٱلَّذِينَ يُنفِقُونَ أَمْوَٰلَهُم بِٱلَّيْلِ وَٱلنَّهَارِ سِرًّا وَعَلَانِيَةً فَلَهُمْ أَجْرُهُمْ عِندَ رَبِّهِمْ
وَلَا خَوْفٌ عَلَيْهِمْ وَلَا هُمْ يَحْزَنُونَ ۞

Those who spend their wealth in charity day and night,
secretly and openly—their reward is with their Lord, and
there will be no fear for them, nor will they grieve. [2:274]

This consistency and frequency in spending is key, and it is the best form of charity to awaken and build our faith and reap the benefits mentioned earlier.

It is important to note that the mentalities that prevent us from giving in charity may not be so blatantly obvious. Rarely do we identify our own greed and selfishness as such, and rarely do we see ourselves as the stereotypical miser counting his money. Instead, we justify not giving in our own personalized ways. We might mistake luxuries for necessities, detach ourselves from the suffering of others, be entrenched in a privileged mindset, or find fault in the poor or in the people and organizations involved in Islamic work and charity.

We might look at the norm for charity in our neighborhood or community and think we are quite generous in comparison, when we are actually far from the mark. When we talk about greed and selfishness, we are most certainly talking about these mindsets and all of their personalized variants. Mindfulness, examining the self and holding ourselves to account are keys to identifying the specific forms of greed and selfishness taking root in our own minds and in the social context around us.

Training in Charity

Dr. Abdul-Rahman Hasan Ḥabannakah writes in his book *al-Akhlāq al-Islāmiyyah wa 'Ususuhā* that training the soul to be generous takes time and repetition. In the beginning, it is always difficult for us to be so open-handed, but with every donation that follows, it gets easier. Our love for giving grows slowly until we eventually find delight in doing so.

The Prophet ﷺ pointed out a unique way to visualize the greed in our hearts. He said, **"The comparison of a stingy person to a charitable one is like comparing two men, each wearing iron chainmail covering from their hands to their breasts, and their necks. Every time the charitable one gives charity, it loosens up on his body, but every time the stingy one goes to give charity, it contracts, and every chain clings to its place."**[24]

This *hadith* gives novel insight into the workings of our soul and psyche. Some of us feel tight-chested when we are asked to give charity, as if our arms are frozen or being held down by weights. We fear the unknown because our faith is weak. Our greed, which can be framed as entitlement, fear, or a perception of scarcity, almost literally ties our hands and restricts our own freedom! But those of us who are accustomed to giving charity without reluctance become even more comfortable and find ourselves more at peace with every dollar we give. Our iman and confidence in God's promise grows. We are able to help those around us more freely, while also feeling a sense of delight within ourselves. This *hadith* beautifully demonstrates the liberating effects of training the soul in generosity. Picture the satisfaction of dislodging the tight chain of the armor from your skin, feeling the air and becoming more able to move and breathe with every charity.

The metaphor of the hand being restricted from movement can also be found in the Quran:

وَلَا تَجْعَلْ يَدَكَ مَغْلُولَةً إِلَىٰ عُنُقِكَ وَلَا تَبْسُطْهَا كُلَّ ٱلْبَسْطِ فَتَقْعُدَ مَلُومًا مَّحْسُورًا ۝

Don't keep your hand shackled to your neck, and don't stretch it out in every direction, or else you will end up blameworthy and regretful. [17:29]

Those who keep their hands tied, refusing to spend for God's sake, are short-sighted and actively working against their own benefit. They will be blamed for not helping others and regret missing out on the chance to secure their own happiness.

Make Charity a Daily Practice

Today's culture views charity as a grandiose statement, a thanksgiving ritual or a reaction to plentiful tax returns. We know better than that from the traditions of our faith. Charity should be a frequent practice, even daily! Because the smallest acts of charity can have exponential benefits, in both the spiritual and material worlds, we have no reason to hold back. Especially if we are working to awaken our hearts and revive our iman, the more interactions we have with charity, regardless of the amount, the faster we will reach our goal of self-purification. Allah did not set any minimum requirements to qualify for reaping the rich rewards of charity; rather He kept the door wide open for all to take part according to their capacities:

لِيُنفِقْ ذُو سَعَةٍ مِّن سَعَتِهِ وَمَن قُدِرَ عَلَيْهِ رِزْقُهُ فَلْيُنفِقْ مِمَّا ءَاتَىٰهُ ٱللَّهُ لَا يُكَلِّفُ ٱللَّهُ نَفْسًا إِلَّا مَا ءَاتَىٰهَا

Let the comfortable one give according to his means. As for the one with limited resources, let him give according to whatever Allah has given him. Allah does not require of any soul beyond what He has given it. [65:7]

Regardless of the amount, we should always give something—even half of a date! There are reports about the Companions that say that they would never let a day pass without giving charity, even if it was a cracker or an onion. They understood the importance of a consistent daily practice of charity, no matter how small the amount, for the Prophet ﷺ was reported to have said, **"Everyone will be in the shade of their charity [on the Day of Resurrection] until the people will be judged."**[25] Daily, consistent acts of charity seem small in our minds, but add up both spiritually and materially.

In the highly unlikely scenario that we can find absolutely nothing to give, there are alternatives that will serve the same purpose. One option is to encourage other people to give and be more generous. This is another trope throughout the Quran, as God repeatedly describes the regret of those who fail to do so. The Prophet ﷺ also taught us that acts of service to others can make up for not being able to contribute financially, especially relieving those who need assistance such as the elderly and disabled. Emphasizing the need for charity as a part of our daily routine is this *hadith*: **"Every joint in your body owes charity for every day that the sun rises. To arbitrate fairly between two parties is charity. To help a man mount his riding animal by carrying him or lifting his belongings onto it for him is a charity. A good word is charity. Every step you take to the prayer is charity, and to remove something harmful from the road is charity."**[26]

Make a point to give charity every day, and make use of the many forms of charity mentioned above. Charity is not an act of worship reserved for times of financial ease. Give charity when your budget is tight, for the impact and amount makes no difference. The ultimate objective of charity is not only to help the poor, but also to purify our own selves and treat the diseases of greed and character. This is why God describes those who spend in charity as being better able to control anger,

$$\text{ٱلَّذِينَ يُنفِقُونَ فِى ٱلسَّرَّآءِ وَٱلضَّرَّآءِ وَٱلْكَـٰظِمِينَ ٱلْغَيْظَ وَٱلْعَافِينَ عَنِ ٱلنَّاسِ وَٱللَّهُ يُحِبُّ ٱلْمُحْسِنِينَ}$$

Those who donate in prosperity and adversity, control their anger, and pardon others—and Allah loves those who strive for excellence. [3:134]

One of Aishah's maids tells a story of a poor person who once came to ask Aishah for food on a day when she was fasting. There was nothing in her house but a loaf of bread. When Aishah instructed that it be given to the beggar, her maid objected: "But then you will have nothing to break your fast with." Aishah insisted that it be given to the beggar, and the maid recounts that before the evening came, someone had gifted them a roasted lamb. Aishah called her over and said, "Eat this. This is better than the loaf of bread."[27]

Being charitable in times of difficulty is the ultimate act of trust in Allah's promises. The Messenger of Allah ﷺ said, **"One dirham can beat out one hundred thousand dirhams. A man** might have much wealth, and then take one hundred thousand from it to give in charity, while another man has nothing but two dirhams, taking the better of the two to give in charity."[28] That single coin that the poor man gave might not have a notable impact —or at least not as clear of an impact as the one hundred thousand—but its impact of the deed on the giver is greater than the impact of the wealthy man's deed.

Umm Bujayd, one of the women who pledged an oath of righteousness and faith to the Prophet ﷺ, once said to him, "Sometimes a poor man stands at my door, but I can find nothing to give him." He told her, **"Even if you can only find the burnt hoof of a lamb, put it in his hand."**[29] Note that the Prophet ﷺ could have given her an easy way out, relieving her sense of guilt, but instead he urged her to be creative and give for the sake of giving even if it is something of little value.

E conomically segregated communities are an affliction of our culture, and depending on where you live, you may not have direct contact with people in need. When charity becomes an indispensable practice to you, you will get creative and be willing to go out of your way to get money in the right hands. Set up a charity box in your home, stop by a mosque on your way home from work, or establish a daily direct deposit for charity. When you do meet an individual in need or visit a disadvantaged community, consider it an opportunity from God, for not everyone has direct access to the needy and all of the opportunities that come with those relationships: opportunities to serve, feed, relieve burdens, provide transportation, and support financially. Keep a list of individuals whom you have met who may be of need of assistance, so that you do not forget about them in your charity spending.

Pursue opportunities to give in charity every day the sun rises, urgently and creatively. The Prophet ﷺ said, **"There is not a single day in which the servants arise except that there are two angels who descend. One of them says, God, give compensation to the one who gives!' while the other says, 'God, give destruction to the one who withholds!"**[30]

A Great Personal Loss

Charity is one of the greatest doors to good, and whoever misses out on it is truly deprived. Asmā' bint Abu Bakr, the sister of Aishah, narrates that the Prophet ﷺ said to her, **"Don't withhold, or else you will be withheld from."**[31] In his commentary on this *hadith*, Ibn Hajar points out that the Prophet ﷺ was instructing her to not hold back her charity out of fear that her wealth would deplete. Ibn Hajar goes on to say, "Whoever believes that God will provide for them in ways that they would never expect should then give without keeping track of the amount."[3]

When we give charity, we are the primary beneficiaries:

$$وَأَنفِقُوا خَيْرًا لِّأَنفُسِكُمْ$$

... and spend in charity—that will be best for you. [64:16]

We secure our own futures with charity, ransoming ourselves from the Hellfire. Let us follow the example of Suhayb the Roman, a Companion who gave up all of the wealth and property that he had amassed in Mecca in order to migrate to Medina, just to be in the company of the Messenger of Allah ﷺ. After he did so, God revealed a verse in the Quran alluding to his sacrifice:

$$وَمِنَ ٱلنَّاسِ مَن يَشْرِي نَفْسَهُ ٱبْتِغَآءَ مَرْضَاتِ ٱللَّهِ وَٱللَّهُ رَءُوفٌ بِٱلْعِبَادِ ۝$$

And there are those who trade their lives for Allah's pleasure.
And Allah is Ever Gracious to His servants. [2:207]

Charity is a path to Martyrdom

Have you ever wondered, if you had lived at the time of the Companions, whether you would have been one of those fighting bravely at the side of the Prophet or whether you would have turned away and fled as many did? Charity is the surest test of your grit and resolve. Many of us aspire to die striving, working, fighting and sacrificing for God's cause. But the reality is that we cannot be willing to dedicate our life for a cause if we are not already willing to give up our wealth for it. We must be willing to fight our weaknesses and selfishness, for this is the true essence of striving and a litmus test for whether our aspirations are sincere.

Once this is achieved, everything in this life will be seen for its true worth, and we will be able to prioritize what truly matters. God say about those who will spared from the Hellfire:

$$وَسَيُجَنَّبُهَا ٱلْأَتْقَى ۝ ٱلَّذِى يُؤْتِى مَالَهُ يَتَزَكَّىٰ ۝ وَمَا لِأَحَدٍ عِندَهُۥ مِن$$
$$نِّعْمَةٍ تُجْزَىٰ ۝ إِلَّا ٱبْتِغَآءَ وَجْهِ رَبِّهِ ٱلْأَعْلَىٰ ۝ وَلَسَوْفَ يَرْضَىٰ ۝$$

But the righteous will be spared from it—who donate
their wealth only to purify themselves, not in return
for someone's favours, but seeking the pleasure of their
Lord, the Most High. They will certainly be pleased.
[92:17-21]

What is it that God will please these charitable souls with? It is certainly not wealth, for someone who is willing to give up their wealth knows that pleasure cannot be found in accumulating worldly goods. Thus, God will reward them with a reward far greater—a rank that is metaphysical and other-worldly.

When we shed our worldly attachments through charity, it becomes easy for us to sacrifice for God's pleasure in other ways: through time, physical effort, striving, activism, calling to God, and so on. In many instances throughout the Quran, the struggle of wealth is mentioned before the physical struggle of giving up our lives for God, the former being a sort of prerequisite for the latter:

$$\text{يَـٰٓأَيُّهَا ٱلَّذِينَ ءَامَنُوا۟ هَلْ أَدُلُّكُمْ عَلَىٰ تِجَٰرَةٍ تُنجِيكُم مِّنْ عَذَابٍ أَلِيمٍ ﴿١٠﴾ تُؤْمِنُونَ بِٱللَّهِ وَرَسُولِهِۦ وَتُجَٰهِدُونَ فِى سَبِيلِ ٱللَّهِ بِأَمْوَٰلِكُمْ وَأَنفُسِكُمْ ذَٰلِكُمْ خَيْرٌ لَّكُمْ إِن كُنتُمْ تَعْلَمُونَ ﴿١١﴾}$$

Believers! Shall I guide you to an exchange that will save you from a painful punishment? To have faith in Allah and His Messenger, and strive in the cause of Allah with your wealth and your lives—that is best for you, if only you knew. [61:10-11]

$$\text{ٱنفِرُوا۟ خِفَافًا وَثِقَالًا وَجَٰهِدُوا۟ بِأَمْوَٰلِكُمْ وَأَنفُسِكُمْ فِى سَبِيلِ ٱللَّهِ ذَٰلِكُمْ خَيْرٌ لَّكُمْ إِن كُنتُمْ تَعْلَمُونَ ﴿﴾}$$

March forth whether it is easy or difficult for you, and strive with your wealth and your lives in the cause of Allah. That is best for you, if only you knew. [9:41]

Let's introduce a sense of urgency and creativity to our charity! Take every opportunity to engage in this act of worship and make it a habit that defines your character. Give charity to prove your commitment to growing your relationship with Allah. Give charity upon every new venture, every resolution, every setback, every difficulty, sin, and mistake. It will have positive repercussions on your heart, allowing iman to grow and take root.

Taking the Road Less Traveled

Charity is a practice that, when performed diligently, will take you to the highest peaks of sacrifice and selflessness. Remember that no dollar given in charity is ever lost, as the

Prophet ﷺ taught us how profitable charity really is: "**No one's wealth ever decreases from charity.**"[33] Keep in mind the Prophetic guidelines for giving charity and do not give so much that you become in need of charity yourself: "**The best charity is that which keeps you self-sustainable. The higher hand is better than the lower hand. Start with those for whom you are responsible.**"[34]

....

ENDNOTES

1. al-Bukhari, #6439; Muslim, #1048
2. *Tafsir ibn Kathir* (4/305)
3. Muslim, #2312
4. *Saheeh*, At-Tirmithi (2472)
5. al-Bukhari, #1410, agreed upon
6. Ahmad, #25401
7. Ahmad, #17333; ibn Hibban
8. *Saheeh al-Jami'* (3358)
9. At-Tirmithi, ibn Hibban, al-Hakim; *Saheeh al-Jami'* (866)
10. al-Wābil al-Ṣayyib, p. 57
11. Ibid., p. 59
12. Abu Dawud, Ahmad, an-Nasa'i; *Saheeh al-Jami'* (1642)
13. Muslim, #2984
14. al-Ṭabarāni, *al-Mu'jam al-Kabeer*, #8014; *Saheeh al-Jami'* (3797)
15. *Saheeh*, Tirmithi; *Saheeh at-Targheeb wa al-Tarheeb* (858)
16. Ibn Khuzaymah 4/95 #2433, Al-Hakim 1/576 #1518, and Al-Albani in *Saheeh Al-Targheeb wa al-Tarheeb* #867
17. al-Tirmidhi; Ad-Darimi
18. *Salaah al-Ummah fi 'uluw al-Himmah*, (2/526)
19. al-Bukhari, # 1461; and Muslim #998; *Saheeh at-Targheeb wa al-Tarheeb* (864)
20. *Salaah al-Ummah fi 'uluw al-Himmah*, (2/534)
21. Ibid, (2/533)
22. *Saheeh*; Ahmad and others; *Saheeh al-Jami'* (8144) and *as-Silsilah as-Saheehah* (1143)
23. Ahmad; Tirmithi; *Saheeh al-Jami'* (4515)
24. al-Bukhari, #1443; and Muslim, #1021 (This wording is narrated by Muslim)
25. Ahmad (28/568 #17332)
26. al-Bukhari, #2989; Muslim, #1009
27. Malik, #3655
28. *Hasan*; an-Nasa'i; Ibn Khuzaymah; ibn Hibban; al-Hakim
29. *Saheeh*; Tirmithi; ibn Khuzaymah; *Saheeh at-Targheeb wa al-Tarheeb* (872)
30. Agreed upon
31. al-Bukhari, #1433; Muslim, #1010
32. Fath al-Bārī, v. 3, p. 300
33. *Saheeh*; Tirmithi, ibn Majah; *Saheeh at-Targheeb wa al-Tarheeb* (859)
34. *Saheeh at-Targheeb wa al-Tarheeb* (869)

Night Prayer

وَمِنَ ٱلَّيْلِ فَتَهَجَّدْ بِهِۦ نَافِلَةً لَّكَ عَسَىٰٓ أَن يَبْعَثَكَ رَبُّكَ مَقَامًا مَّحْمُودًا ۝

*And rise at part of the night, offering additional prayers, so
your Lord may raise you to a station of praise.* [17:79]

Standing in prayer at night (*qiyam*) is among the necessary methods of awakening faith. Our pious predecessors were constant with this practice, and they found it to have the greatest effect on reviving hearts.

The Prophet ﷺ said, **"Our Lord the Exalted descends every night to the lowest sky when the last third of the night remains, and He says, 'Who is calling upon me so that I may answer them? Who is asking of me so that I may give to them? Who is requesting my forgiveness so that I may forgive them?"**[1] He also emphasized how important it is in our personal relationships with God: **"The closest the Lord ever is to the servant is in the last depth of the night. If you can be one of those who remembers God in that hour, then do so."**[2]

The night prayer has special value and standing in Islam, but so few people take advantage of it. Ibn Rajab composed a manual called *Laṭā'if al-Ma'ārif* on how to capitalize on one's time and extract maximum rewards. He writes that anyone who has prayed in the precious hours before dawn knows how rewarding it is. They have spent that time—even a portion of it—in the sweet company of their Lord, praising Him, pleading with Him, and pouring their hearts out to Him. Then they go about the rest of their day, surrounded by so many who know nothing of the delight that they just experienced. One scholar is even quoted to have said, "A worshipper finds more ecstasy in praying at night than sinners find in satisfying their fervent desires." He went on to say, "Were it not for that delight of night prayer, I wouldn't care to stay alive." Ibn Rajab then breaks down the parts of the night:

> The middle of the night is for the lovers to converse with their Most Beloved. Then the time before dawn is for sinners to repent from their sins. The middle

is a special time for those at higher levels to spend alone time with their Lord, while just before dawn is a time for everyone to make up for their sins and ask for their needs. Whoever is unable to wake up early enough to be among the group of Lovers should not then give up on being among those who beg for forgiveness. The repenter's canvas is his cheeks, and his paint is his tears.[3]

Irreplaceable Opportunities

Waking up to the breezes of Allah in the predawn time and claiming our share in the reward He reserved for that time is among the greatest means of awakening faith in the hearts. There are so many benefits to praying at night. It removes sins from us like a stormy wind blows dry leaves off of a tree, it illuminates the heart, brings beauty to the face, and negates any traces of laziness. The angels watch from the sky as the worshippers on earth pray to their Lord, marvelling at them like we marvel at the glimmering stars in the dark night sky. There is a range of spiritual feelings experienced by those who pray at night that are indescribable to those who do not.

The prolific poet and philosopher Muhammad Iqbal once said, "No matter who you learn your knowledge and wisdom from, you will not be worth anything until you weep at night." He himself cherished these valuable hours which he would spend in worship; he considered them to be his most prized possession. Iqbal is also quoted by Abu al-Ḥasan al-Nadawi to have said, "Take anything from me, my Lord! But do not strip me of the sweetness of weeping at night, and do not deprive me of its delight." Shaykh al-Nadawi shares that Iqbal would pray that God spread this emotional experience to the younger generation to awaken their hearts and mobilize them.[4]

Sayyid Qutb described praying at night as vital to anyone who preaches or teaches this religion in *Fee Ẓilāl al-Qur'ān*. He writes,

> Standing through the night while people sleep is a cutting off from the haze of daily life. It is a connecting to Allah, finding His Expanse, Light, and His companionship. In the night, you recite the Quran while all is still, as if it is being revealed from the topmost heavens for the first time with no human speech to interrupt it, basking in its rays and meanings in the peace of the night…These elements are vital for carrying the weighty word and carrying out the difficult task that awaited the Messenger ﷺ, and which awaits all those who spread this message in every generation.[5]

Qutb also offers commentary on the following verse, revealed in the earliest days of Islam, that encourages prayer at night:

إِنَّ نَاشِئَةَ ٱلَّيْلِ هِىَ أَشَدُّ وَطْـًٔا وَأَقْوَمُ قِيلًا ۞

*Indeed, worship in the night is more impactful and suitable
for recitation.* [73:6]

He reflects on how appealing sleep is, and how magnetic our beds can be after an exhausting day, but this ayah is a call to our souls to fight those impulses and to stay in control of our body. Responding to God's call and choosing to spend your time with Him is the most suitable time to recite His scripture and words of prayer. That is the time when remembering Him is most sweet, praying is most humbling, and the connection is most clear and conducive to pouring our hearts out to Him. This closeness cannot be achieved in the daytime. Qutb points out that Allah, who created our hearts and our souls, knows what we need most. He, who created time and space, knows when and where we can most effectively improve our spiritual conditions. He, who created the very concept of cause and effect, offers us clear instructions on how to secure the best outcome for ourselves. He knew the toil and burden that awaited the Messenger ﷺ, and He instructed Him and those who will follow in his footsteps to pray at night.

Night Prayer is Honor

The Messenger of Allah ﷺ said, **"The honor of the believer is his prayer at night, and his glory is his disregard for what others possess."**[6] About this *hadith*, al-Munāwi said that honor indicates loftiness and height. When someone stands at night, humbling himself to Allah and admitting his own weakness by seeking shelter in His strength, Allah will give him honor and grant him a high status with His angels and righteous servants. al-Munāwi also notes how glory is tied to renouncing what others have: "When you admit your dependence and incapacity to the Lord of the Worlds, He will grant you His glory and suffice you Himself."[7]

Our honor and glory lies in the hours of the night. Anyone who claims to love something is expected to prove it, and there is nothing more convincing than the late hours of the night to prove your love for God. Those who pray at night walk with honor, for they have proven true to their claim of loving God, while folk like us who sleep through the night are called out on our phoniness. The two groups can never have the same status in God's eyes.

Fertile Grounds for Sincerity

At night is when we plant in the garden of sincerity. We sow the seeds, and our harvest will be in accordance with our efforts. As long as you are increasing your input of worship, the harvest of blessings will continuously accumulate from every direction. God teaches us this formula when He says,

إِن يَعْلَمِ ٱللَّهُ فِى قُلُوبِكُمْ خَيْرًا يُؤْتِكُمْ خَيْرًا

If Allah finds goodness in your hearts, He will give you better... [8:70]

The night has been called the school of sincerity; only those with true love for God will enroll. Ibn Mas'ood compared praying at night to the virtue of giving charity in secret over giving charity publicly.[8] Praying at night has such high status because it is usually done in private, making it more conducive to sincerity. The early Muslims, who had significantly less privacy in their homes than we do now, went to extreme lengths to conceal their night prayers. Al-Ḥasan al-Baṣri, a pioneer in Islamic scholarship, recalls,

> Muslims used to memorize the whole Quran, and their neighbors would not even know about it. Muslims would study, reaching high levels in knowledge without telling anyone. They used to pray long prayers in their homes while hosting guests for the night, and their guests would not realize at all. We have met people who used to do all that was within their power to make sure their actions were private. The Muslims used to supplicate with overwhelming emotion, while those around them could not hear anything of it; it was their secret between them and God alone. This is because God says, "Call upon your Lord humbly and secretly" [7:55], and because God mentioned one of his most beloved servants by saying: "he cried out to his Lord privately." [19:3]

Muhammad bin Wāsi', an Islamic scholar and devout worshipper from the second generation, those who learned directly from the Companions, said, "I met men who would lay their heads with their wives on the same pillow at night, and would drench the area below their cheeks without their wives noticing at all. I met men who would stand with others in a row for prayer, their tears trailing down their cheeks without the man at his side noticing at all."

The night is when worship's potential is at its peak; it is when the treasures of the heart come out. It's when all of our observations and experiences throughout the day are poured out for Allah. This is when we shed our masks and let down our guard in the company of our Beloved Lord. Our letters to him are written with the ink of our tears and carried away with the nightly breeze—this is our response to Allah's call: "Is there anyone asking of Me so that I may give to them?"

The Ultimate Gratitude

Among the objectives of worship in Islam is to express gratitude for Allah's incalculable blessings. Gratitude is shown through action, and a grateful servant is one on whom the effects of his Lord's blessings are manifest.

وَإِذَا مَسَّ ٱلْإِنسَٰنَ ضُرٌّ دَعَا رَبَّهُۥ مُنِيبًا إِلَيْهِ ثُمَّ إِذَا خَوَّلَهُۥ نِعْمَةً مِّنْهُ نَسِيَ مَا كَانَ يَدْعُوٓا۟ إِلَيْهِ مِن قَبْلُ وَجَعَلَ لِلَّهِ أَندَادًا لِّيُضِلَّ عَن سَبِيلِهِۦ قُلْ تَمَتَّعْ بِكُفْرِكَ قَلِيلًا إِنَّكَ مِنْ أَصْحَٰبِ ٱلنَّارِ ۞ أَمَّنْ هُوَ قَٰنِتٌ ءَانَآءَ ٱلَّيْلِ سَاجِدًا وَقَآئِمًا يَحْذَرُ ٱلْءَاخِرَةَ وَيَرْجُوا۟ رَحْمَةَ رَبِّهِۦ قُلْ هَلْ يَسْتَوِى ٱلَّذِينَ يَعْلَمُونَ وَٱلَّذِينَ لَا يَعْلَمُونَ إِنَّمَا يَتَذَكَّرُ أُو۟لُوا۟ ٱلْأَلْبَٰبِ ۞

When one is touched with hardship, they cry out to their Lord, turning to Him. But as soon as He showers them with blessings from Him, they forget the One to whom they earlier, and set up equals to Allah to mislead away from His path. Say, "Enjoy your disbelief for a little while! You will certainly be one of the inmates of the Fire." Or consider those who worship devoutly in the hours of the night, prostrating and standing, fearing the Hereafter and hoping for the mercy of their Lord. Say, "Are those who know equal to those who do not know?" None will pay mind except people of reason. [39:8-9]

These verses describe two categories of people, both whom Allah blessed. The first group found themselves in severe difficulty, under much pressure and anxiety, and when they called out to God, He brought them relief and removed their trial. But then they failed to be grateful and returned to their previous state of sin. The second group of people chose to show their gratitude by "worshipping devoutly in the hours of the night." They humbled themselves for God as a result of realizing His enormous blessings. And so God ends the comparison with a rhetorical question: "Are those who know equal to those who do not know?"

. . . .

The Messenger of Allah ﷺ would stand in prayer at night until his feet swelled. When Aishah asked why he did so, even though God had already guaranteed him His mercy and forgiveness, his response was moving and elucidating: "Should I not be a grateful servant?"[9]

. . . .

Unity in the Night

In writing about the global Muslim community, Abdul-Raheem al-Ṭaḥān writes that our condition is heart-wrenching. He points to the first community of Muslims as the only model to follow, emphasizing that the latter generations will find success in what made the first successful: reforming their hearts and devotion to Allah through the night prayer.

Something striking about the history of prayer in Islam is that the night prayer was obligatory before the order to pray five times a day. There is incredible wisdom in this prescription. When a person is alone with God, he or she develops an intimate and affectionate relationship with Him, and the heart is cleansed in the process. Their effort to come to God is a means of increasing God's guidance:

وَٱلَّذِينَ جَٰهَدُوا فِينَا لَنَهْدِيَنَّهُمْ سُبُلَنَا وَإِنَّ ٱللَّهَ لَمَعَ ٱلْمُحْسِنِينَ ۝

As for those who struggle in Our cause, We will surely guide
them along Our Way. And Allah is certainly with the good-
doers. [29:67]

Once the heart is pure, it becomes easier to follow any divine order. But a tainted heart will find much resistance in following commands of purity. This is how that first generation was able to comply so seamlessly with Allah's commandments, and this is how they reached heights unparalleled by any other generation.

This is the very reason why *iman* (faith) is highly emphasized in the beginning of one's journey to God, before a more technical understanding of religious knowledge. Jundab bin Abdullah explained this when he said: "We were with the Prophet ﷺ when we were young and lively. We learned faith before learning the Quran, and then we learned the Quran and increased our faith even more."[10]

"Learning faith", as Jundab describes it, is through experience: spending lengths of time alone with The Merciful in the still hours of the night. When faith is learned and the heart embraces it fully, the rest of the limbs join in. Allah nurtures the community of believers based on this principle. When someone asked Aishah about the order of the surahs in the Quran, she replied,

> The first to come down from it were the concise surahs that contained the mention of Paradise and Hellfire. Then when the people flocked to Islam, the sanctions and prohibitions came down. If the first thing to come down was: 'Do not drink wine,' they would have said, "We will never leave off wine." If it was: "Do not fornicate," they would have said, "We will never stop fornicating." While I was still a young girl playing in Mecca, this was revealed to Muhammad: "But the Hour is their appointment [for due punishment], and the Hour is more disastrous and more

bitter"[54:46]. Surahs al-Baqarah and an-Nisâ' did not come down until I was with him.[11]

Alcohol was outlawed in the second year after the Prophet's migration to Medina, which is fifteen years after the Prophet ﷺ first began to teach Islam. The ruling for women wearing veils came down in the sixth year after the migration, nineteen years after the first revelation in Mecca. For its first decade, Islam was dedicated to purifying the heart and nurturing faith, as the external obligations can never be rectified without them.

The Way of Those Before Us

Many of the accounts about the Messenger of Allah's ﷺ relationship with the night prayer come to us through his wife Aishah. She was well acquainted with the details of the Prophet's ﷺ private life, and so those who hadn't had the chance to meet him would take advantage of this by asking her to share what she saw from God's Messenger so that they could emulate it.

Two of her students, 'Ubaydullah and 'Atā', once came to her and asked, "Share with us the most amazing thing you saw from the Messenger of Allah ﷺ." She fell into a silent reflection for a short while, and then she spoke: "During one of my nights with him, he requested, 'Aishah, let me worship my Lord.' I said, 'By Allah, I love to be close to you, but I love what makes you happy.' He then stood up, washed himself, and stood to pray. He cried continuously until he drenched his lap, his beard, and the ground on which he stood. Then Bilal came to call him for the prayer, but when he saw him crying he asked, 'Messenger of Allah, why are you crying when God has already forgiven you for your past and for what's to come?' He said, **"Should I not, then, be a grateful servant? Tonight a verse was revealed to me. Woe to whoever reads it and does not reflect upon it:**[12]

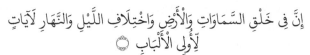

Indeed, in the creation of the heavens and the earth and the alternation of the day and night there are signs for people of reason. [3:190]

Aishah also once told a man, "Never give up the night prayer, for the Messenger of Allah ﷺ would never give it up. Even when he was ill, he prayed while sitting."[13] We also know from the following narration that the Messenger of Allah ﷺ even observed the night prayer while traveling.

One of the Companions narrates a story of when he traveled with the Prophet ﷺ. He wanted to see his nightly routine so he volunteered to stand guard over the Prophet ﷺ for the whole night. He recounts: "After he prayed the Isha prayer, he slept for a short part of the night. Then he woke up, looked into the horizon, and recited,

إِنَّ فِى خَلْقِ ٱلسَّمَٰوَٰتِ وَٱلْأَرْضِ وَٱخْتِلَٰفِ ٱلَّيْلِ وَٱلنَّهَارِ لَءَايَٰتٍ لِّأُولِى ٱلْأَلْبَٰبِ ۝

ٱلَّذِينَ يَذْكُرُونَ ٱللَّهَ قِيَٰمًا وَقُعُودًا وَعَلَىٰ جُنُوبِهِمْ وَيَتَفَكَّرُونَ فِى خَلْقِ ٱلسَّمَٰوَٰتِ

وَٱلْأَرْضِ رَبَّنَا مَا خَلَقْتَ هَٰذَا بَٰطِلًا سُبْحَٰنَكَ فَقِنَا عَذَابَ ٱلنَّارِ ۝ رَبَّنَآ إِنَّكَ

مَن تُدْخِلِ ٱلنَّارَ فَقَدْ أَخْزَيْتَهُۥ وَمَا لِلظَّٰلِمِينَ مِنْ أَنصَارٍ ۝ رَّبَّنَآ إِنَّنَا سَمِعْنَا

مُنَادِيًا يُنَادِى لِلْإِيمَٰنِ أَنْ ءَامِنُوا بِرَبِّكُمْ فَـَٔامَنَّا رَبَّنَا فَٱغْفِرْ لَنَا ذُنُوبَنَا وَكَفِّرْ

عَنَّا سَيِّـَٔاتِنَا وَتَوَفَّنَا مَعَ ٱلْأَبْرَارِ ۝ رَبَّنَا وَءَاتِنَا مَا وَعَدتَّنَا عَلَىٰ رُسُلِكَ وَلَا تُخْزِنَا

يَوْمَ ٱلْقِيَٰمَةِ إِنَّكَ لَا تُخْلِفُ ٱلْمِيعَادَ ۝

Indeed, in the creation of the heavens and the earth and the alternation of the day and night there are signs for people of reason—those who remember Allah while standing, sitting, and lying on their sides, and reflect on the creation of the heavens and the earth. "Our Lord! You have not created this without purpose. Glory be to You! Protect us from the torment of the Fire. Our Lord! Indeed, those You commit to the Fire will be disgraced! And the wrongdoers will have no helpers. Our Lord! We have heard the caller to belief, saying, 'Believe in your Lord alone,' so we believed. Our Lord! Forgive our sins, absolve us of our misdeeds, and allow us to die as one of the virtuous. Our Lord! Grant us what You have promised us through Your messengers and do not put us to shame on Judgment Day—for certainly You never fail in Your promise." [3:190-194]

"The Messenger of Allah ﷺ then bent down to his mat and pulled out a miswāk (a twig from a specific tree that would clean the teeth). He poured out some water from a water pouch into a bowl and brushed his teeth. Then he stood up and prayed until I estimated that he had prayed for just as long as he slept. He then lied down until I estimated that he had rested for the same amount of time that he had just prayed. And then he woke up and did what he had done the first time, reciting the same thing. The Messenger of Allah ﷺ did that three times before the dawn."[14]

What is especially astounding about the Prophet's ﷺ night prayer is how consistent he kept it up through times of extreme difficulty. Ali recalls that fearful day when the Muslims faced an opposition that vastly outnumbered them. He said, "On the day of Badr, al-Miqdād was our only horseman. I remember that every single person among us was sleeping, except for the Messenger of Allah ﷺ. He was praying under a tree, weeping until dawn,"[15] or "calling out to God until dawn," according to another narration. On that night before the Battle of Badr, the Prophet and Abu Bakr stood in prayer, crying out, **"God, Quraysh has brought their most pompous and proud men forth! They discredit and reject your Messenger, so bring the victory that you promised!"**[17] He continued to call upon God until his cloak even fell. Abu Bakr took it and put it back over his shoulders, and told him, "Messenger of Allah, your call upon your Lord is enough. He will certainly carry out His promise." This is the reason Allah sent down the verse,

$$ إِذْ تَسْتَغِيثُونَ رَبَّكُمْ فَاسْتَجَابَ لَكُمْ $$

When you cried out to your Lord for help, He answered you... [8:9]

And so Allah sent them His angels as reinforcements against Quraysh. In Ibn Mas'ood's account of the same situation, he says, "We never heard any man more desperately announce anything lost than when Muhammad ﷺ called upon His Lord on the Day of Badr: "Allah, I beg you for what you promised me!"[16]

This practice of calling upon God with humility and reverence remained a consistent part of the Messenger of Allah's ﷺ practice, and those around him understood its importance well enough to adopt it as a practice themselves. When we fast forward to the victory in Mecca, we see that many of the Prophet's enemies accepted Islam after two decades of denying and undermining him. Hind bint 'Utbah and Abu Sufyan were a married couple who took pride in their abuse and mockery of the Messenger of Allah ﷺ. When, more than twenty years later, Hind voiced her intentions to accept Islam, Abu Sufyan pointed out the irony to her. She responded, "I never saw God being worshipped as He deserves to be worshipped at the Ka'bah until last night. By God, even throughout the night there were people standing and prostrating in prayer!"[17]

Later after the death of the Prophet ﷺ, when the Muslims repeatedly defeated Heraclius's armies, the Byzantine prince asked his generals, "Why is it that we are being defeated as such?!" They said to him, "It is because they stand in prayer all night and fast all day." Even Abbas, the Prophet's uncle, noted how effectively the Companions were nurtured in their faith, connecting worship to the service of others as well. He said, "I was Umar's neighbor, and I never saw anyone more amazing than him. He would spend the night praying, and the days fasting and helping others."[18]

Someone once asked al-Ḥasan al-Baṣri, "Why is it that those who pray at night are the most beautiful people around?" He replied, "Because they spend time one-on-one with the Most Merciful, and so He dresses them in some of His light."[19] This light was so satisfying that those who experienced it could hardly keep it to themselves. One of the early Muslims describes what it was like to be in the same army camp as one of the most brilliant jurists and commentators of the Quran in the third generation. He says, "'Atā' al-Khurasāni would spend all night in prayer. When a third or half of the night passed, he would come to our tent and call out: 'Get up, wash yourselves, and attach fasting the day tomorrow to your prayer tonight! This is much easier than ingesting shards of iron and drinking pus in Hell! Hurry, Hurry! Salvation is on the line!' and then he would go pray."[20]

When asked about his teacher Ali bin Abu Talib, Dirār bin Damrah described him as so: "He was averse to this world and its glamor, and loved the nighttime and its darkness. By God, he had copious knowledge and was deeply contemplative; he would fiddle with his hands as he spoke to himself. He used to like simple clothing and coarse foods, and by God, it felt as if he was just one of us.

He would answer our questions when we asked, initiate conversation with us when we visited him, and would show up when we invited him. But despite how close he kept us and how close we felt to him, we were always shy to speak to him or start conversation with him out of respect and admiration.

His smile looked like a string of pearls. He used to venerate the people of religion and love the poor. No one, no matter how powerful, ever hoped to take advantage of him, and no one, no matter how weak, ever had doubts in his justice.

I swear by God—I once found him after the night's curtain had been drawn and the stars had set, standing in his prayer niche and holding onto his beard. He was murmuring in confidence, but weeping with grief. It's as if I can still hear him now, saying, 'Dunya! Dunya! Is it really me you are after? How mistaken you are—you have no chance! I divorced you permanently, with no chance of coming back to you. Your time is short, your pleasures are worthless, and your risks are lethal. How little we are prepared! How far our destination! How lonely the journey!"[21]

Ibn Kathir records that Nūr al-Deen Zangi, the 12th-century governor of Syria who is credited for uniting the disorganized Muslim army against the Crusaders, was keen to pray during the night. He called upon God desperately, and showed humility to God at all times. He used to cry in his prayers: "God forgive this corrupt and greedy tyrant!" alluding to himself. His wife even used to pray at night, and when she once slept through her usual routine, she woke up regretfully enraged. When her husband asked her about her unusual mood, she mentioned that she had overslept, and so he instituted the practice of striking a bell in the tower some time before dawn in order to wake up anyone who may have hoped to rise at that special time. He even paid a handsome salary to the one who struck the bell.[22]

Sweet Moments

Our moments of regret and brokenness are sweet when we are in the company of God. We are empowered when we realize the full extent of our dependence on the One who holds the world in His hand! The next time you wake up in the night and see that there is still some time before dawn, imagine those select ones who may be standing, begging their Lord urgently for their needs. The petitioners have lined up with their requests to God, so wipe the drowsiness off your face and take the first place in the line—enjoy the undivided attention of your Lord. Ask him like a beggar at the throne of a king. Seek His asylum like a lost refugee. Admit your failures and your fragility; call out to Him and don't hold back your tears. Don't stop knocking on His door, and be insistent when you request of Him. Perhaps He will see your sincerity and will give from His endless reserves:

وَلِلَّهِ خَزَآئِنُ ٱلسَّمَٰوَٰتِ وَٱلْأَرْضِ

But to Allah alone belong the treasuries of the heavens and the earth... [63:7]

How could He ever reject you when it is He who woke you up?! When you find yourself awake at those hours, respond to His call and say, "Yes, my Lord, it's me! I am the one who is asking of you! I am the one seeking your forgiveness! I am the one in need of shelter, so cover me! I am the one who is starving, so feed me! I am the one who is lost, so guide me! I am the one who is poor, so enrich me! I am the one who is weak, so empower me!"

Arrows of the Night Never Miss

The Prophet David once asked Gabriel, "Which part of the night is best?" Gariel responded, "I do not know, but the Throne quakes right before dawn."[23] One scholar said, "There is a breeze that emanates beneath the Throne that only blows before dawn, carrying tears and prayers for forgiveness."[24] Hassan al-Banna once said, "The precious minutes of the night tick by, so don't let them pass by while you are unconscious."

Prepare your requests ahead of time, specify your goals, and sleep lightly, awaiting the moments of solitude with your Beloved Lord. Don't be frightened of the darkness and surrounding silence when you realize you are the only one awake. The angels are actually there with you, proud of you and praying for you. Muhammad bin Qays narrates that he heard that when someone gets up for prayer in the middle of the night, the angels come rushing down from the heavens to listen to his or her recitation. Even the creatures in the house stop to listen along, and when the person finishes praying and begins to supplicate, the angels huddle around him or her and say, "Āmeen." Then when this worshipper lies down to rest after that, the angels say to them: "Sleep sweet one, in peace and pleasure! Sleep well after the best of actions!"[25]

> *"What do you hide?" I asked the night*
> *"What treasures do you hold deep down inside?"*
> *She said, "Nothing in my darkness glows just as bright*
> *As a teardrop that drips from a sincere fearful eye."*

A Treasure Neglected

If we knew that there was a hidden cache of money waiting from which we could take as much as we wished, would we choose sleep over the chance to claim the prize? We ignore the waiting opportunity every night, letting others get to it before us, others who understand its true worth:

$$\text{تَتَجَافَىٰ جُنُوبُهُمْ عَنِ ٱلْمَضَاجِعِ يَدْعُونَ رَبَّهُمْ خَوْفًا وَطَمَعًا}$$

They abandon their beds, invoking their Lord with hope and fear... [32:16]

Night prayer is not reserved for the devout and pure of heart. It is not only for those who have reached high levels in their spirituality. On the contrary, night prayer is for everyone, regardless of where they are on their journey. Some of the early scholars used to say: "Whenever you find yourself having veered off of the path, retrace your steps and let your sins show you the way back."

Ibn Rajab compared the last part of the night to a treasure-filled mine from which seekers extract their various needs.[26] The weak sinners, who are struggling to maintain a connection with their Creator, find consolation in their plea for mercy and forgiveness; the desperate and destitute, who have despaired of help from others, beg their Sustainer to improve their conditions. Those who have become accustomed to rising at night converse with their Beloved. Only the most heedless will opt for more hours of sleep over all of the other resources available to them.

Hassan al-Banna encourages us in *Risālah al-Munājāh*:

Dear brother, the sweetest time to call upon your Lord is when everyone else is asleep. The heedless are asleep, and the whole universe is still. The night darkens and the stars disappear, but your heart is awake and present. You remember your Lord and express your weakness in front of Your Master. You find comfort in Allah's presence, and your heart finds peace in His remembrance. You rejoice in His favor and mercy and cry in humility before Him. You keenly feel His watching over you, and you pour your heart into supplication. You go all out in asking for forgiveness, while asking Him for your needs—He who is capable of anything and who is never preoccupied. If He wills something, He simply says be and it is. Ask Him for this life and ask Him for the next; ask Him on behalf of His cause and His call; ask Him for your hopes, family, people, and country. Ask him for yourself, and ask him for your brothers.

The night is when we advance on our journey with the greatest speed.

$$وَٱسْجُدْ وَٱقْتَرِب ۩$$

Prostrate and draw near. [96:19]

Without this vital provision on our journey, we will never reach our destination, and will remain separated from our Lord, depressed in our faith, demoralized at heart, weak in body. When the Prophet ﷺ encouraged his Companions to pray at night, he made clear to them how essential it is for both our physical and spiritual health. He said, **"Stick with the night prayer, for it is tradition of the righteous people before you, a way to come nearer to God—the Exalted—a means of preventing sin, a remover of bad deeds, and a cleaning of bodily illness."**[27]

Helpful Tips to Wake Up at Night

There are many things that can facilitate our nightly prayer routine, now that we have recognized its true worth and are willing to work for it.

1. ASK ALLAH FOR HELP

How much do you want it? Do you pray to Allah to help you wake up at night? We can assess how badly we really want to pray at night by considering if we have ever asked His help in doing so, just as we ask Him for any other blessing.

◖ Tips for Waking Up ◗

Ask Allah for help
Remember the afterlife
Sleep with wudu
Pray right before Fajr

2. REMEMBER THE AFTERLIFE

To help us wake up at night, we should cut all ties to the material world before we sleep. This is a method that the Messenger of Allah ﷺ practiced himself, reminding himself and others of the Afterlife at night to inspire the thirst for worship. After one third of the night had passed, the Messenger of Allah ﷺ would stand up and say: **"People, remember God! The quake has come, and the next one is to follow. Death has come with all that it contains!"**[28]

3. SLEEP WITH WUDU

The Prophet ﷺ also taught us to end our night in a state of remembering God by making wuḍu' and reciting various verses and words of remembrance before sleeping. This remembrance and state of purity keeps the devil away and can make our hearts more agile in waking up.

4. LINK YOUR NIGHT PRAYERS WITH FAJR

By waking up an hour or a half hour before Fajr, one can fit in at least two rakahs of prayer and sample the experience of waking up at night, while only waking up once for both the night prayer and fajr. As you develop your habit, you may find yourself longing for more time and waking up earlier.

....

ENDNOTES

1. al-Bukhari, #1145; Muslim, #758
2. al-Tirmidhi, #3579; *Saheeh al-Jami'* (173)
3. p. 49
4. *Rawa'i' Iqbal* p. 46
5. Fee Ẓilāl al-Qur'ān, v. 6, p. 3745
6. *Saheeh al-Jami'* (3710) and *as-Silsilah as-Saheehah* (1903)
7. Fayh al-Qadeer, v. 4, p. 212
8. 'Abdur-Razzāq, al-Musannaf, v. 3, p. 36, #4735
9. al-Bukhari, #4837; Muslim, #2820
10. Ibn Mājah, #61
11. al-Bukhari, #4993
12. Agreed upon
13. Abu Dawud (1307); Ahmad (26114)
14. *Saheeh*; al-Albani
15. *Saheeh*; Ahmad, Ibn Khuzaymah, an-Nasa'i
16. The Seerah of Ibn Hishām
17. *Ruhban al-Layl* (1/310); Ibn Abdul-Barr, al-Istee'āb, v. 6, p. 293
18. Ḥilyat al-Awliyā', v. 1, p. 54
19. *Ruhban al-Layl* (1/521)
20. Ibid

21. Ibn Abu Dunya, Maqtal Ali, #105
22. al-Bidāyah wal-Nihāyah, v. 12, p. 279
23. Ahmad bin Ḥanbal, al-Zuhd, #365
24. Ibn al-Jawzi, al-Mudhish, p. 432
25. al-Marwazi, MukhtaṢar Qiyām al-Layl, v. 1, p. 66
26. LaṬā'if al-Ma'ārif, p. 50
27. al-Tirmidhi, #3549
28. al-Ḥākim, #3578

Fasting

In our journey of prioritizing faith, we want to reach the point where our iman exceeds our selfish desires. The previous methods—fear, Quran reflection, prayer, and so on—directly strengthened our faith. Fasting works differently. It is a tranquilizer for the *nafs*—our selfish drive—and gives our iman a chance to breathe and grow. In this battle for our hearts, we must not only bolster our iman and willpower, but also strategize to weaken the opposing forces. Fasting is the best method for the latter.

When God mentions the obligation to fast, He mentions its objective along with it:

$$يَـٰٓأَيُّهَا ٱلَّذِينَ ءَامَنُوا كُتِبَ عَلَيْكُمُ ٱلصِّيَامُ كَمَا كُتِبَ عَلَى ٱلَّذِينَ مِن قَبْلِكُمْ لَعَلَّكُمْ تَتَّقُونَ ۝$$

O believers! Fasting is prescribed for you—as it was for those before you—so perhaps you will become mindful. [2:183]

In his commentary *In the Shade of the Quran*, Sayyid Qutb describes fasting as, "a means of preparing a people who were obligated with striving for God's cause; preparing them to establish His religion here on earth, to transcend physical needs, and to navigate this road full of pits and thorns."[1]

Fasting is a cultivator of willpower and a vaccine against our desires. The Prophet ﷺ informed us of its universal effectiveness when he said, **"Be keen to fast, for there is nothing like it."**[2] He also taught us that it is a means of erasing our sins: **"A man's issues with his family, his wealth, his own self, his children, and his neighbor are all erased by fasting, prayer, charity, encouraging virtue, and preventing vice."**[3]

The honor that we receive when we fast should be enough of a motivation to do so regularly. The Messenger of Allah ﷺ said, **"God, Mighty and Majestic, and His angels all pray for the ones who eat the pre-dawn meal,"**[4] alluding to the fact that the only reason people would eat at that time is to fast the day ahead of them. Fasting also distances us from the Hellfire and increase our chances of entering Paradise. The Prophet ﷺ said, "Allah places a ditch as wide as the sky and the earth between anyone who fasts one day for God's sake and the Hellfire."[5] He also said, "There is a gate in Paradise called al-Rayyān through which those who fast will enter on the Day of Resurrection—no one other than them will enter. It will be asked, 'Where are the ones who used to fast?' and then they will stand and enter it—no one besides them. After they enter, the door will be shut—no one other than them will enter it."[6]

The Dangers of a Full Stomach

A Companion by the name Miqdād bin Ma'deekarib narrates that the Messenger of Allah ﷺ said: "The human being does not fill any container worse than his own stomach. Some food to straighten his spine is enough for the human being. If it is unavoidable, then let it be one third food, one third drink, and one third for his breath."[7]

Another Companion recalls that he ate barley bread with some tender meat, and then went to be with the Prophet ﷺ. While there, he burped, and so the Prophet ﷺ told him, "Restrain your burp, for those who are most full in this life will be the most hungry on the Day of Resurrection."[8] One scholar points out that though many foods are permissible to eat, we should not take that as a license to fill our body with food to the point that it induces sleep and prevents us from worship. We should eat only enough to quiet our hunger, and our objective should be to have enough energy for worship.

The Advantages of an Empty Stomach

Imam al-Ghazali mentions a number of benefits in refraining from filling our stomachs. An empty stomach keeps the heart pure and soft, the mind sharp, and the soul awake, while being constantly full leads to absent-mindedness and a heaviness of heart. These side effects apply to children as well. Luqmān, who is mentioned in the Quran as being a paragon of wisdom, taught his son a number of valuable lessons that have been recorded in various traditions. He said to his son, "A full stomach sedates the mind, drowns out wisdom, and weighs the body down from worship."

A full stomach also diminishes the heart's sensitivity to the sweet taste of worship. Think about how spiritually engaged you are while fasting and compare that to how many prayers and moments of remembrance we hardly reacted to at all. One of the earliest masters of the spiritual sciences once expressed how shocked he was by people who, "fill all the space between their mind and heart with food, and then expect to taste the delight of worship."

Restraining our food consumption also reduces our urges towards sinful pleasures and helps us maintain self-control. Sins are nothing but cravings. Nothing foments these cravings more than food, so decreasing our intake will certainly drain their ferocity. Our success and failure in all aspects, including strengthening our iman, depends on our level of self-discipline.

When we feed our bodies, we also feed and nurture the desires that are connected to our bodies. Aishah goes so far as to say that the worst thing to happen to Muslims after the passing of the Messenger of Allah ﷺ was the widespread abundance of food. She said, **"When people fill their stomachs, their bodies become fat, the hearts become hard, and their passions run wild."**[9] Keeping our stomachs empty helps suppress our sexual desires and keep our frivolous speech at a minimum, which prevents us from falling into sins like backbiting, cursing, lying, and other sins of the tongue. It's also a lot more difficult to restrain yourself against sexual desire when your body is so accustomed to having its cravings satiated. Even if someone does not fall into the bigger sin of adultery or fornication, we can still commit sin easily with our eyes or even our imaginations. Keeping the mind real and alert with hunger will preoccupy it from any sinful fantasies.

Not filling our stomachs also helps us to sleep less. The extra hours of sleep caused by overconsumption could be used in exercise, worship, or learning something new. Excessive sleep keeps us lethargic and spiritually disengaged. Time is our most precious resource, and we must use it to our advantage if we are to strengthen iman. Sleep is good when it is used to recharge and refresh, but too much brings on lethargy. Sleep is often compared to death because of all the hours of our day that it kills, preventing us from doing anything else.

Overconsumption plagues our society today; we experience the physical and spiritual consequences. Many of the most prevalent diseases we find among our communities today are lifestyle diseases; they are due to the quantity or the quality of the food we eat, as well as the unprecedented lack of physical activity in our daily lives. How many people do you know personally who have to pray sitting down due to their physical conditions—they might not have felt the comfort of bowing in full prostration in years! Just a quick search on the percentage of our populations who are on some sort of medication is a good indication of the gravity of this issue. Perhaps the solution lies in consuming less, rather than adding another daily medication.

Minimizing our intake of food also helps us stay content with little. A person used to a full stomach will constantly be occupied with keeping it full; breakfast will be the first thing on their mind when they wake up, and they will need snacks and beverages to hold off until the next meal. During one of the sermons of Umar bin al-Khattab, he said,

Beware of filling your stomach with food! It inhibits your energy to pray, ruins your body, and causes illness. Allah, Blessed and Exalted, despises the fat scholar. Rather you must stay prudent in your provisions, for it is more conducive to righteousness, keeps you away from excessiveness, and is more energizing for worship. A man is only doomed when he prefers his own desires over his religion.[10]

Al-Fuḍayl bin 'Iyāḍ said, "Two things harden the heart: speaking too much and eating too much."[11] It is also narrated that Luqmān instructed his son, "Do not eat past your fill; give your leftovers to the dogs."[12] Another Islamic scholar said, "Whoever can control their stomach can control their religious commitment. Whoever can control their stomach has control of their good manners. Anyone who does not realize the harm their stomach can cause to their piety is spiritually blind."[13]

Moderate Consumption

Ibn Qudāmah writes in *Minhāj al-Qāṣideen* about some ascetics who go overboard in minimizing their food and drink, essentially starving themselves. He said, "The true form of moderation in consumption is to stop while there is still some desire for more." He then narrated the *hadith* mentioned above about keeping one-third of our stomach for food, one-third for water, and one-third empty to breathe. Not eating enough can make us too weak to carry out our obligations.

There is some wise advice that Ibn Qudāmah then offers for those of us who are already accustomed to being full all of the time. He suggests that we should decrease our intake gradually over time until we reach that ideal point of moderation, where we are neither distracted by our hunger nor our full stomachs. This path of balance will sustain our motivation and help keep our minds clear, for "the best of all matters is that which is balanced."[14]

Prophetic Balance

In *Laṭā'if al-Ma'ārif*, Ibn Rajab demonstrates how the Prophet ﷺ struck the perfect balance of his physical and spiritual practice. He would fast some days and opt out of others, using his time at night to both pray and sleep, and showing us how marriage should be more than just a physical relationship. He would eat whatever was available, including sweets, honey, meat, and chicken, but sometimes was driven to such extreme levels of hunger from poverty that he tied a rock to his stomach to alleviate the pain.

Ibn Rajab then relates an inspiring *hadith* that shows us how to engage with our food and hunger spiritually. The Prophet ﷺ said, **"My Lord offered to make the basin of Mecca's valley** gold for me, but I said, 'No, my Lord, instead let me be hungry for one day and full another. When I go hungry, I will become humble and remember you, and when I am full I will praise you and thank you.'"[15] Ibn Rajab comments on this *hadith*: "He chose the best option for himself: to live between gratitude, patience, and contentment with God."[16]

As long as we feed the physical cravings of our soul, we are only increasing our attachment to the earth. There is no better weapon to weaken our own passions than hunger. We should periodically deprive the body to wean it from desires, and the correct way to do this is the model of fasting prescribed in Islam.

A good start in establishing a habit of fasting and limiting consumption is to fast Mondays and Thursdays every week. The Prophet ﷺ was keen on this habit, according to Aishah and Usamah bin Zayd. If that isn't feasible, we can fast the three White Days of every Islamic month (the 13th, 14th, and 15th), keeping in mind that every good deed is worth ten times its own value. So if we fast only three days, it would be as if we fasted every month; and if we do so consistently, we would have the reward of fasting the whole year. With these small steps, we can incrementally restrain our nafs and provide our iman with fertile ground to blossom.

Perhaps we can eventually reach the point of detachment from worldly pleasures where we fast every other day like the Prophet David. There are also other important days to fast throughout the year, such as the day of Arafah any six days during the month of Shawwāl, and the first ten days of the month of Muharram. Ramadan, of course, is the annual divine prescription for the collective Muslim community, increasing our faith, limiting our nafs, and heightening our mindfulness of God. No matter how rampant our appetites may be, Ramadan forces us to rein in our nafs and observe for one month the effects of muted desire and empty stomachs on our lifestyle and spirituality.

....

ENDNOTES

1. *Fee Thilal al-Quran* v. 1, p. 167
2. Ahmad, #22140
3. al-Bukhari, v.1, p. 111, #525; Muslim, v. 4, p. 2218
4. *Saheeh al-Jami'* (3683)
5. *Saheeh al-Jami'* (6333)
6. al-Bukhari, #1896; and Muslim, #1152
7. Ahmad, #1896; *Saheeh al-Jami'* (5550)
8. *Hasan; As-Silsilah as-Saheehah* (343)
9. Ibid., #22
10. Ibid., #81
11. Ibn Ḥibbān, Rawdat al-'Uqalā', v. 1, p. 43
12. Ibn Abu Dunya, al-Jaw', #74
13. Hilyat al-Awliyā', v. 6, p. 157
14. Mukhtaṣar Minhāj al-Qaṣideen, pp. 177-178
15. Ahmad, #22190
16. p. 140

Loving the Mosques

اللَّهُ نُورُ ٱلسَّمَوَتِ وَٱلْأَرْضِ مَثَلُ نُورِهِۦ كَمِشْكَوٰةٍ فِيهَا مِصْبَاحٌ ٱلْمِصْبَاحُ فِى زُجَاجَةٍ ٱلزُّجَاجَةُ كَأَنَّهَا كَوْكَبٌ دُرِّيٌّ يُوقَدُ مِن شَجَرَةٍ مُّبَرَكَةٍ زَيْتُونَةٍ لَّا شَرْقِيَّةٍ وَلَا غَرْبِيَّةٍ يَكَادُ زَيْتُهَا يُضِىٓءُ وَلَوْ لَمْ تَمْسَسْهُ نَارٌ نُّورٌ عَلَىٰ نُورٍ يَهْدِى ٱللَّهُ لِنُورِهِۦ مَن يَشَآءُ وَيَضْرِبُ ٱللَّهُ ٱلْأَمْثَلَ لِلنَّاسِ وَٱللَّهُ بِكُلِّ شَىْءٍ عَلِيمٌ ۝

Allah is the Light of the heavens and the earth. His light is
like a niche in which there is a lamp, the lamp is in a crystal,
the crystal is like a shining star, lit from a blessed olive tree
belonging neither to the east nor the west and whose oil
would almost glow, even without being touched by fire. Light
upon light! Allah guides whomever He wills to His light.
And Allah sets forth parables for humanity. For Allah has
knowledge of all things. [24:35]

This widely celebrated verse speaks about God's light, to which He guides whomever He wills among His servants. So who exactly is it whom God chooses to guide to His light? Who are those blessed ones who experience Allah's light? Notice how Allah continues: He tells us that His light shines:

فِى بُيُوتٍ أَذِنَ ٱللَّهُ أَن تُرْفَعَ وَيُذْكَرَ فِيهَا ٱسْمُهُۥ يُسَبِّحُ لَهُۥ فِيهَا بِٱلْغُدُوِّ وَٱلْءَاصَالِ ۝ رِجَالٌ لَّا تُلْهِيهِمْ تِجَرَةٌ وَلَا بَيْعٌ عَن ذِكْرِ ٱللَّهِ وَإِقَامِ ٱلصَّلَوٰةِ وَإِيتَآءِ ٱلزَّكَوٰةِ يَخَافُونَ يَوْمًا تَتَقَلَّبُ فِيهِ ٱلْقُلُوبُ وَٱلْأَبْصَرُ ۝

Through houses which Allah has ordered to be raised, and
where His Name is mentioned. He is glorified there morning
and evening by men who are not distracted—neither by
buying nor selling—from Allah's remembrance, or performing

prayer, or paying alms-tax. They fear a Day when hearts and
eyes will tremble. [24:36-37]

Not only are the people described with such valuable qualities, but God makes a point to mention that these special people are found within the mosques. The mosques are God's houses on earth, and anyone who visits is sure to be His honored guest. Salmān al-Fārisi narrates that the Prophet ﷺ said, **"Whoever performes wudu' in his home, perfects his wudu', then comes to the mosque is a visitor of Allah, and it is a right upon the host to be generous to the visitor."**[1] Ibn 'Abbās also described the mosques as "God's houses on earth," and said that they "glow for the inhabitants of the sky like the stars glow for the inhabitants of the earth."[2] If we wish to illuminate our hearts with the light of faith, then we must strive to emulate the qualities of these people described in this ayah, including frequenting the mosque.

The mosque is not only a place to pray. Consider how the Messenger of Allah ﷺ described one of the groups of people who will receive God's shade on the day when there will be no shade but His: **"a person whose heart is attached to the mosque."**[3] Imam al-Nawawi says in his commentary that this alludes to an intense love for the mosque that should lead us to perform our prayers regularly in congregation. Our love for the mosque is more than just nostalgic; it is an impetus for us to enhance our worship. "[Being attached to the mosque] does not mean," says an-Nawawi, "to just sit inside of the mosque."[4] In Ibn Ḥajar's commentary of this *hadith* in *Fatḥ al-Bāri*, he highlights the figurative language of the *hadith*, focusing on the word "attached." "It is as if the heart is something hanging inside the mosque–like the candles therein—and this shows how his heart may be regularly contained therein, even when his body is not there."[5]

The Mosque's Role in Awakening Faith

The act of going to the mosque is an important way to connect our hearts to Allah. The Messenger of Allah ﷺ once said to the Companions, **"May I direct you to that with which God erases sins and raises ranks?"** They eagerly responded, **"Of course, Messenger of Allah!"** He said, **"Perfecting wudu despite the inconveniences, taking many steps to the mosque, and waiting for one prayer after the next. That is the anchor! That is the anchor!"**[6] Imam al-Qurtubi explained that the word anchor is used here because these actions keep the heart from drifting away from its good intentions, and keep the body steady in acts of obedience."[7]

Our mercurial hearts are indeed in need of an anchor. The Arabic word for heart is *qalb*, which comes from the root meaning "to flip over." The Arabs used this word to refer to the heart because of its fickle nature. The Prophet ﷺ said, **"The heart (qalb) was thus named because of its constant flipping. The heart is just like a feather in a field; it catches on to the trunk of one tree, and then the wind flips it over and upside down."**[8]

The heart tosses from one state to another, a product of the constant struggle between our inner forces of faith and desire. Guidance battles against the lure of satan in this armageddon of the soul, and our hearts are constantly pulled between the two camps. It is to no surprise that the Prophet's ﷺ most frequent supplication in prayer was: **"Turner of hearts, make my heart firm upon your religion."**[9]

A firm heart is one that does not sway from its condition. In describing the tremendous challenge given to Moses's mother to place her baby into a basket and let him float away on the river, God demonstrates how He rewards those who submit wholly to His command:

$$وَأَصْبَحَ فُؤَادُ أُمِّ مُوسَىٰ فَرِغًا إِن كَادَتْ لَتُبْدِى بِهِۦ لَوْلَآ أَن رَّبَطْنَا عَلَىٰ قَلْبِهَا لِتَكُونَ مِنَ ٱلْمُؤْمِنِينَ ۝$$

*And the heart of Moses' mother ached so much that she
almost gave away his identity, had We not anchored her heart
in order for her to have faith.* [28:10]

Were it not for Allah making her heart firm and anchoring it to faith, Moses's mother would have succumbed to her panic and grief.

One early Islamic scholar once asked his student if he knew why the following verse was revealed:

$$ٱصْبِرُوا۟ وَصَابِرُوا۟ وَرَابِطُوا۟$$

Patiently endure, persevere, stand on guard... [3:200]

When the student said he didn't know, the scholar said, "My dear son, I heard Abu Hurayrah say that there was never a situation in battle in which they had to 'stand on guard,' and that it actually means to stand by for one prayer after the next."[10]

Anchored to the Mosque

There are many *hadiths* that mention the great virtue of walking to the mosque, praying there, and staying inside even after prayer. This indicates the role that the mosque is supposed to have in our lives. We must include going to the mosque in our daily routines and keep a strong connection with it.

Walking (or driving) to the mosque and spending time within its walls increases our number of good deeds and deletes our bad deeds. The Messenger of Allah ﷺ said, **"For whoever goes to the communal mosque, one step will erase a bad deed, and another step will be recorded as a good deed for him, both going and returning."**[11] Attending the mosque also enhances our quality of life and ensures a beautiful ending for us; the Prophet ﷺ describes in a *hadith* how the elite believers busy themselves: "The acts that raise ranks and atone sins, moving their feet towards the communal prayers, perfecting the wudu in unfavorable conditions, and waiting for one prayer after the next—whoever maintains these will live in goodness and die in goodness, and his sins will be just as they were on the day his mother gave birth to him."[12]

Developing this deep relationship with the mosque also helps us earn God's warm and cheerful welcome. The Messenger of Allah ﷺ said, "No one makes wudu, doing so with excellence and perfection, and then comes to the mosque wanting only to pray therein, except that God welcomes him warmly and cheerfully, just like the family welcomes the traveller when he arrives."[13] The angels join in on this cheer, praying for those who stay in the area in which they prayed after finishing The Messenger of Allah ﷺ said, "The angels pray for you for as long as you are in the area in which you prayed—and as long as you don't invalidate your wudu—saying, 'Allah, forgive him! Allah show him mercy."[14]

The Prophet ﷺ promised a special light on the Day of Resurrection as a reward for those who have a special relationship with the mosques. He said, "Give those who always walk to the mosque in the dark the good news of a perfect light on the Day of Resurrection."[15] Even more reassuring than this, the Prophet ﷺ informed us: "There are three people, all of whom God guarantees to sustain and suffice for as long as they live, and enter them into Paradise when they die: Someone who enters his house and says the greeting of peace is guaranteed by God, someone who goes out to the mosque is guaranteed by God, and someone who goes out for God's cause is guaranteed by God."[16]

Allah takes special pride in His servants who take the time out of their day to pray in the mosque. Abdullah bin 'Amr narrates that the Companions once prayed the Maghrib prayer with the Messenger of Allah ﷺ, and some left afterwards while others stayed. The Messenger of Allah ﷺ came running back, out of breath and holding his garment up to his knees. He said to them, "Rejoice, group of Muslims! That was your Lord—He opened one of the doors of the heavens to show you off to the angels! He says, 'These are my servants. They just completed one obligation, and they are waiting for another.'"[17]

Going to the mosque also earns us God's mercy and a safe passage over the bridge of Hell—the bridge from which many who thought they were safe to enter Paradise will fall into the Fire. The Messenger of Allah ﷺ once said, "The mosque is the home of every pious person. God guarantees comfort and mercy to those for whom the mosque is their home, as well as safe passage over the Bridge of Hell into God's pleasure—into Paradise!"[18] There is also a special relationship that those who frequent the mosque have with the angels themselves. The Prophet ﷺ said, likening those who are always found inside the mosque to its actual pillars, "There are pillars in the mosques around whom the angels gather. When they don't show up, the angels notice their absence; if they fall ill, they visit them; and if they are in need, they assist them."[19] In order to strengthen faith, we must anchor our hearts to the mosques, make them our homes, and be just like the Companions were in their love for God's houses on earth. For them, the mosque represented safety and tranquility, and it was to the mosque they fled whenever they felt panic.

We ought to reserve our seats in the first row of the mosque whenever possible. The Messenger of Allah ﷺ said, **"Allah and His angels pray for the first row."**[20] He also said, **"The first row is just like the row of angels. If you knew its virtue, you would rush for it."**[21] Ahmad Abdul-Rahman al-Banna said in his commentary on this *hadith*: "They are like the angels in their nearness to Allah, and the mercy that descends upon them."[22]

If none of the incentives mentioned above is enough to motivate us, then know that regularly attending the mosque and developing a meaningful relationship with it is a sign of sincerity and faith. The Messenger of Allah ﷺ said, **"If you see a man attending the mosque regularly, then attest to his faith, for God, the Exalted, says,[23]**

$$\text{إِنَّمَا يَعْمُرُ مَسَاجِدَ اللَّهِ مَنْ آمَنَ بِاللَّهِ وَالْيَوْمِ الْآخِرِ}$$

The mosques of Allah are only maintained by those who believe in Allah and the Last Day... [9:18]

....

ENDNOTES

1. al-Tabarāni, al-Kabeer, #6139
2. Ibid., #10608
3. al-Bukhari, #660; Muslim, #1031
4. Imam al-Nawawi's commentary on Sahih Muslim, v. 7, p. 121
5. *Fath al-Bāri*, v. 2, p. 145
6. Muslim (1/219 #251)
7. al-Jāmiʻ liʼAhkām al-Qurʼān, v. 4, p. 206
8. Ahmad, #19661
9. Ahmad, #26519
10. Ibn al-Mubārak, al-Zuhd, #408
11. Ahmad, #6599; Ibn Hibban (5/387); deemed *saheeh* by al-Arna'oot
12. Ahmad, #3484; deemed *saheeh* by al-Albani in *Takhreej Mishkat al-Masabeeh*
13. Ahmad, #8065; Ibn Khuzaymah (2/374 #1491); Ibn Hibban (4/484 #1607); *Saheeh al-Targheeb wa al-Tarheeb*
14. al-Bukhari, #445; Muslim, 669
15. Abu Dawud (1/421 #561); at-Tirmithi (1/435 #223); deemed *hasan* by al-Arna'oot
16. Abu Dawud (4/150 #2494); Ibn Hibbān, #499; deemed *saheeh* by al-Albani in *Takhreej Mishkat al-Masabeeh* (727)
17. Ahmad, #6750; Ibn Majah (1/513 #801); deemed *saheeh* by al-Munthiri and al-Arna'oot
18. al-Tabarāni, #6143; al-Bayhaqi in *Shuʻab al-Iman* (4/381 #2689); *as-Silsilah as-Saheehah* (716)
19. Ahmad, #9424; *as-Silsilah as-Saheehah* (2401)
20. Ahmad, #18364; deemed *hasan* al-Munthiri and *saheeh* by al-Arna'oot
21. Ahmad, #21266; Abu Dawud (1/416 #554); deemed *saheeh* by al-Munthiri and al-Arna'oot
22. *al-Fath al-Rabbāni fee sharh Musnad al-Iman Ahmad*
23. Ahmad, #11651; ibn Majah #802; at-Tirmithi #2617

Special Seasons

Ibn Rajab composed a manual on how to take advantage special times and seasons throughout hours of the day, the weeks, months and years. He writes therein that God made certain months more virtuous than others, and quotes three Quranic verses to clarify:

إِنَّ عِدَّةَ ٱلشُّهُورِ عِندَ ٱللَّهِ ٱثْنَا عَشَرَ شَهْرًا فِي كِتَـٰبِ ٱللَّهِ يَوْمَ خَلَقَ ٱلسَّمَـٰوَٰتِ وَٱلْأَرْضَ مِنْهَآ أَرْبَعَةٌ حُرُمٌ ذَٰلِكَ ٱلدِّينُ ٱلْقَيِّمُ فَلَا تَظْلِمُوا فِيهِنَّ أَنفُسَكُمْ

Indeed, the number of months ordained by Allah is twelve—in Allah's Record since the day He created the heavens and the earth—of which four are sacred. That is the Right Way. So do not wrong one another during these months. [9:36]

ٱلْحَجُّ أَشْهُرٌ مَّعْلُومَٰتٌ

The pilgrimage is made in appointed months. [2:197]

شَهْرُ رَمَضَانَ ٱلَّذِي أُنزِلَ فِيهِ ٱلْقُرْءَانُ

Ramadan is the month in which the Quran was revealed...
[2:185]

Ibn Rajab also points out that there are certain days and nights that are more virtuous than others. Laylat al-Qadr, for example, is better than one thousand months of regular nights, and God also swears by the first ten days of the month of Dhul-Hijjah to distinguish them from other days. Ibn Rajab says,

For every one of these special times, God made a specific act of worship to be performed in order to come closer to him. God sends His comforting breezes of bounty and mercy therein to whomever He wishes. The successful ones are those who take advantage of these special months, days, and hours, and use them to come closer to their Lord through those specific acts of worship. Perhaps he might catch one of those breezes, attaining success and salvation from the Hellfire and its tormenting storms.[1]

These "breezes" that he mentions are referenced in the *hadith* of the Messenger of Allah ﷺ: **"Your Lord sends breezes during special days throughout the year, so catch them. Perhaps one of you might be touched by a breeze, after which he will never be troubled."**[2] We must be vigilant to seek out these times of virtues in order to get a boost in our iman.

There are even some hours throughout the day that are more virtuous than others, and the scholars call them, "the hours of traveling to God," in order to distinguish them. Friday is the one day throughout the week that is more valuable than the others, and among the months of the year, Ramadan is foremost.

◁ Special Times ▷

After dawn
Asr every day
Last part of the night
Friday
Asr on Friday
Ramadan
Hajj and Dhul-Hijjah

Special Hours of the Day

There are three times throughout the day in which God urges us to exert extra effort in worship:

$$\text{وَسَبِّحْ بِحَمْدِ رَبِّكَ قَبْلَ طُلُوعِ ٱلشَّمْسِ وَقَبْلَ غُرُوبِهَا}$$
$$\text{وَمِنْ ءَانَآئِ ٱلَّيْلِ فَسَبِّحْ وَأَطْرَافَ ٱلنَّهَارِ لَعَلَّكَ تَرْضَىٰ ۝}$$

And glorify the praises of your Lord before sunrise and before sunset, and glorify Him in the hours of the night and at both ends of the day, so that you may be pleased. [20:130]

The Prophet ﷺ emphasized these times of day to be used as worship to his Companions as well. He once said, **"No one will be saved by their actions."** The Companions asked, **"Not even you, Messenger of Allah?"** He said, **"Not even me, unless God envelops me in His mercy. Aim straight and do your best—work in the morning, in the evening, and for a part of the night. Moderation! Moderation, and you shall reach the goal."**[3]

In another *hadith*, the Messenger alludes to the importance of worshipping during these times by saying, **"The religion is ease. No one goes to an extreme in the religion except that it overwhelms** him. So aim straight, come close, and rejoice. Seek help in the daytime, nighttime, and during part of the night."[4] Ibn Rajab says about this *hadith*, "These three times are the times for traveling to God through worship. It is the last part of the night, the first part of the day, and the last part of the day." He then cites the verses:

وَٱذْكُرِ ٱسْمَ رَبِّكَ بُكْرَةً وَأَصِيلًا ۝ وَمِنَ ٱلَّيْلِ فَٱسْجُدْ لَهُۥ وَسَبِّحْهُ لَيْلًا طَوِيلًا ۝

Mention the Name of your Lord morning and evening, and
prostrate before Him during part of the night, and glorify
Him long at night. [76:25-26]

وَسَبِّحْ بِحَمْدِ رَبِّكَ قَبْلَ طُلُوعِ ٱلشَّمْسِ وَقَبْلَ ٱلْغُرُوبِ ۝ وَمِنَ ٱلَّيْلِ فَسَبِّحْهُ وَأَدْبَارَ ٱلسُّجُودِ ۝

Glorify the praises of your Lord before sunrise and
before sunset. And glorify Him during part of the night
and after the prayers. [50:39-40]

Ibn Rajab then suggests some of the voluntary actions that we can perform during the first and last part of the daytime. Ibn Rajab mentions the words of remembrance that are said after Fajr and Asr; these morning and evening remembrances are collected under different titles, such as *al-Mathurat* and *Athkar al-sabah wa al-masaa'*, and there are many Prophetic narrations extolling the virtues in these remembrances. The early generations emphasized the latter part of the day, giving it more attention than the former. Abdullah bin Mubārak even said, "We heard that whoever ends their day upon the remembrance of God will have his whole day recorded as being in remembrance." The Prophet ﷺ said, **"Remembrance after the dawn prayer is more beloved than freeing four slaves, and after the Asr prayer is more beloved than freeing four slaves."**[5]

Then Ibn Rajab speaks about the third hour mentioned, the last part of the night. He points out how important it is to ask for forgiveness in this hour, as God says about those who strive for excellence:

وَبِٱلْأَسْحَارِ هُمْ يَسْتَغْفِرُونَ ۝

And they pray for forgiveness before dawn. [51:18]

This is the time when God descends, waiting to be asked for help and forgiveness. This time of worship is so important that it was rarely overlooked by the early Muslim community. One of the scholars at that time was incredulous that some people would sleep away this special time, saying, "I never thought that anyone would be asleep before dawn."

The Prophet ﷺ encouraged us to take advantage of these nightly hours of safety and tranquility, comparing our state in this world to someone who is travelling in dangerous territory: **"Whoever is in fear sets out at night, and whoever sets out at night reaches home."**[6] During Ali bin Abu Talib's final years as Caliph, one of his commanders walked in on him at night and found him standing in prayer. Out of sympathy for Ali, he said, "Leader of the Believers! You fast in the day, pray at night, and exhaust yourself even between the two?!" After Ali completed his prayer, he turned and said, "The journey of the afterlife is a long one, and we must travel at night in order to complete it."[7]

The wife of Habeeb Abu Ahmad al-Farisi used to wake her husband up at night while saying, "Get up, Habeeb, for the journey is long, our provision is little, and the righteous caravans have already departed before us and here we are left behind."[8]

Morning Remembrance

In *Madārij al-Sālikeen*, Ibn al-Qayyim directs us to the importance of a focused effort in the early morning, warning us against wasting this time by sleeping. One of the worst things we can do after praying the morning prayer is sleeping before the sun rises. Ibn al-Qayyim calls this "the time to reap the spoils—a time of great opportunity for those who are trekking hard on the journey to God."[9] Even though they may have just spent a part of the night in worship, those who truly yearn for God don't allow themselves to miss out on the opportunity during that time. It is the first part of their day, the key to that day's goodness, and the time in which blessings come down. How positive and productive our day is depends on how we spend that critical hour before sunrise.

The Prophet ﷺ taught us the vital role of this period of the day by urging us to spend it remembering God. He said, **"Whoever prays the dawn prayer in congregation and then sits to remember God until the sun rises, and then prays two units of prayer, will have the equivalent of the rewards of a Hajj and Umrah pilgrimage."** Then he added, **"Completely, completely, completely!"**[10] Ibn al-Qayyim recounts a time when he once visited his teacher Ibn Taymiya. He prayed the Fajr prayer, and then sat to remember God until about noon. Then he turned to Ibn al-Qayyim and said, "This is my breakfast, and without my breakfast, I would lose my strength."

Fridays

Out of all of the days in the week, Friday has a special honor. There is an hour therein where all sincere requests from God are accepted, and we must strive not to let that hour pass us by. The Messenger of Allah 🕊 said, **"There is an hour on Friday during which no Muslim asks God for anything good except that He gives it to him."**[11] Imam al-Nawawi extracts from this *hadith* that it is recommended to make a lot of supplication at all times on Friday from the break of dawn until sunset out of hope to catch this blessed hour.[12] The actual timing of the hour is a matter of debate among scholars. Some hold it to be after dawn and before sunrise, some say it is after the sun passes its zenith, some say after the Asr prayer, and there are other opinions as well. Imam Ahmad's observation is that this hour is after the Asr prayer. He cites the fact that the Prophet's daughter Fatimah used to be keen on making supplication during that hour. She used to instruct her servant to pay attention to the sun and let her know when it began to fall, and would then busy herself with supplication and seeking forgiveness until it set.[13]

We must follow suit and make a conscious effort to set a specific routine for ourselves. Of the most important practices is to prepare and get ready for Jumu'ah (Friday congregational prayer), going to the mosque early looking our best. The Messenger of Allah 🕊 said, **"Whoever bathes and washes himself on Friday, leaving and arriving early—walking, not riding—and then comes close to the imam and listens attentively without speaking will then receive the reward of fasting and praying for a full year with every step."**[14]

Ramadan

The month of Ramadan is the best month of the year. The Messenger of Allah 🕊 said, **"May whoever enters Ramadan and then leaves it without being forgiven be damned!"**[15] During Ramadan the demons are caged, while the atmosphere is filled with prayers, Quran, and God's remembrance. This environment, along with the very act of fasting itself, is highly conducive to taming our souls. We have already discussed the impact of fasting on our hearts and in controlling our nafs, but the time of year that is Ramadan is full of blessings and opportunities beyond fasting. It is the most excellent opportunity of the year to strengthen our faith, but we must prepare for it well by listing our personal spiritual goals and setting a schedule that will make reaching them possible. Note the special times of each day within Ramadan; we must take advantage of every single moment in that blessed month.

The Vacation of a Lifetime

Given how much time and energy we spend toiling for worldly pursuits, it is only appropriate to take time off from work in order to give the soul some rest and tranquility. But it would be a grave mistake to waste your vacation trying to soothe your spiritual component through material pleasures, attempting to fill the intangible void inside of us with temporary gratification. Instead let us use our time off to visit God's Sacred Sanctuary and the Mosque of our beloved Prophet Muhammad ﷺ.

For some people, the Hajj and Umrah pilgrimages are just one-time events to check off on their to-do list, while those who know the value of the pilgrimage yearn to make the trip to Mecca and Medina and plan carefully to make it a reality. They know that no matter how much the trip costs, and no matter what else they might be missing out on, they will always come back having gained rather than lost. The Messenger of Allah ﷺ said, **"Make the Hajj and Umrah pilgrimages repeatedly, for doing so expels poverty and sins just like the oven expels the filth of iron."**[16]

Iman Boosts

These special times are periodic boosts that we can use to advance in our quest of seeking strong *iman*. Look at them as more than just multiplied reward; Allah scattered these kernels throughout the year for us so that we may find one to be the catalyst for reviving our faith. An experience during one of these periods of heightened spiritual engagement could help us return to the life that we were always meant to live: a life with the singular purpose of worshipping our Lord. It might be the starting line for our journey to God, having an impact on our faith that even those around us will notice; our souls will be more calm, and we will be more dedicated to obeying God. We must be vigilant to not allow these opportunities to slip away from us, and we ask God for His assistance in taking advantage of them.

....

ENDNOTES

1. *Lata'if al-Ma'arif* by Ibn Rajab
2. al-Tabarāni, *al-Mu'jam al-Kabeer*, v. 19, p. 233; *as-Silsilah as-Saheehah* 1890
3. al-Bukhari, #6463; Muslim, #2816
4. al-Bukhari, #39
5. Ahmad, #22194
6. al-Tirmidhi, #2450; *as-Silsilah as-Saheehah* 954
7. *al-Mahajjah fee Sayr ad-Duljah* 65-67
8. Ibid
9. *Madārij al-Sālikeen* p. 248
10. al-Tirmidhi, #586; deemed *saheeh* by al-Albani in *as-Saheehah* 3403
11. al-Bukhari, #935; Muslim, #852 in this wording
12. al-Adhkār, p. 129
13. al-Ghazāli, *Ihyā' 'Uloom al-Deen*, v. 1, p. 222
14. Ahmad, #16173; at-Tirmithi (2/367 496) and others
15. Ahmad, #7451
16. Ahmad #167; ibn Majah; deemed *saheeh* by al-Arna'oot

Good Company & Tarbiyah

وَٱصْبِرْ نَفْسَكَ مَعَ ٱلَّذِينَ يَدْعُونَ رَبَّهُم بِٱلْغَدَوٰةِ وَٱلْعَشِيِّ يُرِيدُونَ وَجْهَهُۥ وَلَا
تَعْدُ عَيْنَاكَ عَنْهُمْ تُرِيدُ زِينَةَ ٱلْحَيَوٰةِ ٱلدُّنْيَا وَلَا تُطِعْ مَنْ أَغْفَلْنَا قَلْبَهُۥ عَن
ذِكْرِنَا وَٱتَّبَعَ هَوَىٰهُ وَكَانَ أَمْرُهُۥ فُرُطًا ۝

And patiently stick with those who call upon their Lord
morning and evening, seeking His pleasure. Do not let your
eyes look beyond them, desiring the luxuries of this worldly
life. And do not obey those whose hearts We have made
heedless of Our remembrance, who follow their desires, and
whose state is total loss. [18:28]

Positive spiritual environments and good company are our stabilizers; they help us act upon all of the actions mentioned previously and stay constant in the course of our journey to Allah. Our minds and hearts are constantly flooded with a violent stream of materialist values that inhibit our ascension towards our Lord. In order for us to be able to resist this force, we must join hands with those who only want to please their Lord. To warn us about these dangerous conditions in which we live, and the importance of sticking with those who do good, Allah says,

وَٱلْعَصْرِ ۝ إِنَّ ٱلْإِنسَـٰنَ لَفِى خُسْرٍ ۝ إِلَّا ٱلَّذِينَ ءَامَنُوا وَعَمِلُوا ٱلصَّـٰلِحَـٰتِ
وَتَوَاصَوْا بِٱلْحَقِّ وَتَوَاصَوْا بِٱلصَّبْرِ ۝

By the passing time! Surely humanity is in loss, except those
who have faith, do good, and urge each other to the truth, and
urge each other to perseverance. [103:1-3]

The Dangers of Traveling Alone

Though we shall all be judged before God individually, we should not be traveling alone in this life. When we are alone, our human nature makes it difficult to remain consistent, flitting from one concern to another and experiencing lapses in motivation and energy. But when we are with our brothers and sisters, our mutual support of each other ensures that no one in the group falls behind; when we are lagging there are those who are motivated who can lift us up. They hold our hands and keep us steady until we regain our previous levels of enthusiasm.

Another reason that we need good company on this journey is the fact that we learn so much about ourselves from interacting with others. Our efforts, Islamic work, and deeds are amplified when we are in a group. In *Manhaj al-Tarbiyah al-Islāmiyyah*, Muhammad Qutb writes, 'Being part of a *jama'ah* (a group and a movement) is essential to character and personal development." He continues to explain that our character is assessed through actual interactions with others, in which our values are put to the test.

Within the group should be those who are more seasoned than us who monitor our habits and offer advice and suggestions for improvement. It is easy for someone to be charming for a short period of time while they are aware that their actions are being observed. But it is through authentic and meaningful interactions over a length of time that someone's true personality is shaped; pressure and difficulties will bring out a person's true colors. A *murabbi* (a mentor who facilitates a process of *tarbiyah)* will be more able to help with self-development in the context of a group.

The lonely traveler is easy prey for Satan. The closer we come to God, the more aggressively Satan launches his assault against us, and so not even the pious person is safe to travel without company. Ibn al-Qayyim beautifully demonstrates how for every one of God's commands, Satan has two ways of defeating us: either through negligence or excessiveness. 'Satan does not care how he defeats us..." Ibn al-Qayim points out,

> When he comes to the heart, he opens it up. If he finds
> therein any quality of laziness, carelessness, or negligence,
> he takes advantage of that and attempts to make us fall
> short until we eventually find ourselves insufficient with

regards to all of our duties; and if he finds therein any sort of ambition, passion, or energy, he tries to convince us that what we are doing is not enough, and that we can take on more than what the normal standard is.[1]

Satan's singular goal is to divert us from the straight path, so he does not care if we stray to the left or right.

Most of the practical steps in awakening faith that were laid out in the preceding chapters can benefit greatly from the presence of friends, gatherings, and communities that create environments evoking these spiritual meanings and facilitating consistency. Many of us are inexperienced in self-development and need help with accountability and in charting our path forward. We need the help of someone else to organize our priorities and show us how to apply these strategies of awakening faith in a balanced way.

We are dynamic beings with diverse needs and responsibilities, and we must find the balance in all of these different realms by following a methodology and set of standards. Our knowledge, self-development, teamwork skills, and understanding of dawah are all areas that require our attention, and so it is helpful to proceed with the help of a gradual, balanced curriculum, Even if we excel in one area of personal development, it is likely that we will not be able to address all areas of our development on our own without methodology and mentorship.

There is even a science in Islamic studies called *Fiqh al-Awlawiyaat* (Fiqh of Priorities), which helps us determine what actions and issues should be given more attention in our individual and societal lives. Someone may find immense sweetness in waking up early to pray before dawn, but if this voluntary act is causing him or her to sleep through the day, missing classes or work, and perhaps even missing an obligatory prayer, it is clear that their priorities are misaligned. Ibn Taymiyah says about intellect: "The intelligent one is not the one who knows good from bad, but the one who knows the better of two good things and the worse of two bad things."[2] Such wisdom is difficult to attain on our own, and when we do attain that knowledge, we still require mentorship and practice to understand the applications of that knowledge.

The Need for Good Company

Good friends and company are more important now than ever, with the Muslim body scattered and shattered. We have no central government or institutions, and our communal spiritual momentum has dwindled. People have grown further from religion in unprecedented numbers and in ways that those before us could never have imagined.

Islam is not limited to spirituality and self-improvement alone. Benefiting and helping others improve is part and parcel of our practice of Islam, as there is a concept in our tradition of "promoting good and preventing evil," which is an obligation for every Muslim. These responsibilities don't fall to the wayside, no matter how diligently we pray and fast and no matter how bleak our surroundings may be. We must strive to change the conditions around us to be aligned with God's true faith on all possible levels, freeing all who are oppressed and supporting every just cause—and this is for the general good of every human being.

Of God's mercy to us is that He placed among us role models and revivalist who put forth a vision and model of positive change. Among these figures is Hasan al-Banna, who sparked a revivalist and reform movement in Egypt called the Muslim Brotherhood in the 1930's which would reinvigorate the understanding and application of Islam around the world. Imam al-Banna studied the reality of his surroundings and took note of the various reform methodologies of his time. He observed that these methodologies addressed certain areas of reform while neglecting others, often focusing on the knowledge and theoretical aspects of righteousness while neglecting the practical dimensions. This connection between knowledge and action was the missing link within existing religious reform movements. He came to the conclusion that reform of the ummah, the global Muslim community, begins with practical reform of the self, and reform of the self must take place within an environment of *tarbiyah*, holistic development and training. He writes in one of his letters:

> The objective of this movement is essentially to produce a new generation of believers with the correct Islamic principles. We are attempting to mold the global Muslim community upon the complete form of Islam in every facet of life.

صِبْغَةَ ٱللَّهِ وَمَنْ أَحْسَنُ مِنَ ٱللَّهِ صِبْغَةً وَنَحْنُ لَهُۥ عَٰبِدُونَ ۝

This is the way of Allah. And who is better than Allah in his way? [2:138]

> The way to do this is to change the societal standards of good and to raise the next generation of *dawah* helpers, activists and teachers, upon these principles so that they will be role models for others to hold tight to the same principles, remain firm upon them, and to stay compliant with God's law. *Tarbiyah* (holistic

ummah:

the collective body of Muslims, across time and space

أمة

dawah:

an invitation, a call; the mission of calling people to worship God and follow His guidance

دعوة

development and training) is the best way to revive the Muslim *ummah*. Our goal is to develop a new generation of people who strive against their *nafs* and who are capable of influencing others and taking on any challenge.[3]

...We are in the phase of formation and development. Do not be distracted from the work of development and preparation; put ninety percent of your energy into developing yourself and others. The remaining ten percent is for other matters. This is so that we are toughened up, fully prepared and equipped for when Allah opens the hearts of our people, and He is the best of Openers...Our battle is one of self-discipline. Working on ourselves is our first responsibility, so strive against your own self![4]

The Meaning of Tarbiyah

Imam al-Bayḍāwi, one of the foremost scholars of Quranic Commentary, defines *tarbiyah* as a gradual growth into the ideal form.[5] It also means to translate one's acquired knowledge of something into practice. Knowledge is nothing but ink on paper until it is translated into real-world application, and tarbiyah is the process that enables that application.

Turning knowledge into practice was one of the highest priorities for God's Messengers. Prophet Abraham called out to God:

$$\text{رَبَّنَا وَٱبْعَثْ فِيهِمْ رَسُولًا مِّنْهُمْ يَتْلُوا عَلَيْهِمْ ءَايَـٰتِكَ وَيُعَلِّمُهُمُ ٱلْكِتَـٰبَ}$$
$$\text{وَٱلْحِكْمَةَ وَيُزَكِّيهِمْ إِنَّكَ أَنتَ ٱلْعَزِيزُ ٱلْحَكِيمُ ۝}$$

"Our Lord! Raise from among them a messenger who will
recite to them Your revelations, teach them the Book and
wisdom, and purify them. Indeed, You alone are the Almighty,
All-Wise." [2:129]

Notice how Abraham put knowledge before self-purification, even though we are in need of both of them. Later come the verses that mention the goals of the Messengers, wherein God says,

$$\text{كَمَآ أَرْسَلْنَا فِيكُمْ رَسُولًا مِّنكُمْ يَتْلُوا عَلَيْكُمْ ءَايَـٰتِنَا}$$
$$\text{وَيُزَكِّيكُمْ وَيُعَلِّمُكُمُ ٱلْكِتَـٰبَ وَٱلْحِكْمَةَ وَيُعَلِّمُكُم مَّا لَمْ تَكُونُوا}$$
$$\text{تَعْلَمُونَ ۝}$$

Since We have sent you a messenger from among yourselves—
reciting to you Our revelations, purifying you, teaching you the
Book and wisdom, and teaching you what you never knew [2:151]

Notice now that when Allah spoke, He put self-purification before knowledge to emphasize its precedence.

For most people, the application of knowledge requires consistency, accountability and follow-up. How many times have we sat in lectures and heard reminders, and then afterwards changed nothing major about ourselves? It's because many of us don't have tools and mentors to take us gently by the hand and firmly push us to apply what we learn. A conviction in the mind is not enough to change our spiritual failures and bad habits, and behaving well once or twice is not enough to make good behavior a part of your nature. Conviction must be followed by long-term practice and implementation of that behavior until it becomes our second nature. Good actions will then become second nature for us, without having to think about them beforehand. But this does not happen overnight; it requires patience, persistence, commitment, and accountability. Jawdat Said writes,

> What is important is not just to have the idea. It comes down to turning the thoughts into faith that permeates your entire behavior. When people possess an idea, it does not necessarily mean that it has any impact on their faith or behavior. How often do people speak about justice and equality, but when it comes to applying it, their cultural values prove to be more deeply rooted."[6]

Muhammad Qutb writes along the same lines in his *Manhaj al-Tarbiyah al-Islāmiyyah*. He points out that developing good character requires a long period of conditioning until it becomes a habit. Cleansing our souls takes consistent effort, and the stains will not come out with just one attempt, as they are intertwined with our spiritual fabric. The goal is to repair the human soul and heart, which are not mechanical devices with buttons and gears that you can leave running while you tend to your other affairs. They are dynamic, multi-faceted, immaterial substances with various demands, each requiring special attention and supervision. This is what Muhammad Qutb says makes tarbiyah difficult but at the same time absolutely necessary. He concludes, "It is either persistent effort, or loss."[7]

Three Elements of Tarbiyah

◁(Tarbiyah Elements)▷

Deeply rooted faith
Personal development
Consistent action

Hassan al-Banna writes, "All of the sermons, lessons and lectures describing the problems and prescribing the solutions will not achieve anything or bring about any benefit on their own." He continues to identify three essential ingredients required for a movement to bring about change in people: deep faith, personal development, and continuous action. These are three universal principles of tarbiyah that "can not be changed or substituted."[8]

Deep faith is listed first as a foundation for the process of self-development and discipline we know as tarbiyah. Spiritual development must be tended first before other aspects, and its ultimate objective is to keep our hearts connected to Allah. Once that is established, the rest of the foundations for tarbiyah become easier to complete, for when the heart is sound, the rest of the body is sound and more willing to comply. When the faith component of tarbiyah is established, the connection between the heart and its Creator is open. Changing actions and behaviors can now be achieved through light touches: gentle, sometimes indirect, instruction and reminders. This is the curriculum given by God to the Companions. They might not have been able to comply with the prohibition of alcohol and the change of the direction of prayer so readily if their Lord had not developed and softened their hearts first.

Personal development is the second foundational concept to tarbiyah, and it is the key to developing a Muslim identity. We can also call it self-purification or *tazkiyah*. Through this approach we escape the rut of complacency and move into the mindset of growth. This phase is a fight against our *nafs*—our egoistic self—and a campaign to purify our character from seven major illnesses: attachment to the immediate life, seeking validation of others, ingratitude, conceit, arrogance, delusion, and lust. Purging our character of these diseases might take some time, for there is no shortcut in the process. Self-discipline is difficult and requires effort. It is the ultimate form of internalizing the phrase, "There is no source of power or might but God," and translating it into daily practice and a way of life. Allah will help us in this pursuit if we work hard and strive:

$$وَٱلَّذِينَ جَٰهَدُوا فِينَا لَنَهْدِيَنَّهُمْ سُبُلَنَا$$

As for those who struggle in Our cause, We will surely guide them along Our Way. [29:69]

If we have laid the first foundation of *iman* well, it should help keep us motivated in our self-development struggle. A reservoir of strong *iman* will lift our morale and fuel our commitment to improving ourselves.

Consistent action is the third foundation for *tarbiyah*, and it can also be framed as playing a role in *dawah* and activism. The goal of this method of *tarbiyah* is to develop the Muslim so that he or she is capable of striving for the sake of Allah, inviting others to Islam and working for the betterment of society.

When we talk about *dawah*, we mean it in its broadest sense: educating the Muslim community about Islam's application in every aspect of life; working to revive Islamic principles; calling others to apply the rulings of Allah and to establish justice on earth; advocating for the oppressed and serving the needs of people; and educating non-Muslims about God.

Dawah (calling to Allah) is one of the greatest endeavors anyone can undertake. One who does so follows the path of God's messengers, which is why God says,

$$وَمَنْ أَحْسَنُ قَوْلًا مِّمَّن دَعَآ إِلَى ٱللَّهِ وَعَمِلَ صَٰلِحًا وَقَالَ إِنَّنِي مِنَ ٱلْمُسْلِمِينَ ۞$$

And whose words are better than someone who calls to Allah,
does good, and says, "I am truly one of those who submit"?

[41:33]

$$قُلْ إِنِّي لَن يُجِيرَنِي مِنَ ٱللَّهِ أَحَدٌ وَلَنْ أَجِدَ مِن دُونِهِۦ مُلْتَحَدًا ۞ إِلَّا بَلَٰغًا مِّنَ ٱللَّهِ وَرِسَٰلَٰتِهِۦ وَمَن يَعْصِ ٱللَّهَ وَرَسُولَهُۥ فَإِنَّ لَهُۥ نَارَ جَهَنَّمَ خَٰلِدِينَ فِيهَآ أَبَدًا ۞$$

Say, "No one can protect me from Allah, nor can I find any
refuge other than Him. I am only to convey from Allah and
His messages." [72:22-23]

Sayyid Qutb points out in his explanation of the latter verse,

> There is a gravity conveyed here that overwhelms the hearts with the importance of the message and dawah. The Messenger ﷺ was tasked with conveying the divine message to humanity: he is obligated to convey, no one can protect him from God, and the only way for him to be saved from punishment was to spread the message. The Prophet ﷺ says, 'this is my only refuge and my only protection—it is not by my command, but by the command of God that I convey this message. It is Allah's will, there is no escape from it, and no one can protect me from Allah! We can sense the urgency and gravity of the mission of dawah conveyed in these verses.
>
> After the Prophet, this mission of spreading God's religion falls on our shoulders, and it is not a voluntary mission. It is our responsibility; a pressing and clear-cut directive from Allah. There is no escaping it, and we will be held accountable for it. This mission of conveying guidance and goodness to people is not a volunteer position or a source of personal fulfilment; it is the highest mandate. This is how the Prophet ﷺ explained the responsibility of dawah; as a mandatory mission, rooted in reverence and glory, assigned by the Most High.[9]

The three elements of tarbiyah are all interconnected. Personal development and consistent action in dawah are sustained by the first foundation of deep faith. Sustained by deep-rooted *iman*, the process of refining our personalities and engaging in good deeds and activism will come more easily. To focus on the first component is not neglecting the others, but rather it is an ordering of priorities. We awakening the faith in our hearts first in order for it to become the generator that sustains our efforts in the long-term process of *tarbiyah*. Working in Islamic work and *dawah* requires a motivational force to keep us going for long periods of time, for there are challenges and roadblocks that will inevitably be met with along the path. When we face injustices and work hard to expose corruption and relieve the suffering of others, we risk burnout and low morale if we do not continually renew our *iman*.

Opting to isolate ourselves from society, abandoning good company and retreating into our own shells is not the solution; what use is a renewal of faith if you will not move forward with it? This is a shirking of the responsibility of dawah to Allah, especially in such a time when the Muslim ummah is deeply in need. The Companions and those who came after them understood this concept very well, and would heavily criticize anyone who chose seclusion over community involvement, even if their excuse was to "focus on worship."

....

A bdullah bin Mas'ood once heard that some men left the city of Kufa to focus on their own worship in a nearby village, and so he visited them. They were delighted by his arrival, and when he asked them what caused them to move away, they said, "We wanted to avoid the distraction of other people and just focus on worship." Abdullah said, "If others did as you are doing, then who would fight off the enemies? I will not leave until you come back!"[10]

....

There is another important point to take note of with regards to interacting with others around us: when we abandon the path of working and striving in all of its forms, we will have trouble understanding the Quran. Reading the Quran while distant from the realities and challenges of society leads to a limited perspective. The Quran is a book of guidance and healing. It contains a solution for any problem that a person or society might face. But when someone remains tucked away and isolated, what social challenges are they facing for the Quran to be able to solve? How will they be able to truly practice the verses of patience, steadfastness, and struggle? These verses are not to be understood in a vacuum, and one will only truly understand them when they have lived alongside the verses in real life. To understand anything completely, you must be able to apply it and envision its context and full implications.

We can now see why it is crucial to engage all of the foundations of tarbiyah at the same time. Each provides a unique perspective of understanding that helps to form our foundational knowledge. Though the focus on faith in the *tarbiyah* process might take precedence over the other two components, it should be a temporary emphasis until we develop a solid connection with Allah and purify our intentions. *Iman* must be the driving force for our actions, rather than doing things out of shame, habit, or to please others. With *iman* in the forefront, we will be rewarded for every action we do, regardless of its size. Allah says,

ذَٰلِكَ بِأَنَّهُمْ لَا يُصِيبُهُمْ ظَمَأٌ وَلَا نَصَبٌ وَلَا مَخْمَصَةٌ فِي سَبِيلِ ٱللَّهِ وَلَا
يَطَؤُونَ مَوْطِئًا يَغِيظُ ٱلْكُفَّارَ وَلَا يَنَالُونَ مِنْ عَدُوٍّ نَّيْلًا إِلَّا كُتِبَ لَهُم
بِهِۦ عَمَلٌ صَٰلِحٌ إِنَّ ٱللَّهَ لَا يُضِيعُ أَجْرَ ٱلْمُحْسِنِينَ ۝

That is because whenever they suffer from thirst, fatigue, or hunger in the cause of Allah; or tread on a territory, unnerving the disbelievers; or inflict any loss on an enemy—it is written to their credit as a good deed. Surely Allah never discounts the reward of the good-doers. [9:120]

A Faith-First Tarbiyah Approach

Beginning with faith is appropriate because when the faith of individuals increases, so does the brotherhood between them. This brotherhood is based on *iman* and sincerity and creates a *tarbiyah*-conducive environment, with a special feeling and sweetness.

The hearts of the Ansar (the Companions who had been living in Medina before the Prophet's migration) reached that level and sweetness of faith, and so they welcomed their brothers and sisters who fled their homes in Mecca in search of refuge in an unprecedented and unparalleled way. God said about them,

وَٱلَّذِينَ تَبَوَّءُو ٱلدَّارَ وَٱلْإِيمَٰنَ مِن قَبْلِهِمْ يُحِبُّونَ مَنْ هَاجَرَ إِلَيْهِمْ وَلَا يَجِدُونَ فِي
صُدُورِهِمْ حَاجَةً مِّمَّآ أُوتُوا وَيُؤْثِرُونَ عَلَىٰ أَنفُسِهِمْ وَلَوْ كَانَ بِهِمْ خَصَاصَةٌ وَمَن
يُوقَ شُحَّ نَفْسِهِۦ فَأُوْلَٰٓئِكَ هُمُ ٱلْمُفْلِحُونَ ۝

As for those who had settled in the city and in the faith before they arrived, they love whoever emigrates to them, never having a desire in their hearts for whatever is given to the emigrants. They give them preference over themselves even though they may be in dire need. And whoever is saved from the selfishness of their own souls, it is they who are truly successful. [59:9]

Starting with *iman* as the first step in *tarbiyah* also makes it easy to perform our other obligations. This was the methodology followed by the Messenger of Allah ﷺ in developing the spiritual wellness of his Companions. He worked to connect their hearts to God first, and then directed them to the required actions. Many of his instructions begin with, "Whoever believes in God and the Last Day must…" so that the heart fixed in faith eagerly awaits the instructions to come. As one of many *hadiths* that open with a line that appeals to faith, Abu Dharr narrates that the Messenger of Allah ﷺ said, **"Whoever believes in Allah and the Last day must not harm his neighbor, and treat women well!"**[11]

Tarbiyah Support Groups

It is especially important to develop good friendship and companionship that fosters our tarbiyah, provides mentorship and supports us in these three aspects of deep faith, self-development, and consistent action. These tarbiyah support systems often begin in the form of a family, a circle of friends, or a group of people who come together to work for good. After that, it is expected that Allah will allow these circles to expand and become regenerative sources of faith, allowing other seekers to discover *iman* and begin their own quest of self-purification and *tarbiyah*.

Being in a group removes the intimidation around awakening faith. Many people may be inexperienced in taking the first steps, or think that it is too nebulous or daunting an undertaking. Having a mentor and being part of a *tarbiyah* support system will guide an individual through the practical application and break down some of the mental barriers. He or she will not feel alone in their journey to Allah, heartened by the physical presence and examples of others.

> Engaging with the Quran and learning the art of Quranic reflection benefits from some level of mentorship and group setting. Observing how others connect with the Quran, summoning verses in discussions around different Islamic meanings and drawing connections to personal experiences will help us improve our own ability to engage with the Quran and extract insights during our own recitations. The art of reflecting deeply on the Quran, especially for non-Arabic speakers, can be learned through application, continuous practice, and observing others, all which are readily found in a support group setting.

Moreover, there are pitfalls along the way that may affect one individual alone, but a support system and mentorship can counteract those imbalances. To give one example, the extremes of either having too much fear of God to the point that it paralyzes you spiritually or believing oneself to be guaranteed paradise can both be avoided through balanced methods, such as visiting a graveyard as a group, visiting sick members of the community, or holding a workshop on writing one's will. Imagine the impact that these communal hands-on experiences and ensuing discussions will have on those who are on both ends of the spectrum of fearing God.

A community can also work together to encourage attending the mosque and taking advantage of the blessed times throughout the year, methods of increasing *iman* that were recounted in an earlier chapter. The active leaders in the community can send reminders to their groups to take a break from the world for a few minutes before Maghrib on Friday to supplicate during the hour when prayers are answered. Community members can take turns weekly holding *iftar* dinners on Thursdays to motivate their friends and families to fast. Some mosques have even begun to hold weekend group prayers after midnight in order to take full advantage of that blessed hour in the last third of the night when God's presence is most imminent. There can be classes for Quran recitation or on the meanings of the daily words of prayer after the Fajr prayer until sunrise, giving people an extra reason to stay in the mosque for that time so that they can all reap the hefty reward for doing so. All of these are feasible ways to create a community environment that nurtures the souls of its members.

Tarbiyah and Balance

It is also the responsibility of a *tarbiyah* support group to educate and emphasize the correct understanding of the religion, especially the concept of balance. The Prophetic approach is the only effective antidote for rigidity and extremism. Ibn Rajab writes in *al-Maḥajjah fee Sayr al-Duljah* that the most beloved actions to Allah are those that are accurate, balanced, and don't entail undue hardship, for Allah says,

$$يُرِيدُ ٱللَّهُ بِكُمُ ٱلْيُسْرَ وَلَا يُرِيدُ بِكُمُ ٱلْعُسْرَ$$

Allah intends ease for you, not hardship... [2:185]

Ibn Rajab points out that the Prophet ﷺ prohibited going to extreme measures for worship, such as celibacy, refusing to sleep in order to pray the whole night, and fasting every day. He said, **"I, on the other hand, fast sometimes and eat sometimes. I pray and I sleep, and I marry women. So whoever is averse to my way then has nothing to do with me."**[12]

The Prophet ﷺ also said, **"Aim straight, do your best, and rejoice."**[13] Ibn Rajab says that to "aim straight" means to be accurate in your actions, taking a balanced and moderate approach in worship, neither falling short of what is required nor exceeding the boundaries of the Prophet's ﷺ beautiful example. He also explains that the Prophet ﷺ said "rejoice," because anyone who obeys God as accurately as possible should be delighted, as he will surpass someone who exerts all of their time and energy to ritual worship while neglecting other responsibilities. The path of balance and doing one's best is the correct approach, and the guidance of Muhammad ﷺ is better than that of anyone else. Our rank with God is not based on the quantity of our actions, but rather on the quality of our sincerity to Him and the degree to which we emulate the practice of His Messenger ﷺ.

Ibn Rajab also states that when someone has knowledge of God and His religion, and gives definition to that knowledge by internalizing a fear, hope, and love for Him, this person is better than someone who has none of that but exhausts themselves physically in what they believe is worship. This is why those who knew Abu Bakr used to say that he did not attain his place above everyone else in the community by virtue of any action, but rather it was through something that settled firmly in his heart. Ibn Mas'ood even said to his students once, "You fast and pray more than Muhammad's Companions did, but they are still better than you." They asked, "How is that?" He responded, "They were less interested than you are in this world, and more eager than you are for the next."[14]

The Companions were not interested in the temporal and inferior pleasures of this life; even when they did engage them, their hearts were preoccupied with a yearning for the next life. This is what they learned from the Prophet ﷺ, for he was able to maintain his singular focus on God while engaging with the creation empathetically and with deep consideration. He managed to carry the burdens of his prophethood while keeping full command of his roles as a political, military, community leader; husband and father; mentor, teacher, and friend. The righteous leaders who took his place thereafter followed suit.

The most impactful figures in Islamic history were not always those who performed the greatest quantity of ritual worship, but they reached the crests of piety and faith, such that their hearts took residence in the next life before their bodies could catch up. The best are those who follow the path of the Prophet ﷺ and the most virtuous Companions in their balanced approach to ritual worship and consistent efforts to improve the condition of their hearts and their communities. Ibn Rajab completes his analysis of this concept with a beautiful analogy: "We only reach our destination when we journey with our hearts, before our bodies."[15]

Tarbiyah in our Social Gatherings

A powerful technique to keep our communities focused on spiritual growth and refinement is to begin our social gatherings with the remembrance of God. This helps everyone present transition from the exhausting chaos of the world they live in to the comforting relief of God's remembrance. There might be among those present some who subconsciously believe that they are disqualified from God's mercy because of their sins and distance from the religion. Engaging them regularly, even with a short word or two to help them realize that God's door is always open and encourage them to seek another chance.

If we take advantage of these opportunities to influence the individuals in our community who are hanging to faith by a thread, we will be developing their hearts and minds to better understand the religion and the world around them.

$$\text{لِنَجْعَلَهَا لَكُمْ تَذْكِرَةً وَتَعِيَهَا أُذُنٌ وَاعِيَةٌ ۝}$$

So that We may make this a reminder to you, and that attentive ears may grasp it. [69:12]

Gradually wearing down the crust of ignorance in the hearts of people will eventually produce a more tender-hearted community. This long-term effect of starting our gatherings by mentioning God is in addition to the immediate fruit that the Prophet ﷺ informed us about:

> God has angels who tour the earth, other than those who record people's deeds. They walk the streets searching for people in remembrance, and when they find people remembering God, they call out to one another: "Come to what you seek!" and they encircle them with their wings up to the lowest sky. Their Lord asks them, even though He knows more than they do, "What are my servants saying?" They respond, "They are glorifying you, magnifying you, praising you, and declaring your majesty." He asks, "Have they seen me?" They say, "No, by God they have not seen you." He asks, "Then how would it be if they did see me?" and they respond, "If they saw you, they would be even more intense in their worship, declaring your majesty more intensely and glorifying you more often."
>
> Allah then asks, "What are they asking of me?" and they say, "They are asking you for Paradise." He asks, "Have they seen it?" and they respond, "No, by God, our Lord, they have not seen it." He asks, "Then how would it be if they saw it?" They respond, "If they saw it, they would be more eager for it, requesting it more intensely and yearning for it." He asks, "What are they seeking protection from?" They respond, "From the Hellfire." Allah then asks, "Have they seen it?" and they respond, "No, by God, our Lord, they have not seen it." He asks, "Then how would it be if they saw it?" They say, "If they saw it, they would flee from it more fearfully and be terribly afraid of it." He says, "Then I call you to witness that I have forgiven them!" One angel out of them all then notices, "But there is this man among them who only came for some other reason." God says, "They are a people whose company brings no sorrow."[16]

It is understood from this *hadith* that even the passerby who just happened to end up in the company of the righteous was included in God's expansive forgiveness. We should strive to transform more of our gatherings, in every setting and with every group of people, into gatherings of remembrance, so that more people are encircled by wings of angels and Allah's forgiveness and guidance.

Tarbiyah, Good Company and Paradise

Perhaps the most appropriate spiritual topic to speak about in any social gathering is Paradise. We should dream of Paradise together, mentioning what we know of it and reminding each other about its descriptions. Just a brief mention of this inspires a yearning in the heart for it and helps put the temporal pleasures of this world into perspective. A culture of speaking about Paradise will help people realize in which of the two they should invest their time and effort. The pleasures of this world will come to their eventual end. Paradise, on the other hand, is not only beautiful and pristine, but the people therein will never have to worry about any expiration dates:

خَٰلِدِينَ فِيهَا لَا يَبْغُونَ عَنْهَا حِوَلًا ۝

They will be there forever, never desiring anywhere else. [18:108]

The people of Paradise will never grow old, fall ill, or die. They will not experience any form of worry, grief, or loss once they have entered the realm of eternity. Everyone will experience joy and vast vistas to explore and rest our eyes upon, to extents that exceed our most ambitious imaginations:

وَإِذَا رَأَيْتَ ثَمَّ رَأَيْتَ نَعِيمًا وَمُلْكًا كَبِيرًا ۝

And everywhere you look, you will see delight and a vast kingdom. [76:20]

There will be castles unlike anything you've seen before, whose descriptions cannot be encompassed by any human language. Our imaginations are bound by our own experiences, so we even though we may try to imagine Paradise, remember that the sum total of any beauty found on earth is not even worth the wing of a fly to God. So when Paradise is described as having castles, rivers, food, and drink, realize that the only similarity shared between what is here and what is there is the name.

To demonstrate the vastness of Paradise, the Messenger of Allah said, **"There is a tree in Paradise in whose shadow a rider would trail for one hunred years. If you wish, recite [this verse]:**[17]

وَظِلٍّ مَّمْدُودٍ ۝

... and extended shade... [56:30]

The most distinguished reward in Paradise is the chance for the believers to finally see the face of Allah—the Lord to whom they dedicated their lives without ever having seen Him before. The Prophet ﷺ said, **"When the people of Paradise enter Paradise, God, the Exalted, says, 'Do you want me to give you something more?' They will respond, 'Have you not already delighted our faces? Have you not already brought us into Paradise and saved us from the Hellfire?' He will then lift the veil, and they will not have been given anything more beloved to them than to look upon their Lord."**[18] All of the painful and dark moments of this life will fade when the believers' sights rest upon their Lord:

$$\text{مَن كَانَ يَرْجُو لِقَاءَ اللَّهِ فَإِنَّ أَجَلَ اللَّهِ لَآتٍ}$$

Whoever hopes for the meeting with Allah—Allah's appointed
time is sure to come. [29:5]

Paradise is where we will also have the pleasure of meeting our beloved Prophet, Muhammad bin Abdullah ﷺ. We will finally see that smile and voice we heard so much about and could only imagine in our own minds prior to that moment—the man who taught us everything worth knowing, and so we prayed for him night and day, yearning to see him in a dream. He will be standing there to embrace us and welcome us. He may invite us to sit in the company of the other prophets, the Companions, and all of the heroes throughout history whose stories inspired us growing up. We may not think that we belong there, or even that it is possible for us to be in the company of those who are so superior to us in rank. But this is, after all, Paradise:

$$\text{لَهُم مَّا يَشَاءُونَ فِيهَا وَلَدَيْنَا مَزِيدٌ}$$

There they will have whatever they desire, and with Us is
more. [30:35]

Think about the moment when you will finally see those you love most again. After years of death and separation, families of righteous believers will be reunited at the gates of Paradise. This is a thought that soothes the grief of anyone who has lost someone dear to them, and the image of that scene can be enough to encourage them to continue their loved one's legacy of righteousness by improving their own actions. Allah says,

$$\text{وَالَّذِينَ آمَنُوا وَاتَّبَعَتْهُمْ ذُرِّيَّتُهُم بِإِيمَانٍ أَلْحَقْنَا بِهِمْ ذُرِّيَّتَهُمْ وَمَا أَلَتْنَاهُم مِّنْ}$$
$$\text{عَمَلِهِم مِّن شَيْءٍ}$$

As for those who believe and whose descendants follow them
in faith, We will elevate their descendants to their rank, never
discounting any of their deeds. [52:21]

The Messenger of Allah ﷺ even describes how we will reach one another in Paradise when the desire to see each other arises. He said,

> When the people of Paradise enter Paradise and some of them will feel a yearning to see the others, the bed of one will travel to the other, and the bed of the other will travel to him until they meet together. One of them will say to his Companion, "Do you remember when it was that God forgave us?" The other will say, "On that day when we were in that place, and we called out to Allah, Mighty and Majestic. Then He forgave us."[19]

In Paradise we will also see the condition of the tyrants and sinners being punished in the Hellfire. We will see Pharaoh and his supporters, and every transgressor who sold their afterlife for short-lived power and pleasures. We will see those whom Allah describes so often in the Quran:

$$\text{ٱلَّذِينَ طَغَوْا۟ فِى ٱلْبِلَـٰدِ ۝ فَأَكْثَرُوا۟ فِيهَا ٱلْفَسَادَ ۝}$$

They all transgressed throughout the land, spreading much corruption there. [89:11-23]

This is not spiteful, but rather to gratify those who suffered grievously at the hands of these oppressors. It is only befitting that their example be used to relieve the hearts upon which they inflicted pain.

Reminding those around us about Paradise and its encompassing delights will help develop communities of individuals who dream of the hereafter and compete with one another to work hard, help each other, and do good. Allah demands such an environment, inciting us towards it:

$$\text{وَسَارِعُوٓا۟ إِلَىٰ مَغْفِرَةٍ مِّن رَّبِّكُمْ وَجَنَّةٍ عَرْضُهَا ٱلسَّمَـٰوَٰتُ وَٱلْأَرْضُ أُعِدَّتْ لِلْمُتَّقِينَ ۝}$$

And hasten towards forgiveness from your Lord and a Paradise as vast as the heavens and the earth, prepared for those who are mindful. [3:133]

Such reminders also help us stay patient through the pressure and trials that we encounter on our journey to God, helping us realize that we do not belong here in this world and that we will soon enough return to our first home.

Rejoice! For the Garden of Paradise, your first home
Is filled with comforts, delights, and glittering gold

We may now be prisoners of our enemy, but we hope
That we will soon be welcomed back to our first abode

The Messenger of Allah ﷺ would remind his Companions constantly of Paradise, shifting their perspectives away from the transient pleasures of this world. When he was once gifted a silk garment, they began to crowd around him and marvel at how soft it was. The Messenger of Allah ﷺ noticed this and said, **"The handkerchiefs of Sa'd bin Mu'ādh in Paradise are better than this,"**[20] reminiscing about one of his Companions who had died from his battle wounds.

He also taught them a valuable lesson in mentioning even the person with the lowest rank in Paradise. Abdullah bin Mas'ood reports that the Prophet ﷺ said,

> I certainly know of the last of the people of the Hellfire to exit it, and the last of the people of Paradise to enter it. A man will exit the Hellfire crawling, and God will say to him: "Go, enter Paradise." He will reach it, but it will appear to him that it is full. He will go back and say: "My Master, I found it to be full!" God will repeat: "Go, enter Paradise." He will reach it, but it will again appear to him that it is fully occupied. He will go back and say: "My Master, I found it to be full!" Then He will say: "Go, enter Paradise, for you will have what is equal to the world, and ten times its like" (or: "ten times as much as what is equal to the world"). The man will ask: "Are you mocking me?" (or: "do you laugh at me?"), while you are the King?"[21]

Abdullah bin Mas'ood then commented: "I saw the Messenger of Allah ﷺ smiling so widely that his molar teeth showed. It is said that this is the lowest status of the people of Paradise."

....

The Prophet ﷺ also related a story of when Prophet Moses asked God about the last man to enter Paradise. God responded: "He is a man who will come after the inhabitants of Paradise have been admitted into it. He will be told: "Enter Paradise," but he will say: "How, my Lord, when the people have already settled in their abodes and taken their rewards?" He will be asked: "Would you like to receive what a king on earth would have owned?" He will respond: "I would be pleased, O my Lord!" Then He will say: "Then you shall receive that, plus one more like it, plus one more like it, plus one more like it, plus one more like it…"

The Prophet ﷺ said that the fifth time repeating it, the man said: "I am pleased, my Lord!" Then Allah will say: "You shall have this ten times over! You shall have whatever your soul desires and your eye yearns for!" The man will then say: "I am pleased, my Lord!"[22]

....

If this is the state of the lowest ranking person in Paradise, isn't it something worthy of working for? The Prophet ﷺ challenged the Companions: "**Isn't there anyone who will strive for Paradise? Paradise is not imaginable. It is—by the Lord of the Kaaba!—a shimmering light, a fluttering basil blossom, a looming palace, a flowing river, ripe and abundant fruit, a beautiful spouse, and plenty of fine garments in an eternal realm filled with splendor and brilliance in a magnificent, lofty, and peaceful abode.**" They said, "We will be the ones who strive for it, Messenger of Allah!" He said, "Say, 'God willing.'"[23]

May we advance in our faith journey with the company of good people, striving and struggling against our own selves, until we feel the breezes of Paradise on our cheeks, God willing.

....

ENDNOTES

1. *al-Wābil al-Ṣayyib*, p. 25
2. *Mahjmooʻ al-Fatāwa*, v. 20, p. 53
3. *Majmooʻ Rasāʼil al-Imām al-Shaheed Ḥasan al-Bannā*
4. *Bayān lil-Ikhwān*
5. *Tafseer al-Baydāwi*, v. 1, p. 28
6. *Be Like Adam's Son*
7. *Manhaj al-Tarbiyah al-Islāmiyyah*, v. 2, p. 85
8. *Risālah bayn al-Ams wal-Yawm*, p. 161
9. *Fee Ẓilāl al-Qurʼān*, v. 6, pp. 3736-3737
10. Ibn al-Mubārak, *al-Zuhd*, #1104
11. al-Bukhari, #5186; Muslim, #1468
12. al-Bukhari, #5063: Muslim #1401
13. al-Bukhari, #6467; Muslim, #2818
14. al-Ḥākim, *al-Mustadrak*, #7880
15. *al-Mahajjah fi Siyar ad-Duljah*, Ibn Rajab, p. 57
16. Ahmad, #7424
17. al-Bukhari, #3252; Muslim, #2826
18. Muslim 181
19. Ibn Abu Dunya, *Sifat al-Jannah*, #223
20. al-Bukhari, #3249; Muslim, #2468
21. al-Bukhari, #6571; Muslim, #186
22. Muslim, #189
23. Ibn Mājah, #4332

Hope

The first chapter addressed in detail the concept of fearing God, and so in order to strike the right balance, we must also speak about hope before the end of this book. These two concepts are inseparable and must be engaged in tandem in order for our *iman* to be sustainable and stable.

Those who contemplate the Quran know the recurrent themes of fear and hope that appear side by side. They may take the form of warnings and incentives, or descriptions of Paradise and Hellfire within the same passage. This pattern can also be noticed in the teachings of the Prophet ﷺ and in how he instructed His Companions. He once said, **"Were the believer to know of the punishment that Allah has, no one would ever aspire for His Paradise. If the unbeliever knew of the mercy that Allah had, no one would ever give up on His Paradise."[1]** He also said, **"Paradise is closer to you than your own shoelace, as is the Hellfire."[2]**

This is the way of the Quran, and by practicing emotions of both fear and hope in our relationship with Allah, we may reach the level of those whom Allah describes:

تَتَجَافَىٰ جُنُوبُهُمْ عَنِ ٱلْمَضَاجِعِ يَدْعُونَ رَبَّهُمْ خَوْفًا وَطَمَعًا وَمِمَّا رَزَقْنَٰهُمْ يُنفِقُونَ ۝

They abandon their beds, invoking their Lord with hope and fear, and donate from what We have provided for them. [32:16]

The Quran teaches the heart to engage with both hope and fear, pulled in both directions, suspended between the two.

وَيُحَذِّرُكُمُ ٱللَّهُ نَفْسَهُۥ وَٱللَّهُ رَءُوفٌ بِٱلْعِبَادِ ۝

And Allah warns you about Himself. And Allah is Ever

Gracious to His servants. [3:30]

إِنَّ رَبَّكَ لَسَرِيعُ ٱلْعِقَابِ وَإِنَّهُۥ لَغَفُورٌ رَّحِيمٌ ۝

*Indeed, your Lord is swift in punishment, but He is certainly
All-Forgiving, Most Merciful.* [7:167]

نَبِّئْ عِبَادِىٓ أَنِّىٓ أَنَا ٱلْغَفُورُ ٱلرَّحِيمُ ۝ وَأَنَّ عَذَابِى هُوَ ٱلْعَذَابُ ٱلْأَلِيمُ ۝

*Inform My servants that I am truly the All-Forgiving, Most
Merciful, and that My torment is indeed the most painful.*
[15:49-50]

إِنَّ ٱلْأَبْرَارَ لَفِى نَعِيمٍ ۝ وَإِنَّ ٱلْفُجَّارَ لَفِى جَحِيمٍ ۝

*Indeed, the virtuous will be in bliss, and the wicked will be in
Hell* [82:13-14]

Allah instructs us to internalize both hope and fear and have them both be a part of our
heart's emotional state when we call upon Him:

وَٱدْعُوهُ خَوْفًا وَطَمَعًا

And call upon Him with hope and fear. [7:56]

And He praises the most righteous throughout history in that they engaged both facets of
this relationship with their Lord.

إِنَّهُمْ كَانُوا يُسَٰرِعُونَ فِى ٱلْخَيْرَٰتِ وَيَدْعُونَنَا رَغَبًا وَرَهَبًا وَكَانُوا لَنَا
خَٰشِعِينَ ۝

*Indeed, they used to race in doing good, and call upon Us
with hope and fear, totally humbling themselves before Us.*
[21:90]

أَمَّنْ هُوَ قَٰنِتٌ ءَانَآءَ ٱلَّيْلِ سَاجِدًا وَقَآئِمًا يَحْذَرُ ٱلْءَاخِرَةَ وَيَرْجُوا رَحْمَةَ
رَبِّهِۦ قُلْ هَلْ يَسْتَوِى ٱلَّذِينَ يَعْلَمُونَ وَٱلَّذِينَ لَا يَعْلَمُونَ

*Consider those who worship devoutly in the hours of the
night, prostrating and standing, fearing the Hereafter and
hoping for the mercy of their Lord? Say, "Are those who
know equal to those who do not know?"* [39:9]

An Imbalance of Hope and Fear

We must travel to Allah with both wings of fear and hope. Focusing on only one of the two makes us prone to hazardous risks. When we base our thoughts and perspectives upon the fear of God alone, it will likely lead most people to become discouraged and demoralized, eventually burning out and giving up. When we limit our understanding of God solely to the vastness of His mercy and forgiveness, then it will likely lead most people into feeling too complacent, self-satisfied, and lazy in striving for the betterment of their spiritual state and standing with Allah. Both imbalances are dangerous.

Allah warns us in the Quran about these two extremes. About feeling too confident, He says,

$$\text{فَلَا يَأْمَنُ مَكْرَ ٱللَّهِ إِلَّا ٱلْقَوْمُ ٱلْخَٰسِرُونَ ۝}$$

None would feel secure from Allah's planning except the losers. [7:99]

And about those who would believe that God's mercy was beyond reach, He says:

$$\text{إِنَّهُۥ لَا يَاْيْـَٔسُ مِن رَّوْحِ ٱللَّهِ إِلَّا ٱلْقَوْمُ ٱلْكَٰفِرُونَ ۝}$$

None would lose hope in Allah's mercy except those with no faith. [12:87]

Islam teaches us balance: we should neither feel too safe from God's punishment nor should we ever give up on God's mercy.

> There are certain times when we should lean on one of these emotions more than the other. In our acts of worship, good deeds, and acts of service, perhaps we should remind ourselves to fear that no matter how much good we do, the quality may still be deficient. This will help prevent us from being self-satisfied due to our own deeds. But during times of difficulty, crisis, and struggle, we should remember God's infinite mercy and hope that He would extend it to us even though we don't deserve it.

When we make *dua* (supplication), we must call out to Allah with both feelings of fear and hope. Imam Ahmad bin Hanbal said, "One must travel to God between fear and hope. If either outweighs the other, then the traveler is doomed." Our mindset should constantly alternate between the two states throughout our entire lives. If we find ourselves leaning more towards one, we have to balance ourselves with reminders of the other.

Hope and Fear in Dawah

When addressing those who may be distant from God, it is important to instill that sense of fear within them by reminding them of their need for God, the danger of losing His guidance, and the painful consequences of turning away from Him. At the same time, we must also be sure to inspire hope in them for God's mercy and generosity so that they don't ever think that it is too late or futile to turn back. Sometimes a person might assume that his fate in Hell is sealed, and that God would never forgive him, and so he will persist in destructive behavior and sink deeper into disobedience. This person may require more hope than fear in their system in order to recalibrate to the ideal balance.

This strategy of balancing fear and hope when calling others to God is exactly how the God's messengers are described in the Quran. Allah says that they were,

$$\text{رُّسُلًا مُّبَشِّرِينَ وَمُنذِرِينَ}$$

Messengers delivering good news and warnings... [4:165]

The Messengers reminded their people of God's overwhelming power and majesty, while calling them to earn His forgiveness:

$$\text{قَالَتْ رُسُلُهُمْ أَفِى ٱللَّهِ شَكٌّ فَاطِرِ ٱلسَّمَـٰوَٰتِ وَٱلْأَرْضِ يَدْعُوكُمْ لِيَغْفِرَ لَكُم}$$
$$\text{مِّن ذُنُوبِكُمْ}$$

*Their messengers asked, "Is there any doubt about Allah, the
Originator of the heavens and the earth? He is inviting you in
order to forgive your sins..."* [14:10]

God also recounts the story of Noah, and the strategies with which he tried to bring his people back to the pure form of worship. Noah lamented to God,

$$\text{وَإِنِّى كُلَّمَا دَعَوْتُهُمْ لِتَغْفِرَ لَهُمْ جَعَلُوٓا۟ أَصَـٰبِعَهُمْ فِىٓ ءَاذَانِهِمْ وَٱسْتَغْشَوْا۟ ثِيَابَهُمْ}$$
$$\text{وَأَصَرُّوا۟ وَٱسْتَكْبَرُوا۟ ٱسْتِكْبَارًا ۝}$$

*And whenever I invite them to be forgiven by You, they press
their fingers into their ears, cover themselves with their clothes,
persist spitefully, and act very arrogantly.* [71:7]

The Heavy Trust

God offered the trust to the skies, the earth, and the mountains but they declined in anguish, realizing the great risk of such a burden. Then when God presented the offer to human beings, they accepted:

$$إِنَّا عَرَضْنَا ٱلْأَمَانَةَ عَلَى ٱلسَّمَوَتِ وَٱلْأَرْضِ وَٱلْجِبَالِ فَأَبَيْنَ أَن يَحْمِلْنَهَا وَأَشْفَقْنَ$$
$$مِنْهَا وَحَمَلَهَا ٱلْإِنسَنُ إِنَّهُ كَانَ ظَلُومًا جَهُولًا ۝$$

Indeed, We offered the trust to the heavens and the earth and
the mountains, but they all declined to bear it, being fearful
of it. But humanity assumed it; they are truly wrongful and
ignorant [33:72]

God knew that this was a heavy burden, and that there would be many forces that would hinder us humans from being able to uphold it. And so the verse that follows the above explains why He chose for us to undertake it:

$$لِّيُعَذِّبَ ٱللَّهُ ٱلْمُنَفِقِينَ وَٱلْمُنَفِقَتِ وَٱلْمُشْرِكِينَ وَٱلْمُشْرِكَتِ وَيَتُوبَ ٱللَّهُ عَلَى$$
$$ٱلْمُؤْمِنِينَ وَٱلْمُؤْمِنَتِ وَكَانَ ٱللَّهُ غَفُورًا رَّحِيمًا ۝$$

So that Allah will punish hypocrite men and women and
polytheistic men and women, and Allah will turn in mercy to
believing men and women. For Allah is All-Forgiving, Most
Merciful. [33:73]

Because He knew that we would inevitably fall short in our duty, He promised that he would "turn in mercy" to us and forgive us when we ask for it.

The human being's acceptance of this burden is the reason for our noble status with God. God says that He honored us:

$$وَلَقَدْ كَرَّمْنَا بَنِى ءَادَمَ وَحَمَلْنَهُمْ فِى ٱلْبَرِّ وَٱلْبَحْرِ وَرَزَقْنَهُم مِّنَ ٱلطَّيِّبَتِ$$
$$وَفَضَّلْنَهُمْ عَلَى كَثِيرٍ مِّمَّنْ خَلَقْنَا تَفْضِيلًا ۝$$

Indeed, We have dignified the children of Adam, carried them
on land and sea, granted them good and lawful provisions,
and privileged them far above many of Our creatures. [17:70]

And He ordered the angels to bow to our father:

$$وَإِذْ قُلْنَا لِلْمَلَئِكَةِ ٱسْجُدُوا لِءَادَمَ فَسَجَدُوٓا إِلَّآ إِبْلِيسَ أَبَى وَٱسْتَكْبَرَ وَكَانَ$$
$$مِنَ ٱلْكَفِرِينَ ۝$$

And when We said to the angels, "Prostrate before Adam," so
they all did... [2:34]

He subdued the skies and the earth for our use:

$$وَسَخَّرَ لَكُم مَّا فِى ٱلسَّمَٰوَٰتِ وَمَا فِى ٱلْأَرْضِ جَمِيعًا مِّنْهُ$$

*He subjected for you whatever is in the heavens and whatever
is on the earth—all by His grace.* [45:13]

And engulfed us in endless layers of His constant blessings, even though we don't realize it:

$$وَأَسْبَغَ عَلَيْكُمْ نِعَمَهُۥ ظَٰهِرَةً وَبَاطِنَةً$$

*And He has lavished His favours upon you, both seen and
unseen...* [31:20]

All of this is so to facilitate our duty to uphold this weighty responsibility of worshiping Allah without ever having seen Him, and to test whether or not we will comply.

Human Weakness

When God charged the human being with the responsibility to carry this burden, He knew of our weakness, for He Himself created us. He says,

$$وَخُلِقَ ٱلْإِنسَٰنُ ضَعِيفًا ۝$$

... for humankind was created weak. [4:28]

Allah knows that our souls are constantly burning with passion, and that Satan will take advantage of that to goad us into satisfying every paltry craving. Satan even took an oath before God to lead us astray:

$$قَالَ فَبِمَآ أَغْوَيْتَنِى لَأَقْعُدَنَّ لَهُمْ صِرَٰطَكَ ٱلْمُسْتَقِيمَ ۝ ثُمَّ لَآتِيَنَّهُم مِّنۢ بَيْنِ أَيْدِيهِمْ وَمِنْ خَلْفِهِمْ وَعَنْ أَيْمَٰنِهِمْ وَعَن شَمَآئِلِهِمْ ۖ وَلَا تَجِدُ أَكْثَرَهُمْ شَٰكِرِينَ ۝$$

*He said, "For leaving me to stray I will lie in ambush for them
on Your Straight Path. I will approach them from their front,
their back, their right, their left, and then You will find most
of them ungrateful."* [7:16-17]

And God knows of the beauty and glamor that He put on earth to tempt us and test our will:

$$إِنَّا جَعَلْنَا مَا عَلَى ٱلْأَرْضِ زِينَةً لَّهَا لِنَبْلُوَهُمْ أَيُّهُمْ أَحْسَنُ عَمَلًا ۝$$

We have indeed made whatever is on earth as an adornment
for it, in order to test which of them is best in deeds. [18:7]

Allah knows all of this, and that we will be subjected to trials and pressures until our last breath. But He did not create us to fail. Allah benefits nothing from our suffering and punishment in the Hellfire, and everything He does is to facilitate the success of those who want it—everything He does is out of His mercy and love:

$$\text{إِنَّ رَبِّي رَحِيمٌ وَدُودٌ}$$

Surely my Lord is Most Merciful, All-Loving. [11:90]

And so because the skies, the earth, and the mountains declined God's offer, they will perish and cease to exist on the Day of Judgment. But human beings will live for eternity. If they passed the test and fulfilled their trust, they will enjoy eternal bliss in Paradise and the pleasure of Allah. This burden, then, is actually a great opportunity that was extended to us humans, raising us above all of God's other creation if we do pass the test. This is understood explicitly from the verse,

$$\text{إِنَّ الَّذِينَ آمَنُوا وَعَمِلُوا الصَّالِحَاتِ أُولَٰئِكَ هُمْ خَيْرُ الْبَرِيَّةِ}$$

Indeed, those who believe and do good—they are the best of
beings. [98:7]

Human beings are superior even to the angels, if they believe and do good! The journey that we undertake of first getting to know Allah, then choosing to obey Him, internalizing the transformative emotions of fear, reverence, and hope, is an experience that the angels are deprived of. Someone who chooses instead to degrade himself or herself to the status of the rest of the animals on earth, seeking only to fulfill physical needs and tending only to a material existence in light of the great honor extended to him or her, deserves a humiliating consequence.

Though the skies and the earth declined this treasure that is surrounded with danger—the honor of a close connection with the Lord of the Worlds—we humans have the chance to obtain it. Allah did not leave us to navigate this perilous path on our own; His help and assistance, and His mercy and forgiveness, are with us at all times. He paved the road for our success, and so all we need to do is to take the step forward.

God Rejoices with Our Repentance

Of the most clear signs that God loves us and wants the best for us is His intense joy when we repent and return to Him. The Messenger of Allah ﷺ said,

God is more delighted by the repentance of His servant when he repents to Him than one of you who was on their riding animal in an open desert, and then it slipped away from him while it was carrying all of his provision, food and drink. He eventually gives up hope on it, and stops to rest in the shade of a tree, having given up any hope of finding his riding animal. While he is resting, he turns suddenly to find it standing beside him. He then grabs it by the reins, and exclaims in amazement: "O Allah, You are my servant and I am Your lord!" He mispoke out of extreme joy.[3]

Would there be any reason for God to be delighted by our repentance other than because of His love for us? He is waiting for us to return to Him and wants to see us succeed.

Our Master takes such joy and pride when we return to Him, and no human relationship is comparable in the love and protectiveness between Allah and His servants. His love for us is unfathomable by our human mind, so many stay distant in their heedlessness and obsession with the physical world. When their hearts do awaken to the greater reality, their return to God is made easy. The Prophet ﷺ told us that God says, "If you come closer to me by a handspan, I will come closer to you by an arm span. If you come closer to me by an arm span, I will come closer to you by a wingspan. If you come to me walking, I will come to you running."[4] Imam al-Nawawi comments that "come to you running" means for God to shower us with mercy by shortening the distance we must travel to finally reach Him.[5]

An Open-Door Policy

Allah knows our weakness and the trials that we will encounter, and so He made it easy for us to come back to His path no matter how far we might stray from it. His door is always open. Anyone who wants to repent and return to God will find no obstacles between him and his Lord. The Messenger of Allah ﷺ said, "God extends His hand out at night for the sinner of the daytime to repent, and He extends His hand out in the daytime for the sinner of the night to repent, all until the sun rises from the west."[6]

God is well aware of Satan's attempts to convince some people that their sins are too abominable and numerous for forgiveness, leading them to dig themselves further into the rut of sin and discarding any ambition for the afterlife. God knows this, and so the Messenger of Allah ﷺ told us that He said, "Child of Adam, for as long as you hope in me and call on me I will forgive you for all that you have done, and I will not care. Child of Adam, even if your sins reached the clouds in the sky, but you asked me for forgiveness, I would forgive you, and I would not care. Child of Adam, if you came to me with an earth full of sins, but met me while not having worshipped anything but me, I would reciprocate with forgiveness just as large."[7]

Allah is waiting for us. He will accept our apologies to Him, and rejoice at our returning back to Him. And rather than setting the score back to zero, He will even turn all of our sins into good deeds, giving us a head start on the road toward Him. He truly does love to forgive our sins, and He is always waiting for us to accept His offer of forgiveness:

$$وَمَن يَعْمَلْ سُوٓءًا أَوْ يَظْلِمْ نَفْسَهُۥ ثُمَّ يَسْتَغْفِرِ ٱللَّهَ يَجِدِ ٱللَّهَ غَفُورًا رَّحِيمًا ۝$$

Whoever commits evil or wrongs themselves then seeks Allah's forgiveness will certainly find Allah All-Forgiving, Most Merciful. [4:110]

The Messenger of Allah ﷺ said, "A servant may commit a sin and then say: "O Allah, forgive me for my sin!" He, Blessed and Exalted, then says: "My servant committed a sin, but realized that he has a Lord who forgives sins and punishes for sins." Then he sins again and says: "O my Lord, forgive me for my sin!" He, Blessed and Exalted, then says: "My servant committed a sin, but realizes that he has a Lord who forgives sins and punishes for sins." He then sins again and says: "O my Lord, forgive me for my sin!" He, Blessed and Exalted, then says: "My servant committed a sin, but realizes that he has a Lord who forgives sins and punishes for sins. Do as you wish, for I have forgiven you!"[8]

No matter how much you sin, God will forgive everytime you ask Him to. Imam al-Nawawi said about the last phrase, "Do as you wish…" that no matter what we do and how many times we sin and repent, God will always forgive us, because repentance wipes everything clean.[9]

Responding to God's Call

Have you ever realized that God actually calls us to His mercy and forgiveness? He says,

$$وَٱللَّهُ يَدْعُوٓاْ إِلَى ٱلْجَنَّةِ وَٱلْمَغْفِرَةِ بِإِذْنِهِۦ$$

Allah invites to Paradise and forgiveness by His grace. [2:221]

Notice how the messengers used to speak about God to their people:

قَالَتْ رُسُلُهُمْ أَفِى ٱللَّهِ شَكٌّ فَاطِرِ ٱلسَّمَـٰوَٰتِ وَٱلْأَرْضِ يَدْعُوكُمْ لِيَغْفِرَ لَكُم مِّن ذُنُوبِكُمْ

*Their messengers asked, "Is there any doubt about Allah, the
Originator of the heavens and the earth? He is inviting you in
order to forgive your sins…"* [14:10]

However, this open invitation only lasts until the moment the Angel of Death comes to take our souls. The Prophet ﷺ said, **"Allah accepts the servant's repentance as long as his soul has not come out."**[10] This is our Loving Lord who is supporting us to succeed in carrying this burden. He will overlook our shortcomings and flaws out of His compassion and sympathy for us, but only if we act before it is too late.

While the Messenger of Allah ﷺ was once sitting among his companions, a group of prisoners from a recent battle passed by. There was a woman with them who was dismayed because she had lost her son. When she finally found her son in the large group, she grabbed the baby tightly, held him close to her chest, and began to nurse him. Everyone watched, stricken by this emotional sight, and so the Messenger of Allah ﷺ said to his Companions, **"Do you think this woman would ever throw her child into a fire?"** They responded, "No; she would do all she can not to do so." He said, **"God is more compassionate with His servants than this woman is with her child."**[11]

Yes! God is more compassionate and loving toward us than our own mothers, fathers, brothers, and spouses. It is enough to know that He has reserved ninety-nine parts of mercy for us on the Day of Judgment, the Day when we will need it most. The Messenger of Allah ﷺ said, **"On the day that Allah created the skies and the earth, He created one hundred mercies, with the distance between the sky and the earth between each one. He placed one mercy on earth, and with it the mother shows affection for her child, as do the wild animals and birds to each other. On the Day of Resurrection, He will complete it with this mercy."**[12]

Despite our being ridden with flaws and our falling short in gratitude toward Him, He still values our attempts and boasts of us to the angels! Allah praises us by name to them, even though the angels are more perfect in their obedience. He encourages us to hasten towards Him, knowing that this is better for our wellbeing and happiness than anything else in the world:

وَسَارِعُوٓا۟ إِلَىٰ مَغْفِرَةٍ مِّن رَّبِّكُمْ وَجَنَّةٍ عَرْضُهَا ٱلسَّمَـٰوَٰتُ وَٱلْأَرْضُ أُعِدَّتْ لِلْمُتَّقِينَ ۝

*And hasten towards forgiveness from your Lord and a
Paradise as vast as the heavens and the earth, prepared for
those mindful.* [3:133]

We are to hasten toward him, and compete for His favor, not allowing doubt to hold us back or slow us down in our journey toward Him:

سَابِقُوٓا إِلَىٰ مَغْفِرَةٍ مِّن رَّبِّكُمْ وَجَنَّةٍ عَرْضُهَا كَعَرْضِ ٱلسَّمَآءِ وَٱلْأَرْضِ

Compete with one another for forgiveness from your Lord and a Paradise as vast as the heavens and the earth... [57:21]

And His warnings to us of the Hellfire stem from His compassion and desire for us to succeed. Notice in this ayah how God clarifies that the mention of His punishment is to incite us towards actions that will make us safe from its heat:

لَهُم مِّن فَوْقِهِمْ ظُلَلٌ مِّنَ ٱلنَّارِ وَمِن تَحْتِهِمْ ظُلَلٌ ذَٰلِكَ يُخَوِّفُ ٱللَّهُ بِهِۦ عِبَادَهُۥ يَـٰعِبَادِ فَٱتَّقُونِ ۞

They will have layers of fire above and below them. That is what Allah warns His servants with. So fear Me, O My servants! [39:16]

Allah does not want us to fail:

وَلَا يَرْضَىٰ لِعِبَادِهِ ٱلْكُفْرَ وَإِن تَشْكُرُوا يَرْضَهُ لَكُمْ

He is not pleased by unbelief for His servants, and if you are grateful, He will be delighted by it for you. [39:7]

He constantly encourages us towards good deeds, even though He does not benefit from our meager attempts! He gives us wealth and then speaks as if we are doing Him a favor with our charity. Then He takes what we give and invests it with incalculable returns:

مَّن ذَا ٱلَّذِى يُقْرِضُ ٱللَّهَ قَرْضًا حَسَنًا فَيُضَـٰعِفَهُۥ لَهُۥٓ أَضْعَافًا كَثِيرَةً

Who will lend to Allah a good loan which Allah will multiply many times over? [2:245]

That spare coin that we gave to someone in need to be a mountain's worth of reward waiting for us on the Day of Resurrection.

وَمَآ أَنفَقْتُم مِّن شَىْءٍ فَهُوَ يُخْلِفُهُۥ وَهُوَ خَيْرُ ٱلرَّٰزِقِينَ ۞

And whatever you spend in charity, He will compensate for it. For He is the Best Provider. [34:39]

Allah even explicitly expresses how He loves for His servants to succeed and attain Paradise:

وَٱللَّهُ يُرِيدُ أَن يَتُوبَ عَلَيْكُمْ

And it is Allah's Will to turn to you in grace... [4:27]

Because He knows how weak we are and how much pressure we are under, He multiplied each good deed to be ten times its worth, while keeping the value of our sins static. The Messenger of Allah ﷺ said,

> God recorded the good deeds and the bad deeds, and then made that clear. Whoever intends to do a good deed, but does not do it, then Allah will record it for him as a complete good deed. If one intends to do it and then actually does it, then God will record it for him as ten good deeds multiplied, up to seven hundred multiples, or even far beyond that. Whoever intends to do a bad deed and then does not do it, God will record it for him as a complete good deed, and if he intends to do it and then does, then God will record it as a single bad deed for him.[13]

In another narration, he ﷺ said, **"Only someone deserves to be doomed is doomed by Allah."**[14] Allah only punishes those who insist on their own destruction.

Of the most stunning ways that God demonstrates His generosity and open-handedness with His servants is how He so readily rewards the smallest of deeds. For example, the Messenger of Allah ﷺ said, **"Whoever says, '*Subhān Allahi wabihamdih,*' [Glorified and praise is to Allah] one hundred times in one day will have all of his sins removed, even if they are like the foam of the sea."**[15] The rewards are often even correlated symbolically with the action itself. The Prophet ﷺ also said, **"Whoever makes wudu, striving for perfection in doing so, then his sins will leave his body; they even leave from under his fingernails."**[16]

We also find that God placed immense reward in remembering Him at specific times, helping us to infuse meaning and spirituality within our daily routines and mundane chores. The Prophet ﷺ said, **"Whoever enters the market and says, 'There is nothing worthy of worship but God, alone, without any partners. To Him belongs all authority and praise. He gives life and death, and He is the Ever-living who does not die. In His hand lies all good, and He is powerful over everything,' then Allah will record one million good deeds for him, erase one milion bad deeds from him, and raise him one million ranks."**[17] Is this amount of reward comprehensible to our human minds? Perhaps not, but we are dealing with our Gracious Lord:

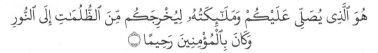

He is the One Who showers His blessings upon you—and His angels pray for you—so that He may bring you out of darkness and into light. For He is ever Merciful to the believers. [33:43]

Atonement

Part of God's boundless mercy and love is that He placed good for us in that which we view as bad. Every form of pain and discomfort is ultimately a means of securing bliss. The Messenger of Allah ﷺ said, "**No hardship, worry, grief, harm, or sorrow ever afflicts the Muslim except that Allah removes his sins with it—even when he is pricked by a thorn!**"[18] Marvel at how caring and wise God is with us when you read that the Prophet ﷺ said, "**When a servant's sins accumulate, and he does not have any deeds to erase them with, God, Mighty and Majestic, tests him with sadness in order to forgive him.**"[19] God fills our lives with tests and events that remove our sins. We may not realize, and our wretched, heedless hearts may not even have the desire to be forgiven, but God still sends us what is best for us in order to bring us closer to Him.

There is so much opportunity to be forgiven for our sins in the trivial actions that we do every day. The Messenger of Allah ﷺ said, that, "**The acts of atonement are: when the feet walk to the communal prayers, sitting in the mosque after the prayers, and perfecting your wudu in unfavorable conditions.**"[20] He also said, "**The five prayers, one Friday to the next, and one Ramadan to the next are atonements for whatever is between them if the major sins are avoided.**"[21] There is even one day in the year during which we can undo all of our past year's sins, and automatically cancel those of the next year: "**I expect that for fasting on the day of 'Arafah, God will forgive of the previous year and the year after it. And I expect that for fasting on the day of 'Āshoorā', God will forgive the previous year.**"[22]

A Patient, Forbearing Lord

Were God to deal with us in strict justice only, we would have been destroyed long ago. But instead He gives us many chances and is patient with us, waiting for us to finally wake up from our ignorance and return to Him. He says,

$$وَلَوْلَا كَلِمَةٌ سَبَقَتْ مِن رَّبِّكَ لَكَانَ لِزَامًا وَأَجَلٌ مُّسَمًّى ۟$$

Had it not been for a prior decree from your Lord and a term already set, their doom would have been inevitable. [20:129]

Do you realize what this means? God's mercy is more than His anger. His tolerance and patience with us is one of the greatest proofs of His love. Consider how many people only became religious shortly before their death, ending their life having converted their lifetime of sins into heaps of good deeds. God could have kept them in their state of heedlessness, but instead He granted them a beautiful ending and admittance into His Paradise. Although it might be to a lesser degree, these people are similar to the story of the man who killed one hundred people before finally repenting to God. He died before he could even complete the instructions of the scholar who directed him to leave the wretched town he was in, but God accepted his repentance nonetheless, even though he never reached his destination.

The Story of Al-Kifl

The Prophet 🌿 shared with us the story of al-Kifl,[23] a man living in one of the Israelite towns, who used to do as he pleased without any consideration for the boundaries of permissible and prohibited. He was notorious for his reckless, immoral behavior, and you could rarely ever find anyone who had anything good to say about him. One night, after everyone had gone home and locked their doors, al-Kifl heard a knock on his door. He opened it and was surprised to see a young woman standing there, covered in shame and visibly embarrassed. He asked what had brought her to his doorstep, and she told him that she was currently having some financial difficulties and could find no one other than him to borrow money from.

Al-Kifl saw this as a golden opportunity! Here was this woman who came to his house willingly in the dark of the night, when no one would see or hear her. He welcomed her with a smile and let her into his home. He told her that he had absolutely no problem lending her money, but that there was one condition: that she let him have his way with her. The woman pleaded with him to show some compassion and to reconsider his stipulation, but he paid no mind to her desperate requests. Seeing no way out of her dilemma, she agreed, though her heart was torn to pieces. When he came close to her, he felt her shoulder blades trembling, and so he asked her what was wrong. She told him that she had never even thought that she would do something like this, and that she was terrified of God and His punishment.

This made al-Kifl pause for a moment, and he began to inch away from her slowly. For some reason, those words of hers sunk deep into his heart. After a short, uneasy silence, he said to her, "If you feel that way while you are being forced, then how should I feel? Don't I have more of a reason to fear God than you?" He then gave her the money she asked of him and let her leave unharmed.

After the relieved woman had left, al-Kifl sunk further into a state of unsettling confusion. He thought critically about how he was living his life, fear and regret creeping into his heart. Those words of hers flipped his world upside down, and all he could think about was how much time he had spent being heedless of God, and how far he had transgressed God's boundaries. Every sin and crime that came to mind only made him feel more remorseful, making his pain harder to bear and forcing more tears out of him. He began to pray, begging God urgently for His forgiveness.

It was at that moment that al-Kifl received another visitor. This time it wasn't a woman. Nor was it a man, rather, the Angel of Death had come to take his life. Along with him entered the angels of mercy, celebrating and announcing the good news of God's forgiveness and mercy for him. Allah had accepted his regretful repentance and pardoned all of his previous sins, and out of His mercy, He took al-Kifl's life before he could commit anymore sins. He ended al-Kifl's life at the moment when He was most pleased with him.

This is your Lord. He is compassionate and merciful, and he wants to forgive us all. He says so clearly in His message to us,

$$وَٱللَّهُ يُرِيدُ أَن يَتُوبَ عَلَيْكُمْ$$

Allah wants to turn to you in grace [4:27]

God wants us to end up with Him in Paradise:

$$وَٱللَّهُ يَدْعُوٓا۟ إِلَى ٱلْجَنَّةِ وَٱلْمَغْفِرَةِ بِإِذْنِهِ$$

Allah invites to Paradise and forgiveness by His grace. [2:221]

Notice in this ayah that the object of the verb "invites," is not mentioned, alluding to the universal opportunity afforded to every soul to enter God's Paradise. We shouldn't then be surprised by al-Kifl's redemption. God is waiting for all of His slaves to make the slightest turn back to Him with sincerity so that He could embrace us and pardon our sins.

The story of al-Kifl doesn't end there. When the people woke up the next morning and came out of their houses to work as they would usually do, one of them passed by the house of al-Kifl and noticed some words written on his door. He came closer, and as soon as he read the words, his jaw dropped. He stood there, baffled and in utter disbelief of what was before him. Written on the door were the words, "God has forgiven al-Kifl."

Everyone gathered around to read it for themselves as they couldn't believe the news. They knocked on the door, but no one was there to open it. When they forced the door open, their shock only intensified when they found al-Kifl dead. They ran to the Prophet who was with them at the time to ask him about what had happened to al-Kifl, and Allah revealed to him the events of the previous night. The crowd broke out into tears, and their love for the Lord grew stronger. They were now certain of the extent of His mercy, and they all rushed to repent. They said to themselves, "If God forgave al-Kifl after all that he did, then God's door to forgiveness is open for everyone!"

This event could have taken place without anyone knowing. Many people die without anyone around them knowing their ultimate status with God. But our loving Lord wants us to be certain in the vastness of His mercy in order to push us to flee to Him. He made this a sign so that everyone who witnessed it and heard about it could contemplate on its lessons and indications. It is a brilliant sign of God's love for His servants, and that He is waiting for the slightest sincere act of repentance from us to welcome us back into His mercy and erase all of our sins.

This story could have been limited to those who saw it first hand. But our loving Lord wanted us, the followers of Muhammad ﷺ, to hear about it and retell it in order for us to love Him more and run to Him. What more can you ask for from your Lord? What are you waiting for? Turn back to Him without any fear of disappointment. He is waiting for you.

Is There a Contradiction?

You might think that this discussion of God so readily forgiving His servants contradicts what we previously said in the chapter on fear about the consequences of sins and God's severe wrath. But in reality, there is no contradiction at all. It is certain that God wants us to succeed in this test He gave us, and because He knows our own weaknesses and the discomfort and challenges that we will face, He made the road to repentance and returning to Him easy. Anyone who asks for forgiveness is forgiven, and anyone who asks to be pardoned is pardoned. This is His promise to us.

But sometimes people insist on swimming against the tide, acting in opposition to God's orders and letting their arrogance prevent them from returning to Him in humility. The small reminders that God sends their way do them no good, and so they dig themselves deeper into the muddy ditch of delusion—what can their end be other than destruction?

Imagine if you were a teacher, and there was a student whom you loved and wanted to succeed because you were friends with his parents. You tried helping and supporting him, but always found that he just didn't care to pass the class. He was excessively absent, and whenever he did come to class, he never paid attention. He would distract his classmates and interrupt the lesson, and whenever you asked him about any of the class material, he couldn't answer. Time after time, you let it slide, using all of the recommended tactics to correct his misconduct, but he insisted on continuing down the road of failure. How would you grade him at the end of the year?

God is obviously incomparable to any of His creation, but consider the ayah,

$$وَلَا يَرْضَىٰ لِعِبَادِهِ ٱلْكُفْرَ$$

He is not pleased for His servants to disbelieve. [39:7]

God wants us to succeed in this test of our will and faith. He multiplies the value of good deeds by ten, keeps his door open to everyone at all times, and allows us to make up for our transgressions with the simplest acts of atonement. Is there any other reason why God would allow some to live years in sin, and then repent sincerely and wholeheartedly right before their death? He even sends us reminders to help find our way back to Him and redirect us to His mercy. He says,

$$وَلَنُذِيقَنَّهُم مِّنَ ٱلْعَذَابِ ٱلْأَدْنَىٰ دُونَ ٱلْعَذَابِ ٱلْأَكْبَرِ لَعَلَّهُمْ يَرْجِعُونَ ۝$$

We will certainly make them taste some of the minor torment before the major torment, so perhaps they will return. [32:21]

Everyone receives these signs and reminders, but so many refuse to return. The Messenger of Allah ﷺ once said to his companions, **"All of my nation will enter Paradise, except for whoever refuses."**[24] They asked him, "But who would ever refuse?" He said, **"Whoever obeys me will enter Paradise, and whoever disobeys me has then refused to."** He also said, **"All of you will enter Paradise except for whoever strays from Allah like a camel strays from its owner."**[25] So what does someone who insistently strays and turns away from God in defiance of Him deserve?

$$فَكَفَرُوا وَتَوَلَّوا وَّٱسْتَغْنَى ٱللَّهُ وَٱللَّهُ غَنِىٌّ حَمِيدٌ ۝$$

They persisted in disbelief and turned away. And Allah was not in need, for Allah is Self-Sufficient and Praiseworthy. [64:6]

Respond to Your Lord

We still have a chance to correct our ways and pass this test. But all of these generous opportunities that God affords to His servants so that they repent and return to Him end upon death. God highlights the regret of those who fail to take advantage of His willingness to forgive:

$$أَن تَقُولَ نَفْسٌ يَحَسْرَتَىٰ عَلَىٰ مَا فَرَّطتُ فِى جَنْبِ ٱللَّهِ وَإِن كُنتُ لَمِنَ ٱلسَّٰخِرِينَ ۝$$

So that no soul will say, "Woe to me for neglecting what Allah offered... [39:56]

There will come a time when our remorse will do us no good:

$$هَٰذَا يَوْمُ لَا يَنطِقُونَ ۝ وَلَا يُؤْذَنُ لَهُمْ فَيَعْتَذِرُونَ ۝$$

On that Day they will not speak, nor will they be permitted to offer excuses. [77:35-36]

God says about the the people in the Hellfire:

فَإِن يَصْبِرُوا فَٱلنَّارُ مَثْوًى لَّهُمْ وَإِن يَسْتَعْتِبُوا فَمَا هُم مِّنَ ٱلْمُعْتَبِينَ ۝

Even if they endure patiently, the Fire will be their home. And even if they plead to appease, they will never be allowed to. [41:24]

So what are we waiting for? He wants to forgive us. He wants to accept our apologies. He wants to guide us. But do we want to be guided and forgiven? Are we motivated enough? All we have to do is ask with sincerity. The Quran calls us to:

ٱسْتَجِيبُوا لِرَبِّكُم

Respond to your Lord... [42:47]

وَسَارِعُوٓا إِلَىٰ مَغْفِرَةٍ مِّن رَّبِّكُم

And hasten towards forgiveness from your Lord... [3:133]

فَفِرُّوٓا إِلَى ٱللَّهِ

Flee to Allah! [51:50]

وَأَنِيبُوٓا إِلَىٰ رَبِّكُم

Turn to your Lord... [39:54]

So what will our response to these calls be? What is our answer when He asks:

أَلَا تُحِبُّونَ أَن يَغْفِرَ ٱللَّهُ لَكُمْ

Would you not love to be forgiven by Allah? [24:22]

Will we answer His invitation?

يَدْعُوكُمْ لِيَغْفِرَ لَكُم مِّن ذُنُوبِكُمْ

He is inviting you in order to forgive your sins... [14:10]

Will we answer in time? Or will we say when it is too late:

رَبَّنَآ أَخِّرْنَآ إِلَىٰٓ أَجَلٍ قَرِيبٍ نُّجِبْ دَعْوَتَكَ وَنَتَّبِعِ ٱلرُّسُلَ

"Our Lord! Delay us for a little while. We will respond to Your call and follow the messengers!" [14:44]

A Hopeful Journey

We saw in the chapter on fearing God many verses calling us to fear and revere God. While fear is an effective force to bring us to worship our Lord, rush to do good, and comply with His command, some of you may be at a stage in life where fear would lead to succumbing to one of the gravest errors: despairing in God's mercy. Unfortunately, because many Muslims are disconnected from our source of guidance, the Quran, they can be easily misled into believing that God's anger is greater than His mercy.

God quotes Abraham when he said,

$$وَمَن يَقْنَطُ مِن رَّحْمَةِ رَبِّهِ إِلَّا ٱلضَّآلُّونَ ۟$$

Who would despair of the mercy of their Lord except the misguided? [15:56]

Ali bin Abu Talib said, "The one with true knowledge of the religion is one who does not cause others to despair in God's mercy, nor cause them to feel validated in their disobedience of God, nor cause them to feel safe from God's punishment."[26] Just as we are in need of nurturing the fear of God in our hearts, we must also nurture the hope in Allah and develop a habit of assuming the best of Him. Abdullah ibn Mas'ud once said, "There are three great sins: despairing of relief from Allah, losing hope in the mercy of Allah, and feeling secure from God's plan."[27]

Hope plays an equally important role in our relationship with God, and it has immense effects on how we worship and connect with Him. These effects manifest in occasional breezes that pass over our hearts and fill us with love for Allah, an excitement to serve Him, and a yearning to meet Him. Building a positive perspective of God is actually how we carry out the instructions of the Messenger of Allah ﷺ when he said to Jabir bn Abdullah three days before he passed, **"Let none of you die except that He assumes the best of God."**[28] He also said, **"Assuming the best of God is from the perfection of worship."**[29] There are many examples throughout the Quran, the words of the Prophet ﷺ, and those of His Companions that encourage us and help us feel positively towards God. When one of the early scholars of Islam was on the verge of death, he instructed his son to recite to him the verses of mercy from the Quran so that his soul would leave his body with high hopes in God and His mercy.

Some of these verses are as follows. In one example, God commands His Prophet to relay the following message to us:

$$قُلْ يَٰعِبَادِىَ ٱلَّذِينَ أَسْرَفُوا عَلَىٰ أَنفُسِهِمْ لَا تَقْنَطُوا مِن رَّحْمَةِ ٱللَّهِ إِنَّ ٱللَّهَ يَغْفِرُ ٱلذُّنُوبَ جَمِيعًا إِنَّهُۥ هُوَ ٱلْغَفُورُ ٱلرَّحِيمُ ۟$$

"O My servants who have exceeded the limits against their souls!
Do not lose hope in Allah's mercy, for Allah certainly forgives
all sins. He is indeed the All-Forgiving, Most Merciful." [39:53]

In his book *al-Burhān fee 'Uloom al-Qur'ān*, the Mamluk scholar Muhammad al-Zarkashi writes that one of the most hope-inspiring ayahs in the Quran is the ayah of debt, the longest verse in the Quran that at face value is mostly technical guidelines for contractual agreements:

يَـٰٓأَيُّهَا ٱلَّذِينَ ءَامَنُوٓا۟ إِذَا تَدَايَنتُم بِدَيْنٍ إِلَىٰٓ أَجَلٍ مُّسَمًّى فَٱكْتُبُوهُ وَلْيَكْتُب بَّيْنَكُمْ
كَاتِبٌۢ بِٱلْعَدْلِ وَلَا يَأْبَ كَاتِبٌ أَن يَكْتُبَ كَمَا عَلَّمَهُ ٱللَّهُ فَلْيَكْتُبْ وَلْيُمْلِلِ ٱلَّذِى
عَلَيْهِ ٱلْحَقُّ وَلْيَتَّقِ ٱللَّهَ رَبَّهُۥ وَلَا يَبْخَسْ مِنْهُ شَيْـًٔا فَإِن كَانَ ٱلَّذِى عَلَيْهِ ٱلْحَقُّ سَفِيهًا
أَوْ ضَعِيفًا أَوْ لَا يَسْتَطِيعُ أَن يُمِلَّ هُوَ فَلْيُمْلِلْ وَلِيُّهُۥ بِٱلْعَدْلِ وَٱسْتَشْهِدُوا۟ شَهِيدَيْنِ
مِن رِّجَالِكُمْ فَإِن لَّمْ يَكُونَا رَجُلَيْنِ فَرَجُلٌ وَٱمْرَأَتَانِ مِمَّن تَرْضَوْنَ مِنَ ٱلشُّهَدَآءِ أَن
تَضِلَّ إِحْدَىٰهُمَا فَتُذَكِّرَ إِحْدَىٰهُمَا ٱلْأُخْرَىٰ وَلَا يَأْبَ ٱلشُّهَدَآءُ إِذَا مَا دُعُوا۟ وَلَا تَسْـَٔمُوٓا۟ أَن
تَكْتُبُوهُ صَغِيرًا أَوْ كَبِيرًا إِلَىٰٓ أَجَلِهِۦ ذَٰلِكُمْ أَقْسَطُ عِندَ ٱللَّهِ وَأَقْوَمُ لِلشَّهَٰدَةِ وَأَدْنَىٰٓ أَلَّا
تَرْتَابُوٓا۟ إِلَّآ أَن تَكُونَ تِجَٰرَةً حَاضِرَةً تُدِيرُونَهَا بَيْنَكُمْ فَلَيْسَ عَلَيْكُمْ جُنَاحٌ أَلَّا
تَكْتُبُوهَا وَأَشْهِدُوٓا۟ إِذَا تَبَايَعْتُمْ وَلَا يُضَآرَّ كَاتِبٌ وَلَا شَهِيدٌ وَإِن تَفْعَلُوا۟ فَإِنَّهُۥ فُسُوقٌۢ
بِكُمْ وَٱتَّقُوا۟ ٱللَّهَ وَيُعَلِّمُكُمُ ٱللَّهُ وَٱللَّهُ بِكُلِّ شَىْءٍ عَلِيمٌ ۞

O believers! When you contract a loan for a fixed period of time, commit
it to writing. Let the scribe maintain justice between the parties. The
scribe should not refuse to write as Allah has taught them to write.
They will write what the debtor dictates, bearing Allah in mind and not
defrauding the debt. If the debtor is incompetent, weak, or unable to
dictate, let their guardian dictate for them with justice. Call upon two
of your men to witness. If two men cannot be found, then one man and
two women of your choice will witness—so if one of the women forgets
the other may remind her. The witnesses must not refuse when they are
summoned. You must not be against writing for a fixed period—whether
the sum is small or great. This is more just in the sight of Allah, and
more convenient to establish evidence and remove doubts. However, if
you conduct an immediate transaction among yourselves, then there
is no need for you to record it, but call upon witnesses when a deal is
finalized. Let no harm come to the scribe or witnesses. If you do, then
you have gravely exceeded. Be mindful of Allah, for Allah teaches you.
And Allah has knowledge of all things. [2:282]

Imam al-Zarkashi points out that Allah used this long passage (actually, the longest ayah in the Quran) to direct us towards something that is purely for our own worldly good.

He instructs us to write down our loans, "whether the sum is small or great."[30] This is the clearest manifestation of God's compassion for us, as He dedicated this lengthy ayah for our seemingly trivial worldly benefit, managing our minor affairs in a way that protects and ensures our wellbeing.

In his discussion of verses that incite hope in our hearts, al-Zarkashi also includes this concise and moving ayah:[31]

قُل لِّلَّذِينَ كَفَرُوٓا۟ إِن يَنتَهُوا۟ يُغْفَرْ لَهُم مَّا قَدْ سَلَفَ

Tell the disbelievers that if they desist, their past will be forgiven. [8:38]

If God is so hospitably inviting the disbelievers to forgiveness through simply testifying to His oneness, could you imagine how He will treat those who already submit to Him?

Verses on Hope and Fear

Below is a list of verses to contemplate in order to reactivate our hope in God. One may read the entire Quran with a lens of hope and forgiveness, while awakening *iman* and a greater motivation to do one's best for the sake of Allah.

فَهَلْ يُهْلَكُ إِلَّا ٱلْقَوْمُ ٱلْفَٰسِقُونَ ۝

Will anyone be destroyed except the rebellious people? [46:35]

وَرَحْمَتِى وَسِعَتْ كُلَّ شَىْءٍ

But My mercy encompasses everything. [7:156]

إِنَّا قَدْ أُوحِىَ إِلَيْنَآ أَنَّ ٱلْعَذَابَ عَلَىٰ مَن كَذَّبَ وَتَوَلَّىٰ ۝

It has indeed been revealed to us that the punishment will be upon whoever denies and turns away. [20:48]

وَإِنَّ رَبَّكَ لَذُو مَغْفِرَةٍ لِّلنَّاسِ عَلَىٰ ظُلْمِهِمْ

Surely your Lord is full of forgiveness for people, despite their wrongdoing... [13:6]

وَلَسَوْفَ يُعْطِيكَ رَبُّكَ فَتَرْضَىٰ ۝

And your Lord will give to you, so you will be pleased. [93:5]

وَإِذَا جَاءَكَ ٱلَّذِينَ يُؤْمِنُونَ بِـَٔايَٰتِنَا فَقُلْ سَلَٰمٌ عَلَيْكُمْ كَتَبَ رَبُّكُمْ عَلَىٰ نَفْسِهِ ٱلرَّحْمَةَ أَنَّهُۥ مَنْ عَمِلَ مِنكُمْ سُوٓءًۢا بِجَهَٰلَةٍ ثُمَّ تَابَ مِنۢ بَعْدِهِۦ وَأَصْلَحَ فَأَنَّهُۥ غَفُورٌ رَّحِيمٌ ۝

When those who believe in Our ayahs come to you, say, "Peace be upon you! Your Lord has taken upon Himself to be Merciful. Whoever among you commits evil ignorantly, and then repents afterwards and mends their ways, then Allah is truly All-Forgiving, Most Merciful." [6:54]

إِنَّ ٱللَّهَ لَا يَغْفِرُ أَن يُشْرَكَ بِهِۦ وَيَغْفِرُ مَا دُونَ ذَٰلِكَ لِمَن يَشَآءُ

Indeed, Allah does not forgive associating others with Him, but forgives anything else of whoever He wills. [4:48]

وَلَا يَأْتَلِ أُولُوا ٱلْفَضْلِ مِنكُمْ وَٱلسَّعَةِ أَن يُؤْتُوٓا أُولِي ٱلْقُرْبَىٰ وَٱلْمَسَٰكِينَ وَٱلْمُهَٰجِرِينَ فِي سَبِيلِ ٱللَّهِ وَلْيَعْفُوا وَلْيَصْفَحُوٓا أَلَا تُحِبُّونَ أَن يَغْفِرَ ٱللَّهُ لَكُمْ وَٱللَّهُ غَفُورٌ رَّحِيمٌ ۝

Do not let the people of virtue and affluence among you swear to suspend donations to their relatives, the needy, and the emigrants in the cause of Allah. Let them pardon and forgive. Do you not love to be forgiven by Allah? And Allah is All-Forgiving, Most Merciful. [24:22]

وَمَآ أَصَٰبَكُم مِّن مُّصِيبَةٍ فَبِمَا كَسَبَتْ أَيْدِيكُمْ وَيَعْفُوا عَن كَثِيرٍ ۝

Whatever affliction befalls you is because of what your own hands have committed. And He pardons much. [42:30]

إِن تَجْتَنِبُوا كَبَآئِرَ مَا تُنْهَوْنَ عَنْهُ نُكَفِّرْ عَنكُمْ سَيِّـَٔاتِكُمْ وَنُدْخِلْكُم مُّدْخَلًا كَرِيمًا ۝

If you avoid the major sins forbidden to you, We will absolve you of your misdeeds and admit you into a place of honor. [4:31]

وَءَاخَرُونَ ٱعْتَرَفُوا بِذُنُوبِهِمْ خَلَطُوا عَمَلًا صَٰلِحًا وَءَاخَرَ سَيِّئًا عَسَى ٱللَّهُ أَن يَتُوبَ عَلَيْهِمْ إِنَّ ٱللَّهَ غَفُورٌ رَّحِيمٌ ۝

Some others have confessed their wrongdoing: they have mixed

goodness with evil. It is right to hope that Allah will turn to them in mercy. Surely Allah is All-Forgiving, Most Merciful.
[9:102]

وَمَن يَعْمَلْ سُوٓءًا أَوْ يَظْلِمْ نَفْسَهُۥ ثُمَّ يَسْتَغْفِرِ ٱللَّهَ يَجِدِ ٱللَّهَ غَفُورًا رَّحِيمًا ۞

Whoever commits evil or wrongs themselves then seeks Allah's forgiveness will certainly find Allah All-Forgiving, Most Merciful. [4:110]

هُوَ ٱلَّذِى يُصَلِّى عَلَيْكُمْ وَمَلَٰٓئِكَتُهُۥ لِيُخْرِجَكُم مِّنَ ٱلظُّلُمَٰتِ إِلَى ٱلنُّورِ وَكَانَ بِٱلْمُؤْمِنِينَ رَحِيمًا ۞

He is the One Who showers His blessings upon you—and His angels pray for you—so that He may bring you out of darkness and into light. For He is ever Merciful to the believers. [33:43]

Many Hadiths on Hope

The Messenger of Allah ﷺ said, **"Whoever testifies that there is nothing worthy of worship but Allah, alone, without any partners; and that Muhammad is His servant and Messenger; and that Jesus is His servant of Messenger, His word that He sent down to Mary, and a spirit from Him; and that Paradise is true; and the the Hellfire is true, Allah will then enter him into Paradise in light of the actions he was upon."**[32]

The Prophet ﷺ once said to Mu'adh bin Jabal, who was riding behind him on the saddle, **"Mu'adh!"** He responded, "Happily at your service, Messenger of Allah." He repeated, **"Mu'adh!"** He responded, "Happily at your service, Messenger of Allah." He said again, **"Mu'adh!"** He responded, "Happily at your service, Messenger of Allah." Then he said, **"There is no servant who testifies that there is nothing worthy of worship but Allah, and that Muhammad is His servant and Messenger, except that Allah prohibits the fire from him."** Mu'adh asked, "Messenger of Allah, should I not tell the people so that they can then rejoice?" He said, **"Then they will slack."**[33] Mu'adh only relayed it upon his death to avoid withholding a saying of the Prophet from the people.

⟪A Secret Hadith⟫

Explanations of the hadith to the left clarify that the Prophet shared this information with Mu'adh because he knew it would only motivate him to work harder. He discouraged Mu'ath from sharing it with others out of fear that someone weak in faith would hear it and use it as an excuse to slack off on their worship and deeds, relying on this hadith to enter Paradise

Abu Hurayrah narrates that the Messenger of Allah ﷺ said, "I swear by the One in whose hand is my soul, were you not to sin, God would remove you and bring people who sin so that they would ask God for forgiveness, and He would forgive them."[34]

Abdullah bin 'Amr narrates that the Prophet ﷺ once recited the verse wherein God quotes the words of Abraham:

رَبِّ إِنَّهُنَّ أَضْلَلْنَ كَثِيرًا مِّنَ ٱلنَّاسِ فَمَن تَبِعَنِي فَإِنَّهُ مِنِّي وَمَنْ عَصَانِي فَإِنَّكَ غَفُورٌ رَّحِيمٌ ۝

My Lord! They have caused many people to go astray. So whoever follows me is with me, and whoever disobeys me— then surely You are All-Forgiving, Most Merciful. [14:36]

And the words of Jesus:

إِن تُعَذِّبْهُمْ فَإِنَّهُمْ عِبَادُكَ وَإِن تَغْفِرْ لَهُمْ فَإِنَّكَ أَنتَ ٱلْعَزِيزُ ٱلْحَكِيمُ ۝

You punish them, they belong to You after all. But if You forgive them, You are surely the Almighty, All-Wise. [5:118]

The Prophet ﷺ then raised his hands and said, "My Lord! My nation! My nation!" and cried. God, Mighty and Majestic, said, "Gabriel, go to Muhammad and though your Lord knows best, ask him what makes him cry." Gabriel (peace and blessings be upon him) then came to him and asked him, and the Messenger of Allah ﷺ told him even though He knows best. Allah then said, "Gabriel, go to Muhammad and say, 'We will make you pleased regarding your nation, and we will not let you down.'"[35]

Ibn Umar narrates that he heard the Messenger of Allah ﷺ say about the private conversation between God and His servant, "The believer will be brought close to His Lord, Mighty and Majestic, on the Day of Resurrection, until He draws His curtain over him and makes him admit his sins. He will say, 'Do you acknowledge?' and he will respond, 'Yes, my Lord, I acknowledge.' He will then say, 'I concealed it for you in the worldly life, and I will forgive you for it today,' and then he will be given his page of good deeds."[36]

Abu Hurayrah narrates that the Prophet ﷺ said that Allah, Mighty and Majestic, said, "My mercy precedes my wrath."[37] He also narrates that the Messenger of Allah ﷺ said, "God, Mighty and Majestic, said, 'I am as my servant thinks of me, and I am with him when he remembers me.'"[38]

Mu'adh bin Jabal narrates that the Messenger of Allah ﷺ said, "If you wish, I will tell you the first thing that God will say to the believers on the Day of Judgement, and the first thing that they will say to Him." They said, "Yes, Messenger of Allah!" He said, "God will say to the believers, 'Did you desire to meet me?' They will respond, 'Yes, our Lord!' He will say, 'Why?' They will respond, 'We hoped in your pardon and your forgiveness.' He will then say, 'My forgiveness is certainly guaranteed for you.'"[39]

Abdullah b. Mas'ood narrates: We were with the Messenger of Allah ﷺ in a domed tent. He said: "Would you all be pleased to be a fourth of the people of Paradise?" We said: "Yes!" He said: "Would you all be pleased to be a third of the people of Paradise?" We said: "Yes!" He said: "I swear by the One in whose hand is my soul, I hope that you will be half of the people of Paradise. That is because only a Muslim soul will enter Paradise. You are to the people of false worship like white hairs on the skin of a black bull, or like black hairs on the skin of a red bull."[40]

Abu Hurayrah narrates: The Prophet ﷺ once came out to a group of his companions who were laughing and speaking. He said, "I swear by the One in whose hand is my soul, if you know what I knew, you would laugh little and cry a lot." He then left, having caused the men to cry, so Allah sent down to him, "O Muhammad, why did you cause my servants to despair?" The Prophet ﷺ then came back and said, "Rejoice, aim straight, and come as close as you can."[41] Imam al-Bayhaqi said that this hadith is proof that one's fear should not cause them to give up on and despair in God's mercy, just as one's hope should not cause them to feel too safe from God's punishment or emboldened to disobey Him.[42]

Anas narrates that the Prophet ﷺ visited a young man who was on the verge of death. He asked, "How are you feeling?" The man said, "I hope in God, Messenger of Allah, but I fear my sins." The Messenger of Allah ﷺ said, "These two do not come together in anyone's heart at a time like this except that God will give him what he hopes for, and secure him from what he fears."[43]

Sayings of the Righteous

Our tradition is filled with sayings from the companions and the generations who followed that also help regenerate a hopeful perspective of God in our hearts. These sayings can be found in *Husn al-Dhanni billāh* by Ibn Abu al-Dunyā.

Abdullah bin Mas'ood once passed by a storyteller as he was relating a story in public. He said to him, "O preacher, do not cause the people to despair!" Then he recited,

قُلْ يَٰعِبَادِىَ ٱلَّذِينَ أَسْرَفُوا عَلَىٰٓ أَنفُسِهِمْ لَا تَقْنَطُوا مِن رَّحْمَةِ ٱللَّهِ إِنَّ ٱللَّهَ يَغْفِرُ ٱلذُّنُوبَ جَمِيعًا ۞

"O My servants who have exceeded the limits against their souls! Do not lose hope in Allah's mercy, for Allah certainly forgives all sins." [39:53]

Abdullah bin Mas‘ood also said, "God will most certainly forgive on the Day of Resurrection in a way that no human heart could ever imagine."[44] He is reported to have once said, "I swear by the One other than whom there is nothing worthy of worship, a believing servant is not given anything better than high hopes in God! I swear by the One other than whom there is nothing worthy of worship, a servant never expects the best from God except that God will give him what he expects! That is because all good is in His hand."

Ali bin Husayn, the grandson of Ali bin Abu Talib, heard that his friend's son who was a known sinner had passed away. He told his friend, "Your son has three things on his side: his testimony that there is nothing worthy of worship but Allah, the intercession of the Messenger of Allah ﷺ, and the Mercy of Allah that encompasses everything."

Highlighting the unparalleled mercy of God, Sufyān al-Thawri said, "I would not desire for my parents to decide my fate; my Lord is better for me than my parents." Imam al-Shāfi‘i was asked during his fatal illness, "How are you?" He responded, "I am departing from this world and leaving my brothers behind. I am drinking from death's cup, and I do not know whether to congratulate my soul for reaching Paradise, or consoling it for ending up in the Hellfire." Then he recited a poem:

> *Though my heavy heart weighs me down and my veins are constricted*
> *My hope in your mercy elevates me*
> *Though my sins seem to exceed every boundary unrestricted*
> *They cannot be compared to your boundless mercy*

Another early Islamic scholar once said, "When the fear of the believers was weighed against their hope, neither of the two should outweigh the other." Yahya bin Mu‘ādh said, "Fear is replenished from the sea of His justice, and hope is replenished from the sea of His generosity. It has already been decreed that His mercy overtakes His wrath." Mutarrif, one of the masters of Hadith in Baghdad at end of the first century of Islam, once recited the following ayah:

وَإِنَّ رَبَّكَ لَذُو مَغْفِرَةٍ لِّلنَّاسِ عَلَىٰ ظُلْمِهِمْ وَإِنَّ رَبَّكَ لَشَدِيدُ ٱلْعِقَابِ ۞

Surely your Lord is full of forgiveness for people, despite their
wrongdoing, and your Lord is truly severe in punishment.
[13:6]

Then he said, "If the people knew the true extent of God's forgiveness, God's mercy, God's pardon, and God's tolerance, they would rest comfortably and easily. If the people knew the true danger of God's punishment, God's revenge, God's strength, and God's torment, their eyes would never go dry, and they would never be able to enjoy a single meal or drink."

Abu Ali Rudbari, a spiritual master from the fourth century of Islam, is quoted as the first to have made the famous analogy of the importance of balancing both fear and hope: "Fear and hope are like the two wings of a bird. If they are equal, then it flies well, but if one of them is less than the other, it becomes flawed. If both of them vanish, then the bird is as good as dead."

....

ENDNOTES

1. al-Bukhari, #6469; Muslim, #2755 (in this wording)
2. al-Bukhari, #6488
3. Muslim, #2747
4. al-Bukhari, #7405, and Muslim #2675 (in this wording)
5. Riyād al-Sāliheen, p, 216
6. Muslim, #2759
7. al-Tirmidhi, #3540; *as-Silsilah as-Saheehah* 127
8. al-Bukhari, #7507; and Muslim, #2758
9. Riyād al-Sāliheen, pp. 221-222
10. Ahmad, #6160; Ibn Majah #4254; at-Tirmithi #3537; and others; deemed *saheeh* by al-Arna'oot and ath-Thahabi
11. al-Bukhari, #5999; and Muslim #2754
12. al-Bukhari, #6469; and Muslim #2753 (in this wording)
13. al-Bukhari, #6491, and Muslim, #131
14. Ahmad, #2519
15. al-Bukhari, #6405, Muslim #2691
16. Muslim, #245
17. Ahmad #327; Ibn Majah #2235; at-Tirmidhi, #3428; *as-Silsilah as-Saheehah* #3139
18. al-Bukhari, #5641, and Muslim, #2573
19. Ahmad #25236; deemed *saheeh* by al-Arna'oot
20. Ahmad, #22109; Tirmithi #3235; Bukhari
21. Muslim, #233
22. Muslim, #1162
23. Story of Al-Kifl from the following *hadeeths*: Ahmad 4747; Tirmithi 2496, and others
23. al-Bukhari, #7280
25. Ahmad, #22226
26. Ad-Darimi #305 and Abu Dawud in *az-Zuhd* #104
27. Tafseer at-Tabari (8/246)
28. Muslim, #2877
29. Ahmad, #7956; Abu Dawud #4993; at-Tirmithi #583; ibn Hibban #631; al-Hakim #285
30. v. 1, p. 200
31. Ibid.
32. al-Bukhari, #3435; Muslim, #28
33. Bukhari #128; Muslim #32
34. Muslim, #2749
35. Muslim, #202
36. al-Bukhari, #4685; Muslim, #2768
37. al-Bukhari,# 7422; Muslim, #2751
38. al-Bukhari, #7405; Muslim, #2675
39. Ahmad, #22072
40. al-Bukhari, #6528 and #6642; Muslim, #221
41. al-Bukhari, al-Adab al-Mufrad, #254

42. Shu'ab al-Īmān, v. 2, p. 243

43. Ibn Mājah, #4621

44. This and the remainder of the quotes quotes from the end of the chapter can be found in *Husn al-Dhanni billāh* by Ibn Abu al-Dunyā.

A Plea For Iman

Through practicing the methods of awakening the heart recounted in this book, readers will set themselves on the right course for a stronger *iman*. Allah is the source of all goodness, and He gives it to whomever carries in their heart a sincere desire to seek Him and come closer to Him.

إِن يَعْلَمِ اللَّهُ فِى قُلُوبِكُمْ خَيْرًا يُؤْتِكُمْ خَيْرًا مِّمَّا أُخِذَ مِنكُمْ وَيَغْفِرْ
لَكُمْ ۗ وَاللَّهُ غَفُورٌ رَّحِيمٌ ۝

If Allah finds goodness in your hearts, He will give you better
than what has been taken from you, and forgive you. For
Allah is All-Forgiving, Most Merciful. [8:70]

This is why one of the recommendations for making *dua* (supplication) to God is to be persistent in asking, without being impatient. It is one of the ways that we prove our motivation and genuine desire for Allah's mercy. The Messenger ﷺ said, **"Knowledge comes through striving in learning, forbearance comes through striving in forbearance; whoever actively pursues goodness will be given it, and whoever tries to avoid evil will be saved from it."**[1]

In our *dua* and in our striving, we must learn to be beggars before God. Repeating the same supplications with humility is a reflection of our sincerity and neediness. During the rain prayer (*salah al-Istisqaa'*), it is recommended to demonstrate an excess of humility and brokenness before God. We can see in these examples that divine bestowal of what we seek can be dependent on how much we truly, sincerely want and plead for it.

وَالَّذِينَ جَاهَدُوا فِينَا لَنَهْدِيَنَّهُمْ سُبُلَنَا ۚ وَإِنَّ اللَّهَ لَمَعَ الْمُحْسِنِينَ ۝

But We shall be sure to guide to Our ways those who strive
hard for Our cause: God is with those who do good. [29:69]

Our Lord commands us to be patient, but reminds us that patience comes only from Him.

$$وَاصْبِرْ وَمَا صَبْرُكَ إِلَّا بِاللَّهِ$$

So be patient; your patience comes only from God...[16:127]

And the Prophet ﷺ said, **"Whoever strives to be patient, Allah will make him patient."**[2] In our quest for stronger *iman*, greater patience, good character, connection with the Quran, or any other aspect of growing closer to God, we must pursue our heart's aim using all of the necessary means, all the while trusting that He will bestow His blessing and success upon our endeavor. In the meantime, we should not lose hope or grow frustrated mid-way through our journey. Reform of the heart and the nurturing of *iman* take time; but we should not stand by waiting for things to magically happen. We should be in constant motion, striving as best as we can, improving ourselves day by day, in order to place ourselves in the line of God's mercy.

$$إِنَّ رَحْمَتَ اللَّهِ قَرِيبٌ مِّنَ الْمُحْسِنِينَ$$

Indeed, the mercy of Allah is near to the doers of good. [7:56]

We will eventually find what we seek. Then, when our heart is fully awakened and beating with life, we will undoubtedly look around and realize how much we have missed out on. So we start another phase of our journey post-awakening. We roll up our sleeves and start the life's work of living and breathing Islam in full, racing to catch up with the righteous caravans in the trek through life to Allah. We engage in hard work, with the help of Allah: performing consistent good deeds, treating our family better, elevating the quality of our worship, refining our character, seeking knowledge, striving in activism and service, and sacrificing for the sake of Allah. On the way, we will find treasures we never knew of, treasures that many others are missing out on because they have traded away the magnificent and eternal for what is cheap and temporary. And so we also become active callers to God, inviting others to worship Him alone and dedicate their lives to His service.

Along this path, we may miss out on some of the temporal pleasures of this world, but we will be pleased with what God has written for us. Our hearts will be quenched with a peace, purpose, and equanimity, the rarest commodities in our modern time. There will be times when we will taste the euphoric sweetness of *iman* in our hearts. *Thikr* (remembrance of Allah) will calm our souls and the Quran will be music to our ears and the spring of our hearts. If Allah wills for our souls to experience this sweetness along the journey of life, we may say, as worshippers of God have said before us,

"If kings knew what bliss can be found[in faith and worship],
they would fight us for it."

॥·॥·॥

....

ENDNOTES

1. Ibn Abi ad-Dunya in al-Hilm; deemed hasan by al-Albani in as-Saheehah (342)
2. Bukhari 1469, Muslim 1053